AWS Certified Cloud Practitioner

Technology Workbook

Second Edition

www.ipspecialist.net

Document Control

Proposal Name	:	AWS Certified Cloud Practitioner Workbook
Document Version	:	2.0
Document Release Date	:	04-Sep-19
Reference	:	CLF-C01

Registered in England and Wales

Company Registration No: 10883539

Registration Office at: Office 32, 19-21 Crawford Street, London W1H 1PJ, United Kingdom

www.ipspecialist.net

Feedback:

If you have any comments regarding the quality of this book, or otherwise alter it to better suit your needs, you can contact us through email at info@ipspecialist.net.

Please make sure to include the book title and ISBN in your message.

About IPSpecialist

IPSPECIALIST LTD. IS COMMITTED TO EXCELLENCE AND DEDICATED TO YOUR SUCCESS.

Our philosophy is to treat our customers like family. We want you to succeed, and we are willing to do anything possible to help you make it happen. We have the proof to back up our claims. We strive to accelerate billions of careers with great courses, accessibility, and affordability. We believe that continuous learning and knowledge evolution are the most important things to keep re-skilling and up-skilling the world.

Planning and creating a specific goal is where IPSpecialist helps. We can create a career track that suits your visions as well as develop the competencies you need to become a professional Network Engineer. We can also assist you with the execution and evaluation of proficiency level based on the career track you choose, as they are customized to fit your specific goals.

We help you STAND OUT from the crowd through our detailed IP training content packages.

Course Features:

- Self-Paced Learning
  - Learn at your own pace and in your own time
- Covers Complete Exam Blueprint
  - Prep-up for the exam with confidence
- Case Study Based Learning
  - Relate the content with real life scenarios
- Subscriptions that suit you
  - Get more, pay less with IPS Subscriptions
- Career Advisory Services
  - Let industry experts plan your career journey
- Virtual Labs to test your skills
  - With IPS vRacks, you can evaluate your exam preparations
- Practice Questions
  - Practice Questions to measure your preparation standards
- On Request Digital Certification
  - On request digital certification from IPSpecialist LTD.

About the Authors:

This book has been compiled with the help of multiple professional engineers. These engineers specialize in different fields e.g. Networking, Security, Cloud, Big Data, IoT etc. Each engineer develops the content in his/her specialized field that is compiled to form a comprehensive certification guide.

About the Technical Reviewers:

Nouman Ahmed Khan

AWS-Architect, CCDE, CCIEX5 (R&S, SP, Security, DC, Wireless), CISSP, CISA, CISM is a Solution Architect working with a major telecommunication provider in Qatar. He works with enterprises, mega-projects, and service providers to help them select the best-fit technology solutions. He also works closely as a consultant to understand customer business processes and to help to select an appropriate technology strategy that support business goals. He has more than fourteen years of working experience in Pakistan/Middle-East & UK. He holds a Bachelor of Engineering Degree from NED University, Pakistan, and M.Sc. in Computer Networks from the UK.

Abubakar Saeed

Abubakar Saeed has more than twenty-five years of experience, Managing, Consulting, Designing, and implementing large-scale technology projects, extensive experience heading ISP Operations, Solutions Integration, heading Product Development, Presales, and Solution Design. Emphasizing on adhering to Project timelines and delivering as per customer expectations, he always leads the project in the right direction with his innovative ideas and excellent management.

Syed Hanif Wasti

Syed Hanif Wasti is a graduate in computer science working professionally as a Technical Content Developer. He is part of a team of professionals operating in the E-learning and digital education sector. He holds a Bachelor's Degree in Computer Sciences from PAF-KIET, Pakistan. He completed his training of MCP and CCNA and has both technical knowledge and industry sounding information, which he uses efficiently in his career. He has also worked as a Database and Network administrator while getting the experience of software development.

Muhammad Yousuf

Muhammad Yousuf is a professional technical content writer. He is a Certified Ethical Hacker (v 10) and Cisco Certified Network Associate in Routing and Switching, holding a Bachelor's Degree in Telecommunication Engineering from Sir Syed University of Engineering and Technology. He has both technical knowledge and industry sounding information, which he uses perfectly in his career.

Saima Talat

Saima Talat is a postgraduate Computer Engineer working professionally as a Technical Content Developer. She is a part of the team of professionals operating in the E-learning and digital education sector. She holds a Bachelor's Degree in Computer Engineering accompanied by Masters of Engineering in Computer Networks and Performance Evaluation from NED University, Pakistan. With strong educational background, she possesses exceptional researching and writing skills that has led her to impart knowledge through her career.

Free Resources:

With each workbook that you buy from Amazon, IPSpecialist offers free resources to our valuable customers.

Once you buy this book you will have to contact us at support@ipspecialist.net or tweet @ipspecialistnet to get this limited time offer without any extra charges.

Free Resources Include:

Exam Practice Questions in Quiz Simulation: With more than 300+ Q/A, IPSpecialist's Practice Questions is a concise collection of important topics to keep in mind. The questions are especially prepared following the exam blueprint to give you a clear understanding of what to expect from the certification exam. It goes further on to give answers with thorough explanations. In short, it is a perfect resource that helps you evaluate your preparation for the exam.

Career Report: This report is a step by step guide for a novice who wants to develop his/her career in the field of computer network. It answers the following queries:

- What are the current scenarios and future prospects?
- Is this industry moving towards saturation or are new opportunities knocking at the door?
- What will the monetary benefits be?
- Why get certified?
- How to plan and when will you complete the certifications if you start today?
- Is there any career track that you can follow to accomplish specialization level?

Furthermore, this guide provides a comprehensive career path towards being a specialist in the field of networking and also highlights the tracks needed to obtain certification.

Our Products

Technology Workbooks

IPSpecialist's Technology workbooks are the ideal guides for developing the hands-on skills necessary to pass the exam. Our workbook covers official exam blueprint and explains the technology with real life case study based labs. The content covered in each workbook consists of individually focused technology topics presented in an easy-to-follow, goal-oriented, step-by-step approach. Every scenario features detailed breakdowns and thorough verifications to help you completely understand the task and associated technology.

We extensively use mind maps in our workbooks to visually explain the technology. Our workbooks have become a widely used tool to learn and remember the information effectively.

vRacks

Our highly scalable and innovative virtualized lab platforms let you practice the IP Specialist Technology Workbook at your own time and at your own place as per your convenience.

Quick Reference Sheets

Our Quick Reference Sheets are a concise bundling of condensed notes of the complete exam blueprint. It is an ideal and handy document that helps you remember the most important technology concepts related to the certification exam.

Practice Questions

IPSpecialist's Practice Questions have been developed in accordance with the certification exam. The collection of these questions from our technology workbooks is prepared by keeping the exam blueprint in mind, covering not only important but necessary topics as well. It is an ideal document that helps you practice and revise for your certification.

Content at a glance

Contents

About this Workbook

This Workbook provides in-depth understanding and complete course material to pass the AWS Certified Cloud Practitioner Exam (CLF-C01). The workbook is designed to take a practical approach to learning with real-life examples and case studies.

- Covers complete CLF-C01 Exam Blueprint
- Summarized content
- Case study based approach
- Ready to practice labs
- Exam tips
- Mind maps
- 100% pass guarantee

AWS Cloud Certifications

AWS Certifications are industry-recognized credentials that validate your technical cloud skills and expertise while assisting you in your career growth. These are the most valuable IT certifications right now since AWS has established an overwhelming lead in the public cloud market. Even with the presence of several tough competitors such as Microsoft Azure, Google Cloud Engine, and Rackspace, AWS is by far the dominant public cloud platform today, with an astounding collection of proprietary services that continues to grow.

The two key reasons as to why AWS certifications are prevailing in the current cloud-oriented job market are as follows;

- There is a dire need of skilled cloud engineers, developers, and architects – the current shortage of experts is expected to continue into the near future
- AWS certifications stand out for their thoroughness, rigor, consistency, and appropriateness for critical cloud engineering positions

Value of AWS Certifications

AWS places equal emphasis on sound conceptual knowledge of its entire platform, as well as on hands-on experience with the AWS infrastructure and its many unique and complex components and services.

For Individuals

- Demonstrate your expertise on design, deploy, and operate highly available, cost-effective, and secured applications on AWS
- Gain recognition and visibility for your proven skills and proficiency with AWS
- Earn tangible benefits such as access to the AWS Certified LinkedIn Community, invites to AWS Certification Appreciation Receptions and Lounges, AWS Certification Practice Exam Voucher, Digital Badge for certification validation, AWS Certified Logo usage, access to AWS Certified Store
- Foster credibility with your employers and peers

For Employers

- Identify skilled professionals to lead IT initiatives with AWS technologies
- Reduce risks and costs to implement your workloads and projects on the AWS platform
- Increase customer satisfaction

Types of Certification

Role-Based Certifications:

- ***Foundational*** - Validates overall understanding of the AWS Cloud. Prerequisite to achieving the Specialty certification or an optional start towards the Associate certification
- ***Associate*** - Technical role-based certifications. No pre-requisite
- ***Professional*** - Highest level of technical role-based certification. Relevant Associate certification required

Specialty Certification:

- Validates advanced skills in specific technical areas
- Requires one active role-based certification

Certification Roadmap

AWS Certified Cloud Practitioner is a new entry-level certification. Furthermore, there are five different AWS certification offerings in three different tracks. These include Solutions Architect, Developer and SysOps Administrator. AWS also offers two specialty certifications in technical areas that are Big Data and Advanced Networking.

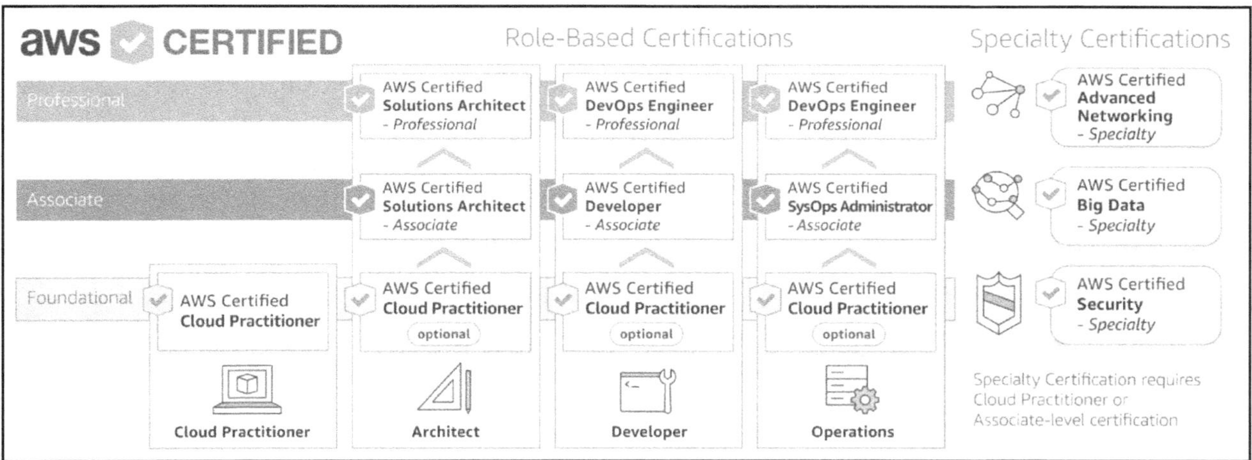

Figure 1: Certification Roadmap

AWS Certified Cloud Practitioner

The AWS Certified Cloud Practitioner (`CLF-C01`) examination is intended for individuals who have the knowledge and skills necessary to effectively demonstrate an overall understanding of the AWS Cloud. Those who are independent of specific technical roles addressed by other AWS certifications (e.g., Solutions Architect - Associate, Developer - Associate, or SysOps Administrator - Associate). This exam enables individuals to validate their knowledge of the AWS Cloud with an industry-recognized credential.

Overview of AWS Cloud Practitioner Certification

This exam certifies an individual's ability & understanding of the followings;

- AWS Cloud and its basic global infrastructure
- Basic AWS Cloud architectural principles
- AWS Cloud value proposition
- Key services on the AWS platform and their common use cases (e.g., compute analytics, etc.)
- Basic security and compliance aspects of the AWS platform and the shared security model
- Billing, account management, and pricing models
- Identify sources of documentation or technical assistance (example, white papers or support tickets)
- Basic/Core characteristics of deploying and operating in the AWS Cloud

Intended Audience

Candidates may be business analysts, project managers, chief experience officers, AWS Academy students, and other IT-related professionals. They may be serving in sales, marketing, finance, and legal roles.

Course Outline

The table below lists the main content domains and their weightings on the exam.

	Domain	% of Examination
Domain 1	Cloud Concepts	28%
Domain 2	Security	24%
Domain 3	Technology	36%
Domain 4	Billing and Pricing	12%
Total		100%

Following is the outline of the topics included in this examination; however, the list is not comprehensive.

Domain 1: Cloud Concepts

1.1 -Define the AWS Cloud and its value proposition
1.2 -Identify aspects of AWS Cloud economics
1.3 -List the different cloud architecture design principles

Domain 2: Security

2.1 -Define the AWS Shared Responsibility model
2.2 -Define AWS Cloud security and compliance concepts
2.3 -Identify AWS access management capabilities
2.4 -Identify resources for security support

Domain 3: Technology

3.1 -Define methods of deploying and operating in the AWS Cloud
3.2 -Define the AWS global infrastructure
3.3 -Identify the core AWS services
3.4 -Identify resources for technology support

Domain 4: Billing and Pricing

4.1 -Compare and contrast the various pricing models for AWS
4.2 -Recognize the various account structures in relation to AWS billing and pricing
4.3 -Identify resources available for billing support

Exam Details

Pricing: USD 100

Exam Length: 90 minutes

Exam Content: There are two types of questions on the examination;

- Multiple-choice: Has one correct response and three incorrect responses (distracters)
- Multiple-response: Has two correct responses out of five options.

Always choose the best response(s). Incorrect responses will be plausible and are designed to be attractive to candidates who do not know the correct response. Unanswered questions are scored as incorrect. There is no penalty for guessing.

Exam Results:

The AWS Certified Cloud Practitioner (CLF-C01) examination is a pass or fail exam. The examination is scored against a minimum standard established by AWS professionals who are guided by the certification industry's best practices and guidelines.

The results of the examination are reported as a scaled score from 100 through 1000, with a minimum passing score of 700. The score shows how you performed on the examination as a whole and whether or not you passed.

Exam Validity: 2 years; Recertification is required every 2 years for all AWS Certifications.

How to become an AWS Certified Cloud Practitioner?

Pre-requisites

No pre-requisite exam is required. Although, it is recommended to have at least six months of AWS cloud experience in any role, including technical, managerial, sales, purchasing, or financial. Also, the candidates should have a basic understanding of IT services and their uses in the AWS Cloud platform.

Exam Preparation Guide

Exam preparation can be accomplished through self-study with textbooks, practice exams, and on-site classroom programs. This workbook provides you with all the information and knowledge to help you pass the AWS Certified Cloud Practitioner Exam. IPSpecialist provides full support to the candidates in order for them to pass the exam.

Step 1: Take AWS Training Class

These training courses and materials will help with the exam preparations:

AWS Training (aws.amazon.com/training)

- AWS Cloud Practitioner Essentials course
- AWS Technical Essentials course
- AWS Business Essentials course

Step 2: Review the Exam Guide and Sample Questions

Review the Exam Blue Print and study the Sample Questions available at AWS website.

Step 3: Practice with Self-Paced Labs and Study Official Documentations

Register for an AWS Free Tier accounts to use limited free services and practice labs. Additionally, you can study the official documentation on the website.

Step 4: Study AWS Whitepapers

Broaden your technical understanding with whitepapers written by the AWS team.

AWS Whitepapers (aws.amazon.com/whitepapers) Kindle, .pdf and other materials

- Overview of Amazon Web Services whitepaper, April 2017
- Architecting for the Cloud: AWS Best Practices whitepaper, Feb 2016
- How AWS Pricing Works whitepaper, March 2016

- The Total Cost of (Non) Ownership of Web Applications in the Cloud whitepaper, Aug 2012
- Compare AWS Support Plans webpage

Step 5: Review AWS FAQs

Browse through these FAQs to find answers to commonly raised questions.

Step 6: Take a Practice Exam

Test your knowledge online in a timed environment by registering at aws.training.

Step 7: Schedule Your Exam and Get Certified

Schedule your exam at a testing center near you at aws.training/certification.

Chapter 1: Cloud Concepts

What is Cloud Computing?

Cloud Computing is a technology through which users can access a network of remote servers hosted on the internet to store, manage and process data, instead of using a local server or a personal computer. Computing resources are delivered on-demand through a cloud service platform with pay-as-you-go pricing.

Advantages of Cloud Computing

1. **Trade capital expense for variable expense**

   Pay for resources consumed, instead of investing in data centers and servers before knowing the exact requirements.

2. **Benefit from economies of scale**

   Variable costs are lower than clients can access on their own. This is because cloud computing providers, such as Amazon, build their own huge data centers which benefit from the economies of scale and lower prices for the client.

3. **Stop guessing capacity**

   Access as many or as few resources depending on current demand, instead of buying too many or too few resources by guessing the needs of the business. Resources can be scaled up and down as required with no long-term contracts.

4. **Increase speed and agility**

   New IT resources are readily available so that resources can be scaled up infinitely according to demand. This leads to a dramatic increase in agility for organizations.

5. **Stop spending money on running and maintaining data centers**

   Eliminates the traditional requirement of spending money on running and maintaining data centers. Instead these are managed by the cloud provider.

6. **Go global in minutes**

   Provide lower latency at minimal cost by easily deploying any cloud-based application in multiple regions around the world.

Types of Cloud Computing

Infrastructure as a Service (IaaS)	Provides basic building blocks for cloud IT by offering access to networking features, computers, and data storage space.
Platform as a Service (PaaS)	Manages its own underlying infrastructure, usually hardware and operating systems, and provides application development platform.
Software as a Service (SaaS)	Offers a complete product as a web service that is run and maintained by the service provider along with the management of the underlying infrastructure.

Figure 1-01: Types of Cloud Computing

Cloud Computing Deployments Models

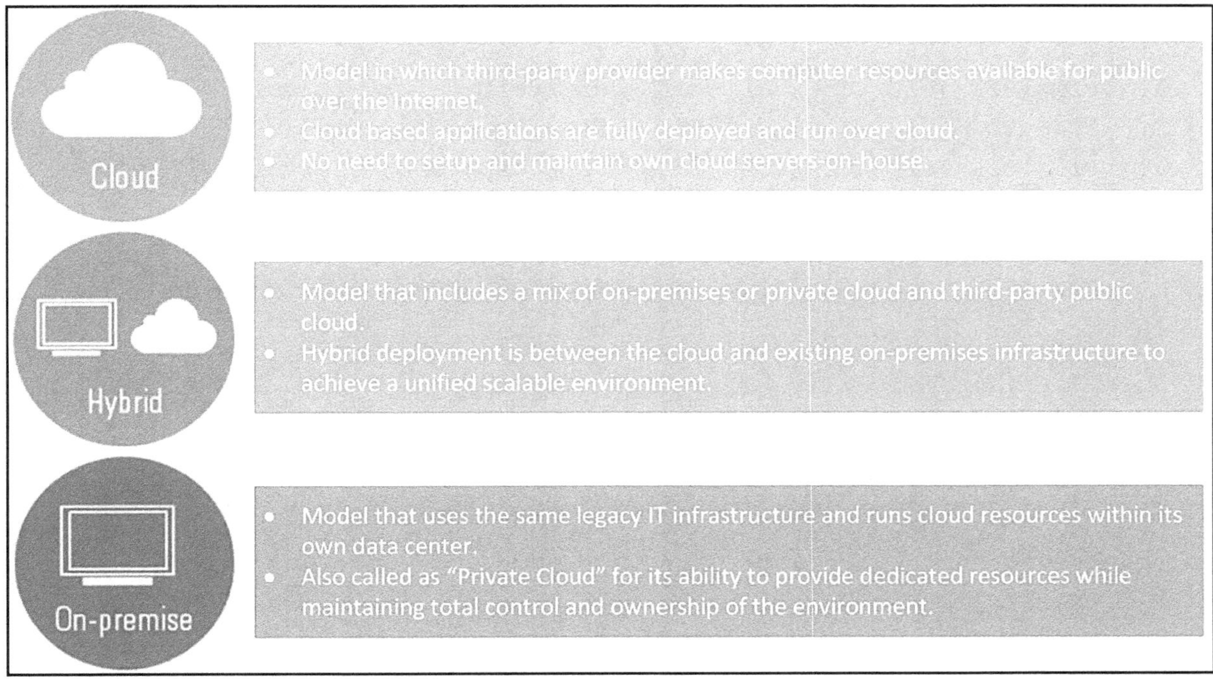

Figure 1-02: Cloud Computing Deployment Models

Amazon Web Services Cloud Platform

Amazon Web Services (AWS) is a secure cloud services platform, offering computing power, database storage, content delivery and other functionalities on-demand to help businesses scale and grow. AWS cloud products and solutions can be used to build sophisticated applications with a large degree of flexibility, scalability and reliability.

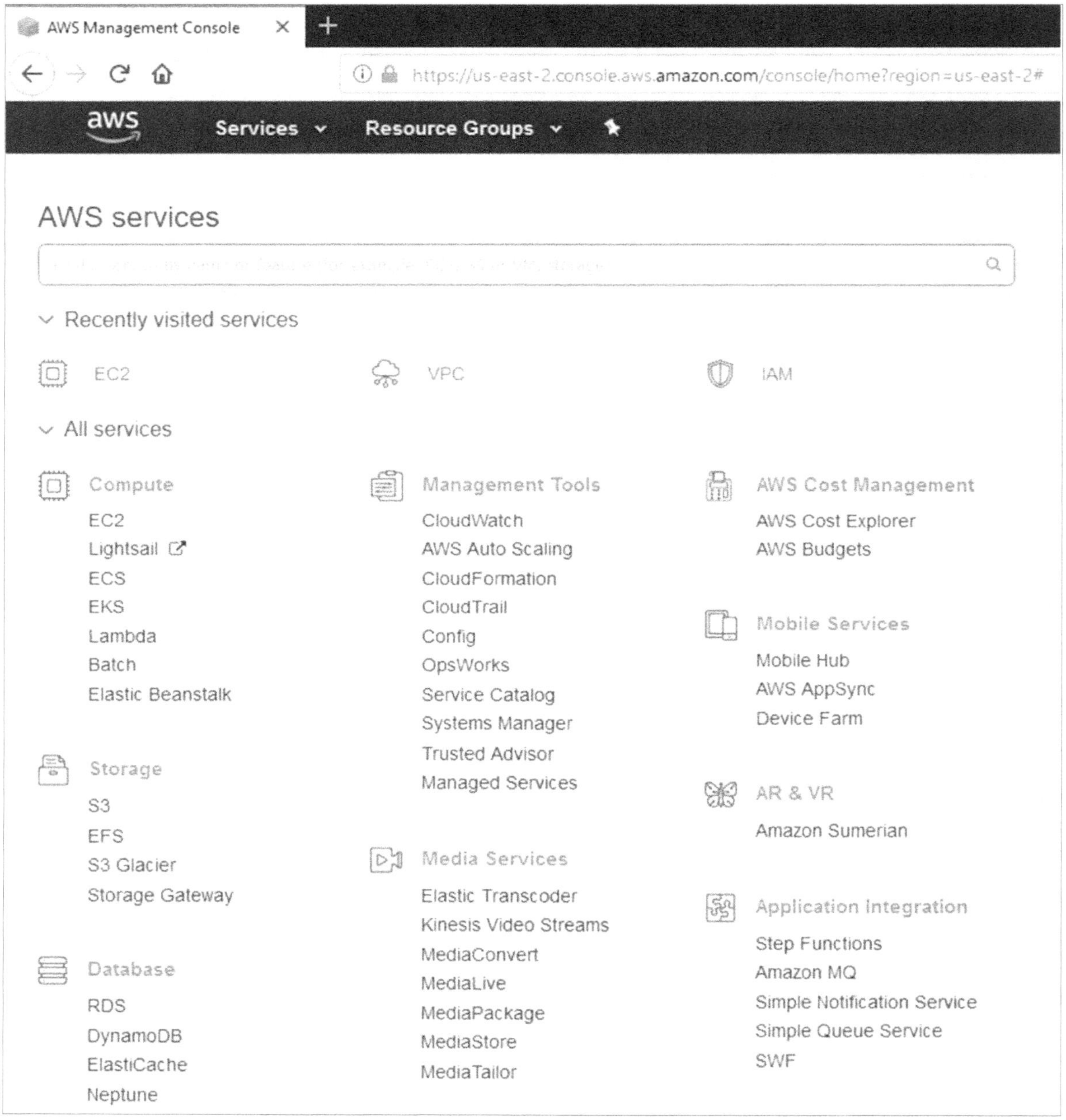

Figure 1-03: AWS Platform

The Cloud Computing Differences

This section will compare cloud computing with the traditional computing environment, reviewing the new computing technology and explaining why these new practices have emerged.

IT Assets Become Programmable Resources:

In a traditional environment, it could take weeks to set-up IT resources such as servers and networking hardware, depending on the complexity of the environment. On AWS, servers, databases, storage and higher-level application components can be created within seconds. These can be used as temporary and disposable resources to meet actual demand, while the business only pays for what it has consumed.

Global, Available, and Unlimited Capacity:

With the AWS cloud platform, businesses can deploy their infrastructure to different AWS regions around the world. The on-demand capacity is virtually unlimited, which enables future expansion of the IT architecture, while the global infrastructure ensures high availability and tolerance to faults.

Higher Level Managed Services:

Apart from computing resources in the cloud, AWS also provides other higher-level managed services such as storage, database, analytics, application and deployment services. These services are instantly available to developers, which can reduce dependency on in-house specialized skills.

Built-in Security:

In a non-cloud environment, security auditing would be a periodic and manual process. The AWS cloud provides extensive security and encryption features with governance capabilities that continually monitor your IT resources. The security policy of each business can be embedded into the design of their unique cloud infrastructure.

The Economic of the AWS Cloud

Comparing the financial aspects of a traditional environment to those of the cloud infrastructure is not as simple as comparing hardware, storage and computing costs. You also have to consider other investments, such as:

- Capital expenditures
- Operational expenditures

- Staffing
- Opportunity costs
- Licensing
- Facility overheads

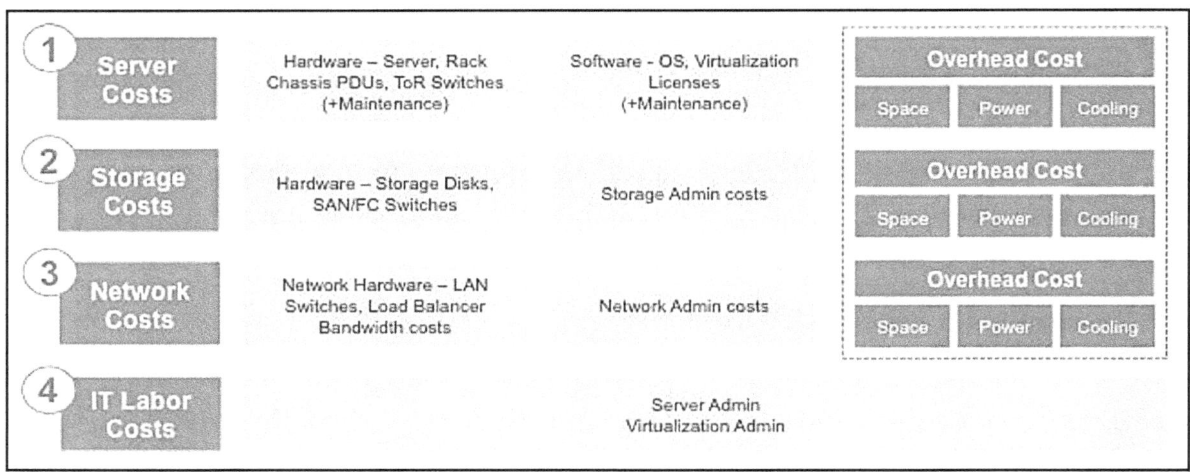

Figure 1-04: Typical Data Center Costs

A cloud environment provides scalable and powerful computing solutions, reliable storage, and database technologies at lower costs than traditional data centers with reduced complexity and increased flexibility. When you decouple from an on-site data center, you will be able to;

- **Decrease your TCO**: Eliminate the costs of building and maintaining data centers or a co-location deployment. Pay for only the resources that you have consumed
- **Reduce complexity**: Reduce the need to manage the infrastructure, investigate licensing issues, or divert resources when needed
- **Adjust capacity on the fly**: Scale resources up or down depending on the needs of the business using a secure, reliable, and broadly accessible infrastructure
- **Reduce time to market**: Design and develop new IT projects faster
- **Deploy quickly, even worldwide**: Deploy applications across multiple geographic areas
- **Increase efficiency**: Use automation to reduce or eliminate any IT management activities that waste time and resources
- **Innovate more**: Businesses can try out new ideas with less risk, as the cloud makes it faster and cheaper to deploy, test and launch new products and services

- Use **your resources strategically**: Switch to a DevOps model to free IT staff from handling operations and maintenance
- **Enhance security**: Cloud providers employ specific teams of people to focus on security and offer best practices to ensure that your businesses practices are compliant

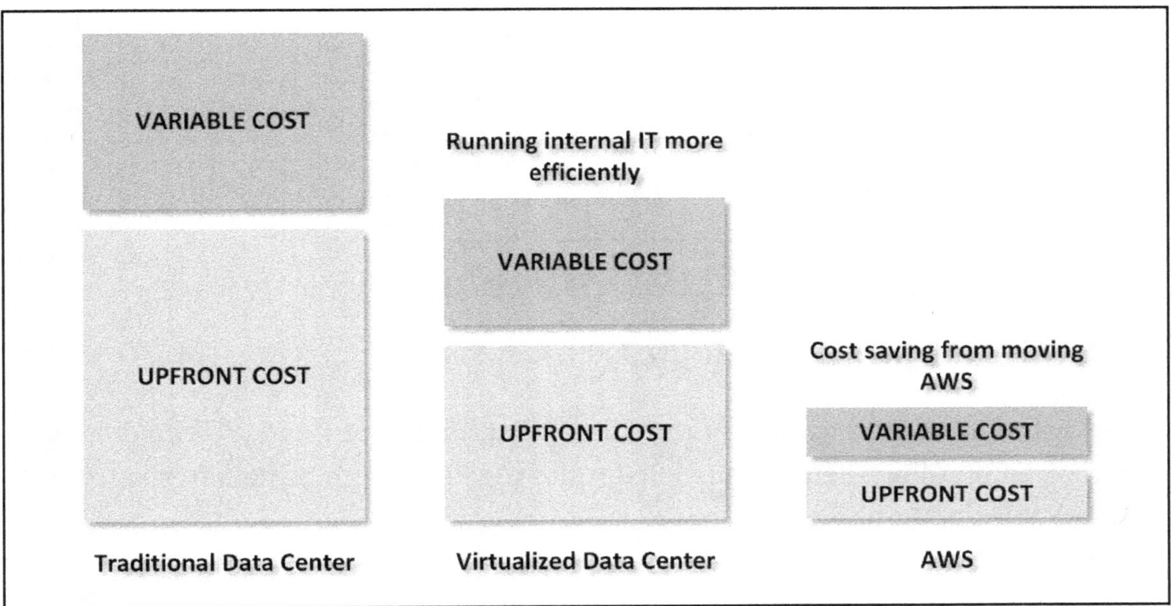

Figure 1-05: Cost Comparisons of Data Centers and AWS

The AWS Virtuous Cycle

The AWS pricing philosophy is driven by a virtuous cycle. Low prices mean a high number of customers will take advantage of the platform, which in turn results in further lowering costs down.

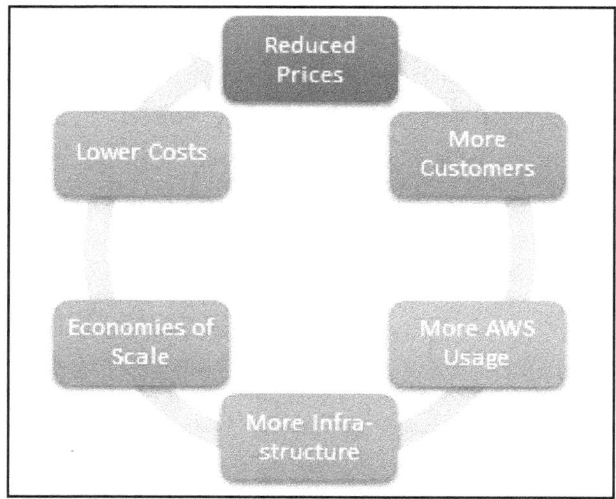

Figure 1-06: AWS Virtuous Cycle

Design Principles of AWS Cloud Architecture

Architects should take advantage of the inherent strengths of the AWS cloud computing platform when building their systems. Below are the key design principles that need to be taken into consideration:

Scalability

Systems need to be designed in such a way that they are capable of growing and expanding over time with no drop in performance. The architecture needs to be able to take advantage of the virtually unlimited on-demand capacity of the cloud platform and be able to scale in a way, which ensures that adding extra resources results in a greater ability to serve additional load.

There are generally two ways to scale IT architecture: vertically and horizontally.

Scale Vertically- Increase specifications such as RAM, CPU, IO, or the networking capability of a single resource.

Scale Horizontally- Increase the number of resources, for example by adding more hard drives to a storage array or adding more servers to support an application.

The way that applications are scaled depends on the applications and their components:

- **Stateless Applications**– An application that needs no memory of previous interactions and stores no sessions, for example an application that responds to a given input with the same response. A stateless application can scale horizontally because any request can be serviced by any of the available computing resources,

for example, Amazon EC2 instances, AWS Lambda functions. As there is no session data to be shared, you can add more resources as needed and terminate them when the capacity is no longer required

- **Stateless Components**- Most applications need to store some kind of state information. For example, web applications need to track previous activities such as whether a user is signed in to a certain website. A portion of these servers can be made stateless by storing state information in the client's browser using cookies. This can make servers relatively stateless because the sessions are stored in the user's browser rather than in the application itself.
- **Stateful Components** – Some layers of the architecture are stateful, such as the database, and because of the potential for an increase in state information, you need databases that can scale. When considering AWS components, Amazon RDS DB can scale up and, if the business adds read replicas, it can also scale out. However, Amazon DynamoDB scales automatically and is therefore a better choice
- **Distributed Processing** – Processing very large amounts of data requires a distributed processing approach wherein big data is broken down into pieces. These pieces are then worked on separately but in parallel by computing instances. On AWS, the core service that handles this is Amazon Elastic Map Reduce (EMR). It manages a fleet of EC2 instances that work on the fragments of data simultaneously

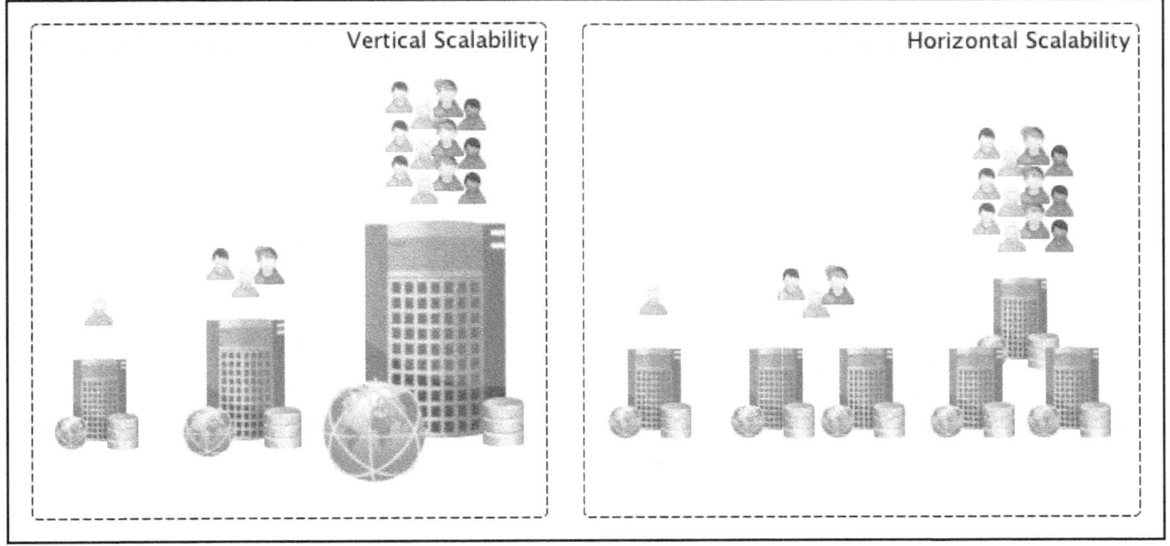

Figure 1-07: Vertical vs. Horizontal Scalability

Disposable Resources Instead of Fixed Servers

In a cloud computing environment, servers and other components are treated as temporary disposable resources instead of fixed components. You can launch as many as you need at any one time and use them for as long as you need. If a server goes down or needs a configuration update, it can be quickly replaced with the latest configuration server instead of updating the old one.

Instantiating Compute Resources- When deploying resources for a new environment or increasing the capacity of the existing system, it is important to keep the configuration and coding as an automated and repeatable process, which will avoid human errors and extensive lead times.

These are a few ways in which a resource can be deployed:

- **Bootstrapping**– Executing bootstrapping after launching a resource with a default configuration, enables you to reuse the same scripts without modifications when you relaunch the applications
- **Golden Image**– Certain resource types such as Amazon EC2 instances, Amazon RDS DB instances, and Amazon Elastic Block Store (Amazon EBS) volumes, can be launched from a golden image. This is a snapshot of a particular state of that resource. It is used in auto-scaling; for example, by creating an Amazon Machine Image (AMI) of a customized EC2 instance, you can launch as many instances as needed with the same customized configurations
- **Hybrid**– A hybrid launching approach uses a combination of both of the above approaches, wherein some parts of the configuration are captured in a golden image, while others are configured dynamically through a bootstrapping action. AWS Elastic Beanstalk follows the hybrid model

Infrastructure as Code– AWS assets are programmable, which allows you to treat your infrastructure as code. This code lets you repeatedly deploy the infrastructure across multiple regions without the need to provision everything manually. AWS Cloud Formation and AWS Elastic Beanstalk are two provisioning resources which use this approach.

Automation

One of the best practices of system design is to automate whenever possible using various AWS automation technologies, to improve the system's stability and efficiency of the organization. Examples of these technologies include AWS Elastic Beanstalk, Amazon

EC2 Auto recovery, Auto Scaling, Amazon Cloud Watch Alarms, Amazon Cloud Watch Events, AWS OpsWorks Lifecycle events and AWS Lambda Scheduled events.

Loose Coupling

Ideally, IT systems should be designed with reduced interdependency. As applications become more complex, they should be broken down into smaller loosely coupled components. This prevents the failure of any one component from cascading down to other parts of the application. The more loosely coupled a system is, the more resilient it will prove to be.

Well-Defined Interfaces– Using technology-specific interfaces such as RESTful APIs allows components to interact with each other to reduce inter-dependability. This hides the details of technical implementation, allowing teams to modify any underlying operations without affecting other components. For example, the Amazon API Gateway service makes it easier to create, publish, maintain and monitor thousands of concurrent API calls while also handling all tasks involved in accepting and processing data including traffic management, authorization, and access control.

Service Discovery– Applications deployed as a set of smaller services need to interact with each other as these services may be running across multiple resources. Implementing Service Discovery allows smaller services to be used through loose coupling irrespective of the details of their network topology. In the AWS platform service, Service Discovery can be achieved using Amazon's Elastic Load Balancer. This uses DNS endpoints; so, if the RDS instance goes down but the Multi-AZ has been enabled on that RDS database, the Elastic Load Balancer will redirect the request to the copy of the database in the other availability zone.

Asynchronous Integration- Asynchronous Integration is a form of loose coupling wherein an immediate response between the services is not needed as only an acknowledgment of the request is sufficient. One component generates events while the other consumes them. Both components interact through an intermediate durable storage layer, not through point-to-point interaction. An example of this is an Amazon SQS Queue which ensures that if a process fails while reading messages from the queue, messages can still be added to the queue for processing once the system has recovered.

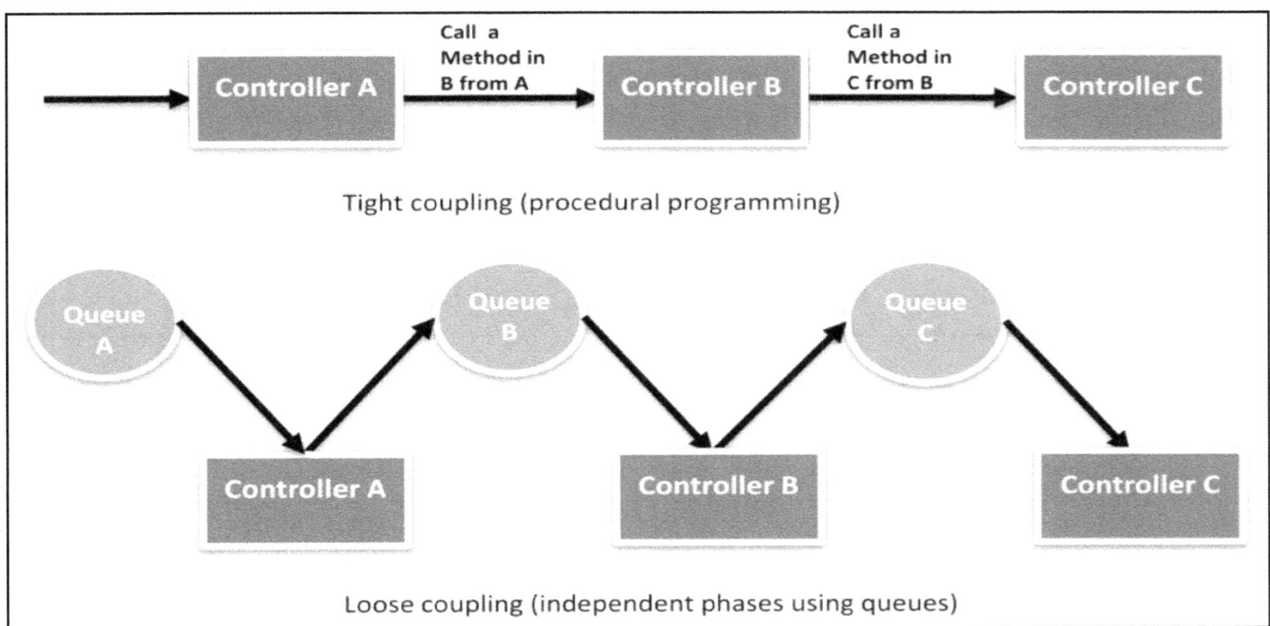

Figure 1-08: Tight and Loose Coupling

Graceful Failure– This increases loose coupling by building applications that handle component failure in a graceful manner. This helps to reduce the impact on end users and increase the ability to progress on offline procedures, if components do fail.

Services, Not Servers

Developing large-scale applications requires a wide variety of underlying technological components. Best design practice involves the leveraging of a broad set of computing, storage, database, analytics, application and deployment services involved in AWS. This will increase developer productivity and operational efficiency.

Managed Services- Always rely on services, not servers. Developers can power their applications with AWS managed services including databases, machine learning, analytics, queuing, search, email, notifications and many more. For example, Amazon S3 can be used to store data without businesses having to consider capacity, hard disk configurations, replication, along with other issues. Amazon S3 also provides a widely available static web hosting solution that can scale automatically to meet traffic demands.

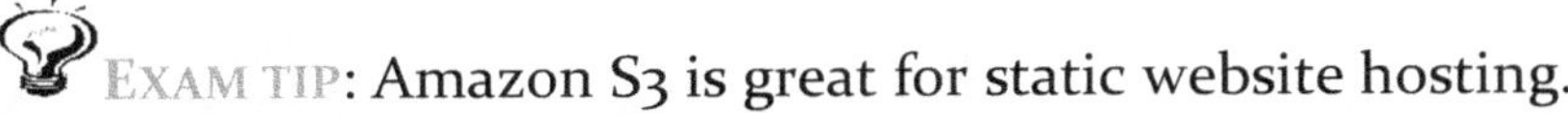
EXAM TIP: Amazon S3 is great for static website hosting.

Serverless Architectures - Serverless architectures reduce the operational complexity of running various applications. Event-driven and synchronous services can both be built without managing any server infrastructure. For example, a code for the architecture can be uploaded to the AWS Lambda computing service that runs the code on your behalf. This means that scalable synchronous APIs powered by AWS Lambda can be developed using Amazon API Gateway. Finally, a complete web application can be produced by combining these APIs with Amazon S3 for serving static content.

> EXAM TIP: For event-driven managed service/serverless architecture, use AWS Lambda. If you want to customize the architecture to your own unique needs, Amazon EC2 offers flexibility and full control.

Databases

AWS-managed database services remove the constraints that come with licensing costs and also add the ability to support diverse database engines. When designing system architecture, keep in mind these different types of database technologies:

Relational Databases

- These are often called RDBS or SQL databases
- They consist of normalized data presented in well-defined tabular structures with rows and columns known as tables
- They provide powerful query language, flexible indexing capabilities, strong integrity controls, and the ability to combine data from multiple tables quickly and efficiently
- Examples include Amazon Relational Database Service (Amazon RDS) and Amazon Aurora
- ***Scalability:*** Can be scaled vertically by upgrading the system to a larger Amazon RDS DB instance or adding more or faster storage. For read-heavy applications, use Amazon Aurora to horizontally scale the system by creating one or more read replicas
- ***High Availability:*** Using Amazon RDS Multi-AZ deployment feature creates a synchronously replicated standby instance in a different Availability Zone (AZ). In case the primary node fails, Amazon RDS performs an automatic switchover to the standby without manual administrative intervention

- ***Anti-Patterns:*** If your application does not need joins or complex transactions, consider a NoSQL database instead. These store large binary files, such as audio, video, and image files, in Amazon S3 and only hold the metadata for the files in the database.

Non-Relational Databases

- These are often called NoSQL databases
- They trade the query and transaction capabilities of relational databases for a more flexible data model
- They utilize a variety of data models, including graphs, key-value pairs and JSON documents
- An AWS example of this is Amazon DynamoDB
- ***Scalability:*** Non-relational databases automatically scale horizontally through data partitioning and replication
- ***High Availability:*** The databases synchronously replicate data across three facilities in a single AWS region to provide fault tolerance in case of a server failure or disruption to an availability zone
- ***Anti-Patterns:*** If your schema cannot be de-normalized and requires joins or complex transactions, consider a relational database. These store large binary files, such as audio, video, and image files, in Amazon S3 and only hold the metadata for the files within the database

> EXAM TIP: If you are given a scenario in which you have to work on complex transactions or use JOINs, then you should opt for Amazon Aurora, Amazon RDS, MySQL or another relational database. However, if you do not have to work with these, then you should use a non-relational database such as Amazon DynamoDB.

Data Warehouse

- This is a special type of relational database, which is optimized for the analysis and reporting of large amounts of data
- It is used to combine transactional data from disparate sources so that they are available for analysis and decision-making

- Running complex transactions and queries on the production database creates massive overheads and requires an immense quantity of processing power, which is why data warehousing is needed
- An AWS example of a Data Warehouse is Amazon Redshift
- ***Scalability:*** Amazon Redshift uses a combination of massively parallel processing (MPP), columnar data storage and targeted data compression encoding to achieve efficient storage and optimum query performance. This increases performance by increasing the number of nodes in the data warehouse clusters
- ***High Availability:*** By deploying production workloads in multi-node clusters, Redshift enables the data written to a node to be automatically replicated to other nodes within the same cluster and is also continuously backed up to Amazon S3. When necessary, Amazon Redshift automatically re-replicates data from failed drives and replaces nodes
- ***Anti-Patterns:*** Amazon Redshift is not meant to be used for online transaction processing (OLTP) functions as it is an SQL-based relational database management system (RDBMS). For a high concurrency workload or a production database, consider using Amazon RDS or Amazon DynamoDB instead

Search

- **A** search service is used to index and search data, both in structured and free text format
- A search service is required because sophisticated search functionality typically outgrows the capabilities of relational or NO SQL databases
- AWS provides two services of this type: Amazon CloudSearch and Amazon ElasticSearch Service (Amazon ES)
- Amazon CloudSearch is a managed search service that requires little configuration and scales automatically; whereas Amazon ES offers an open source API which gives the user more control over the configuration details
- ***Scalability:*** Both CloudSearch and ES use data partitioning and replication to scale horizontally
- ***High-Availability:*** Both services store data redundantly across all availability zones

Removing Single Points of Failure

A system needs to be widely available to withstand any failure of either individual or multiple components, for example hard disks, servers and network links. Resiliency should be built across multiple services as well as in multiple availability zones to automate recovery and reduce disruption at every layer of the architecture.

Introducing Redundancy - You can introduce redundancy by creating multiple resources for the same task. Redundancy can be implemented in either standby or active mode. In standby mode, functionality is recovered through a secondary resource while the initial resource remains unavailable. In active mode, requests are distributed to multiple redundant computing resources when any single one of them fails.

Detect Failure- Processes of detection and reaction to failure should both be automated as much as possible, by configuring health checks and masking failure by routing traffic to healthy endpoints using services like ELB and Amazon Route53. Auto Scaling can also be configured to replace unhealthy nodes using the Amazon EC2 auto-recovery feature or services such as AWS OpsWorks and AWS Elastic Beanstalk.

Durable Data Storage– Durable data storage is vital for data availability and integrity and can be achieved by introducing redundant copies of data. The three most-often used modes of replication are; Asynchronous Replication, Synchronous Replication, and Quorum-based Replication.

- **Synchronous replication** only acknowledges a transaction after it has been durably stored both in the primary location and in its replicas
- **Asynchronous replication** decouples the primary node from its replicas, however this comes at the expense of introducing replication lag
- **Quorum-based replication** combines synchronous and asynchronous replication to overcome the challenges of large-scale distributed database systems

Automated Multi-Data Center Resilience–This resilience is achieved by using the multiple availability zones offered by the AWS global infrastructure. Availability zones are designed to be isolated from potential failures of the other availability zones. For example, a fleet of application servers distributed across multiple availability zones can be attached to the Elastic Load Balancing service (ELB). When health checks of the EC2 instances of a particular availability zone fail, ELB will stop sending traffic to those nodes. Amazon RDS provides automatic failover support for DB instances using

Multi-AZ deployments, while Amazon S3 and Amazon DynamoDB stores data redundantly across multiple facilities.

Fault Isolation and Traditional Horizontal Scaling–Fault isolation can be attained through sharding, which is a method of grouping instances into groups called shards. Each customer is assigned to a specific shard, instead of spreading traffic from all customers across every node. In case of a fault, a shuffle sharding technique allows the client to try every endpoint in a set of shared resources until one succeeds.

Optimize for Cost

Businesses can reduce capital expenses by benefiting from the economies of scale of AWS. The main principles of optimizing for cost include:

Right-Sizing- AWS offers a broad set of options for each instance type. Costs can be reduced by selecting the right configurations, resource types and storage solutions to suit your workload requirements.

Elasticity- Auto Scaling is a feature which will reduce costs by horizontally scaling resources up or down automatically depending upon the need of the business. Businesses can also automate the switching off of non-production workloads when they not in use and AWS managed services to take capacity decisions wherever possible.

Take Advantage of the Variety of Purchasing Options– AWS provides flexible purchasing options with no long-term commitments. These purchasing options can reduce cost while businesses continue to pay for instances. Two ways to pay for Amazon EC2 instances are:

- **Reserved Capacity**– Reserving instances enables you to access a significantly discounted hourly rate when reserving computing capacity, instead of having to pay for On-Demand instance pricing. This is ideal for applications with predictable capacity requirements
- **Spot Instances** - Spot instances are available at discounted pricing and are ideal for workloads that have flexible start and end times. Spot instances allow you to bid on spare computing capacity. If your bid exceeds the current Spot market price, your instance will be launched until the Spot market price increases above your bid price, at which point your instance will be terminated automatically

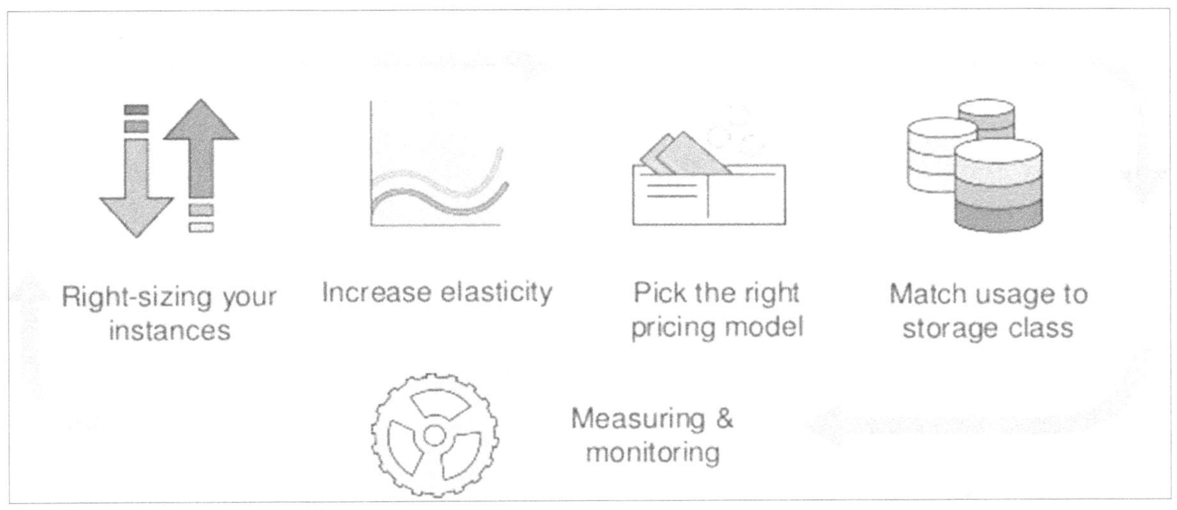

Figure 1-09: Cost Optimization Pillars

Caching

Caching is used to store previously calculated data for future use. This improves application performance and increases the cost efficiency of implementation. Because of this, architects should implement caching in the IT architecture wherever possible.

Application Data Caching– Application data can be stored in the cache for subsequent requests, which improves latency for end users and reduces the subsequent load on back-end systems. Amazon ElastiCache makes it easy to deploy, operate and scale an in-memory cache in the cloud.

Edge Caching– Both static and dynamic content can be cached at multiple edge locations around the world using Amazon CloudFront. This allows popular content to be provided by infrastructure that is closer to viewers, lowering latency and providing sustained high data transfer rates to deliver data to end users at scale.

Security

AWS allows you to improve your infrastructure security in a variety of ways, while also allowing the use of more traditional security tools and techniques.

Utilize AWS Features for in-Depth Defense–AWS allows the user to isolate parts of the infrastructure by building a VPC network topology using subnets, security groups, and routing controls. You can also setup a web application firewall for further protection using AWS WAF.

Offload Security Responsibility to AWS- The security of the underlying cloud infrastructure is managed by AWS; the user is only responsible for securing the workloads that they deploy using AWS.

Reduce Privileged Access– To avoid a breach of security, users should reduce privileged access to any programmable resources and servers for example, by defining IAM roles to restrict root level access.

Security as Code- AWS Cloud Formation scripts incorporate your security policies and reliably deploy them. These security scripts can then be reused along multiple projects as part of the continuous integration pipeline.

Real-Time Auditing– AWS allows you to continuously monitor and automate controls which, in turn, minimizes the exposure to security risks. Services like AWS Config, Amazon Inspector, and AWS Trusted Advisor continually monitor IT resources for compliance and vulnerabilities. Real-time testing and auditing are essential for keeping the cloud environment fast and safe.

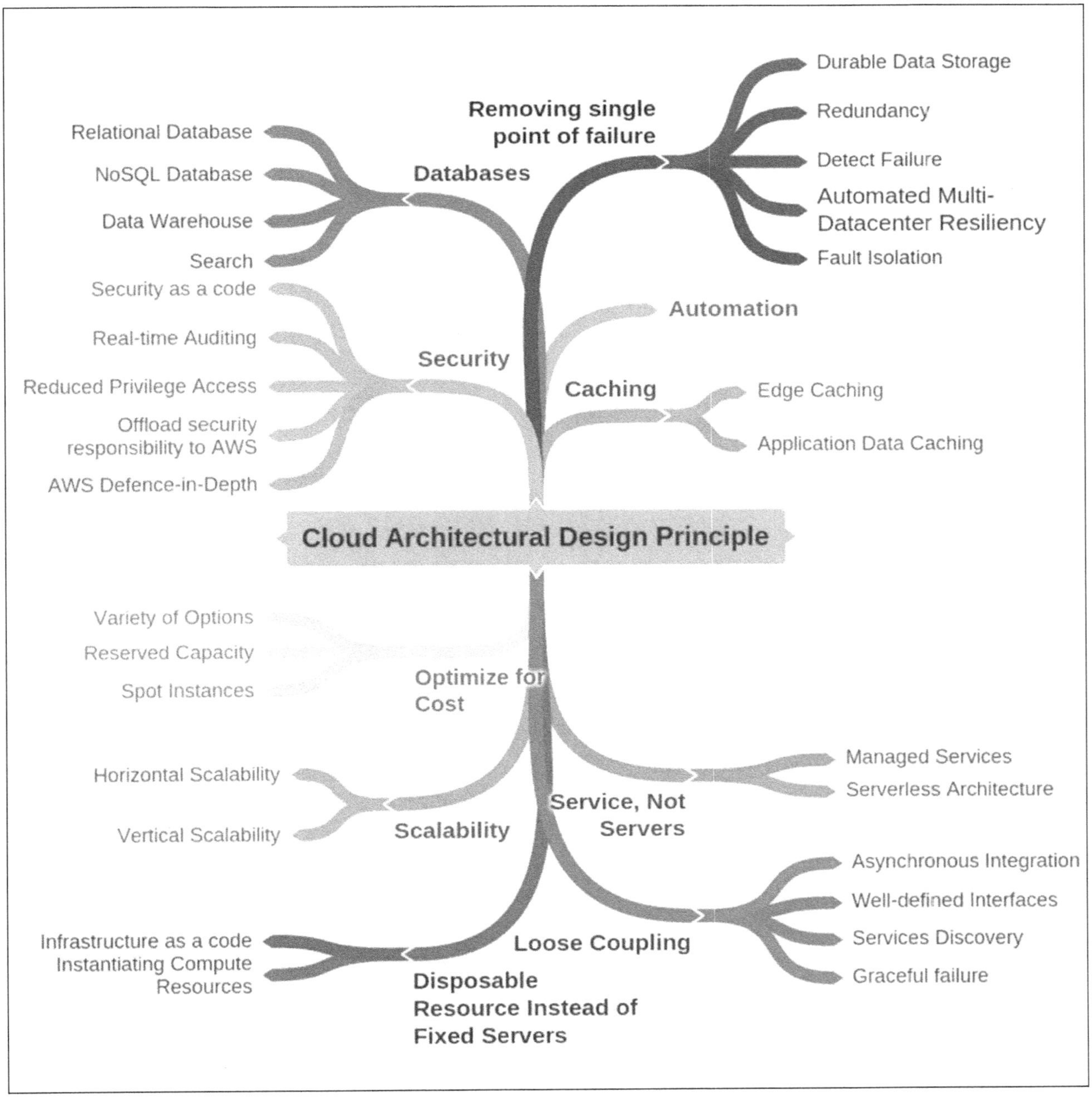

Cloud Architectural Design Principle

Databases
Relational Database
NoSQL Database
Data Warehouse
Search

Removing single point of failure
Durable Data Storage
Redundancy
Detect Failure
Automated Multi-Datacenter Resiliency
Fault Isolation

Security
Security as a code
Real-time Auditing
Reduced Privilege Access
Offload security responsibility to AWS
AWS Defence-in-Depth

Automation

Caching
Edge Caching
Application Data Caching

Optimize for Cost
Variety of Options
Reserved Capacity
Spot Instances

Service, Not Servers
Managed Services
Serverless Architecture

Scalability
Horizontal Scalability
Vertical Scalability

Loose Coupling
Asynchronous Integration
Well-defined Interfaces
Services Discovery
Graceful failure

Disposable Resource Instead of Fixed Servers
Infrastructure as a code
Instantiating Compute Resources

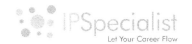

Figure 1-10: Mind Map of Architectural Design Principles

Chapter 2: Security

Introduction to AWS Cloud Security

Security in the cloud is much like security in traditional on-premises data centers, only without the costs of maintaining facilities and hardware. The security provided includes protecting critical information from theft, data leakage, integrity and deletion. In the cloud environment, the cloud provider manages the physical servers or storage devices while the customer uses software-based security tools to monitor and protect the flow of information through the cloud resources.

Benefits of AWS Security

- ***Keep your data safe***- Within the strongly safeguarded AWS infrastructure, data is stored in highly secured AWS data centers
- ***Meet compliance requirements***- AWS infrastructure incorporates dozens of compliance programs, which means that segments of user compliance have already been completed
- ***Save money*** - While using highly secured AWS data centers, users only pay for the services they use without any upfront expenses, which are generally provided at a lower cost than in an on-premises environment
- ***Scale quickly***- AWS allows customers to scale and innovate the cloud environment while maintaining the security of the environment. Infrastructure is designed to keep data safe no matter the size of your system

AWS Shared Responsibility Model

The management of cloud security is slightly different to security in an on-premises data center. Migrating computer systems and data to the cloud requires AWS and customers to work together towards security objectives. The security responsibilities are shared between the user and the cloud service provider. Under this shared responsibility model, AWS is responsible for securing the underlying infrastructure that supports the cloud, and the user is responsible for anything deployed in the cloud or connected with the cloud.

While AWS manages the security of the cloud, security within the cloud is the responsibility of the customer. The control of security tools for protecting the content,

platform, applications systems and networks, lies with the customer. This is no different than it would be in an on-site data center.

Below is the shared security responsibility model describing what AWS and the customer are personally responsible for in the cloud-computing domain.

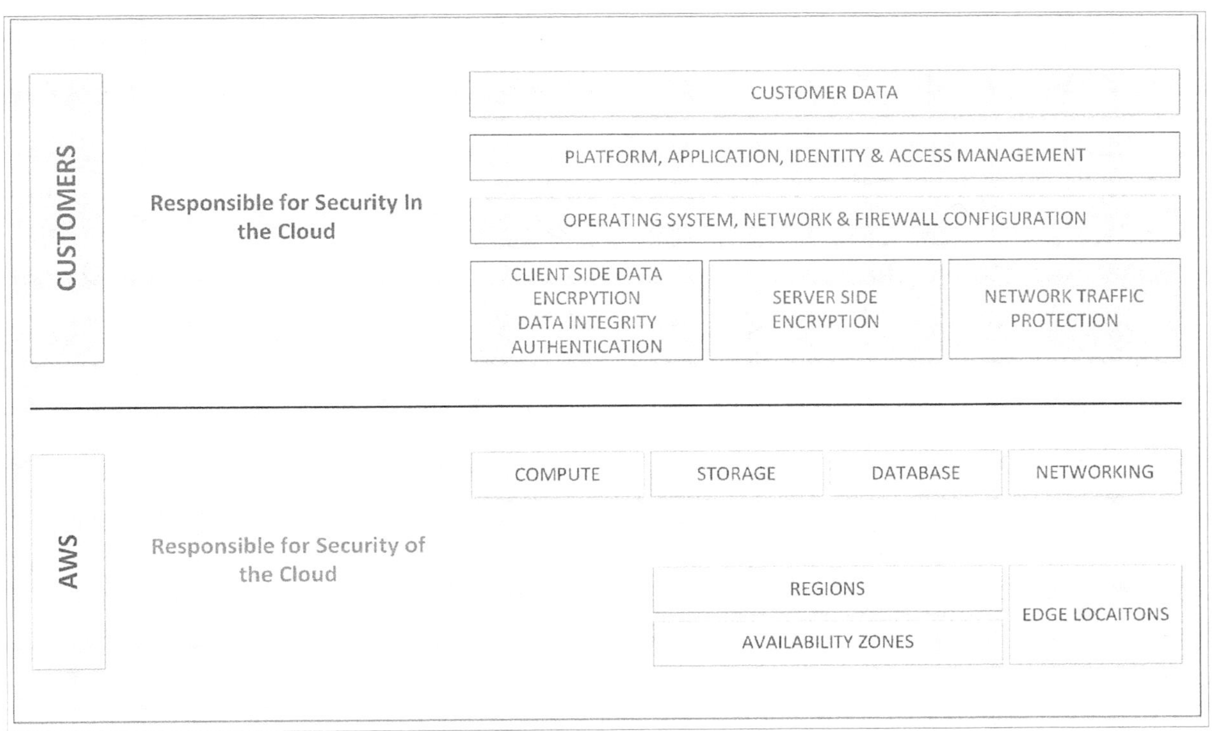

Figure 2-01: AWS Shared Security Responsibility Model

AWS Security Responsibilities

AWS operates, manages, and controls the components of the host operating system and virtualization layer and the physical security of the facilities in which the services operate. In short, AWS is responsible for securing the complete global infrastructure of their business including foundational compute, storage, networking and database services, as well as higher-level services.

Additionally, AWS is also responsible for the security configuration of its products that are considered 'managed services'. Examples of these include Amazon DynamoDB, Amazon RDS, Amazon Redshift, Amazon Elastic MapReduce, Amazon WorkSpaces and several other services. For these services, AWS handles basic security tasks like the guest operating system (OS) and database patching, firewall configuration and disaster recovery.

Customer Security Responsibilities

As part of the AWS "shared responsibility" model, AWS customers retain control over their data and consequently hold all responsibilities relating to that content. Their responsibility is to protect the confidentiality, integrity, and availability of their data in the cloud. They also manage the security of their operating system including updates and security patches and of other associated application software, as well as the configuration of the AWS-provided security group firewall. AWS provides a range of security services and features that customers can use to secure their assets.

The responsibilities and the amount of security configuration work on each customer needs depends on the type of AWS services selected and the sensitivity of their data. If the services fall under the category of Infrastructure as a Service (IaaS), such as Amazon EC2 and Amazon VPC, then all the necessary security configuration and management tasks need to be handled completely by the customer. On the other hand, for AWS managed services such as Amazon RDS or Amazon Redshift, there is no need to worry about the configuration work as it will be managed by AWS.

Irrespective of the AWS services employed, you should always configure security by using AWS Account credentials and setting up individual user accounts with Amazon Identity and Access Management (IAM) so that each user has their own credentials. Some of the AWS assistive tools provided to the customers to enhance security include using Multi-Factor Authentication (MFA) with each account, requiring the use of SSL/TLS to communicate with your AWS resources, setting up API/user activity logging with AWS CloudTrail, leveraging technology such as host-based firewalls, host-based intrusion detection/ prevention and encryption.

EXAM TIP: A way to remember the shared responsibility model is to analyze what it is that you have control over and what you do not. When given a specific scenario, consider whether you have control over that particular task, service or resource. If not, then its Amazon's responsibility. Security 'in' the cloud is your responsibility and security 'of' the cloud is managed by Amazon.

AWS Global Infrastructure Security

The AWS global infrastructure is one of the most flexible and secure cloud computing platforms present today. It offers an exceptionally scalable, highly reliable platform that facilitates customers in deploying applications and data swiftly and securely. The infrastructure includes the services, network, hardware, and operational software such as

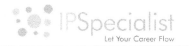

host OS and virtualization software that support the provisioning and use of computing resources.

AWS runs under a shared responsibility security model, in which AWS is in charge of the infrastructure security of the cloud and the user is responsible for securing any workloads deployed in the cloud. This provides the flexibility and agility to implement appropriate security controls, such as strongly restricting access to locations that process sensitive data or setting up less rigid controls for less sensitive data accessed by the public.

The AWS global infrastructure utilizes the best practices pertaining to cloud security along with a range of security compliance standards. AWS monitors and protects the underlying infrastructure every minute of the day using redundant and layered controls, continuous validation and testing and extensive automation. AWS ensures the replication of these controls across every new data center or service.

AWS Compliance Program

AWS computing environments are continuously audited with certifications from accreditation bodies across geographies and verticals, including ISO 27001, FedRAMP, DoD CSM, and PCI DSS. By operating in an accredited environment, customers reduce the scope and cost of any audits they need to perform. AWS continuously undergoes assessments of its underlying infrastructure including the physical and environmental security of its hardware and data centers so customers can take advantage of those certifications and simply inherit the controls. The programs that AWS follow regarding Compliance are divided into three areas:

1. Certifications / Attestation
2. Laws, Regulations and Privacy
3. Alignments / Framework

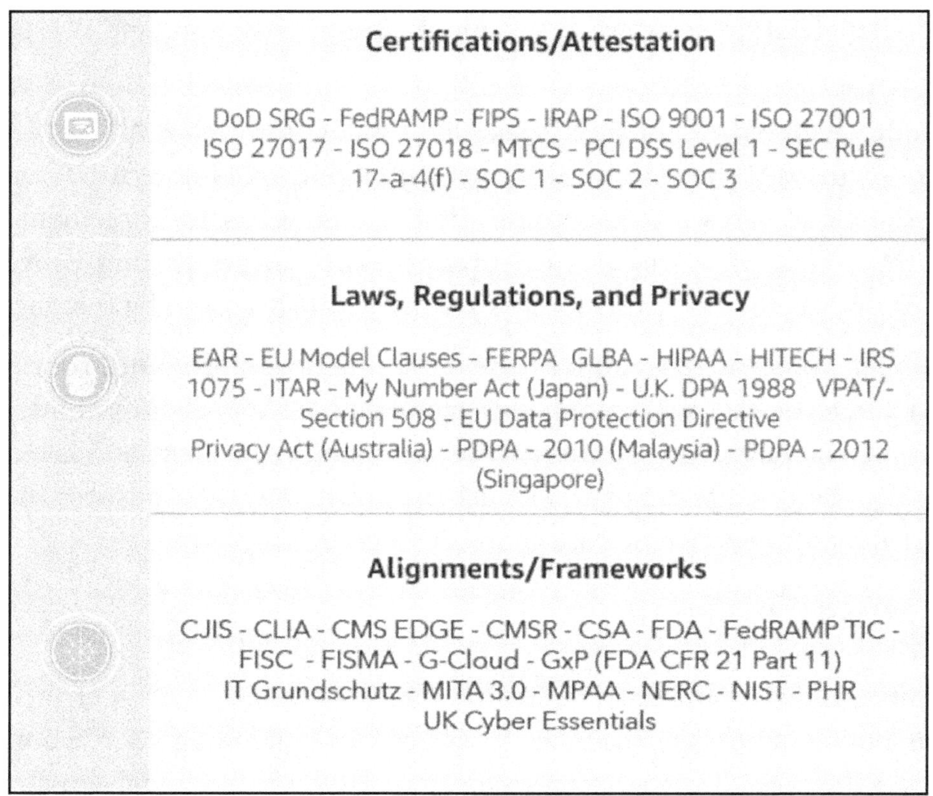

Figure 2-02: AWS Assurance Programs

Certifications / Attestations:

Compliance certifications and attestations are assessed by a third-party, independent auditor and result in a certification, audit report or an attestation of compliance. Major certification and attestations that you need to be aware of for this course include ISO 27001, PCI DSS Level 1, SOC 1, SOC 2, and SOC 3.

- ***ISO 27001*** - ISO 27001 is a security management standard that specifies best practices for security management and comprehensive security controls
- ***PCI DSS Level 1***- The Payment Card Industry Data Security Standard (PCI DSS) is a proprietary information security standard (means security for information that is protected by copyright or trademark) administered by the PCI Security Standards Council. All entities that deal with online payments using credit cards and store, process or transmit cardholder data need to be PCI DSS Level 1 compliant
- ***SOC*** - Reports from AWS System & Organization Control (SOC) are independent third-party examination reports that demonstrate how AWS achieves its key

compliance controls and objectives. The AWS platform is compatible with SOC 1, SOC 2, & SOC3

Laws, Regulations, and Privacy:

AWS customers are still responsible for complying with applicable compliance laws and regulations. The main one you should be aware of is HIPAA.

- ***HIPAA*** - U.S. Health Insurance Portability and Accountability Act (HIPAA) is a set of federal standards, which protect the security and privacy of PHI Protected Health Information (PHI). AWS enables entities and their business associates covered by HIPAA to leverage the secure AWS environment for processing, maintaining, and storing protected health information

Alignments / Frameworks:

Compliance alignments and frameworks consist of published security or compliance requirements for a specific industry or function. The one to focus on is G-Cloud [UK].

- ***G-Cloud [UK]*** -The G-Cloud framework is an agreement between the UK government and cloud-based service providers. The framework enables public bodies to procure commodity-based, pay-as-you-go cloud services on government-approved short-term contracts. In order to host on AWS, public bodies need to meet the G-Cloud [UK] requirements

AWS Access Management

AWS contains a number of cloud services that can be accessed and combined depending on the requirements of your business or organization.

Access Methods

There are three ways of accessing these services:

- ***The AWS Management Console***– AWS offers web access to services through the AWS Management Console. This is a simple and intuitive user interface through which Amazon Web Services can be accessed and managed. There is also a mobile app version, AWS Console Mobile App, to view resources on the move
- ***The Command Line Interface***- The AWS Command Line Interface (CLI) is an integrated tool that manages AWS services by controlling them from the command line. It also provides programmatic access to the services by automating them using scripts

- ***Software Development Kits (SDKs)*** - Software Development Kits (SDKs) contain libraries and sample code for numerous programming languages and platforms such as Java, Python, Ruby, .NET, iOS and Android. They provide programmatic access to AWS services in your applications through an Application Program Interface (API), which is personalized for your programming language or platform

> EXAM TIP: Remember these three access methods: AWS Management console, SDK and CLI.

Getting Started with AWS

Go to 'aws.amazon.com/free' to create an account. A Free Tier account gives you the benefit of a free, hands-on experience of the AWS platform, products, and services. Some of the services are free for the first 12 months while some will always remain free. Regarding compute capacity and database services, you will get 750 hours per month of Amazon EC2 and Amazon RDS respectively and 5 GB of Amazon S3 for storage.

Create a Billing Alarm

After creating your Free Tier account, sign in to the Management Console to set up a billing alarm. Creating a billing alarm will save you from any unnecessary cost by alerting you if you are being charged over a set amount for the services.

Lab 2-1: Creating a Billing Alarm

1. Log in to the “AWS Console”.
2. Click on your account name in the top right corner to display a drop down menu. Select “My Billing Dashboard”.

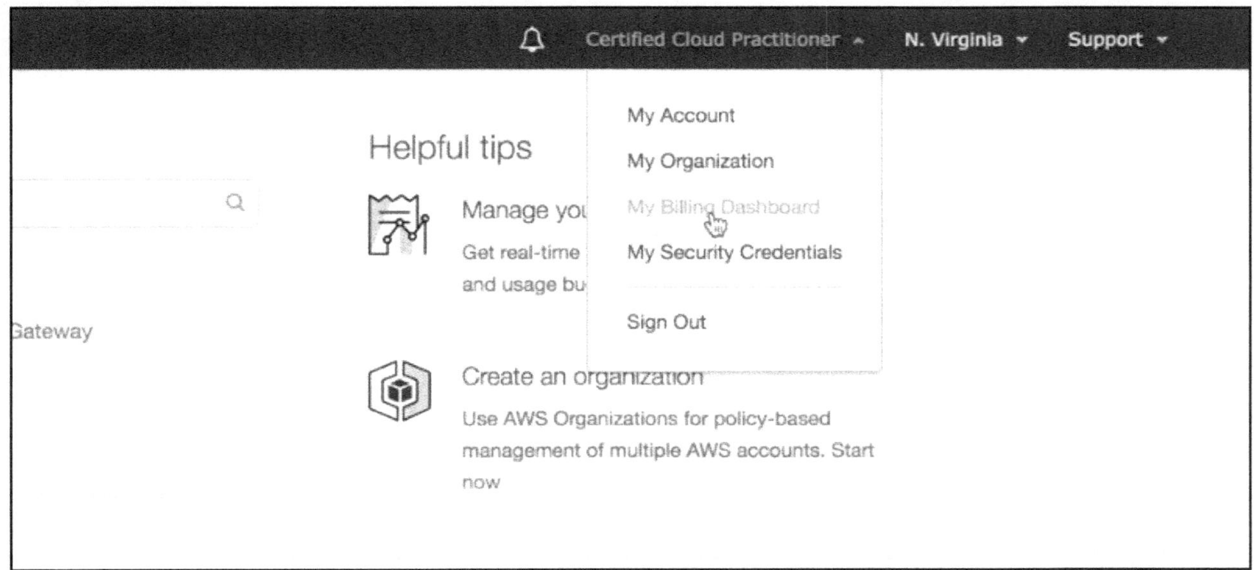

3. Scroll down to the “Alerts & Notifications” section. Click “Enable Now” on the “Monitor your estimated charges” option.

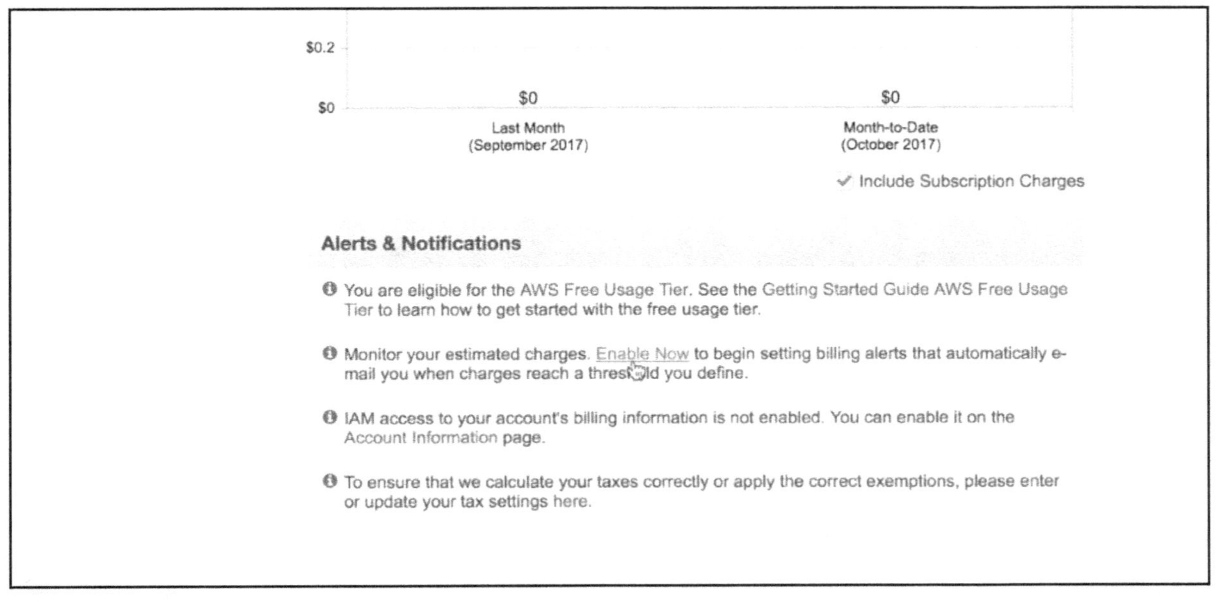

4. Select the checkbox for “Receive Billing Alerts” and click “Save preferences”.

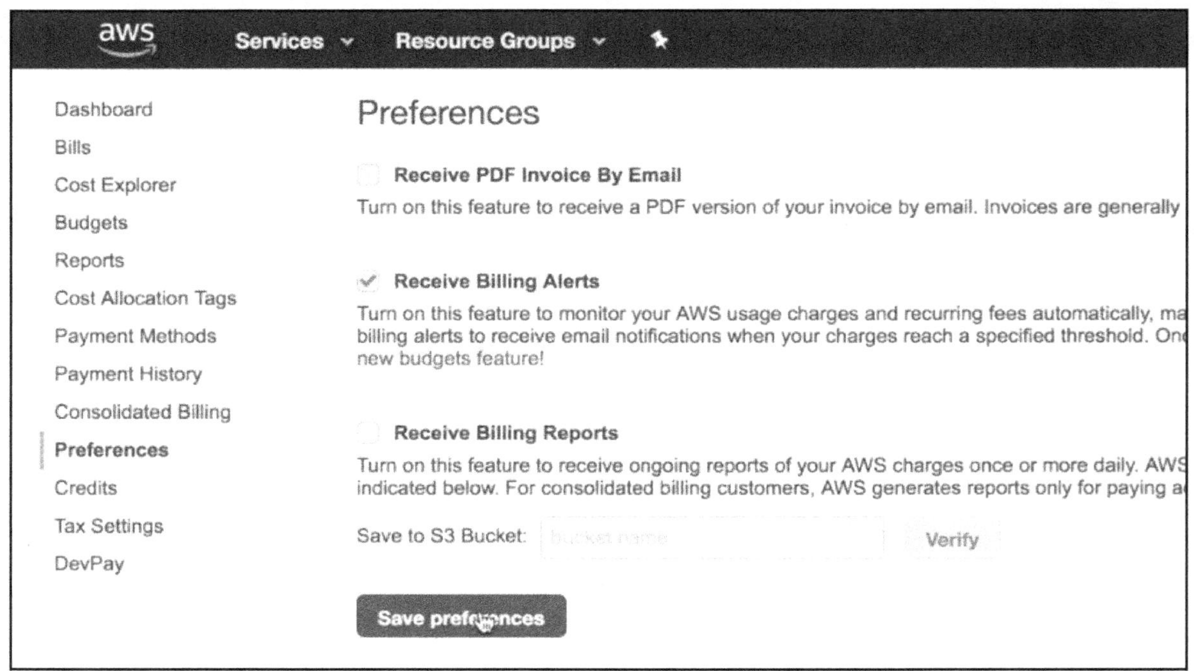

5. Once this is done, go back to the “Manage Billing Alerts” section in the “Receive Billing Alert” option. In the “Alarm Summary’” section, select “Create a billing alarm”.

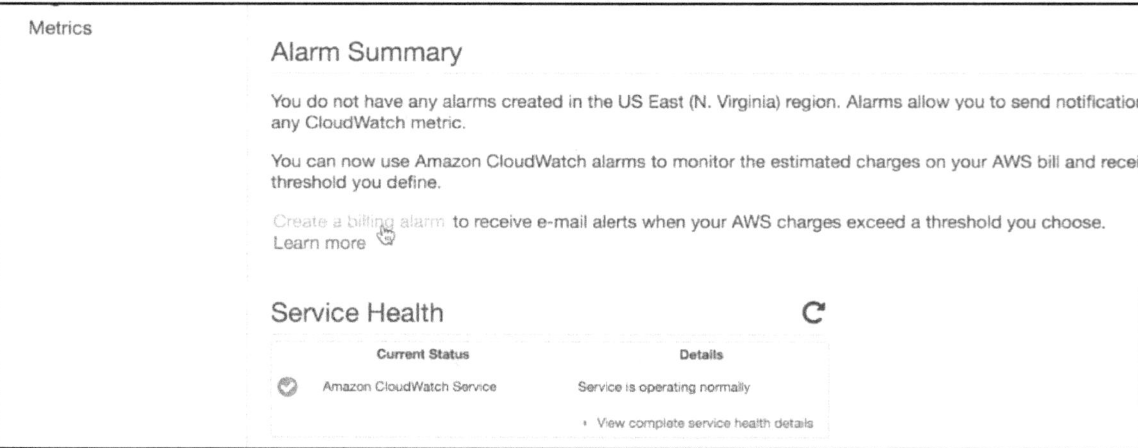

6. Enter the threshold amount after which you want Amazon to alert you, and the email address to which you want the alarm to be sent. Click “Create Alarm” when done.

Create Alarm

Billing Alarm

You can create a billing alarm to receive e-mail alerts when your AWS charges exceed a threshold you choose. Simply:

1. Enter a spending threshold
2. Provide an email address
3. Check your inbox for a confirmation email and click the link provided

When my total AWS charges for the month

exceed: $ 10 USD

send a notification to: type your email address

Reminder: for each address you add, you will receive an email from AWS with the subject "*AWS Notification - Subscription Confirmation*". Click the link provided in the message to confirm that AWS may deliver alerts to that address.

Additional settings

Provide additional configuration for your alarm.

Treat missing data as: missing

showing simple options | show advanced

Alarm Preview

This alarm will trigger when the blue line goes above the red line

EstimatedCharges > 10

More resources

AWS Billing console

Getting started with billing alarms

More help with billing alarms

AWS Billing FAQs

Cancel Previous Next **Create Alarm**

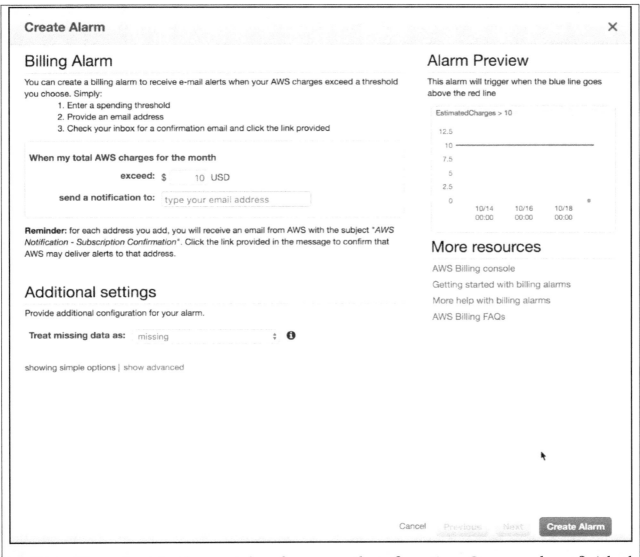

7. You will need to check your inbox for an email confirmation. Once you have finished the email verification process, you will be able to see your alarm.

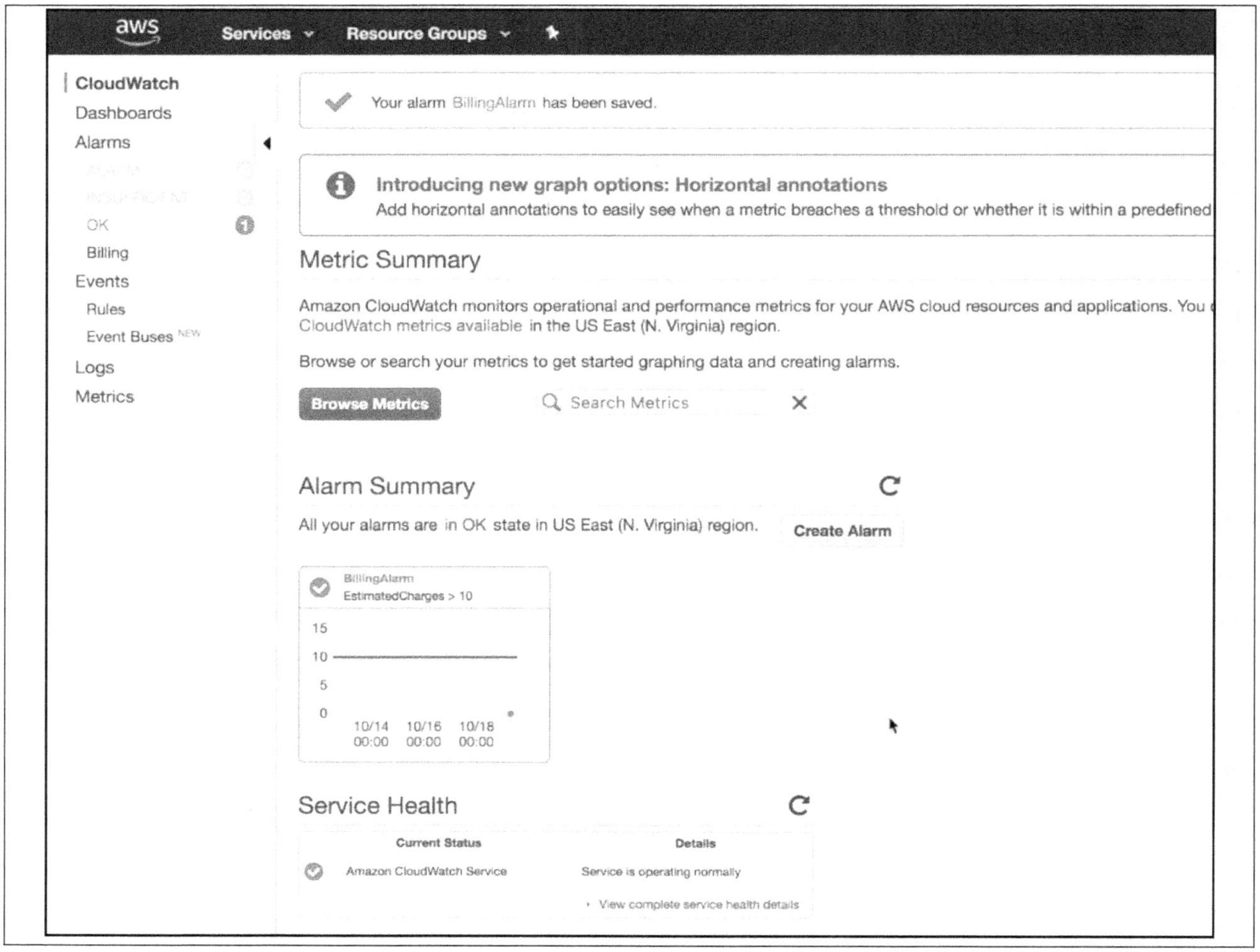

Setting Up On Mac

- For Code Editing:
    - Download TextWrangler from the App Store
    - This will make it easy for you to look at your code when you start building and working with web pages
- For connecting to Windows instances:
    - Download Microsoft Remote Desktop from the App Store
    - This RDP (Remote Desktop Protocol) client will enable you to connect to Windows servers
- For connecting to Linux instances:
    - Go to Finder; under the Applications tab select Utilities. Select the Terminal app from the list

  - Apple's Terminal app will enable you to connect to Linux instances via the SSH protocol

Setting Up On Windows

- For Code Editing:
  - Download Notepad++ from 'notepad-plus-plus.org'
  - This text editor will make it easier to edit your code
- For connecting to remote instances:
  - Download PuTTY from 'chiark.greenend.org.uk'
  - This open-source terminal emulator will enable you to connect to remote instances via the SSH protocol
- For generating an access key:
  - Log in to Create Key Pair on the AWS console and download the key pair
  - Open PuTTYgen and use the downloaded Key Pair to generate and save your access key
  - This key will be used to log in to the web servers

Identity Access Management (IAM)

AWS Identity and Access Management (IAM) is a web service that provides secured control access to AWS resources such as compute, storage, database and application services in the Cloud. IAM manages authentication and authorization by controlling who is signed-in and whether they have permissions to utilize the resources. IAM uses access control concepts such as Users, Groups, Roles and Policies to control which users can access specific services, the types of actions they can perform and which resources are available to them. The IAM service is free from any additional charge. However, your account will be charged, depending on the usage of other AWS services by your users.

When you first create an AWS account, you begin with a single sign-in identity that has complete access to all the AWS services and resources connected with the account. This identity is called the AWS account root user and is accessed by signing in with the email address and password that you used to create the account. Since these credentials have complete access to the AWS account, it is highly recommended that you only use the Root User to create other User accounts for individuals within your organization. Make sure the credentials for the Root User account are kept safe and only used for a few account and service management tasks.

EXAM TIP: Understand what the Root User is and learn the privileges that come with it. It always has full administrator access; therefore, you should not share these account credentials with anyone else. Instead, you should create a user for each individual within your organization and secure the root account using multi-factor authentication.

IAM Features

The IAM service is the key component of the AWS secure global infrastructure. With IAM, you can create and manage users and groups, and set up security credentials such as passwords, access keys and permission policies to allow or deny certain users access to the AWS resources.

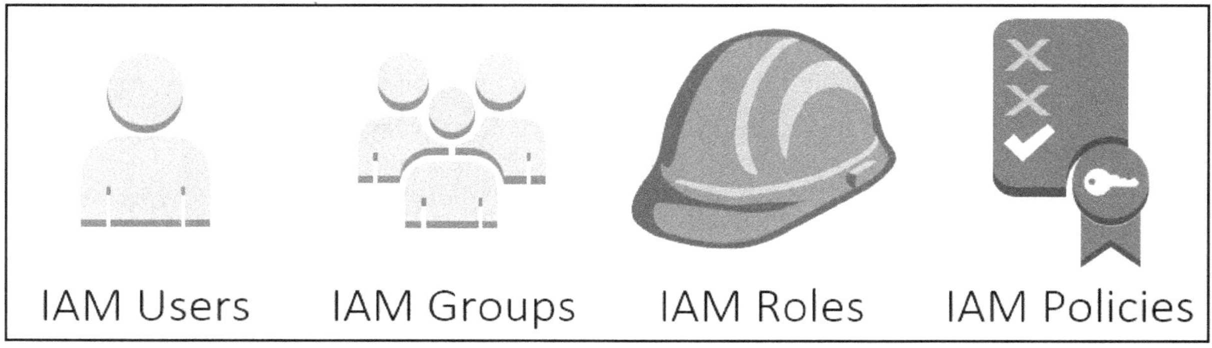

Figure 2-03: IAM Features

What is an IAM User?

An IAM User is a unique identity with limited access to an AWS account and its resources, as defined by their IAM permissions and policies. An IAM user may represent a person, system or application. IAM policies assigned to a user must grant explicit permissions to access services or resources before the user can view or use them.

IAM lets you create individual users within your AWS account, each with their own username, password and access keys. Individual users can log into the console using an account-specific URL that is specific to your account. You can also create access keys for individual users so that they can make programmatic calls and access AWS resources. You can permit a user to access any or all of the AWS services, which have been integrated with IAM or which use IAM in conjunction with external identity sources, such as Microsoft Active Directory, AWS Directory Service or Login with Amazon.

If the users in your organization already have an authentication method, such as a corporate network log-in, you do not have to create separate IAM users for them. Instead, you can federate these user identities into AWS. As a best practice, it is recommended that you also create an IAM user for yourself to ensure you do not use your AWS account credentials for everyday access to AWS.

What is a Group?

A Group is a collection of IAM users. You can use groups to specify permissions for a collection of users, which makes it easier to manage their permissions. For example, you can create a group called Admins and grant that group the types of permissions that administrators typically need. Any user in that group is automatically granted the permissions that are assigned to the group. If a new user joins the organization and needs to have administrator privileges, you can assign them the appropriate permissions by adding the user to the Admins group. Similarly, if a person changes jobs within the organization, instead of editing their permissions manually, you can remove them from any old groups and add them to the appropriate new groups.

Some key aspects of Groups:

- A user can be added or removed from a group at any time
- A user can belong to multiple groups
- A group cannot belong to other groups
- Groups can be granted permissions using access control policies. This makes it easier to manage permissions for a collection of users, rather than having to manage permissions for each individual user
- Groups do not have security credentials, and cannot access web services directly; they exist solely to make it easier to manage user permissions

> EXAM TIP: A group is simply a collection of IAM users. The grouped users will inherit all permissions that the group is granted.

What is an IAM Role?

An IAM Role is an IAM entity that lets you define a set of permissions to allow access to the resources that a user or a service needs. However, these permissions are not attached to a specific IAM user or group. Instead, IAM users, mobile and EC2-based applications, or AWS services (like Amazon EC2) can programmatically assume a role, which will return temporary security credentials that the user or application can use to make

programmatic requests to AWS. These temporary security credentials have a configurable expiration time and are automatically rotated.

Using IAM roles and temporary security credentials means that you do not have to manage long-term credentials and IAM users for every entity that requires access to a resource. Therefore, roles are more secure than using access key IDs and secret access keys and are also easier to manage. You cannot attach multiple IAM roles to a single instance, but you can attach a single IAM role to multiple instances.

Roles are universal, just like everything else in identity access management. Like users, you do not need to specify what region they are in.

 EXAM TIP: IAM resources are global. You can use the IAM Roles across regions.

What are Policies?

An IAM Policy is a rule or set of rules that define the operations allowed or denied on an AWS resource. Permissions are granted through policies. When a policy is attached to an identity or resource, it defines their permissions. AWS evaluates these policies whenever a user makes a request. Permissions in the policies determine whether the request should be allowed or denied. Policies are stored in AWS as JSON documents of either identity-based or resource-based policies.

Policies can be granted to an identity or resource in a number of ways:

- Attaching a managed policy. AWS provides a list of pre-defined policies such as AmazonS3 Read Only Access
- Attaching an inline policy, which is a custom policy created by hand
- Adding the user to a group that already has appropriate permission policies attached
- Cloning the permissions of an existing IAM user

By default, IAM users, groups, and roles have no permissions. To set permissions, you can create and attach policies using the AWS Management Console, the IAM API, or the AWS CLI. Users who have been granted the necessary permissions can create policies themselves to be assigned to IAM users, groups and roles.

Managed policies are IAM resources that regulate permissions using the IAM policy language. You can create, edit, and manage the policies separately from the IAM users, groups, and roles to which they are attached. After you attach a managed policy to

multiple IAM users, groups, or roles, you can update that policy in one place, and the updated permissions will automatically extend to all attached entities. Managed policies are policies that are managed either by the customers (Customer-managed policies) or by AWS (AWS-managed policies).

You should use IAM groups to collect IAM users and define common permissions for them, and use managed policies to share permissions across IAM users, groups and roles. For example, if you want a group of users to be able to launch an Amazon EC2 instance, and you want the role on that instance to have the same permissions as the users in the group, you can create a managed policy and assign it to both the group of users and the role.

> EXAM TIP: To set permissions in a group, you need to apply a policy to that group. Policies are created with JavaScript Object Notation (JSON).

Key Differences between IAM users, IAM groups, and IAM roles

- An IAM user is granted permanent long-term credentials and directly interacts with AWS services
- An IAM group is primarily a management convenience used to control a single set of permissions for a set of IAM users
- An IAM role is an entity with permissions to make AWS service requests. An IAM role does not have any credentials and therefore cannot make direct requests to AWS services. They are meant to be assumed by authorized entities, such as IAM users, applications or AWS services such as EC2. Use IAM roles to delegate access within or between AWS accounts

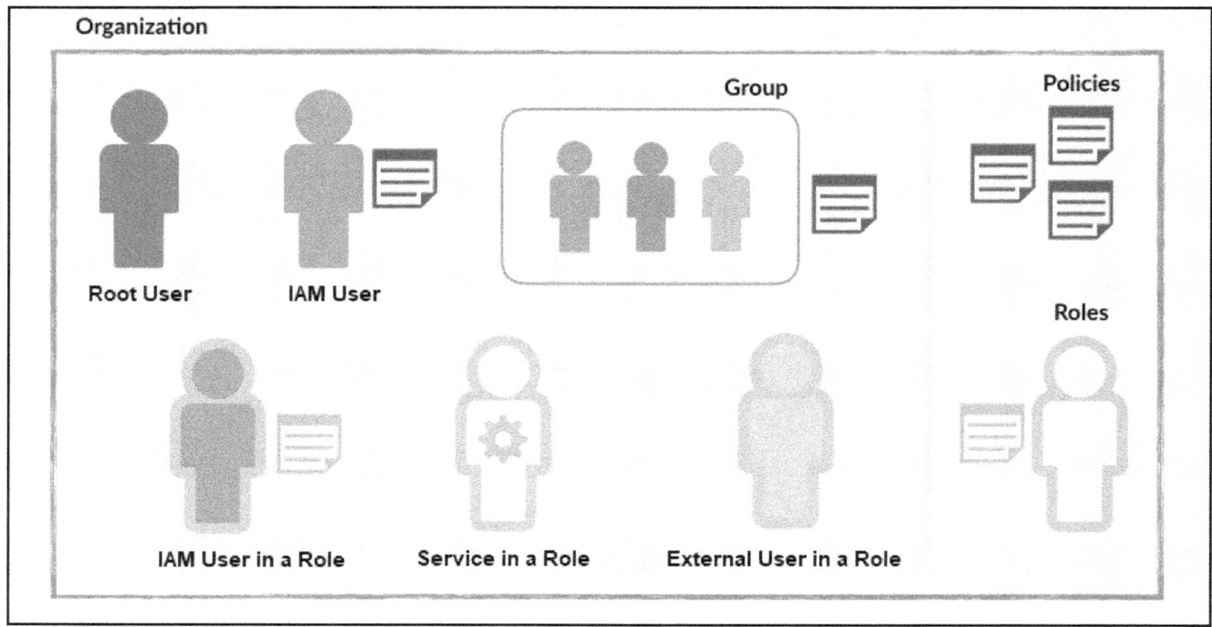

Figure 2-04: IAM Concepts

IAM Functionality

IAM assists in creating roles and permissions. AWS IAM allows you to:

- **Manage IAM users, and their access** – You can create users in IAM; assign them individual security credentials such as access keys, passwords and multi-factor authentication devices; or request temporary security credentials to grant users access to AWS services and resources. You can also manage permissions to control which operations individual users can perform
- **Manage IAM roles and their permissions** – You can create roles in IAM and manage permissions to control which operations can be performed by the entity or AWS service that assumes that role. You can also define which entities are allowed to assume the role
- **Manage federated users, and their permissions** – Federated users with external identities are users you manage in your corporate directory outside of AWS, but who are granted access to your AWS account using temporary security credentials without the need to create an IAM user for each identity. They differ from IAM users, which are created and maintained by your AWS account

IAM Best Practices

AWS publishes a list of best practices to help IT professionals and developers manage access to different AWS resources.

- **Users** – Create individual IAM users
- **Groups** – Use Groups to assign permissions to collections of IAM users
- **Permissions** – Use AWS defined policies to assign permissions whenever possible. You can review IAM Permissions using access levels
- **Auditing** – Turn on AWS CloudTrail to monitor activity within your AWS account
- **Password** – Configure a strong password policy for your users
- **MFA** – Enable MFA for privileged users
- **Roles** – Use Roles for applications that run on Amazon EC2 instances
- **Sharing** – Use IAM roles to share access, instead of sharing credentials
- **Rotate** – Rotate security credentials regularly and remove unnecessary credentials
- **Conditions** – Restrict privileged access and gain extra security by using policy conditions
- **Root** – Lock away your AWS Account Root User access keys and reduce the use of the root account

Lab 2-2: Creating IAM Users

1. Log in to the “AWS Console”.
2. Click on “Services”.
3. Scroll down to “Security, Identity & Compliance”.
4. Select “IAM”.

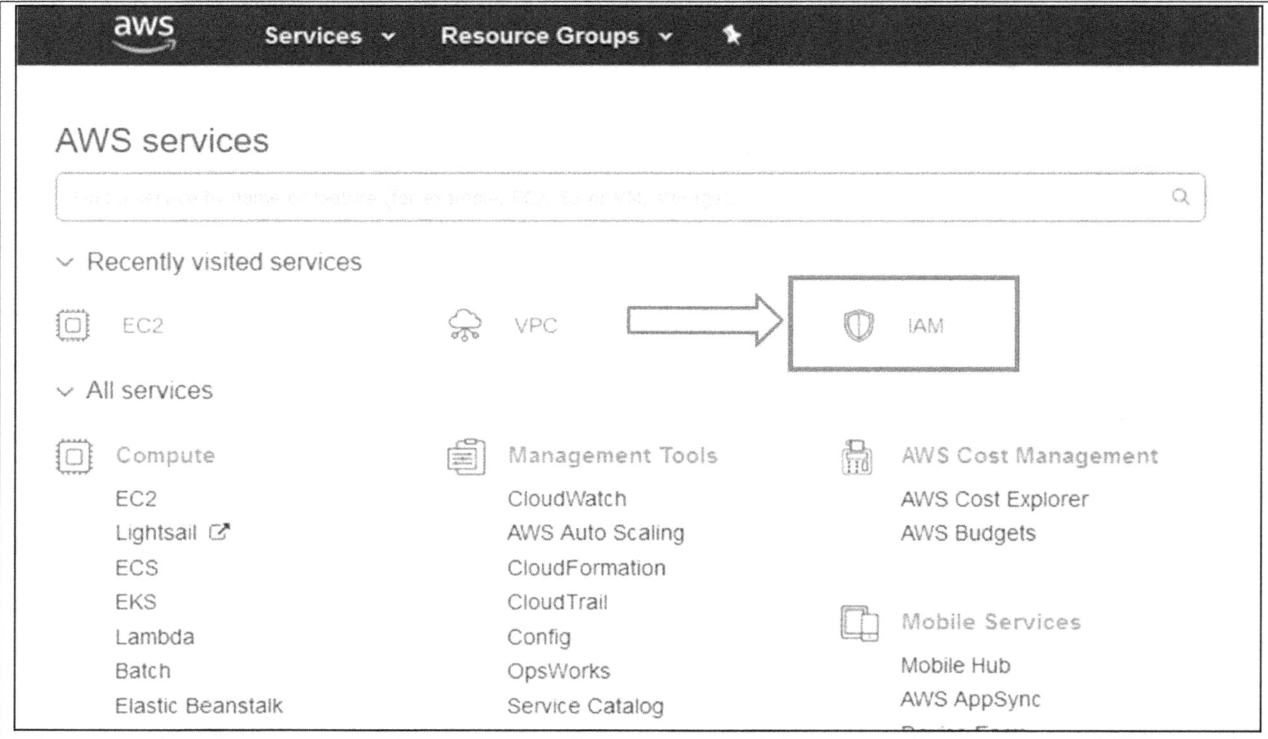

5. You will see the IAM user sign-in link at the top. This is a custom link where your users can sign in. The greyed-out portion of the link contains your account number. For security reasons, you should use an alias name instead of publicizing this number. Click on "Customize" to enter an alias.

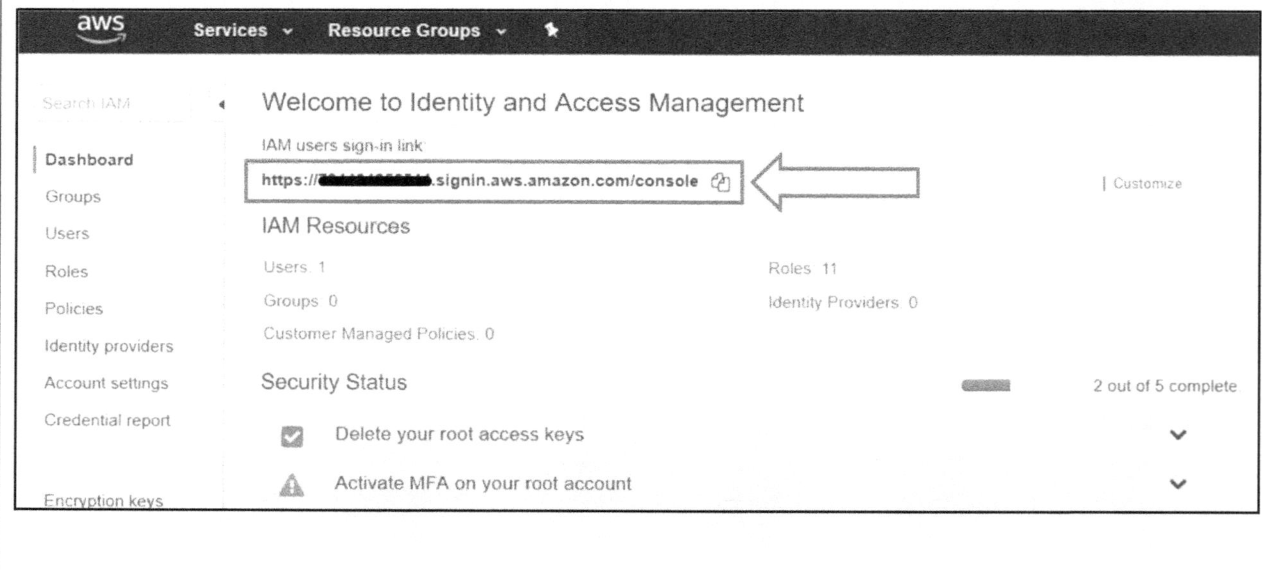

6. Click on the "Yes, Create" button to create an account alias.

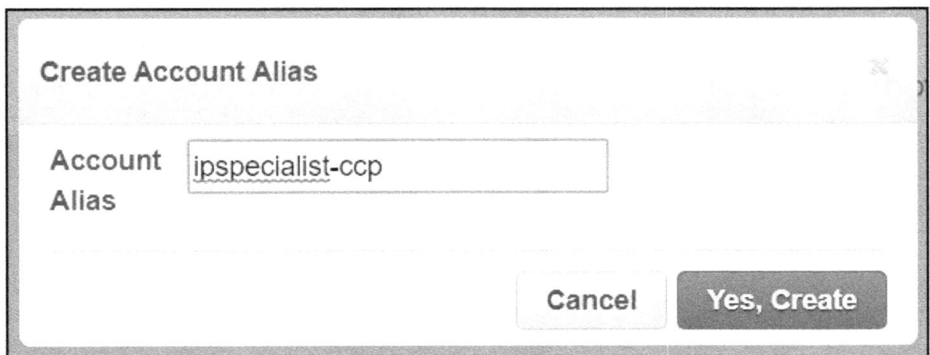

7. Next, you need to activate multi-factor authentication on your root account. Select "Activate MFA on your root account" then click "Manage MFA".

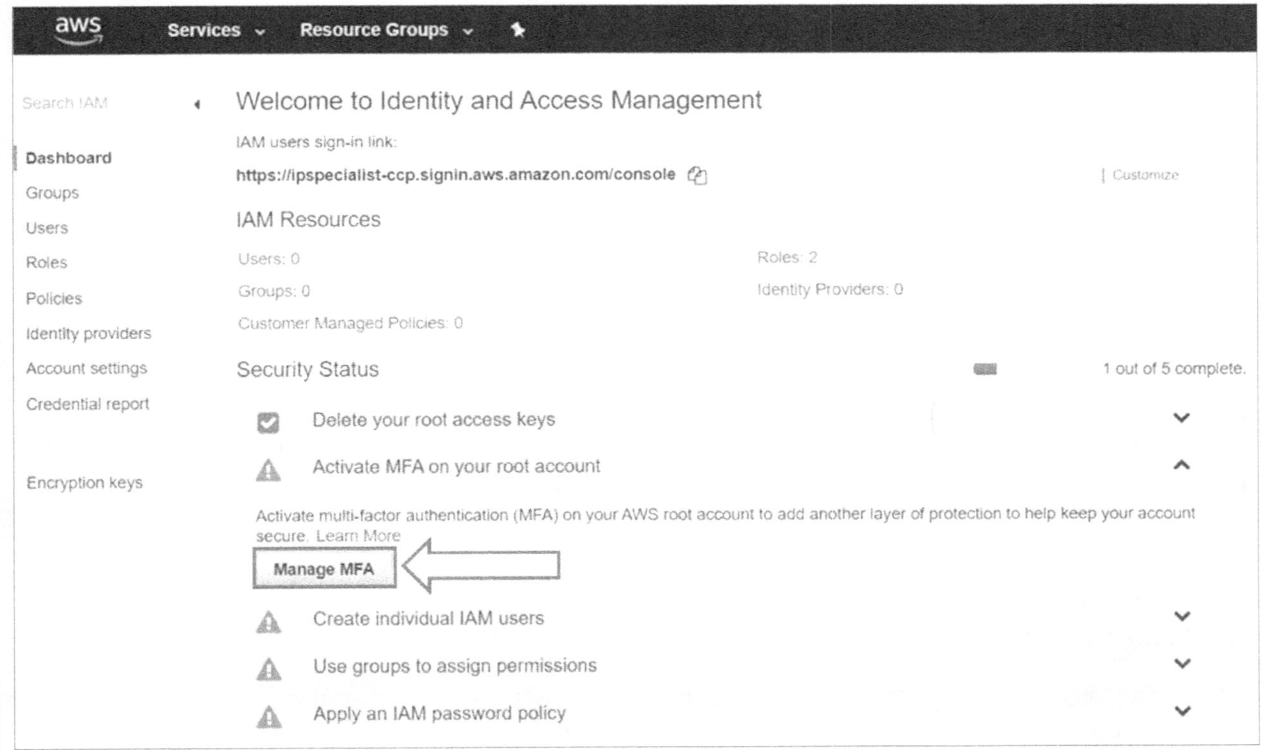

8. You need a physical device to enable hardware MFA. Use your smartphone and Google Authenticator to enable virtual MFA. You can download Google authenticator from the Google Play Store or iTunes Store on your smartphone.

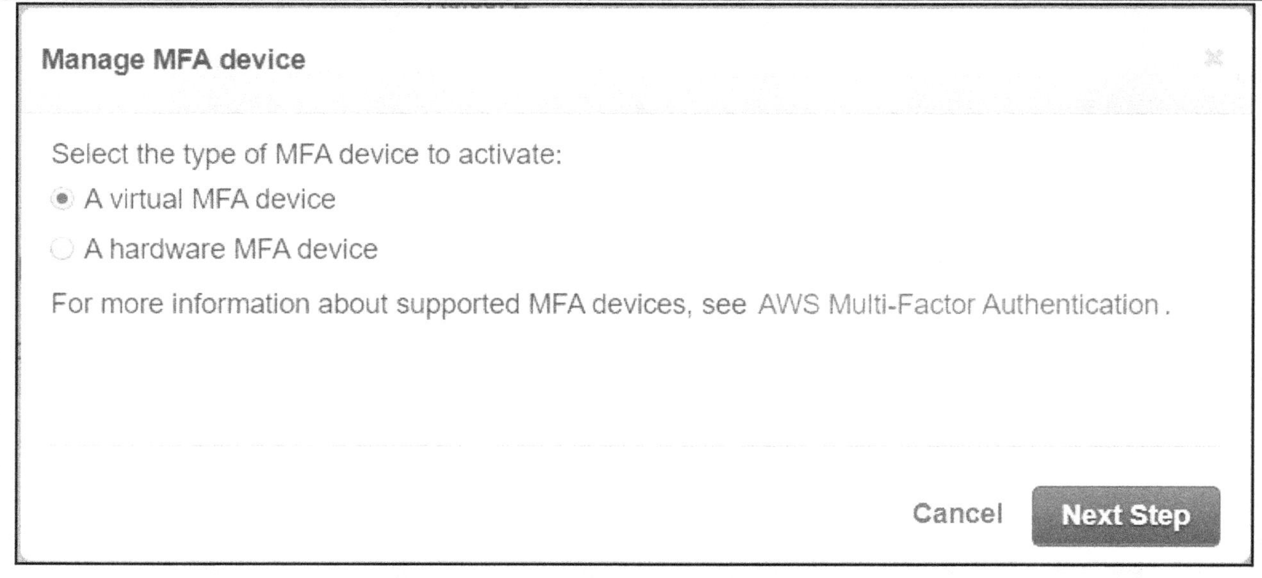

9. After installing the application on your smartphone, click "Next Step". You will need to open "Google Authenticator" on your smartphone.

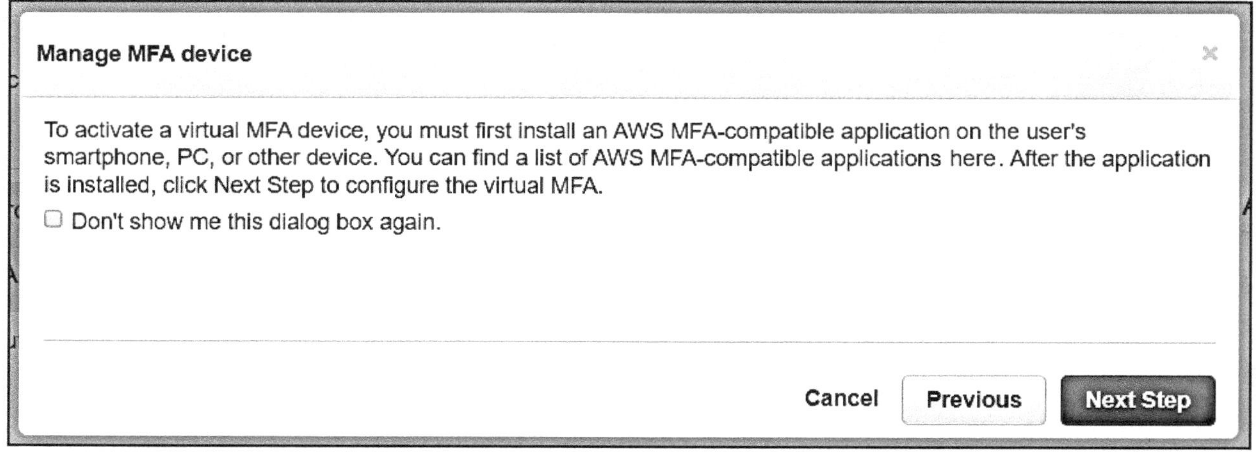

10. Using your smartphone, scan the barcode displayed on the screen. Google Authenticator will provide you with two authentication codes. Enter the codes in the boxes provided then click "Activate virtual MFA".

Manage MFA device

If your virtual MFA application supports scanning QR codes, scan the following QR code with your smartphone's camera.

▸ Show secret key for manual configuration

After the application is configured, enter two consecutive authentication codes in the boxes below and choose **Activate virtual MFA**.

Authentication code 1 370834

Authentication code 2 292960

Cancel | Previous | Activate virtual MFA

11. A pop-up will announce whether MFA was successful. If successful, click "Finish" and refresh your browser. You will see a green tick mark next to the MFA activation tab.

Manage MFA device

The MFA device was successfully associated with your account.

Finish

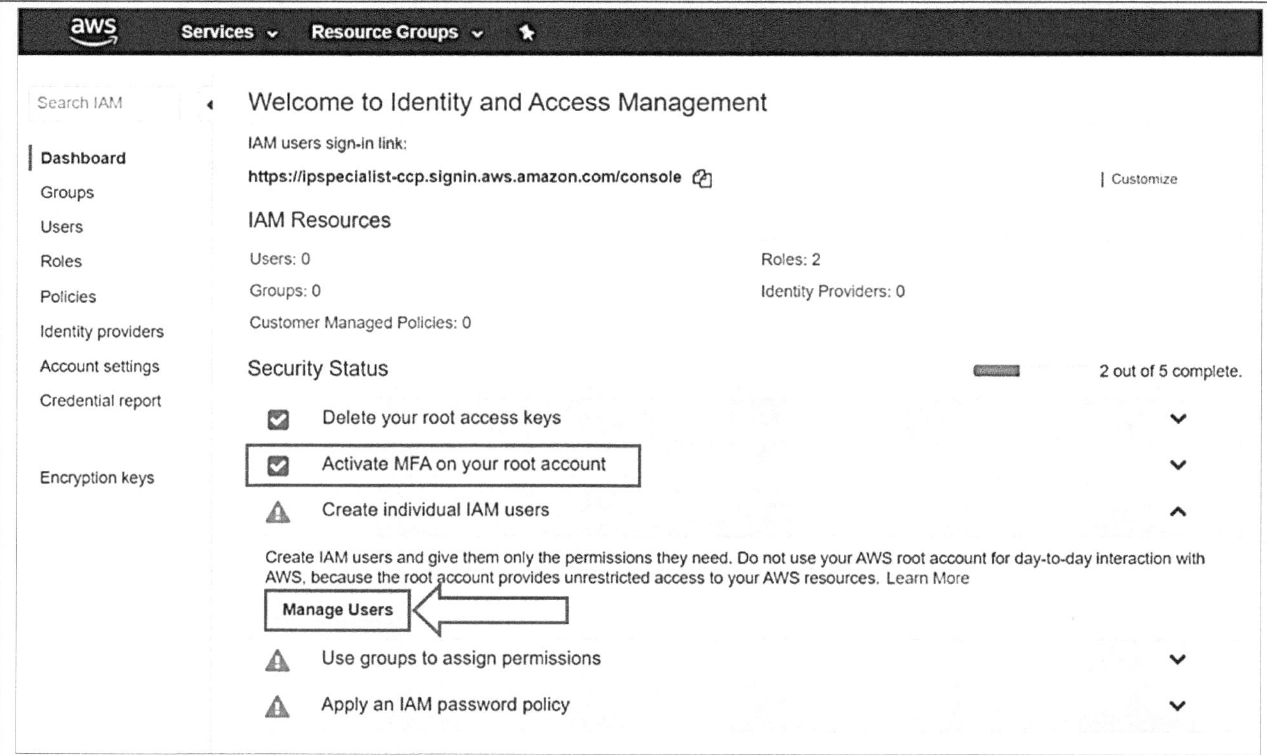

12. The next step is to create users within your root account. Select the "Create individual IAM users" tab and click "Manage Users". Click the "Add user" button at the top to add users.

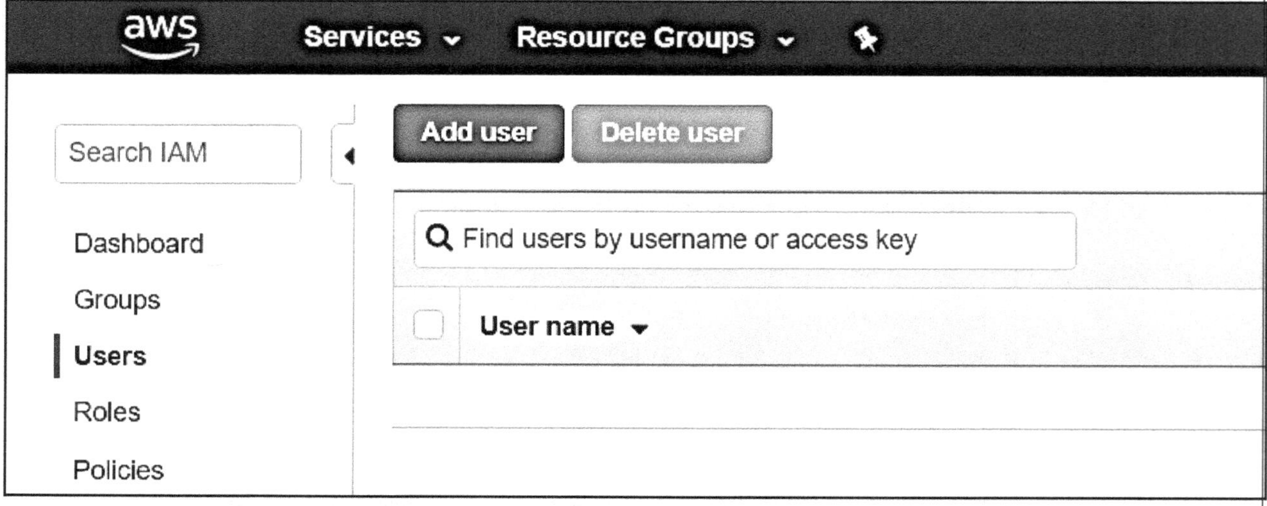

13. Enter a username and select the access type for the user. Programmatic access will generate an access key ID and a secret access key for the user. Accessing AWS via the

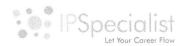

management console will require a password. You can either select an "Auto-generated password" or provide your custom password. Finally, you have the option to enable password reset, which will let the user create a new password when signing in for the first time. Click "Next: Permissions".

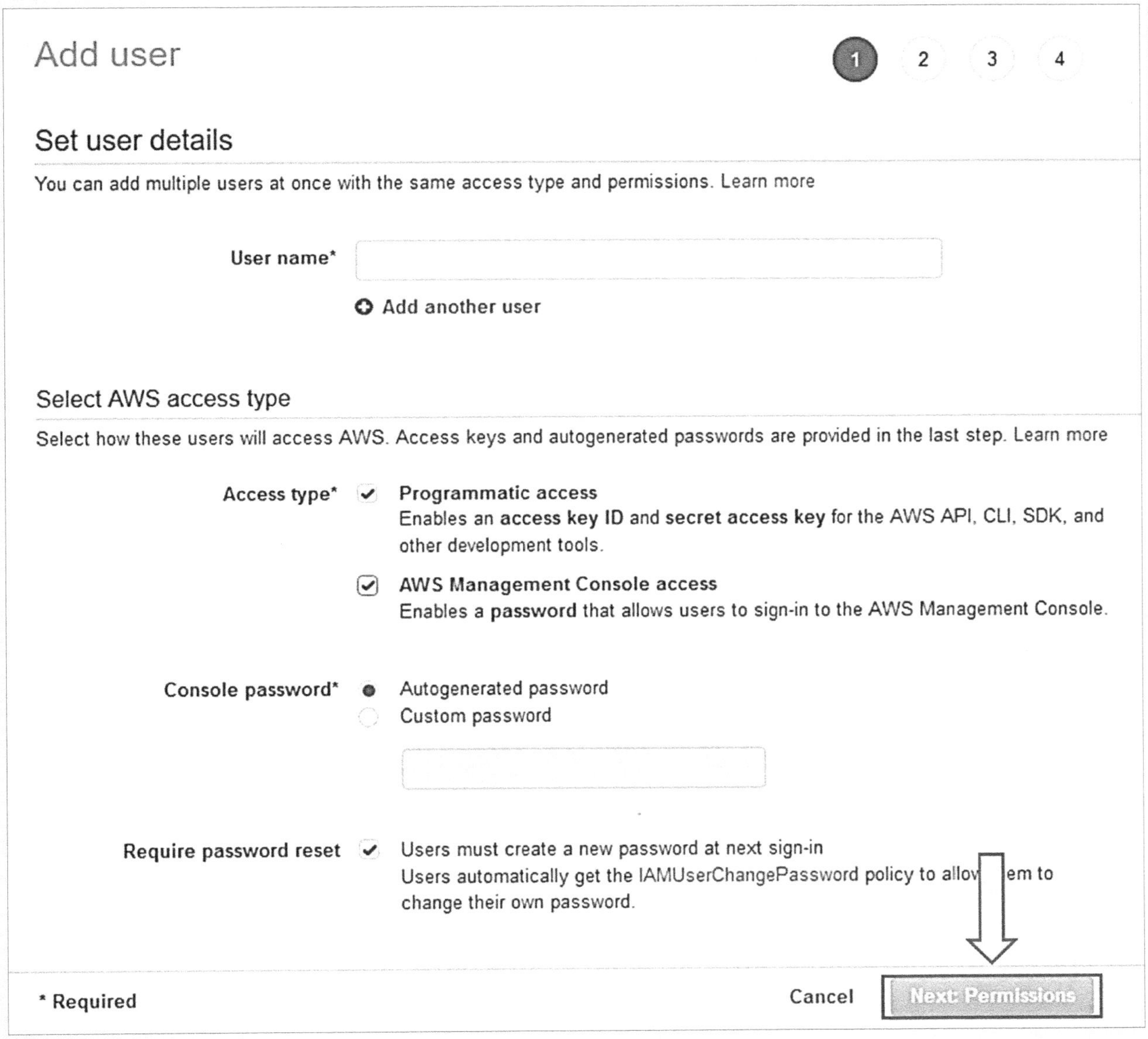

Add user

1 2 3 4

Set user details

You can add multiple users at once with the same access type and permissions. Learn more

User name*

Add another user

Select AWS access type

Select how these users will access AWS. Access keys and autogenerated passwords are provided in the last step. Learn more

Access type* — Programmatic access
Enables an **access key ID** and **secret access key** for the AWS API, CLI, SDK, and other development tools.

AWS Management Console access
Enables a **password** that allows users to sign-in to the AWS Management Console.

Console password* — Autogenerated password
Custom password

Require password reset — Users must create a new password at next sign-in
Users automatically get the IAMUserChangePassword policy to allow them to change their own password.

* Required — Cancel — Next: Permissions

14. To set permissions for the new user, you can either add a user to a premade group, copy permissions from an existing user, or attach existing policies directly. For this tutorial, we will add a user to a group.

15. First we need to create the group. Select "Create group".

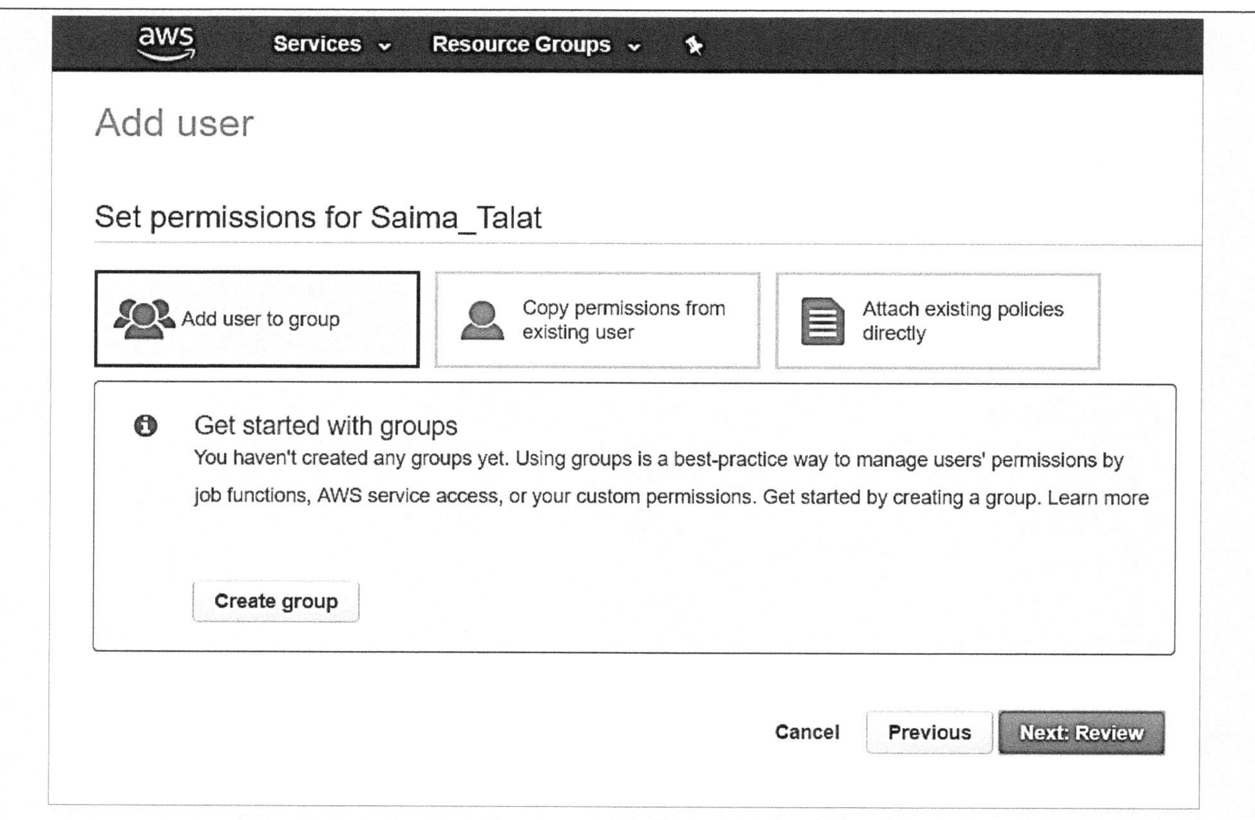

16. Enter a group name and select the policies you want to attach to this group. All users added to this group will inherit the policies of the group. For example, here we have selected the Administrator Access policy for our group named 'Administrators_Group', which provides full access to AWS services and resources. Click "Create group".

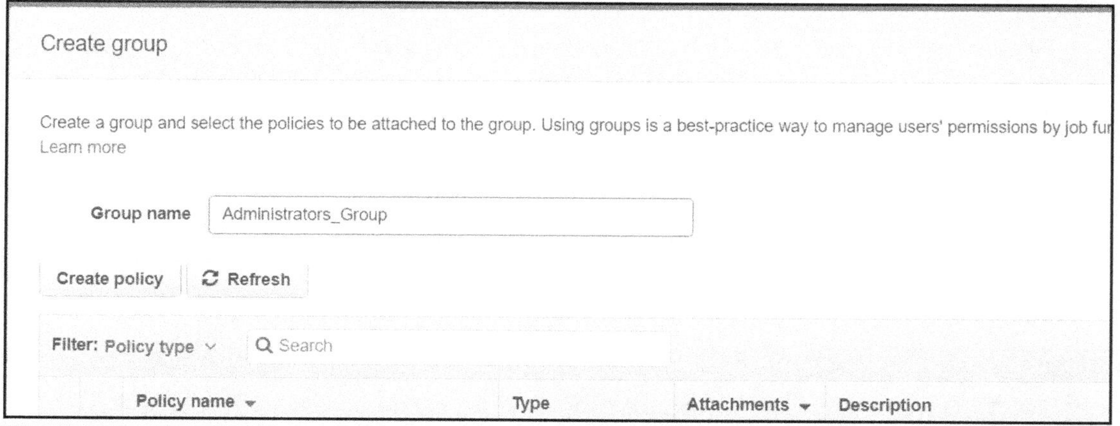

AWS managed	0	Provide gateway execution access to AlexaForBusiness services
AWS managed	0	Provide read only access to AlexaForBusiness services
AWS managed	0	Provides full access to create/edit/delete APIs in Amazon API Gateway via the AWS Mana...
AWS managed	0	Provides full access to invoke APIs in Amazon API Gateway.

Cancel Create group

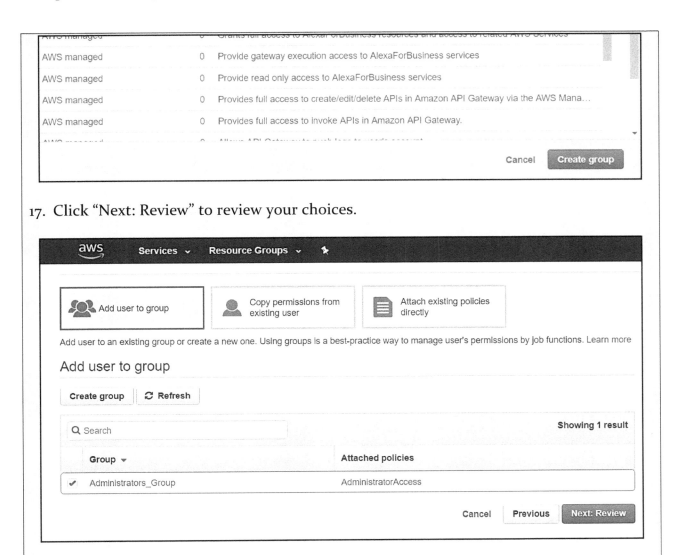

17. Click “Next: Review” to review your choices.

aws Services Resource Groups

Add user to group | Copy permissions from existing user | Attach existing policies directly

Add user to an existing group or create a new one. Using groups is a best-practice way to manage user's permissions by job functions. Learn more

Add user to group

Create group Refresh

Search Showing 1 result

	Group	Attached policies
✔	Administrators_Group	AdministratorAccess

Cancel Previous Next: Review

18. Review the details, select “Create user”.

aws Services Resource Groups

Add user

Review

Review your choices. After you create the user, you can view and download the autogenerated password and access key.

User details

User name	Saima_Talat
AWS access type	Programmatic access and AWS Management Console access
Console password type	Custom
Require password reset	No

Permissions summary

The user shown above will be added to the following groups.

Type	Name
Group	Administrators_Group

Cancel Previous Create user

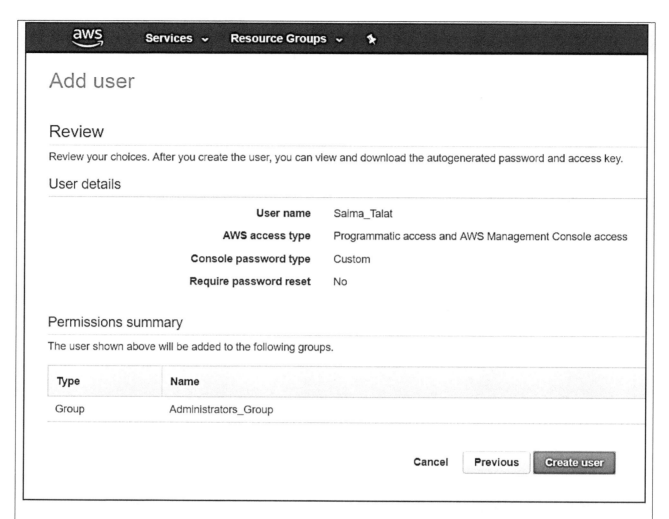

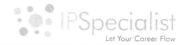

19. An Access key ID and a Secret access key for the user will be generated for programmatic access to AWS. These security credentials must always be kept secured. Click "Download .csv" button to download the user security credentials and then click "Close".

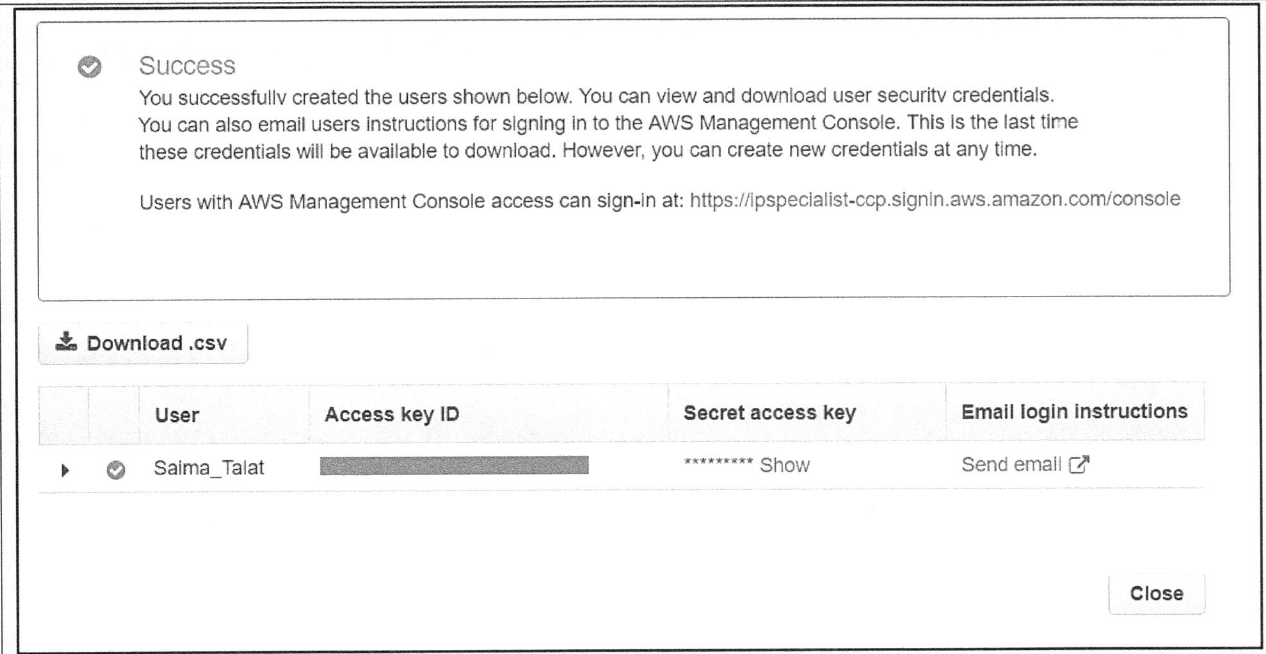

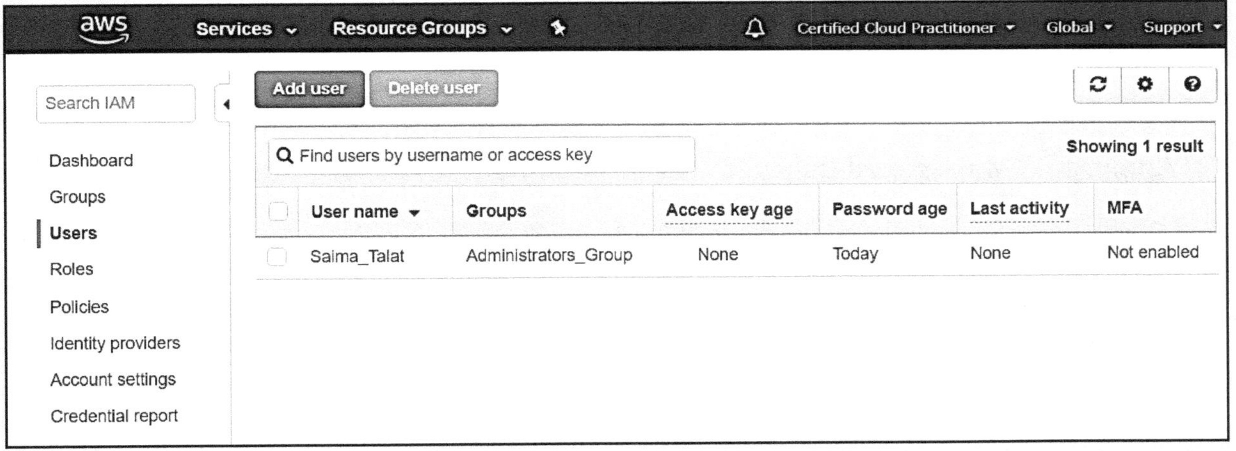

20. You will be able to see your newly-created user here. Select "Dashboard" from the list of tabs on the left to go back to the main IAM window.

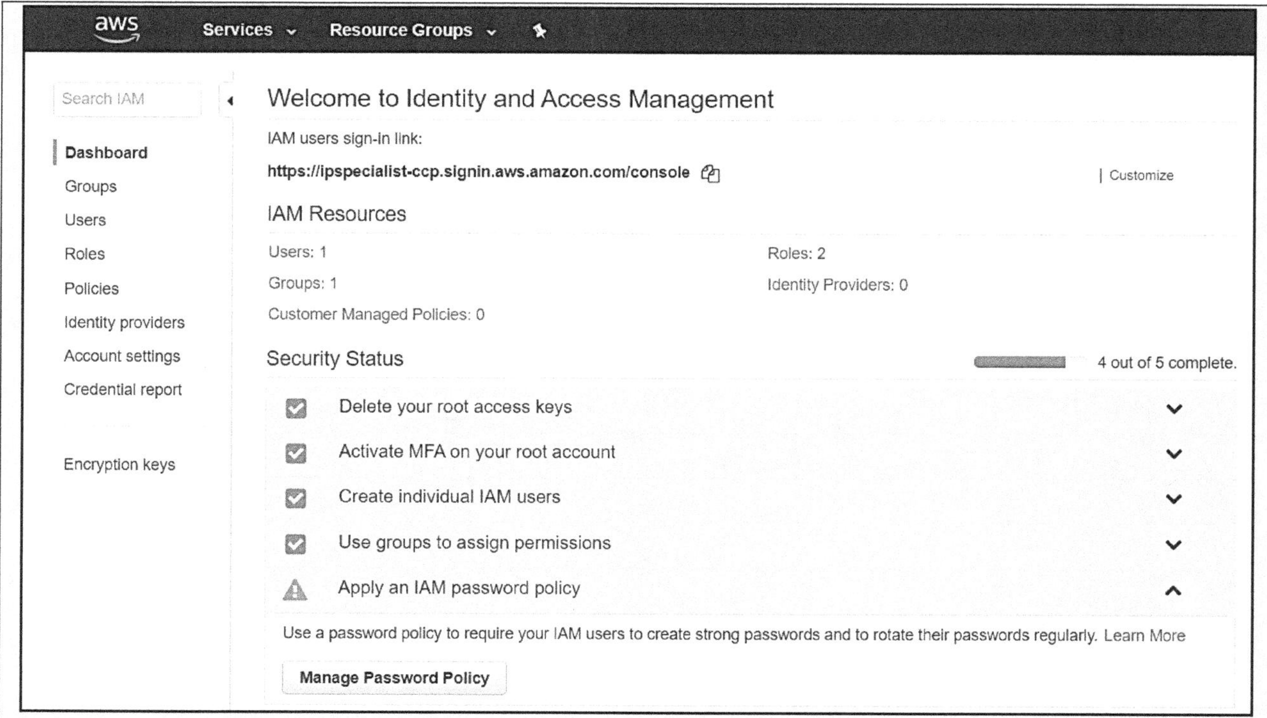

21. After creating a user and assigning permissions using groups, you now have to apply a password policy. This policy defines what passwords your users can create. Select the "Apply an IAM password policy" tab and click "Manage Password Policy".

aws Services Resource Groups

Search IAM

Dashboard
Groups
Users
Roles
Policies
Identity providers
Account settings
Credential report
Encryption keys

Password Policy

You have unsaved changes to your password policy.

A password policy is a set of rules that define the type of password an IAM user can set. For more information about password policies, go to Managing Passwords in Using IAM.

Currently, this AWS account does not have a password policy. Specify a password policy below.

Minimum password length: 6

- [x] Require at least one uppercase letter
- [x] Require at least one lowercase letter
- [x] Require at least one number
- [x] Require at least one non-alphanumeric character
- [x] Allow users to change their own password
- [ ] Enable password expiration

  Password expiration period (in days):
- [ ] Prevent password reuse

  Number of passwords to remember:
- [ ] Password expiration requires administrator reset

Apply password policy   Delete password policy

Security Token Service Regions

You can enable additional regions from which you can request temporary credentials. Activate only the regions you intend to use.

Regions	Status	Actions

Feedback English (US) © 2008 - 2018, Amazo

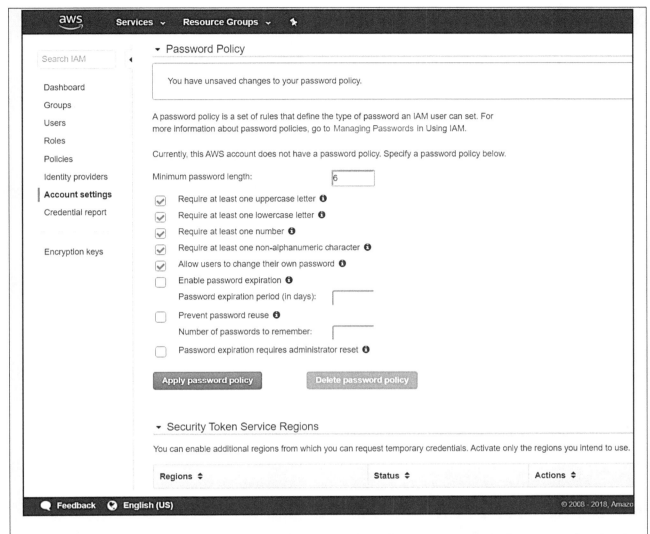

22. Specify the password policy by selecting options for your preferred password criteria. The more criteria you select, the more secure the password will be. Click “Apply password policy”. Once completed, select “Dashboard” to go back to the main IAM window.

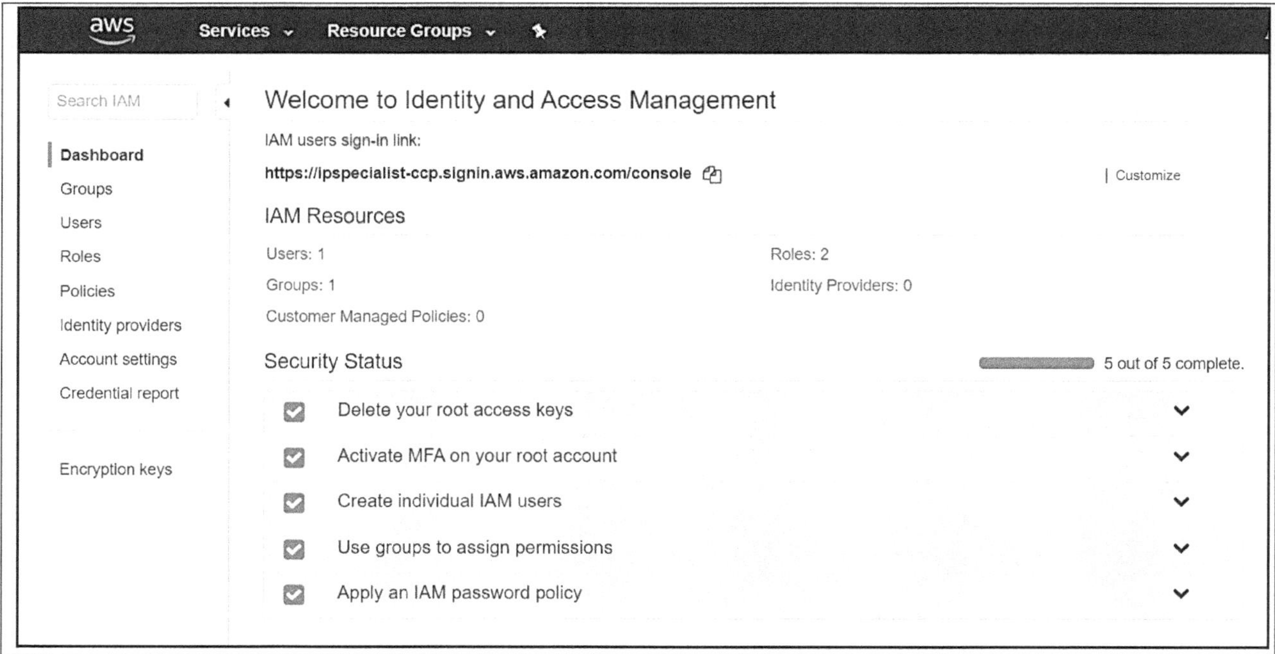

Security Support

AWS provides its customers with a variety of tools and features to assist them in achieving security objectives and maintaining an optimized environment. The four major tools and features covered in this course are described below.

AWS WAF

The AWS Web Application Firewall (WAF) provides protection to web applications against common web threats that disrupt application accessibility, compromise security or consume undue resources. AWS WAF lets you create and define custom web security rules for specific applications, offering you control over web traffic and whether to allow, block, or monitor (count web requests) traffic based on predefined conditions. These conditions can be IP addresses, HTTP headers, HTTP body, URI strings, SQL injection or cross-site scripting. Security rules can also be created to block attacks from specific user-agents, bad bots or content scrapers.

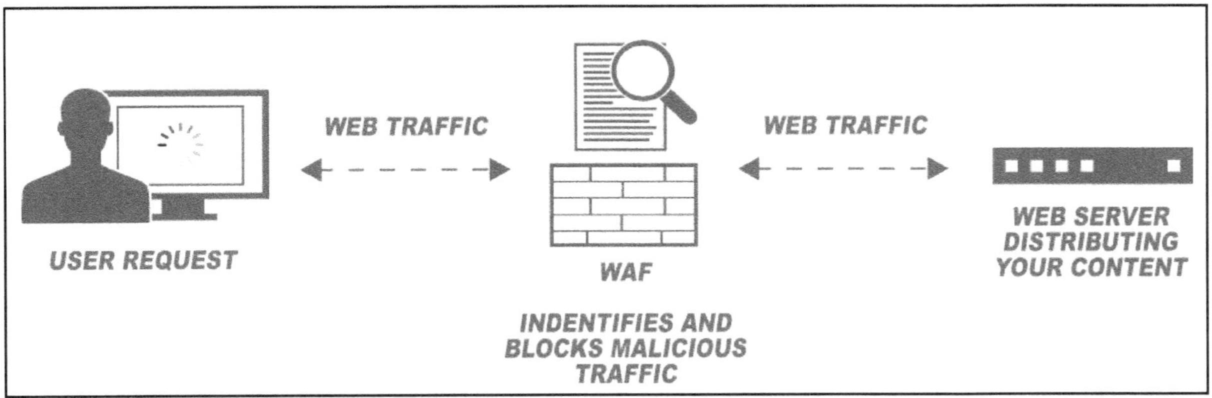

Figure 2-05: Web Application Firewall

AWS WAF contains a full-featured API that automates the creation, deployment, and maintenance of web security rules when required, depending on changes to traffic patterns. AWS WAF can be deployed either on Amazon CloudFront as part of CDN to protect resources and content at Edge locations before they reach the web servers, or as a part of the Application Load Balancer (ALB) to protect origin web servers from running behind the ALBs or the internet-facing servers.

An example scenario of this would be a hacker sending a cross-site scripting attack using an SQL injection. WAF can penetrate to layer seven of the OSI (Open Systems Interconnection) model and analyze network traffic at the application layer. It will inspect the data the hacker is sending and intervene by blocking that traffic. This prevents cross-site attacks or an SQL injection.

AWS WAF also follows the 'pay-as-you-go' model with no upfront commitments. The pricing depends upon the number of rules you deploy and the number of web requests your web application receives.

EXAM TIP: The best way to remember WAF is to think of it as an intelligent Security Group. AWS WAF efficiently prevents common attack patterns like SQL injection and Cross-Site Scripting (XSS) by monitoring the HTTP and HTTPS requests.

AWS Shield

AWS Shield is a managed protection service that safeguards web applications running on AWS against Distributed Denial of Service (DDoS) attacks. It delivers always-on detection with automatic inline mitigations that reduce

application downtime and latency. A Denial-of-Service (DoS) attack is a malicious attempt to disrupt the availability of a targeted system by flooding it with packets or requests, causing the system to crash due to the overwhelming traffic volume. A Distributed-Denial-of-Service (DDoS) attack is generated using several compromised systems or controlled sources.

There are two tiers of AWS Shield:

- AWS Shield Standard
- AWS Shield Advanced
    - AWS Shield Standard is offered to all AWS customers at no additional cost
    - AWS Shield Advanced is an optional paid service accessible to AWS Business Support and AWS Enterprise Support customers with a monthly fee of $3,000

AWS Shield Standard protects against more commonly occurring Infrastructure (OSI layer 3 and layer 4) attacks such as SYN/UDP Floods, Reflection attacks and others, in order to maintain the high availability of applications on AWS.

AWS Shield Advanced delivers enhanced protection against larger and more sophisticated attacks through the flow-based monitoring of network traffic and active application scrutiny, which can notify system hosts of incoming DDoS attacks in near real-time. Customers can take immediate action to mitigate the attack using the highly flexible controls.

Lab 2-3: AWS Shield

1. Log in to the “AWS Console”.
2. Click on “Services”.
3. Scroll down to “Security, Identity & Compliance”.
4. Select “WAF & Shield”.

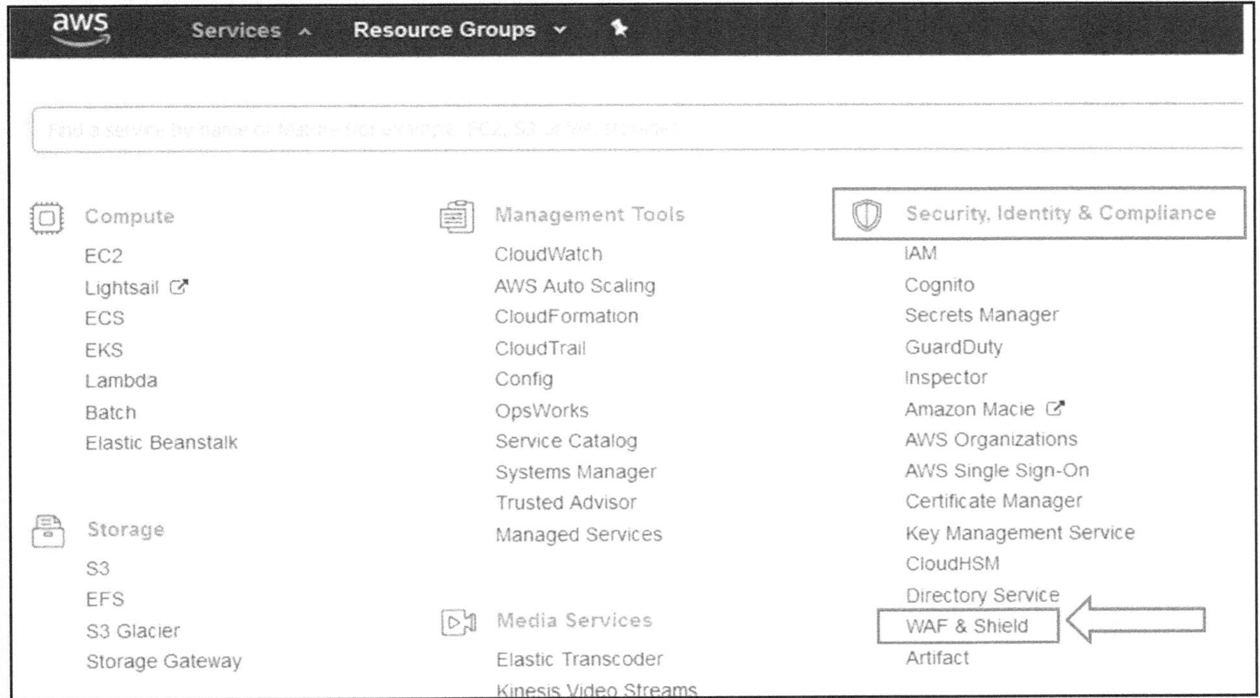

5. Click on “Go to AWS WAF” to configure web application firewall services or select “Go to AWS Shield” to determine Standard and Advance version options.

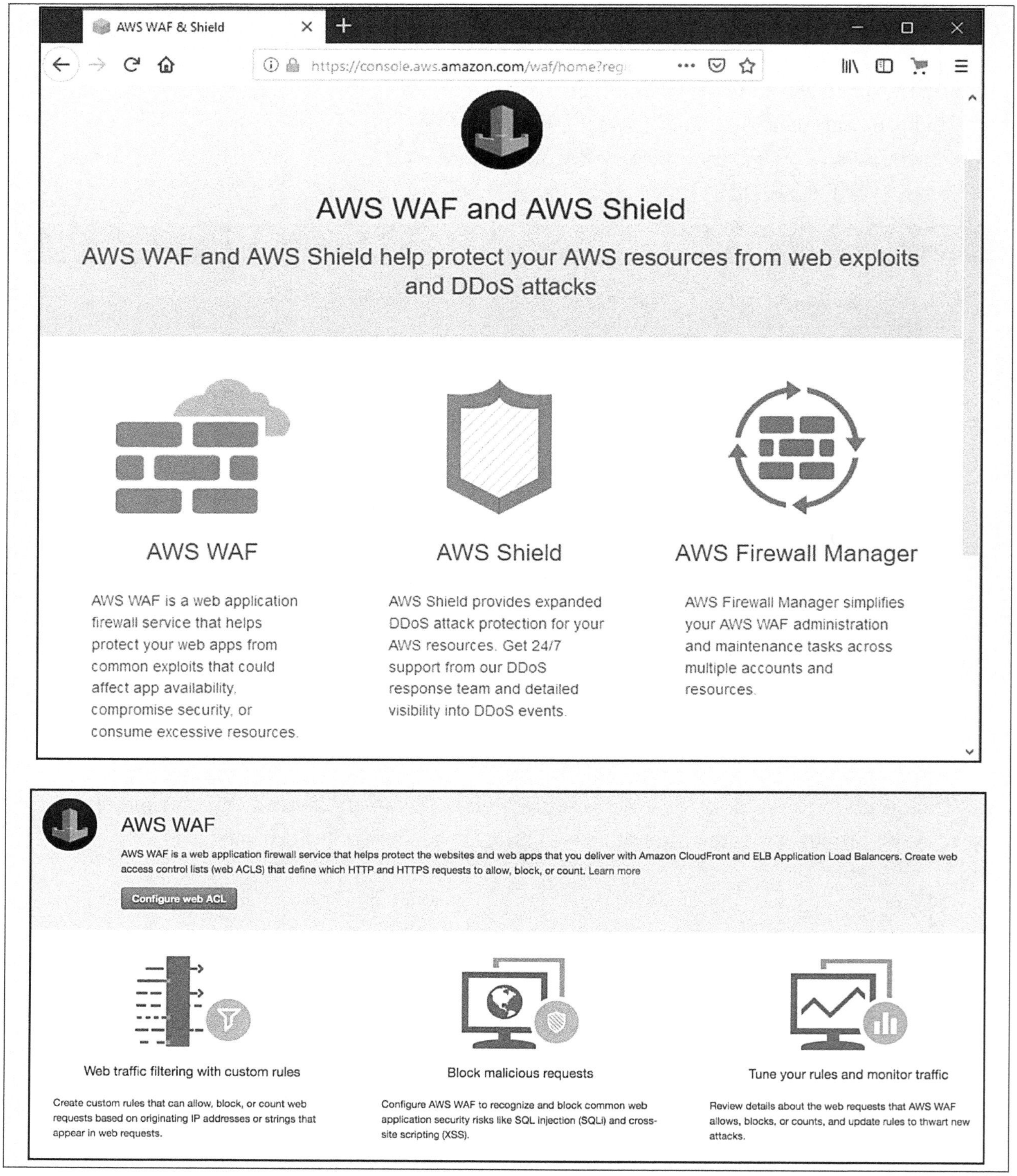

AWS WAF & Shield

https://console.aws.amazon.com/waf/home?regi

AWS WAF and AWS Shield

AWS WAF and AWS Shield help protect your AWS resources from web exploits and DDoS attacks

AWS WAF

AWS WAF is a web application firewall service that helps protect your web apps from common exploits that could affect app availability, compromise security, or consume excessive resources.

AWS Shield

AWS Shield provides expanded DDoS attack protection for your AWS resources. Get 24/7 support from our DDoS response team and detailed visibility into DDoS events.

AWS Firewall Manager

AWS Firewall Manager simplifies your AWS WAF administration and maintenance tasks across multiple accounts and resources.

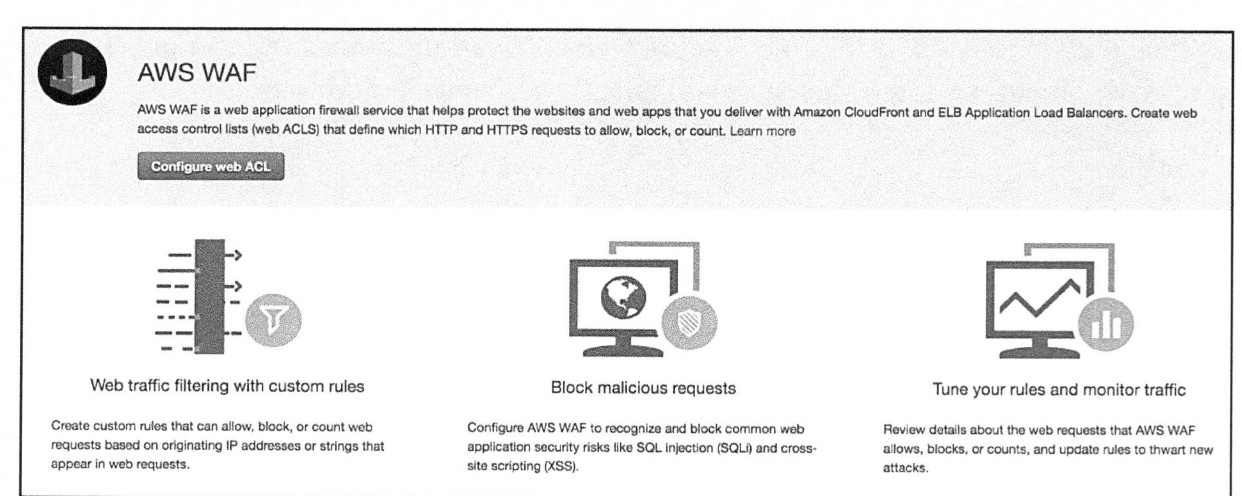

AWS Shield

As an AWS customer, you automatically have basic DDoS protection with the AWS Shield Standard plan, at no additional cost beyond what you already pay for AWS WAF and your other AWS services. For an additional cost, you can get advanced DDoS protection by activating the AWS Shield Advanced plan. The following table shows a comparison of the two plans.

Features	AWS Shield Standard	AWS Shield Advanced
Active monitoring		
Network flow monitoring	✔	✔
Automated application (layer 7) traffic monitoring	-	✔
DDoS mitigations		
Helps protect from common DDoS attacks, such as SYN floods and UDP reflection attacks	✔	✔
Access to additional DDoS mitigation capacity	-	✔
Visibility and reporting		
Layer 3/4 attack notification and attack forensic reports	-	✔
Layer 3/4/7 attack historical report	-	✔
DDoS response team support		
Incident management during high severity	-	✔

EXAM TIP: You only need to know the general overview of AWS WAF and AWS Shield. Remember that AWS Shield Standard is free of charge and is activated automatically; but for the AWS Shield Advanced version, you will have to pay $3000/month. Similarly, AWS WAF also costs money on a pay-per-use system.

AWS Inspector

Amazon Inspector is an automated security assessment service to improve the security and compliance of the applications running on Amazon EC2.

After assessing applications for vulnerabilities or deviations from best practices, it provides a thorough list of security findings, listed in order of severity. Amazon Inspector is API-driven service that makes it easy to deploy, manage and automate.

While using Amazon Inspector, an assessment target is defined, including the collection of AWS resources to be monitored. Eventually, a security assessment run of the target is launched. A complete detailed assessment report is then delivered via the Amazon Inspector console or API. This report includes a list of findings for potential security issues discovered after analyzing and monitoring the network, process activity and file system of the specified target.

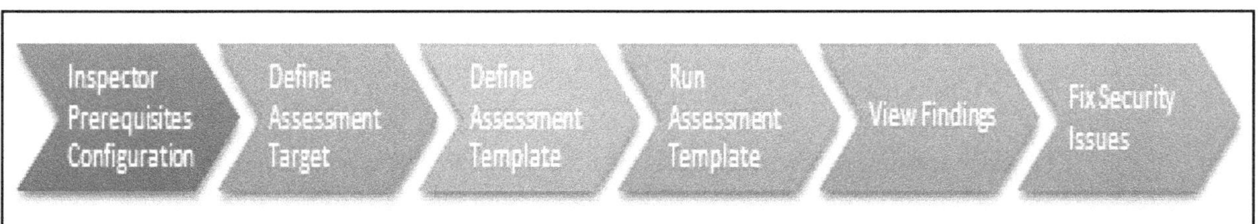

Figure 2-06: AWS Inspector

Lab 2-4: AWS Inspector

1. Log in to the "AWS Console".
2. Click on "Services".
3. Scroll down to "Security, Identity & Compliance".
4. Select "Inspector".

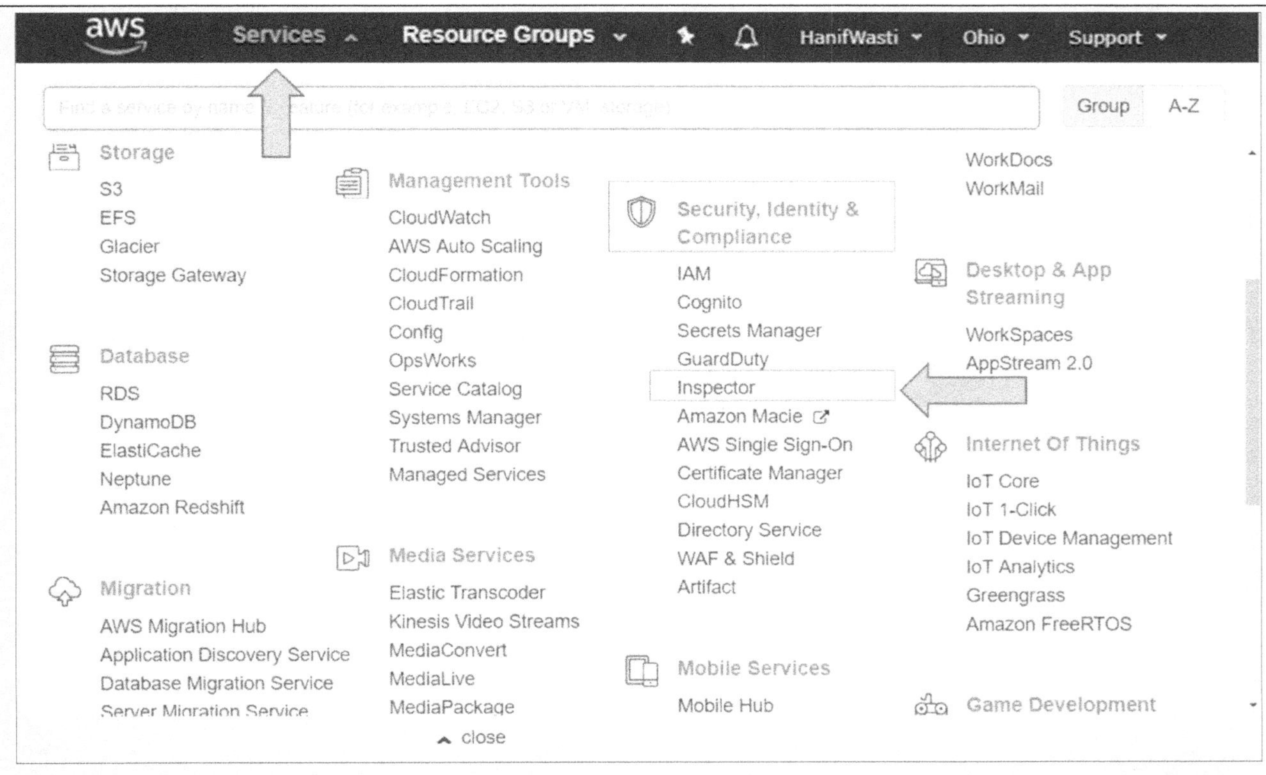

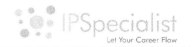

5. Click "Get started" to configure Amazon Inspector by creating a role, tagging your EC2 instances, installing the AWS agent and defining an assessment target.

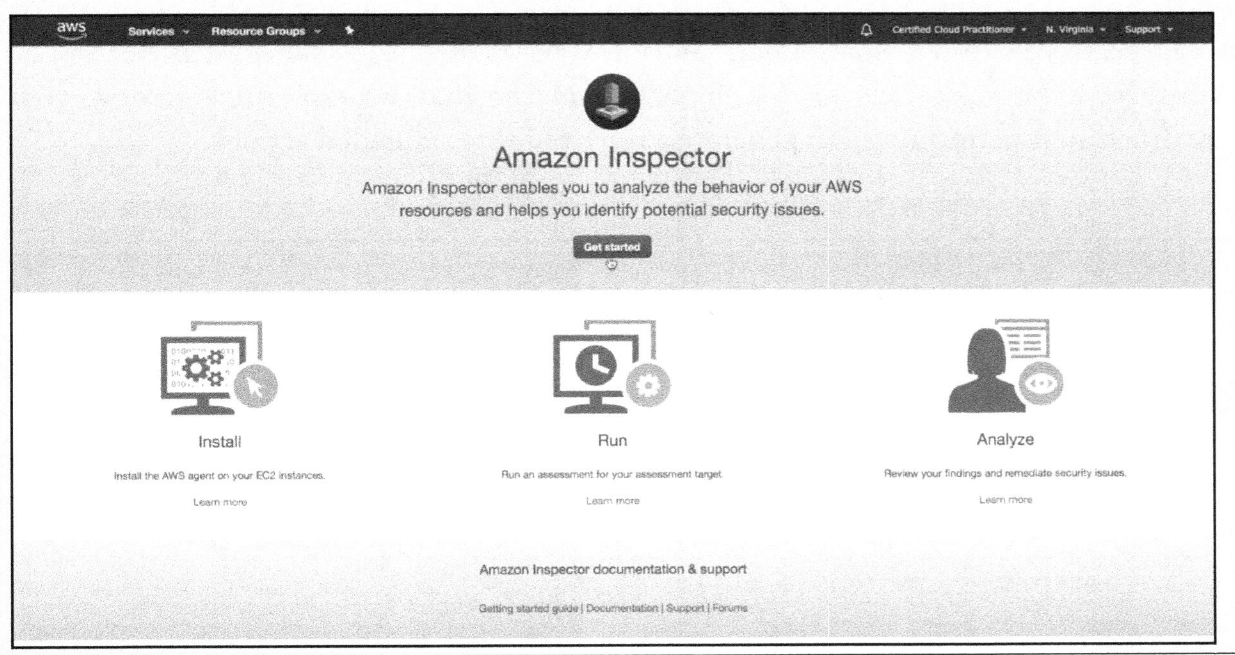

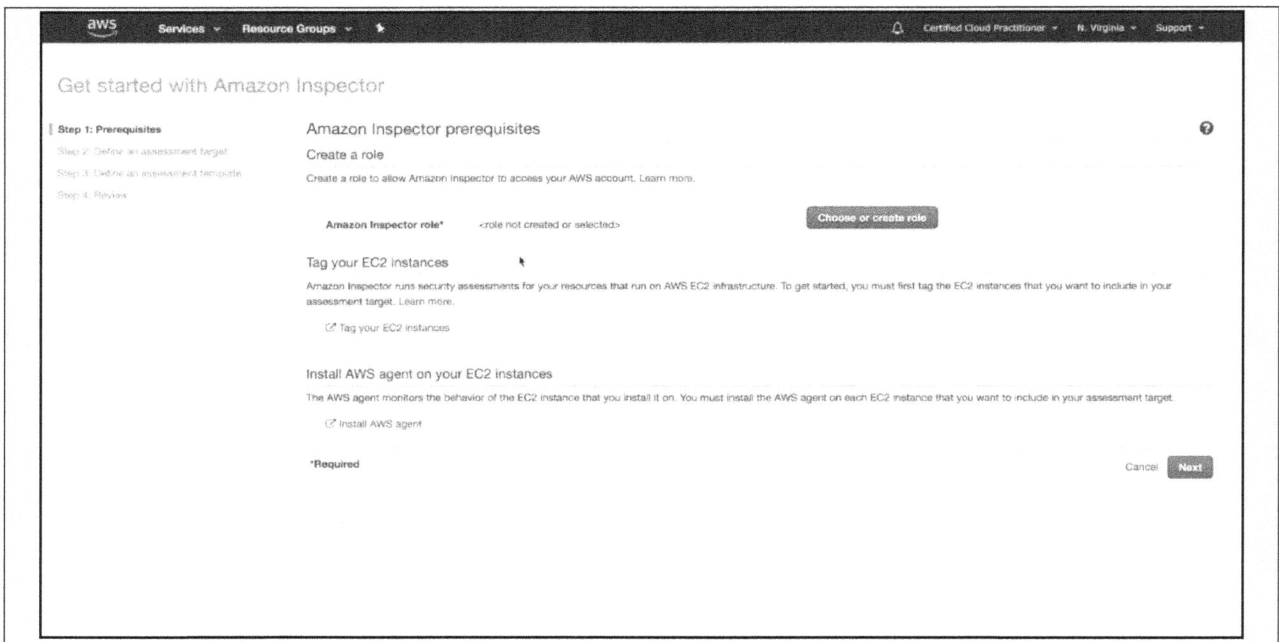

AWS Trusted Advisor

AWS Trusted Advisor is an online resource used for optimizing your AWS environment by following AWS best practices. It helps you to identify how to configure the resources you can use in order to reduce cost, increase performance, and improve security. Trusted Advisor works as a customized cloud expert that inspects your AWS environment and provides real-time guidance. It is not only a security tool but also acts as a complete analyzer that will inform you how your infrastructure is performing and generate a report of recommended actions.

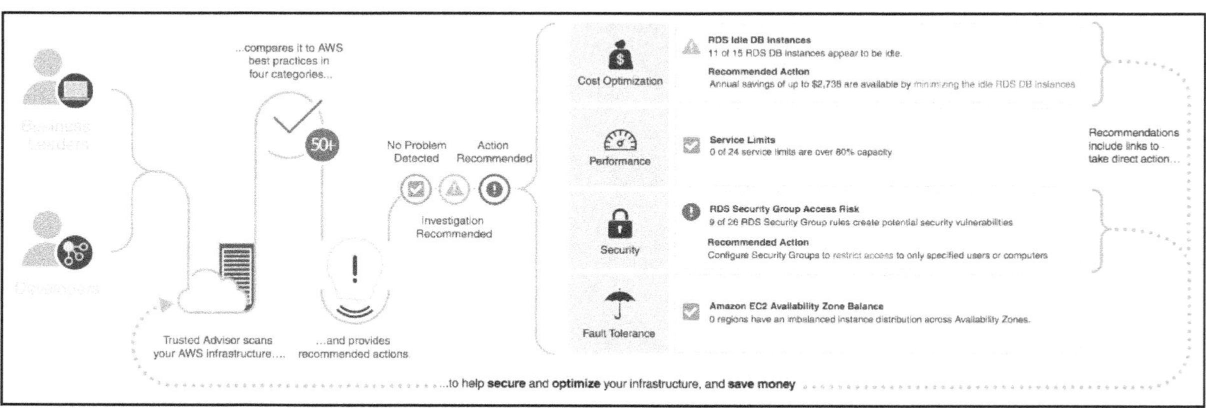

Figure 2-07: An Environment with Trusted Advisor

Trusted Advisor performs a list of checks in the following four categories:

- ***Cost Optimization*** – Recommends how you can save money, by highlighting idle resources and prospects to cut costs
- ***Security*** – Identifies optimum security settings to help close security gaps and make the environment more secure
- ***Fault Tolerance*** – Provides recommendations that help increase the resiliency of AWS solutions by highlighting redundancy shortfalls, current service limits and over-utilized resources
- ***Performance*** – Suggests recommendations for improving the rapidity and responsiveness of applications by detecting common security misconfigurations, as well as suggestions for refining system performance and under-utilized resources

AWS Trusted Advisor is available to customers in two different forms:

Core Checks and Recommendations:

- Available to all AWS Customers at no additional cost
- Access to seven core checks to improve security and performance: S3 Bucket Permissions, Security Groups - Specific Ports Unrestricted, IAM Use, MFA on Root Account, EBS Public Snapshots and RDS Public Snapshots
- Service Limits: Checks for service usage that is more than 80% of the limit

Full Trusted Advisor:

- Available with Business and Enterprise Support Plans only
- Access to a complete set of checks to help optimize your entire AWS infrastructure
- Additional benefits include: Notifications to stay up-to-date and Programmatic Access to retrieve and refresh results of the Trusted Advisor Program

EXAM TIP: Inspector is a security product that you install on your EC2 instances to look for vulnerabilities, whereas Trusted Advisor gives recommendations on security as well as cost optimization, performance and fault tolerance. Trusted Advisor looks into a whole plethora of services and is not only limited to EC2 instances.

Lab 2-04: AWS Trusted Advisor

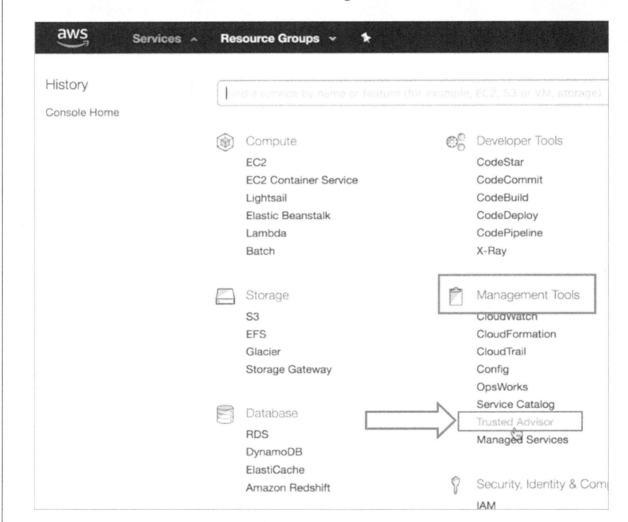

1. Log in to the "AWS Console".
2. Click on "Services" and scroll down to "Management Tools". Select "Trusted Advisor".
3. Click the "Refresh" logo at the top right corner to re-run all the Cost Optimization, Performance, Security and Fault Tolerance checks.

aws Services Resource Groups

Certified Cloud Practitioner Global Support

Dashboard
Cost Optimization
Performance
Security
Fault Tolerance
Preferences

Trusted Advisor Dashboard

Cost Optimization: 0 0 0
Performance: 1 0 0
Security: 4 1 0
Fault Tolerance: 0 0 0

Recommended Actions

Security Groups - Specific Ports Unrestricted — Refreshed: 18 hours ago
Checks security groups for rules that allow unrestricted access (0.0.0.0/0) to specific ports.
3 of 12 security group rules allow unrestricted access to a specific port.

IAM Use — Refreshed: 18 hours ago
Checks for your use of AWS Identity and Access Management (IAM).
At least one IAM user has been created for this account.

MFA on Root Account — Refreshed: 18 hours ago
Checks the root account and warns if multi-factor authentication (MFA) is not enabled.
MFA is enabled on the root account.

Service Limits — Refreshed: 18 hours ago
Checks for usage that is more than 80% of the service limit.
0 of 63 items have usage that is more than 80% of the service limit.

Amazon EBS Public Snapshots

Chapter 3: Technology

Introduction

AWS offers a broad set of global cloud-based products and services that can be used as building blocks for setting up common cloud architectures. The products and services are divided into categories. Some of the categories and their services covered in this course include:

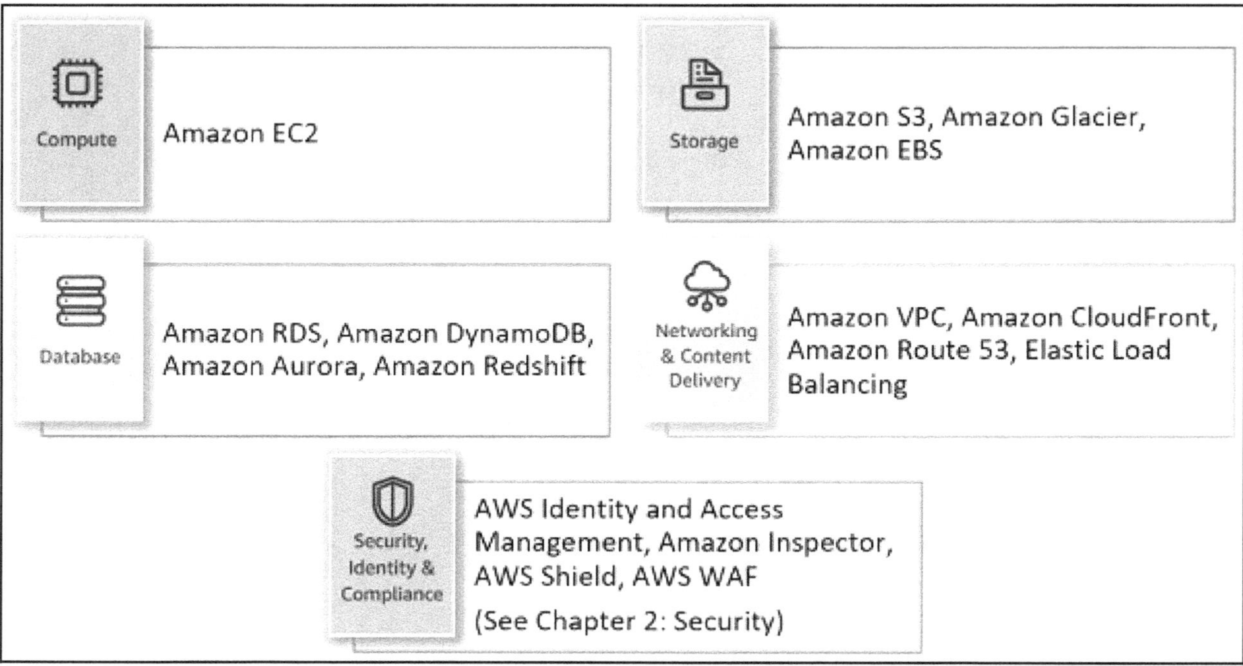

Figure 3-01: AWS

AWS Cloud Deployment and Management Services

AWS caters to customers with distinctive requirements by offering several customization alternatives to ensure it can serve a wide range of use cases. When it comes to deployment and management services, whether for a simple application or a complex set of workloads, AWS offers multiple options for provisioning your IT infrastructure. As the deployment model differs from customer to customer, you can use the various building blocks (Amazon EC2, Amazon EBS, Amazon S3, Amazon RDS) and leverage the integration provided by third-party tools to deploy your application. Alternatively, you could consider the automation provided by the AWS deployment services.

These deployment services are simple ways you can deploy your application on the underlying infrastructure. The AWS deployment tool handles the complex provisioning of the AWS resources, which are required for your application to run.

Despite having a similar functionality, each service has its own unique method for deploying and managing your application. For the Cloud Practitioner Exam, you need to study Elastic Beanstalk and CloudFormation services.

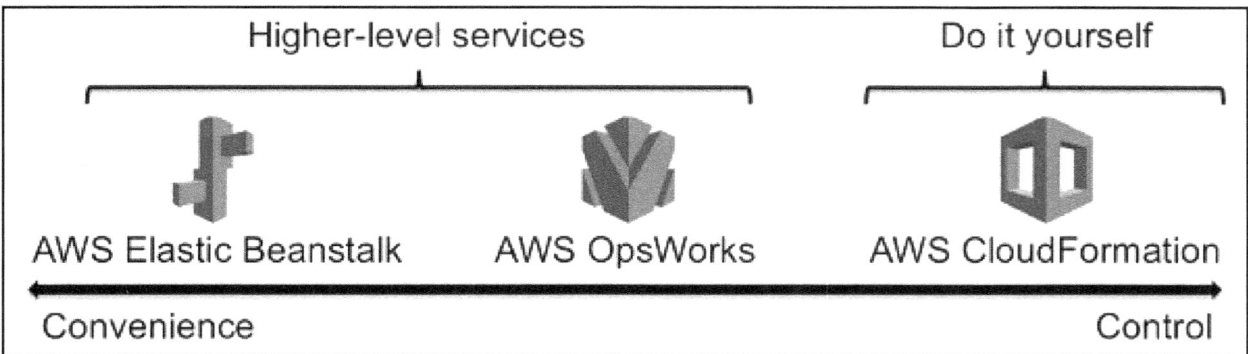

Figure 3-02: AWS Deployment & Management Services Overview

AWS Elastic Beanstalk

AWS Elastic Beanstalk allows developers to deploy everything at the click of a button. It is the simplest way to set up an application on AWS without worrying about managing the underlying infrastructure. Developers only need to upload their code as the service automates the deployment of all resources.

Elastic Beanstalk works best with a standard three-tier PHP, Java, Python, Ruby, Node.js,NET, Go or Docker application running on an app server containing a database. Common use cases include web apps, content management systems (CMS) and API backends.

Elastic Beanstalk uses Auto Scaling and Elastic Load Balancing to handle peaks in workload. It automatically scales the application up or down based on the requirements of the application while allowing the developer to retain full control over the AWS resources.

Lab 3-1: AWS Elastic Beanstalk

1. Log in to the "AWS Console".
2. Click on "Services".
3. Scroll down to "Compute". Select "Elastic Beanstalk".

aws Services Resource Groups

AWS services

Recently visited services

WAF & Shield
IAM
EC2
VPC

All services

Compute
EC2
Lightsail
ECS
EKS
Lambda
Batch
Elastic Beanstalk

Storage
S3

Management Tools
CloudWatch
AWS Auto Scaling
CloudFormation
CloudTrail
Config
OpsWorks
Service Catalog
Systems Manager
Trusted Advisor
Managed Services

AWS Cost Management
AWS Cost Explorer
AWS Budgets

Mobile Services
Mobile Hub
AWS AppSync
Device Farm

AR & VR

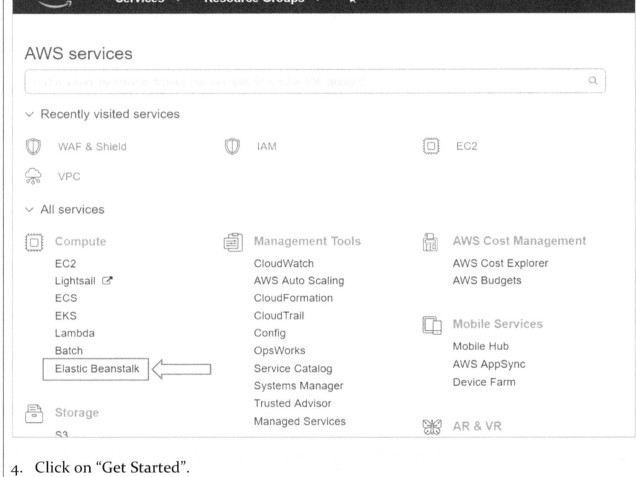

4. Click on "Get Started".

aws Services Resource Groups
IPSPECIALIST Ohio Support
Elastic Beanstalk
Create New Application

Welcome to AWS Elastic Beanstalk

With Elastic Beanstalk, you can **deploy**, **monitor**, and **scale** an application quickly and easily. Let us do the heavy lifting so you can focus on your business.

To deploy your **existing web application**, create an application source bundle and then create a new application. If you're using **Git** and would prefer to use it with our command line tool, please see Getting Started with the EB CLI.

To deploy a **sample application**, click **Get started**, choose a name, select a platform and click **Create app**.

By launching the sample application, you allow AWS Elastic Beanstalk to administer AWS resources and necessary permissions on your behalf. Learn more

Get started

Get Started in Three Easy Steps

Select a Platform

Upload an Application or Use a Sample

Run it!

Start Now by Selecting Your Platform

php Ruby node ...and more

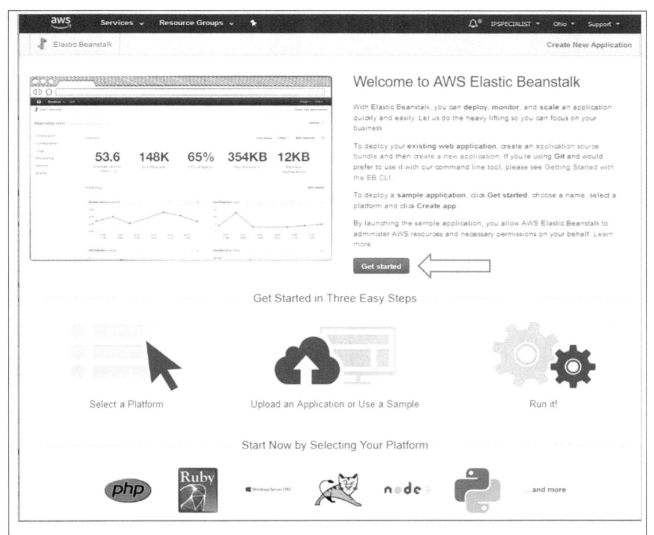

5. Enter the application name, platform and application code.
6. Here we have selected the platform "PHP", and we have used the application code "Sample application". Click "Create application".

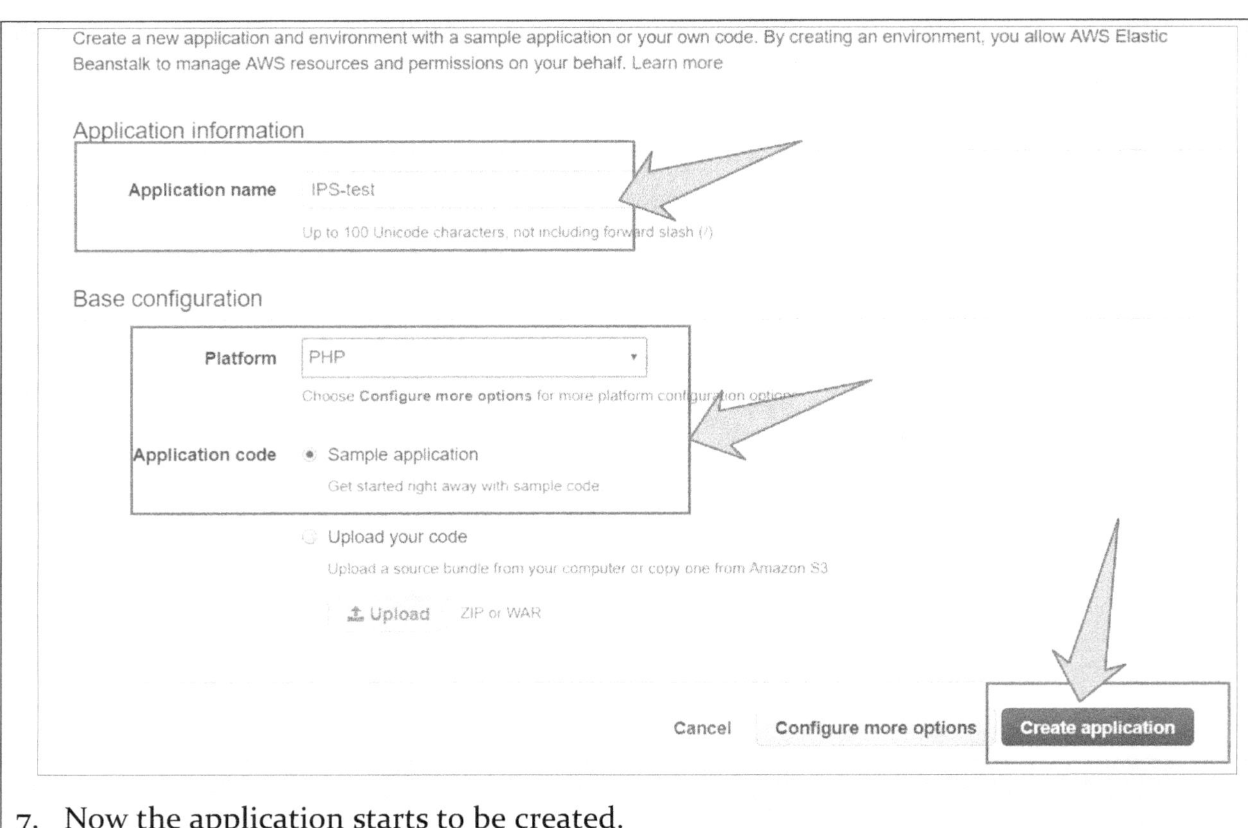

7. Now the application starts to be created.

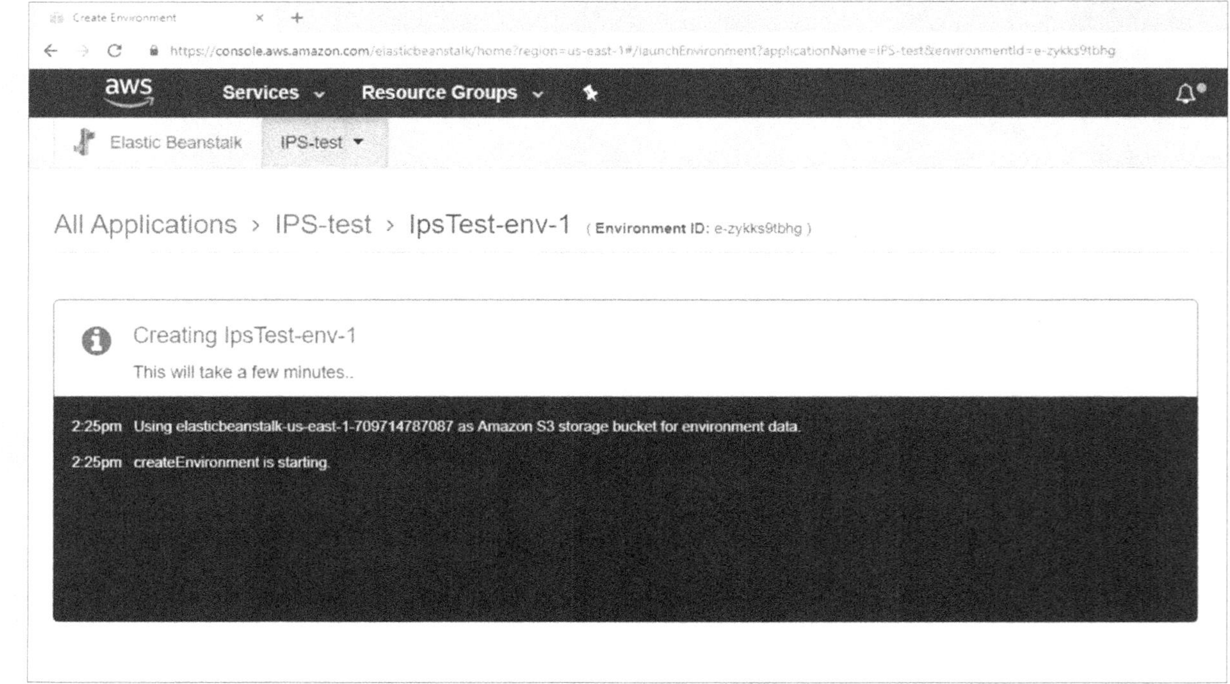

8. Once the application is created and its environment has also been created, click on "All Application" > "IPS-test".

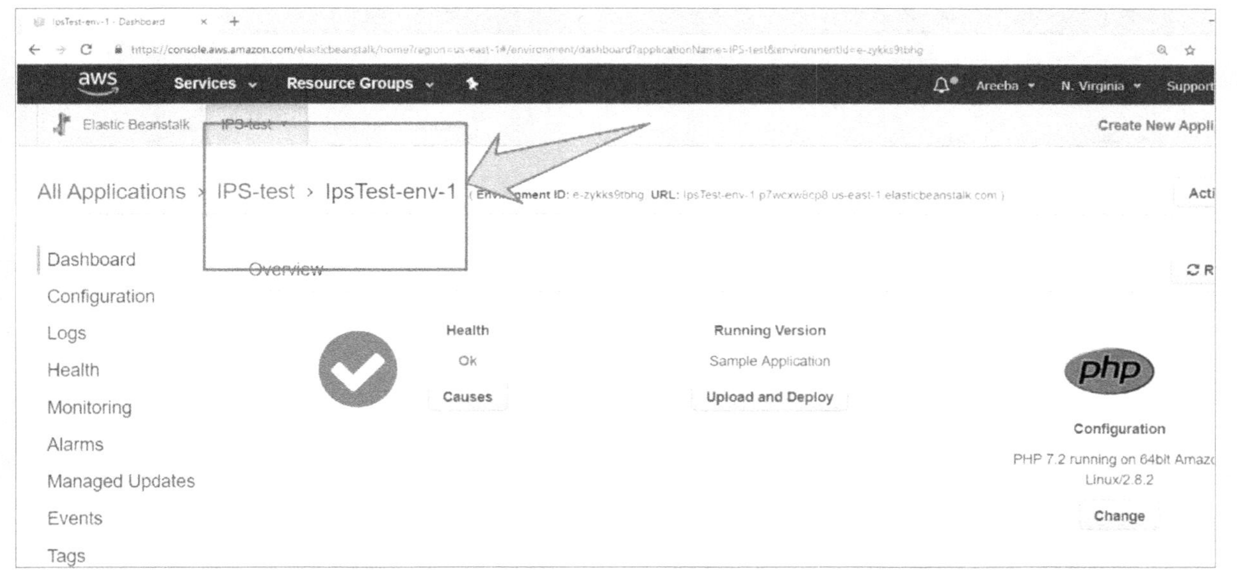

9. Now you can see information related to the environment. In a single application, you can also create multiple environments.

10. Click on the environment and then on its URL.

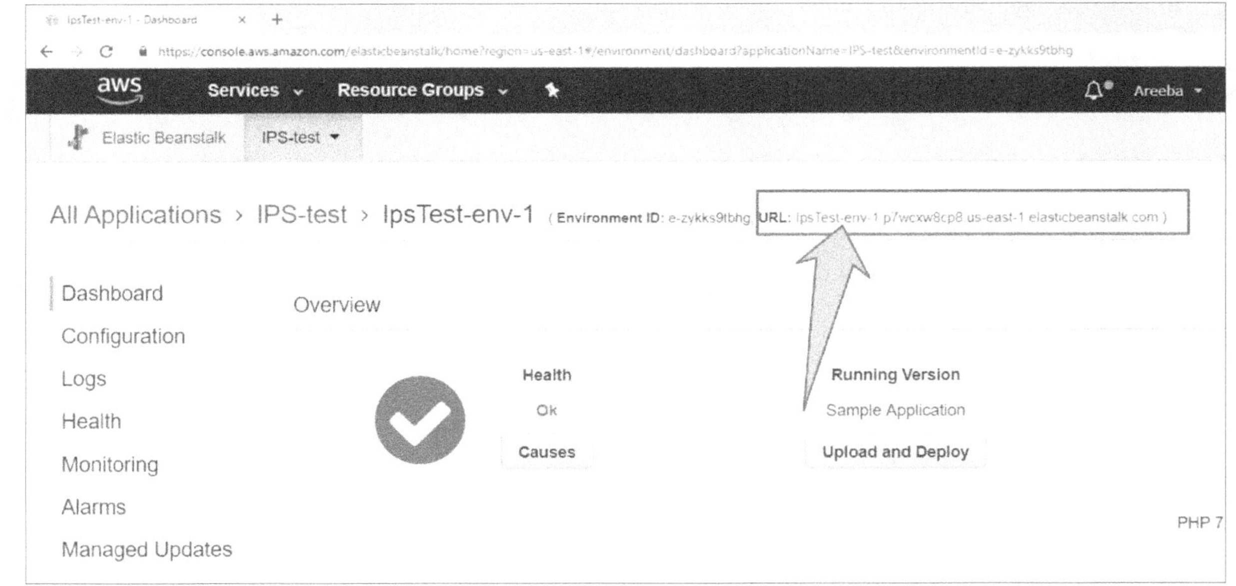

11. You should now see the web page of your application.

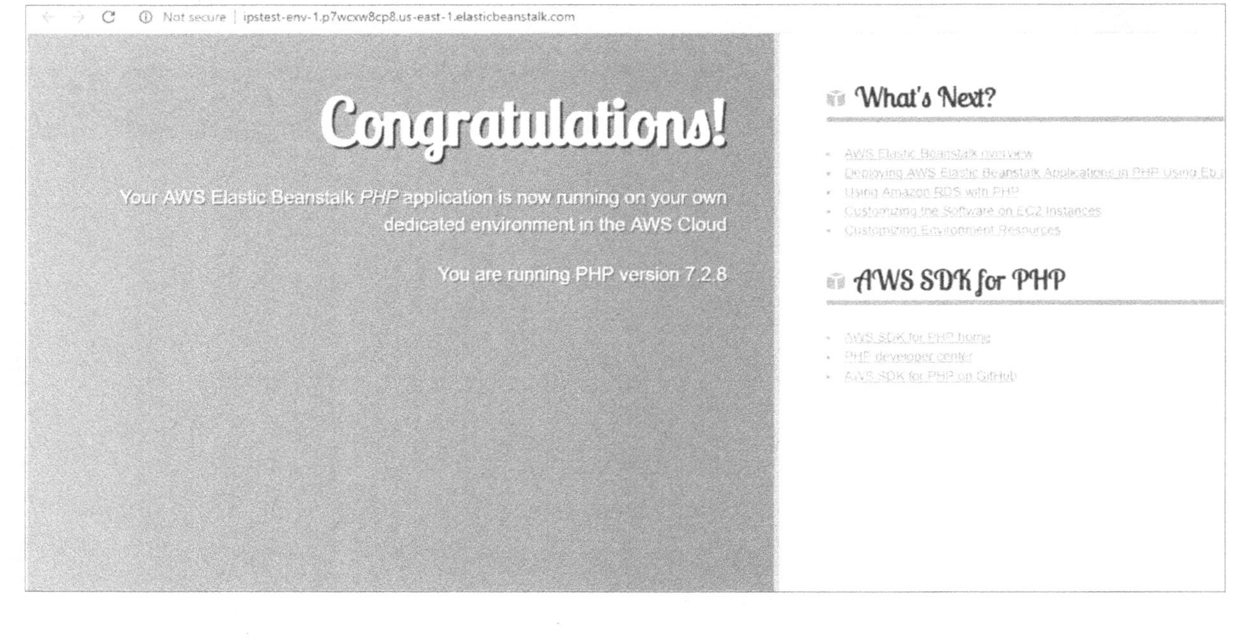

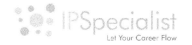

AWS CloudFormation

AWS CloudFormation offers system administrators, developers and network architects a facility to provision and manage a collection of related AWS resources by coding out the infrastructure. This is achieved by creating templates to model the infrastructure, which in turn manages everything from a single Amazon EC2 instance to a complex multi-tier, multi-regional application.

Cloudformation is a powerful tool as it gives you the ability to script your infrastructure so that you can easily replicate your infrastructure stack quickly. The stack is nothing but a collection of templates. Compared to Elastic Beanstalk and AWS OpsWorks, AWS CloudFormation gives you more granular control and flexibility over the provisioning and management of resources.

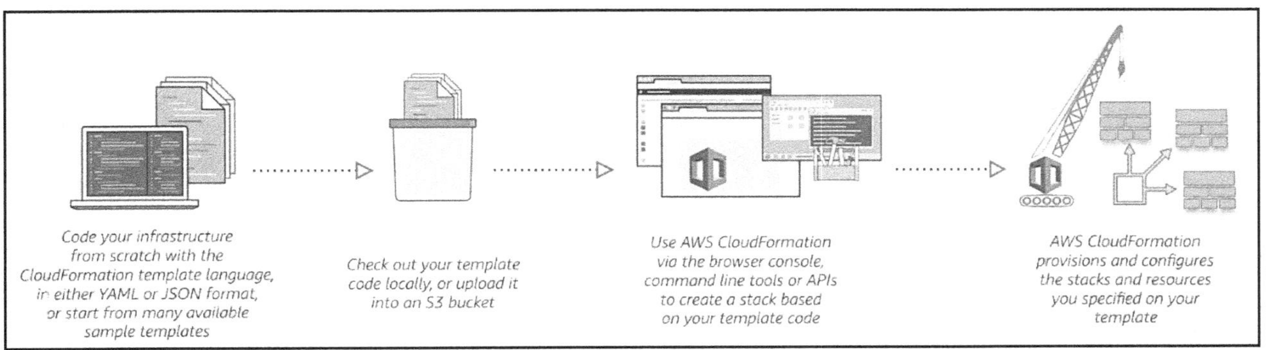

Figure 3-03: How AWS CloudFormation Works

EXAM TIP: AWS CloudFormation and AWS Elastic BeanStalk are completely free services, but the resources they provision are not free. All the resources provisioned under these services, whether EC2 instances, elastic load balancer, or RDS instances, will cost money.

Lab 3-2: AWS Cloud Formation

1. Log in to the “AWS Console”.
2. Click on “Services”.
3. Scroll down to “Management Tools”. Select “CloudFormation”.

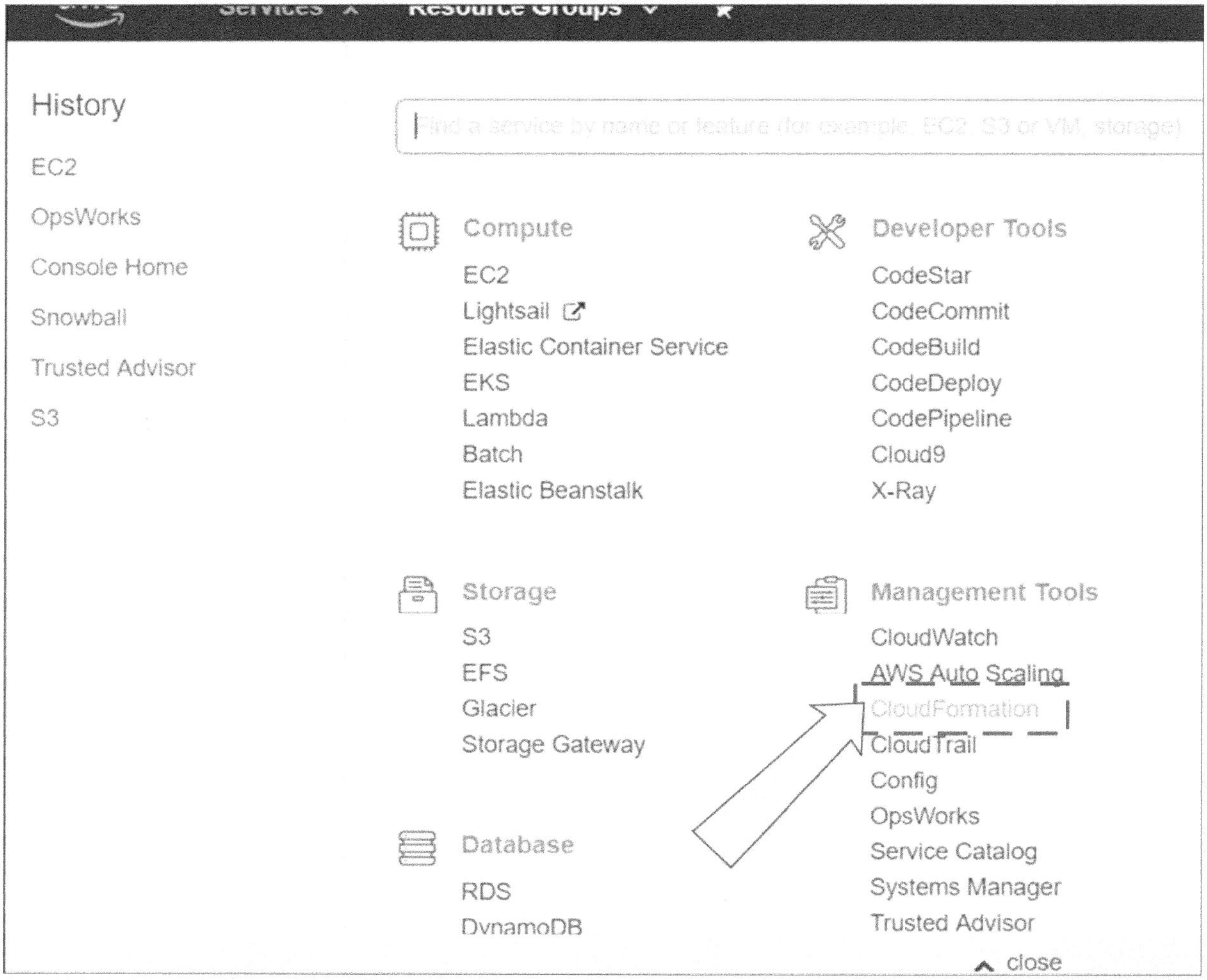

4. From the options given on the main dashboard, click on "Create new stack". The stack is a template that will provision resources for you. Alternately, you could also code your infrastructure in either YAML or JSON format. However, for this course, we will use one of the sample templates as an example.

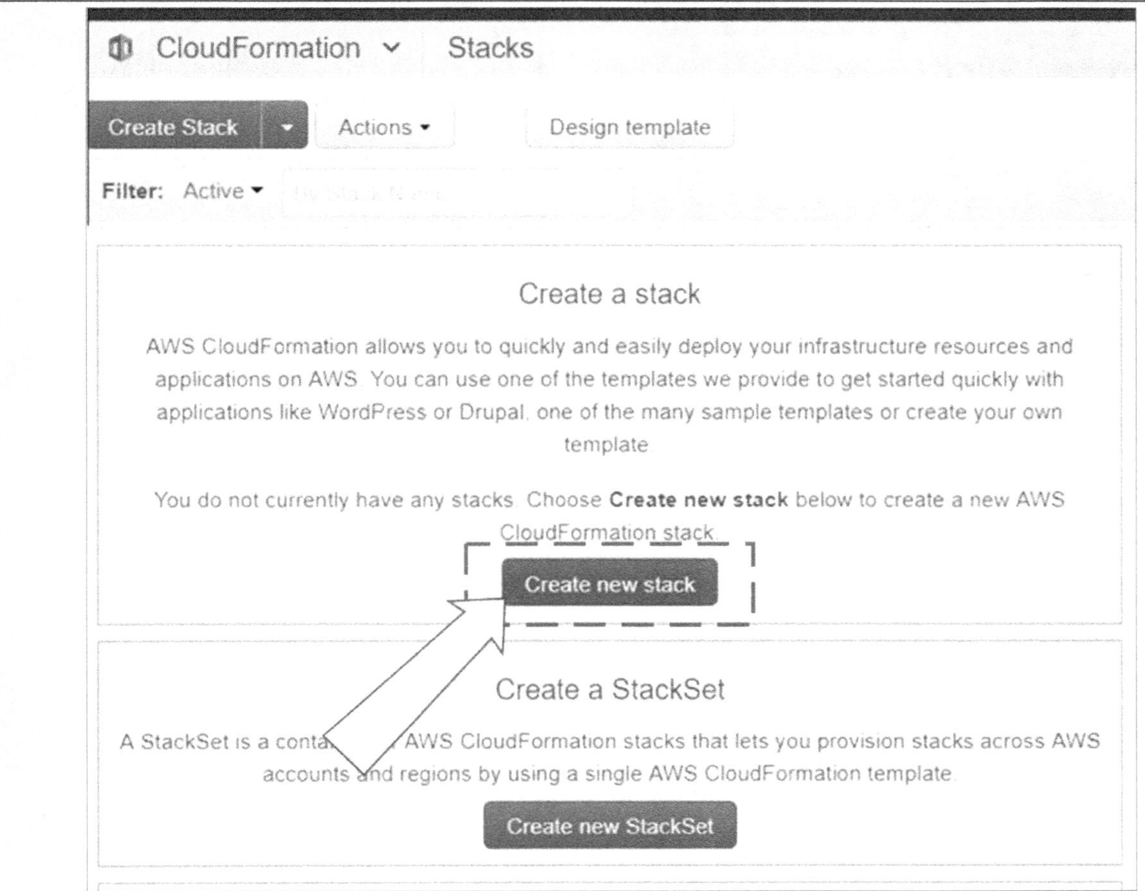

5. Choose a template from the list of drop-down menus. Here, we have selected "WordPress" blog as an example. Click "Next".

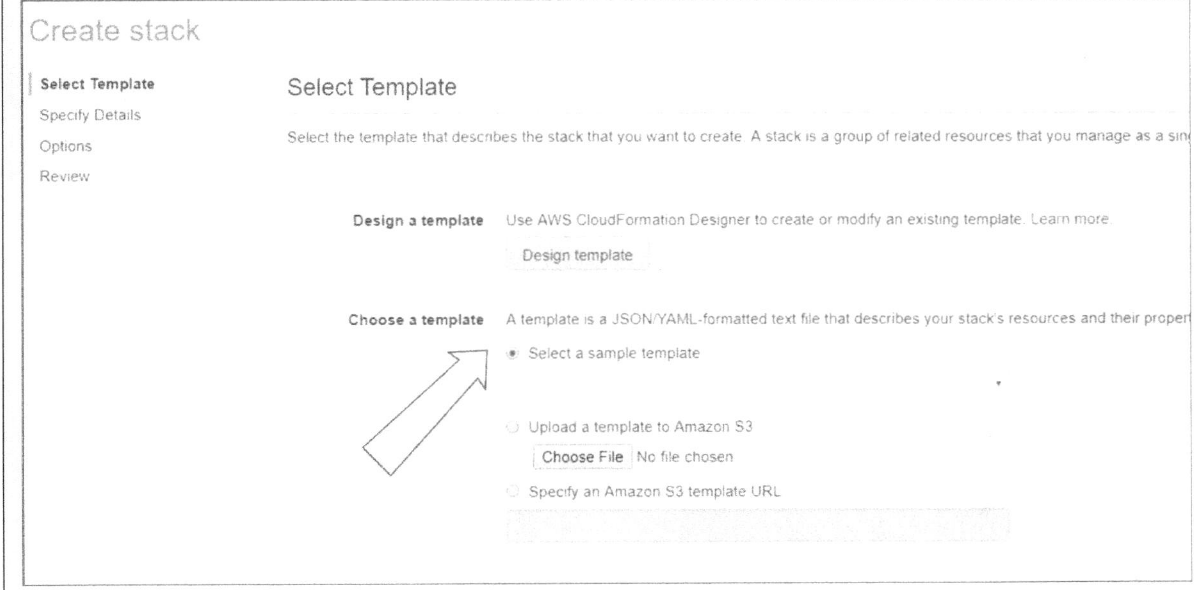

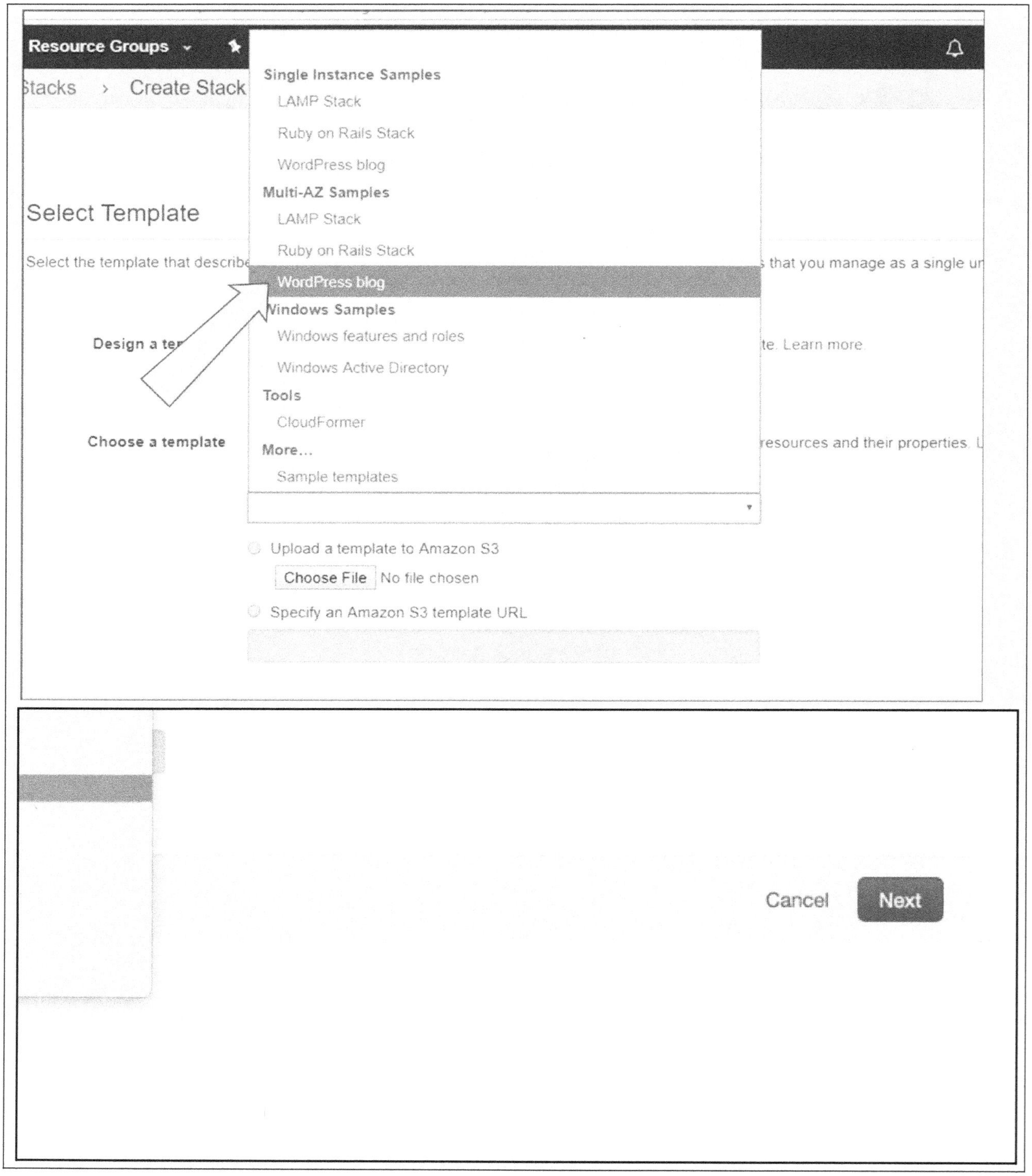

Resource Groups

Stacks › Create Stack

Single Instance Samples

LAMP Stack

Ruby on Rails Stack

WordPress blog

Multi-AZ Samples

LAMP Stack

Ruby on Rails Stack

WordPress blog

Windows Samples

Windows features and roles

Windows Active Directory

Tools

CloudFormer

More...

Sample templates

Select Template

Select the template that describe... that you manage as a single un

Design a te... te. Learn more

Choose a template ... resources and their properties. L

Upload a template to Amazon S3

Choose File No file chosen

Specify an Amazon S3 template URL

Cancel Next

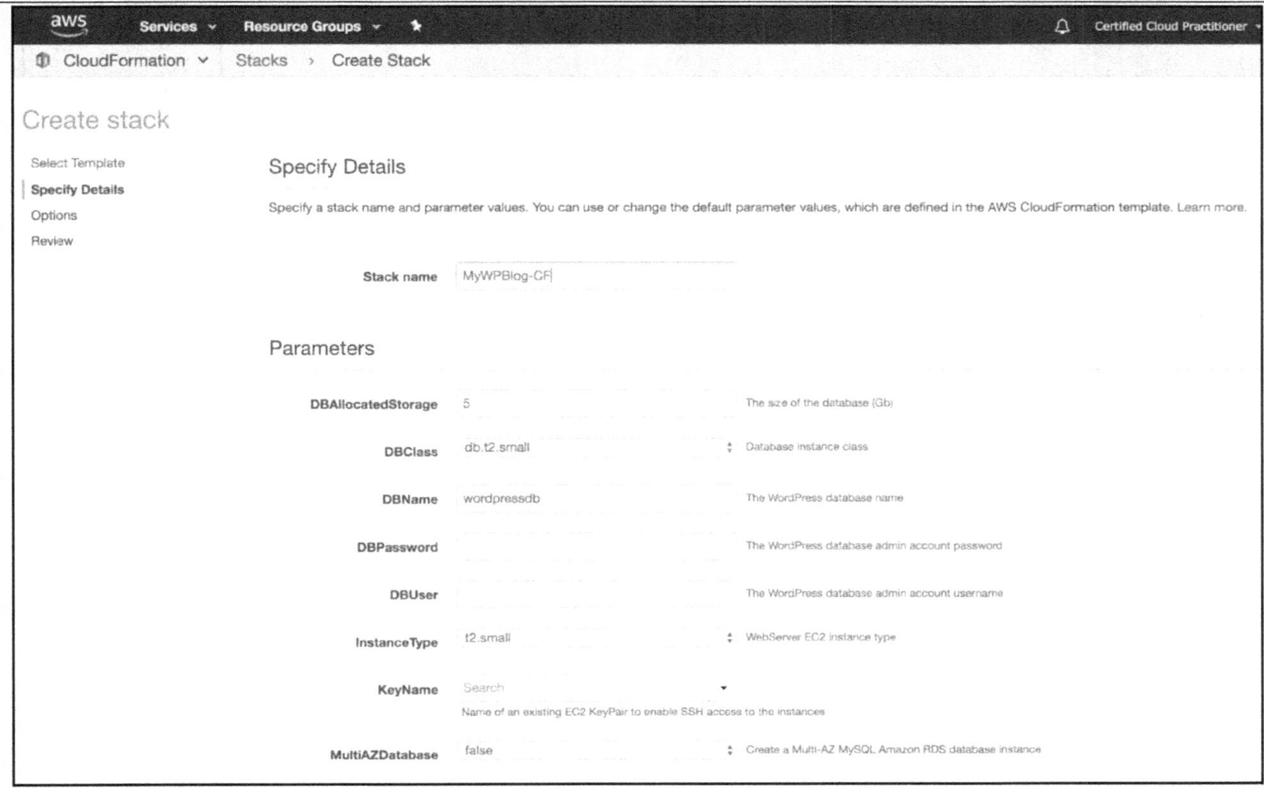

6. Enter the below details and then click "Next".

- Your stack name
- The name, instance type, and size of your database
- The database admin username and password
- The webserver (EC2) instance type and number of webservers
- Key pair to enable SSH access and SSH location
- Subnets that you want to deploy your stack into and their VPC ID

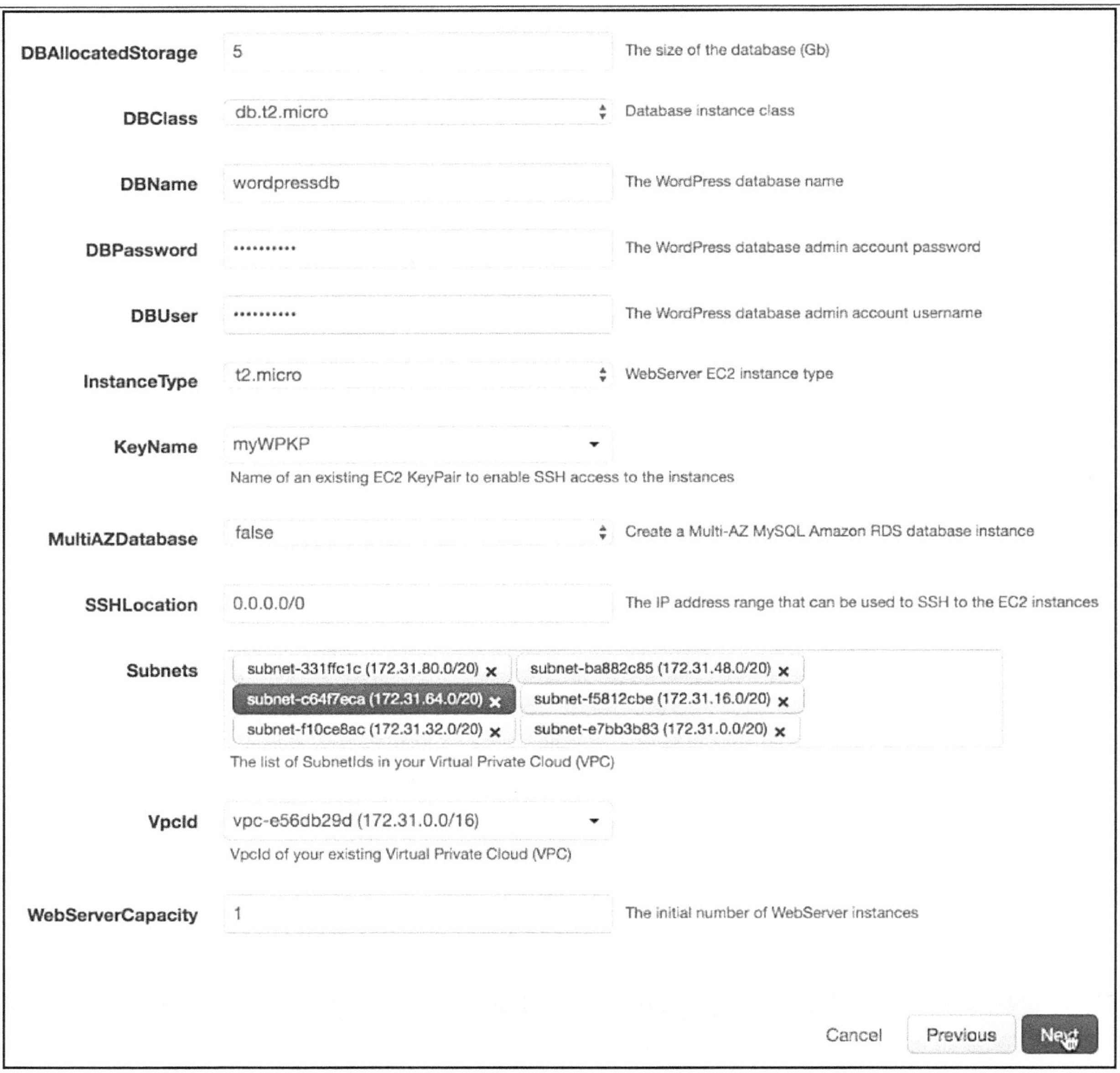

Parameter	Value	Description
DBAllocatedStorage	5	The size of the database (Gb)
DBClass	db.t2.micro	Database instance class
DBName	wordpressdb	The WordPress database name
DBPassword	••••••••••	The WordPress database admin account password
DBUser	••••••••••	The WordPress database admin account username
InstanceType	t2.micro	WebServer EC2 instance type
KeyName	myWPKP	Name of an existing EC2 KeyPair to enable SSH access to the instances
MultiAZDatabase	false	Create a Multi-AZ MySQL Amazon RDS database instance
SSHLocation	0.0.0.0/0	The IP address range that can be used to SSH to the EC2 instances
Subnets	subnet-331ffc1c (172.31.80.0/20) × subnet-ba882c85 (172.31.48.0/20) × subnet-c64f7eca (172.31.64.0/20) × subnet-f5812cbe (172.31.16.0/20) × subnet-f10ce8ac (172.31.32.0/20) × subnet-e7bb3b83 (172.31.0.0/20) ×	The list of SubnetIds in your Virtual Private Cloud (VPC)
VpcId	vpc-e56db29d (172.31.0.0/16)	VpcId of your existing Virtual Private Cloud (VPC)
WebServerCapacity	1	The initial number of WebServer instances

Cancel | Previous | Next

7. These parameters can also be configured inside the JSON document.
8. You can fill in the optional details, but for this example, we have left them blank. Click "Next".

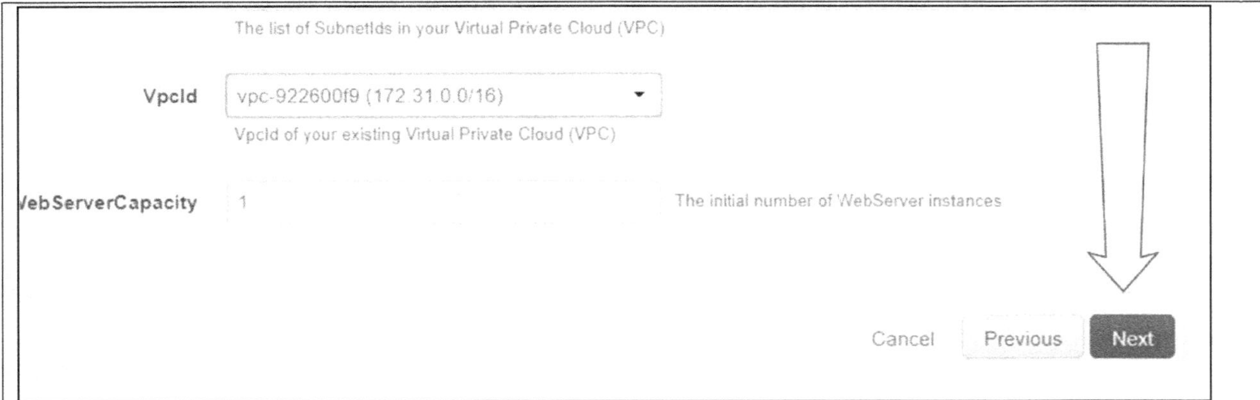

9. You will see a review screen. Scroll down to the bottom and click "Create" to create the stack. This may take between 5 to 20 minutes, depending on the complexity of the stack.

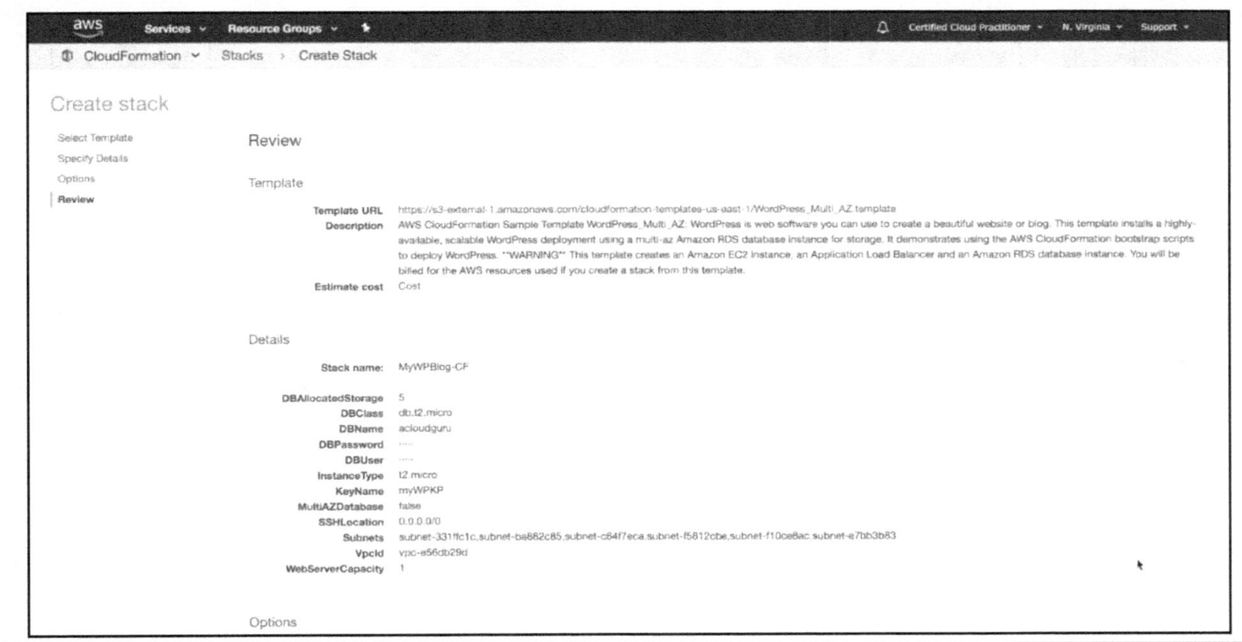

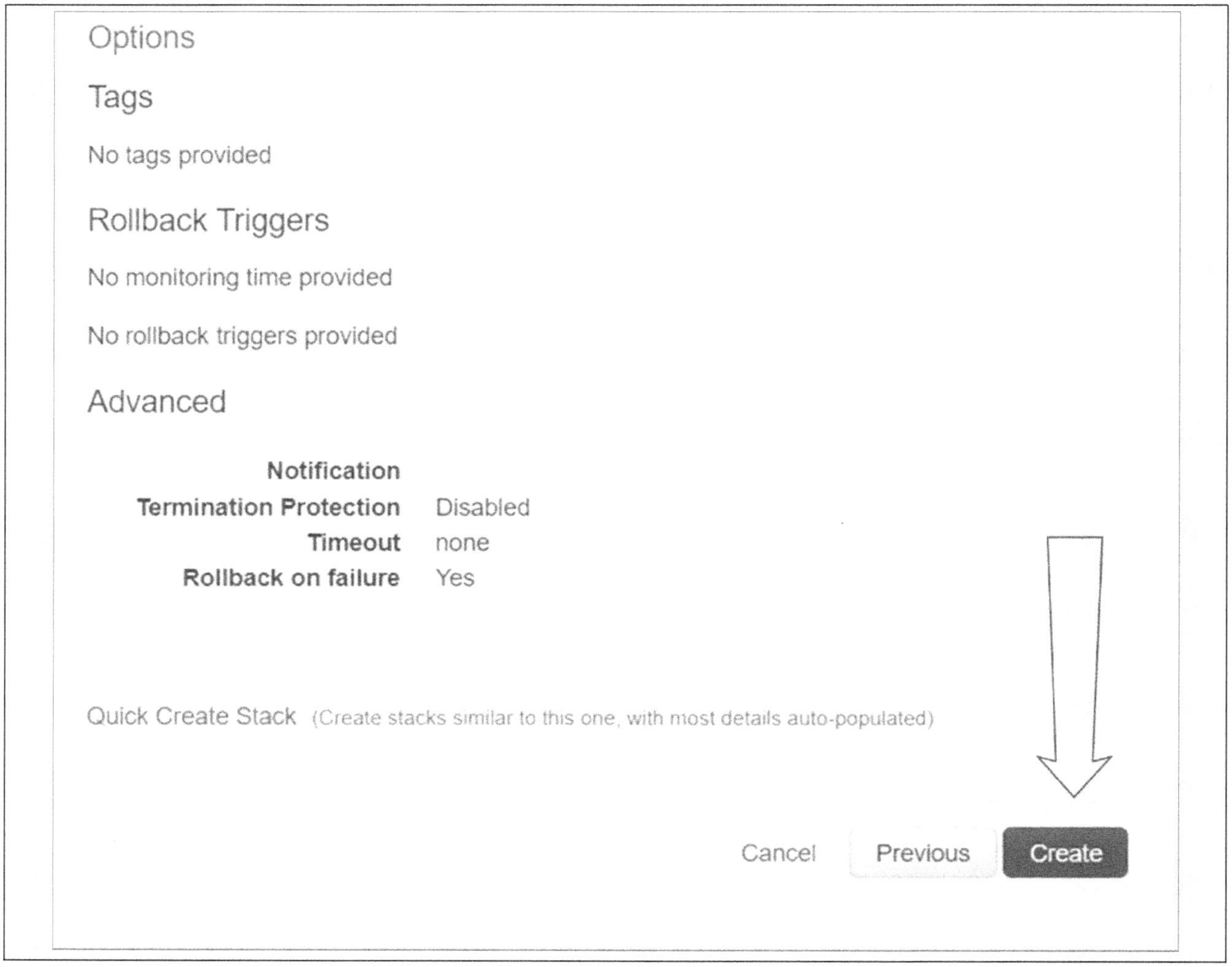

Options

Tags

No tags provided

Rollback Triggers

No monitoring time provided

No rollback triggers provided

Advanced

Notification	
Termination Protection	Disabled
Timeout	none
Rollback on failure	Yes

Quick Create Stack (Create stacks similar to this one, with most details auto-populated)

Cancel Previous Create

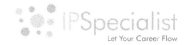

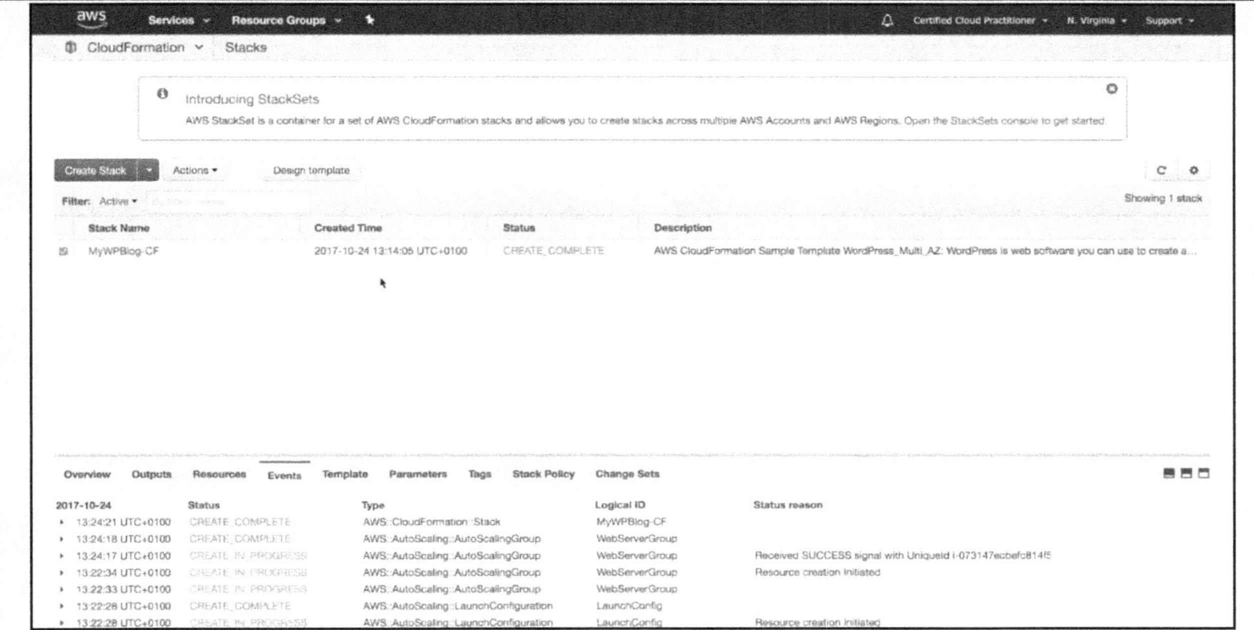

10. Once the stack has been created, select the "Outputs" tab. You will now be able to see your website's URL address.

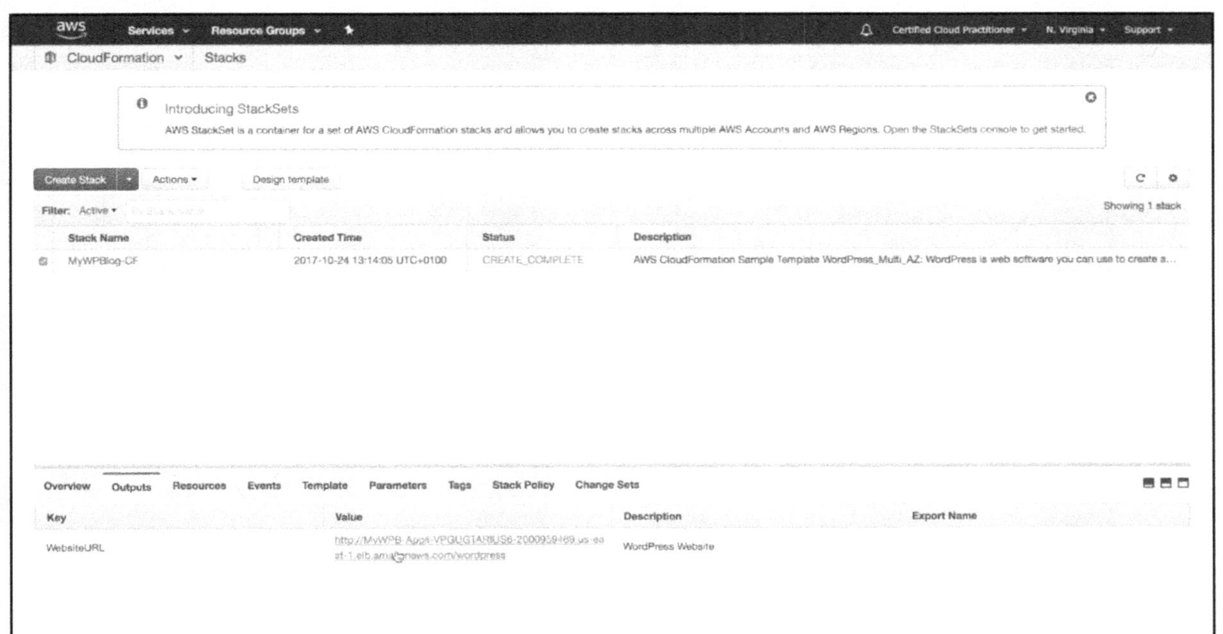

11. This is the website URL of your WordPress site. Click on it to be directed to your WordPress site.

12. You can delete the entire CloudFormation Stack and its provisioned resources anytime.

Welcome

Welcome to the famous five-minute WordPress installation process! Just fill in the information below and you'll be on your way to using the most extendable and powerful personal publishing platform in the world.

Information needed

Please provide the following information. Don't worry, you can always change these settings later.

Site Title

Username

Usernames can have only alphanumeric characters, spaces, underscores, hyphens, periods, and the @ symbol.

Password

Hide

Important: You will need this password to log in. Please store it in a secure location.

Your Email

Double-check your email address before continuing.

Search Engine Visibility

Discourage search engines from indexing this site

It is up to search engines to honor this request.

Install WordPress

AWS Quick Starts

If you are new to AWS and want to deploy a particular type of technology onto the AWS cloud, AWS Quick Starts is a simple way of getting started. Quick Starts are automated reference deployments that act like templates. They are built by AWS solutions architects and their partners to help you to deploy popular solutions of key technologies on AWS cloud, using the AWS best practices for security and high availability.

Each Quick Start launches, configures and runs the AWS services required to deploy a specific workload on AWS. You can build your test or production environment in a few simple steps and start using it immediately. Quick Starts saves time by eliminating hundreds of manual installation and configuration steps.

Quick Starts include:

1. A reference architecture for the deployment
2. AWS CloudFormation templates (JSON or YAML scripts) that automate and configure the deployment
3. A deployment guide, which explains the architecture and implementation in detail and provides instructions for customizing the deployment

Lab 3-3: AWS Quick Start

1. Open your browser to "https://aws.amazon.com/quickstart".

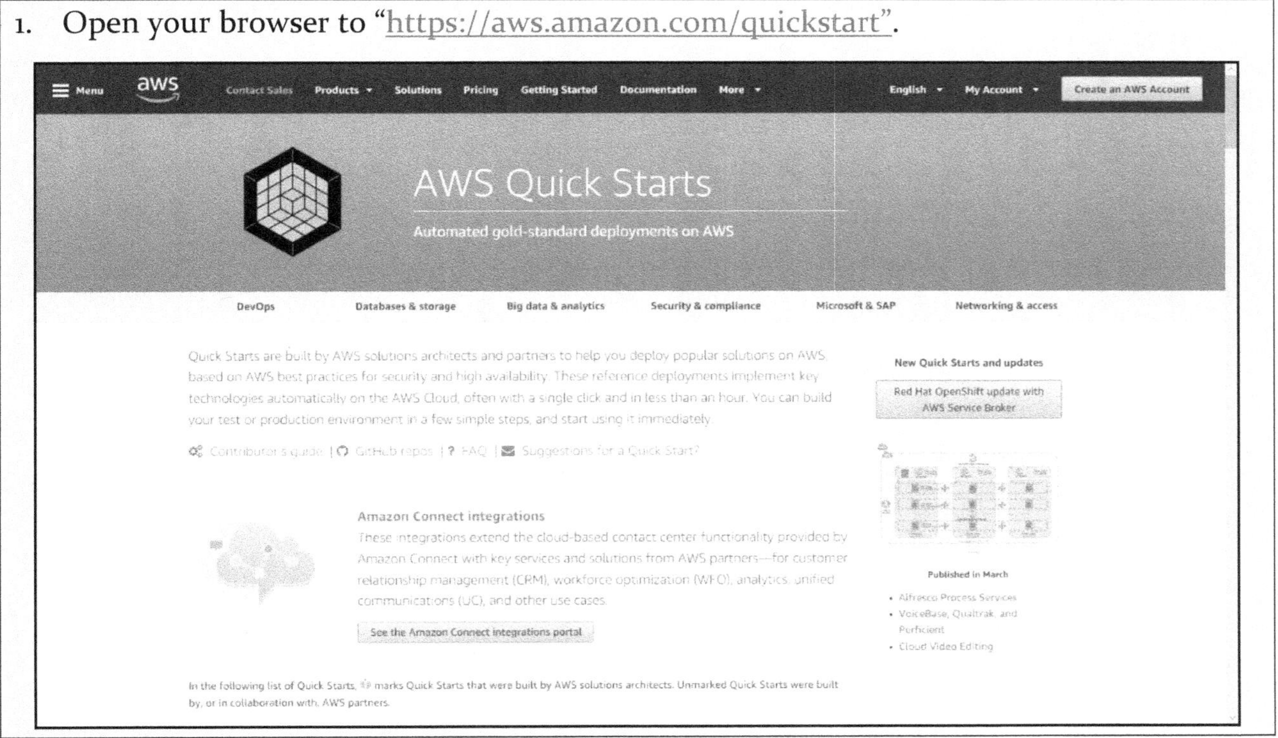

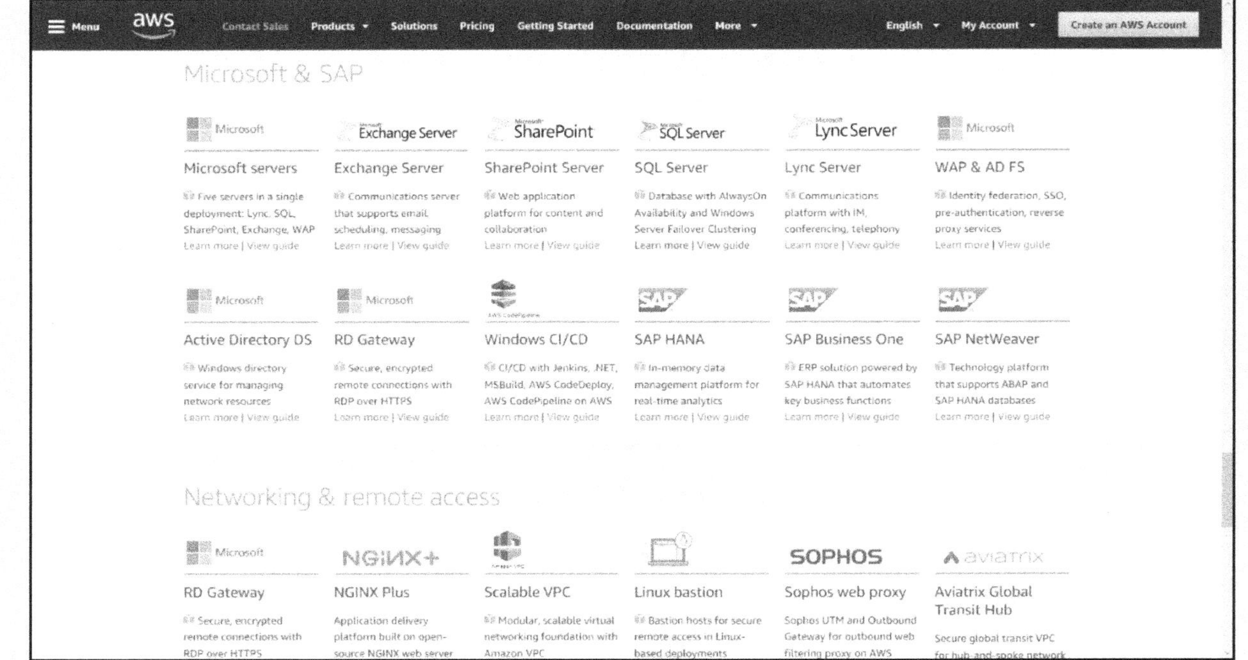

2. You will see a list of popular deployment models. Select the solution you need to deploy by clicking "View guide". For this example, we will deploy a SharePoint server.

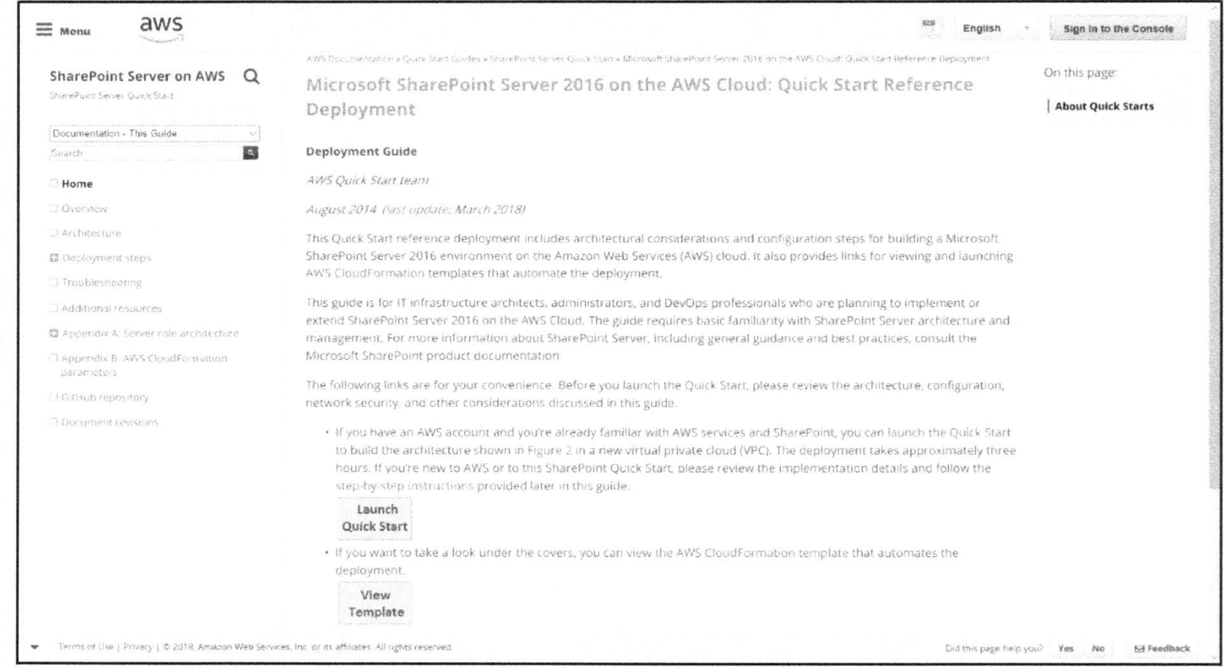

3. You will see a complete guide to the deployment solution you have selected. After reading the guide, click "Launch Quick Start". This will open the AWS console and

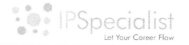

launch AWS CloudFormation, which will be used to setup your SharePoint infrastructure without needing to manually configure the resources.

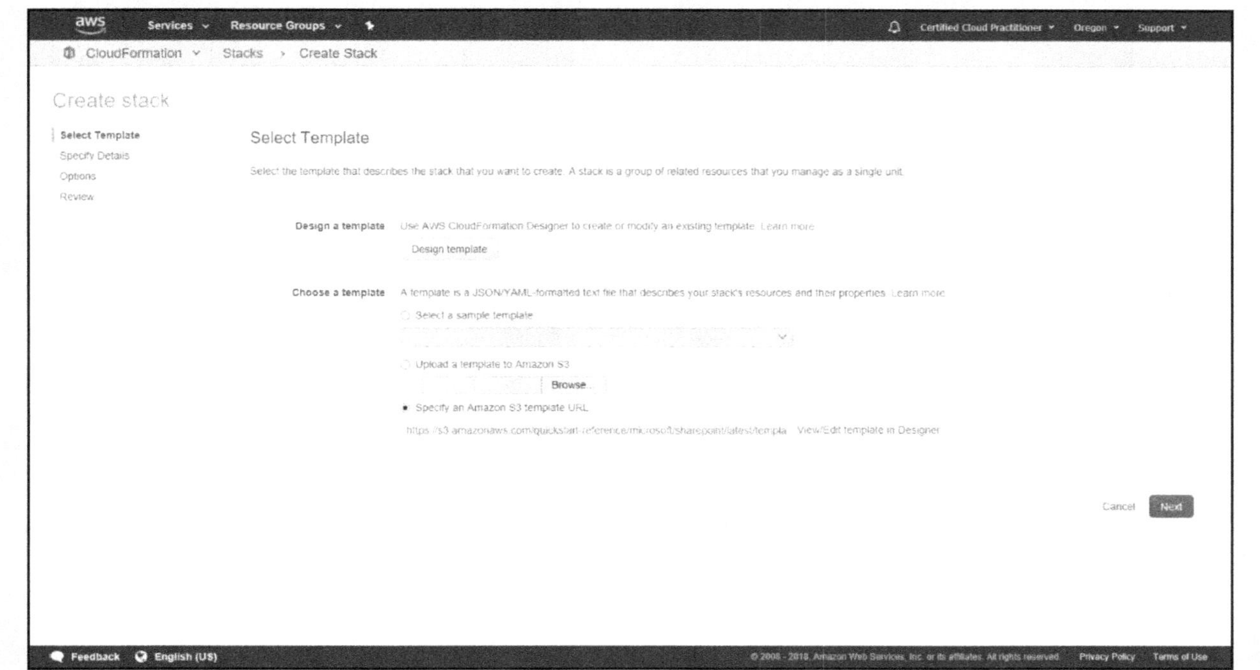

AWS Global Infrastructure

The AWS Cloud spans 18 geographic Regions with 53 Availability Zones and 1 Local Region around the world, with further plans for 12 more Availability Zones and four more Regions in Bahrain, Hong Kong SAR, Sweden, and a second AWS GovCloud Region in the US.

What is a Region?

A Region is a complete independent and separate geographical area. Each region has multiple, physically separated and isolated locations known as availability zones. Examples of regions include London, Dublin and Sydney.

What is an Availability Zone?

An Availability Zone is simply a data center or a collection of data centers. Each availability zone in a region has separate power sources, networking and connectivity to reduce the chances of two zones failing simultaneously. No two availability zones share a data center; however, the data centers within a particular availability zone are connected

to each other over redundant low-latency private network links. Likewise, all zones in a region are linked by highly resilient and very low latency private fiber optic connections for communication. The availability zones are all situated at a certain length or distance from each other.

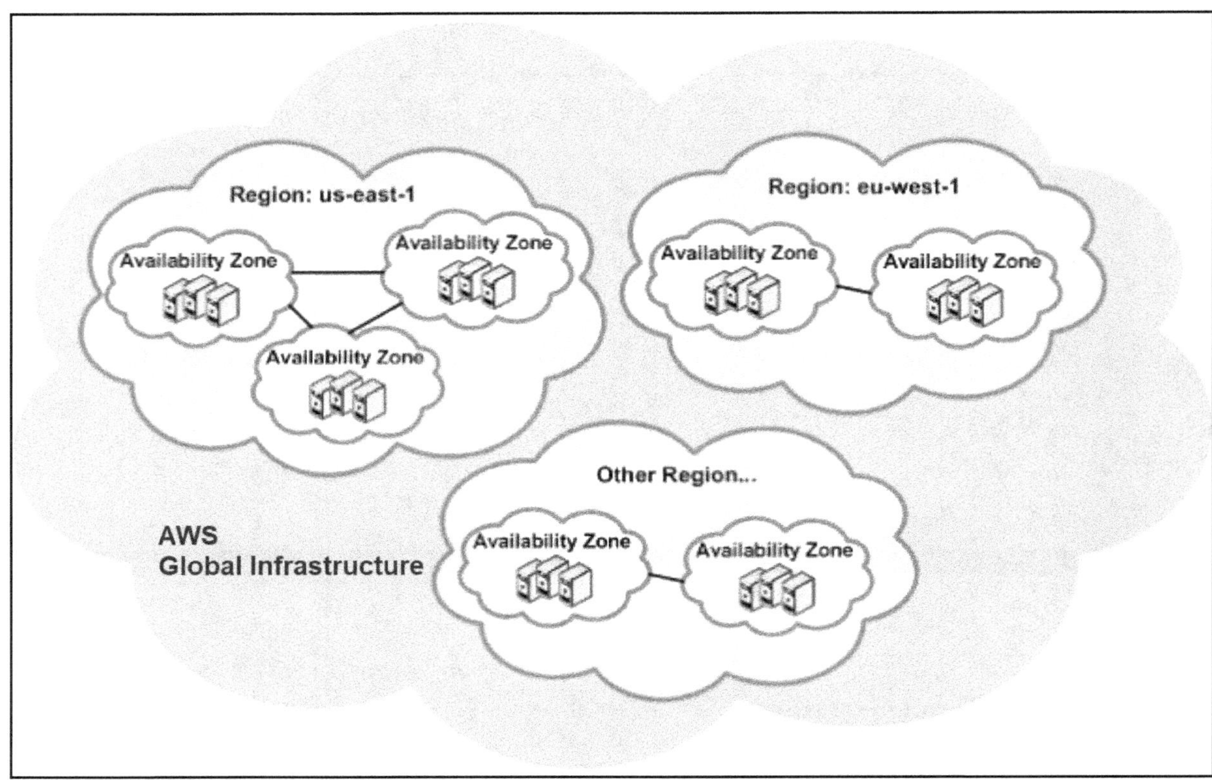

Figure 3-04: Regions and Availability Zones

What is an Edge Location?

Edge Locations are AWS sites deployed in major cities and highly populated areas across the globe. There are many more edge locations than there are regions. Currently, there are more than 102 edge locations. Edge locations are used by AWS services such as AWS CloudFront to cache data and reduce latency for end-user access. They use the edge locations as a global Content Delivery Network (CDN).

Therefore, edge locations are primarily used by end users who are accessing and using your services. For example, your website may be hosted by the Ohio region with an associated configured CloudFront distribution. If a user accesses your website from Europe, they will be redirected to their closest edge location in Europe, where cached data could be read on your website. This significantly reduces latency.

Regional Edge Cache

In November 2016, AWS announced a new type of edge location, called a Regional Edge Cache. This sits between the CloudFront Origin servers and the edge locations. A regional edge cache has a larger cache-width than each individual edge location and retains data that has expired in an edge location.

Therefore, when data is requested that is no longer available, the edge location can retrieve the cached data from the regional edge cache instead of the origin servers, which would have a higher latency.

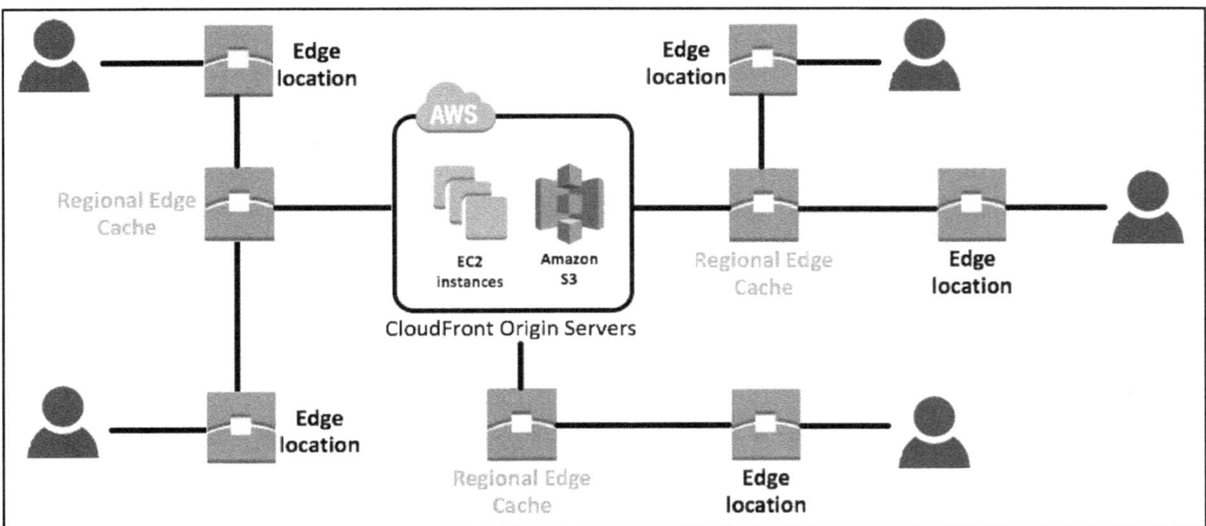

Figure 3-05: Edge Locations and Regional Edge Caches

EXAM TIP: Learn the difference between these three: Region, Availability Zone, and Edge Location.

AWS Compute

The provisioning of computing resources on demand provides access to raw compute power and server capacity. This involves providing virtual or physical resources as a service. AWS offers a range of computing services that allow you to develop, deploy, run and scale your applications and workloads in a cloud environment. It also provides a robust and scalable platform for Virtual Server Hosting, Container Management and Serverless Computing.

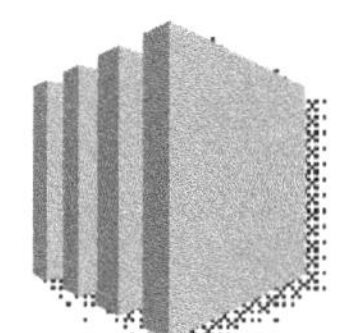

Amazon Elastic Compute Cloud (Amazon EC2)

Launched in 2006, Amazon Elastic Compute Cloud (Amazon EC2) is a web service that provides secure and resizable cloud-based compute capacity in the form of EC2 instances. These are virtual servers in the cloud. Amazon EC2 enables any developer to leverage the compute capacity that Amazon offers to meet their business requirements with no up-front investment and no performance compromises. Amazon EC2 provides a true virtual computing environment, where the web service interfaces can be used to launch instances with a variety of operating systems, to load custom application environments, to manage network access permissions, and run image. Amazon EC2 can consume as many or as few systems as desired.

Amazon EC2 offers the tools to build failure-robust applications that will isolate themselves from common failure scenarios. When designing a system, it is good practice to assume things will fail. In this way, you will always design, implement and deploy systems with an automated recovery and restore strategy. With Amazon EC2, you can provision multiple instances at any one time, so that even if one instance fails, the system will continue running.

EXAM TIP: EC2 is a compute-based service. It is not serverless as you are physically connecting to a virtual server. Always design for failure and provision at least one EC2 instance in each availability zone to avoid a system failure if any single instance goes down.

Benefits of Amazon EC2

- Quickly scales capacity both up and down by booting new server instances within minutes as your requirements change
- Has complete control of the instances with root access
- Provides a wide range of Instance types optimized to fit different use cases

- Integrates with other AWS services to provide a complete solution for a wide range of applications
- A highly reliable environment with rapid and simultaneous replacement and provisioning of multiple instances
- Pay only for the capacity you actually use
- Secure, inexpensive and easy to start up

Pricing Models

There are four different pricing models for EC2 instances:

On-Demand Instances: On-Demand Instances allow you to pay a fixed rate by the hour or by the second, depending upon which instances you run, with no long-term commitments or upfront payments. Depending on your application demands, you can increase or decrease compute capacity and only pay the specified per hour rates for the instances you use.

Reserved Instances: Reserved Instances (RIs) offers significant discounts of up to 75% off the on-demand instance pricing. They provide you with a capacity reservation over a 1- or 3-year term. Reserving servers and paying upfront for all of them entitles you to massively discounted prices.

- Standard reserved instances give you up to 75% off the on-demand prices
- Convertible RIs allow you to change the attributes of the reserved instances, providing the exchange results in the creation of reserved instances of equal or greater value. This gives up to 54% off the on-demand prices
- Scheduled RIs let you purchase capacity reservations on a daily, weekly, or monthly basis, with a specified start time and duration, for a one-year term. The instances are available to launch within the time window you reserve

Spot Instances: Spot Instances enable you to bid your preferred price on spare EC2 instance capacity, giving you even greater savings. The moment that the spot price drops down below your bid amount, your instance is provisioned, but as soon as the spot price moves back above your bid amount, your instance terminates. This allows you to grow your application's compute capacity and throughput and significantly reduce the cost of running your applications. If Amazon EC2 terminates your spot instance, you will not be charged for a partial hour of usage. However, if you terminate the instance yourself, you will be charged for the hour in which the instance ran.

Dedicated Hosts: Dedicated Hosts are physical EC2 servers dedicated to your use. Dedicated hosts can help you reduce costs by allowing you to use your existing server-bound software licenses. They offer you more flexibility, visibility and control over the placement of instances on dedicated hardware.

Recommended Use Cases

On-Demand Instances:

- Users that require flexibility and low costs, without any up-front payments or long-term commitment
- Applications being developed or tested on Amazon EC2 for the first time
- Applications with short-term, spiky or unpredictable workloads that cannot be interrupted

Reserved Instances:

- Applications that require reserved capacity
- Applications with steady state or predictable usage, such as webservers
- Users can commit to a 1- or 3-year contract to further reduce their total computing costs

Spot Instances:

- Applications that have flexible start and end times
- Applications that are only feasible to run at a very low compute-price
- Users who have urgent computing needs for large amounts of additional capacity

Dedicated Hosts:

- Useful for regulatory requirements that may not support multi-tenant virtualization
- Best for licensing that does not support multi-tenancy or cloud deployment
- Can be purchased on demand (hourly)
- Can be purchased as a reservation for up to 70% off the on-demand price

> EXAM TIP: Understand the different pricing models; you will be questioned about the pricing model you should use depending on a given scenario.

EC2 Instance Types

Amazon EC2 offers an extensive variety of instance types optimized for different use cases. Instance types consist of varying combinations of CPU, memory, storage and networking capacity, and may have one or more instance sizes. This gives you the

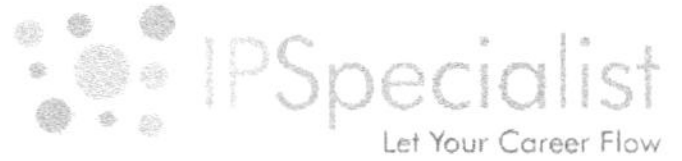

flexibility to select computational resources according to the requirements of your target workload.

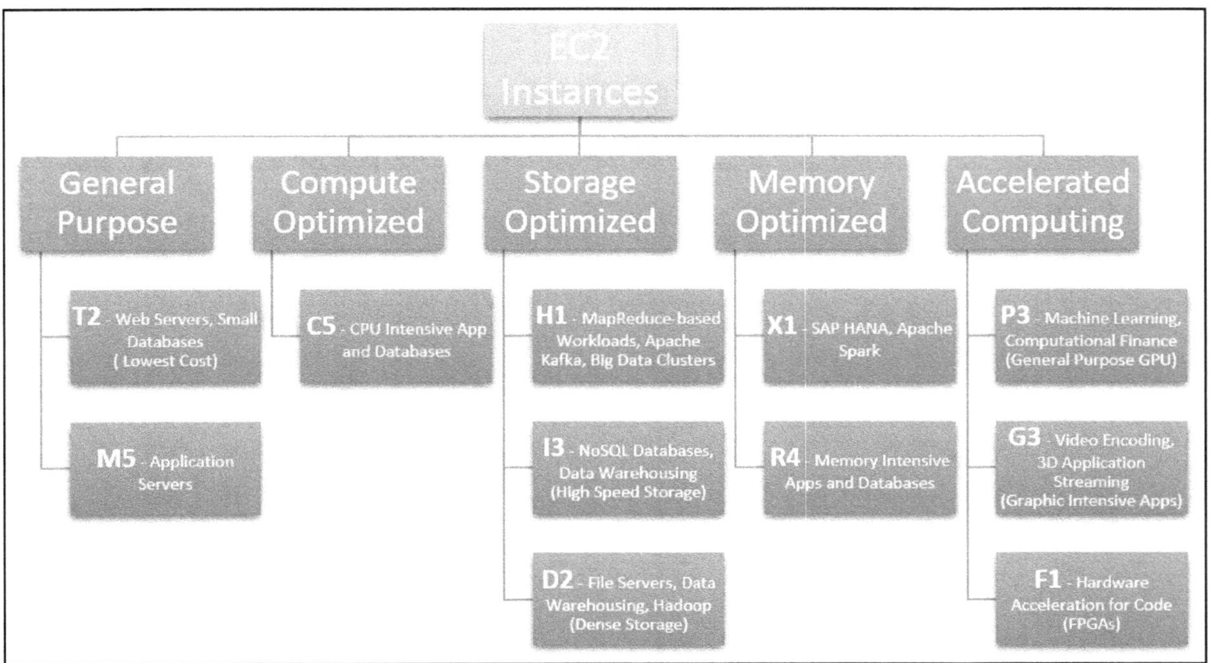

Figure 3-06: EC2 Instances

EXAM TIP: Know that there are different types of EC2 instances for different use cases. For example, R4 for memory, C4 for computing, etc. You do not need to remember all of the instance types.

Lab 3-4: AWS EC2 Instance

1. Log in to the "AWS Console".
2. Click on "Services".
3. Select "EC2" from Compute.

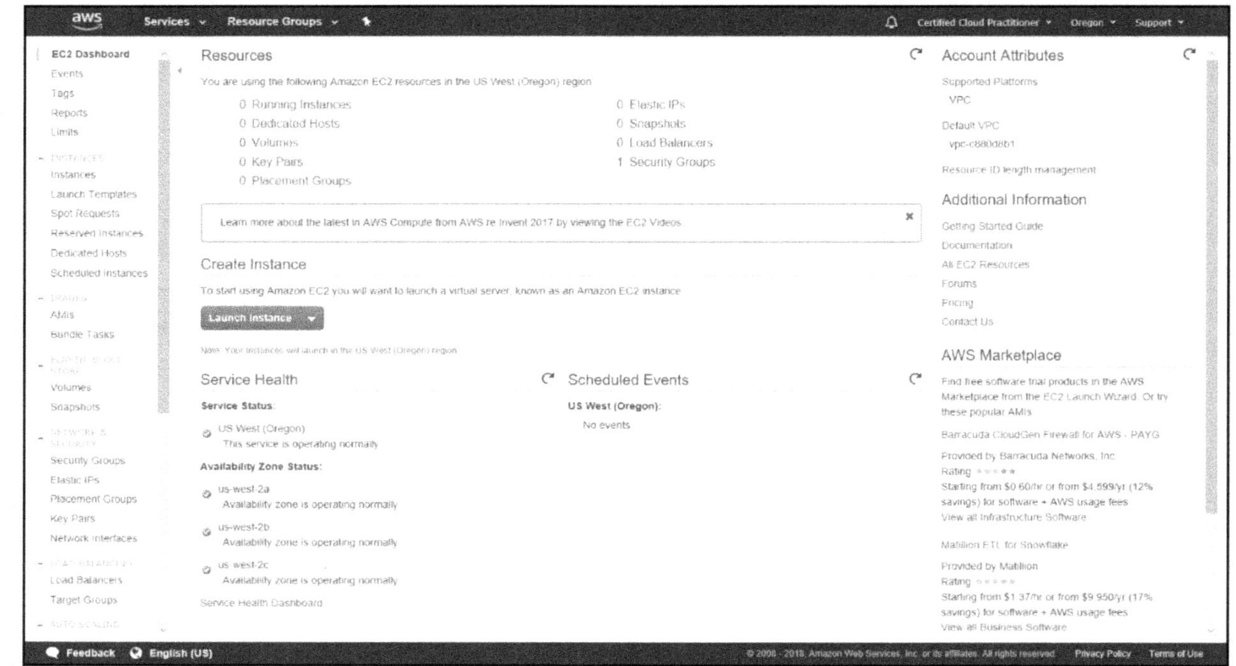

4. You will see one default security group and a default VPC. A VPC is simply a virtual data center in the cloud where we will deploy our EC2 instance. Click "Launch Instance" to get started.

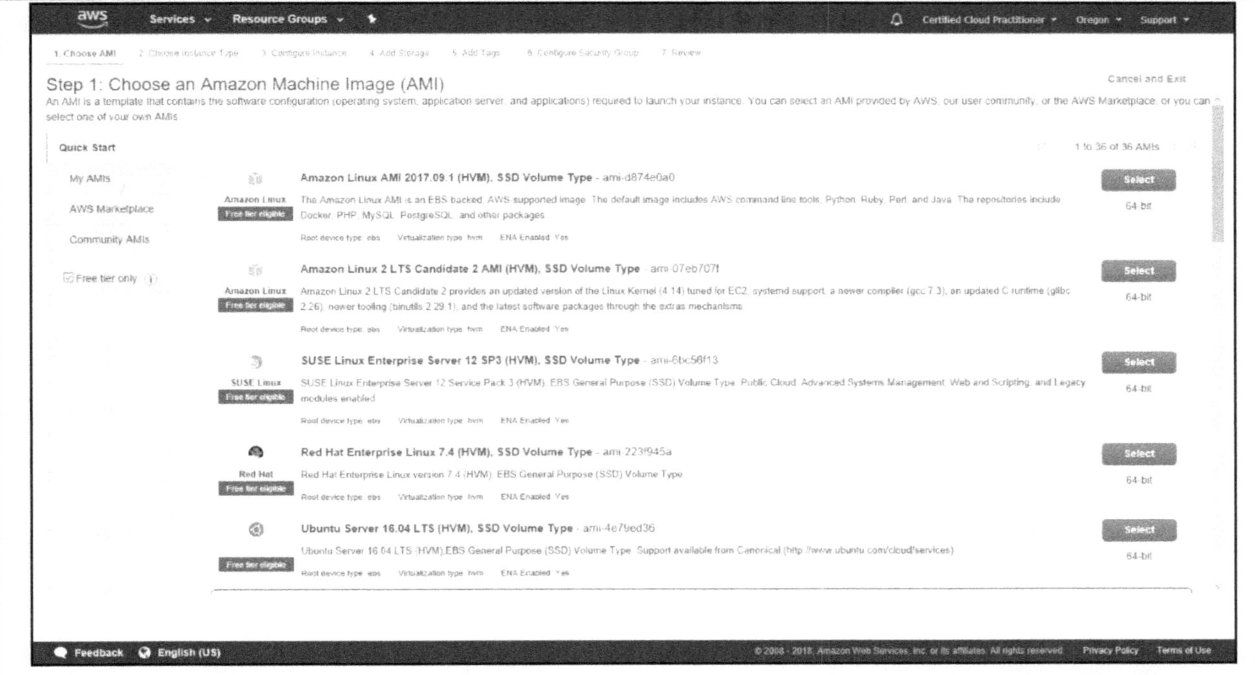

5. From the left tab, select the checkbox for "Free tier only". This will display only the list of AMIs that are eligible for use by the free tier account. Select the Amazon Linux AMI. We will use this AMI because it comes with the AWS command line tools pre-installed.

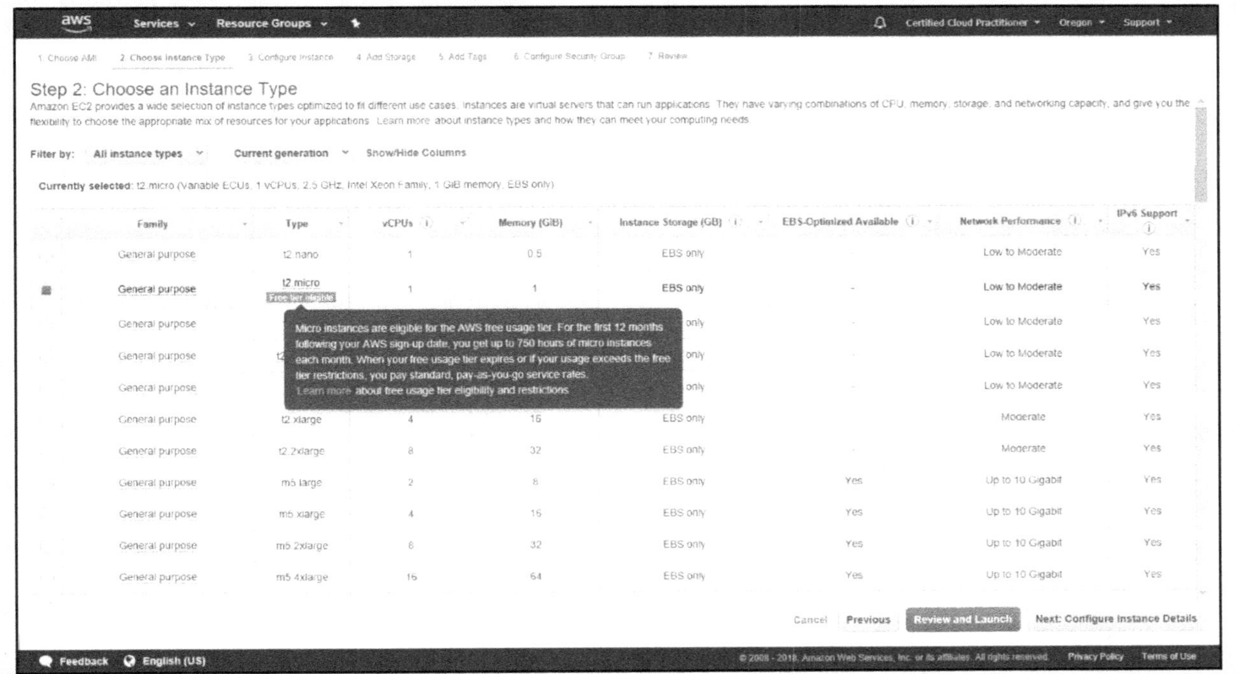

6. Here, you will see a list of different instance types. Select the general purpose "t2.micro" as it is included within the free tier. Click "Next: Configure Instance Details".

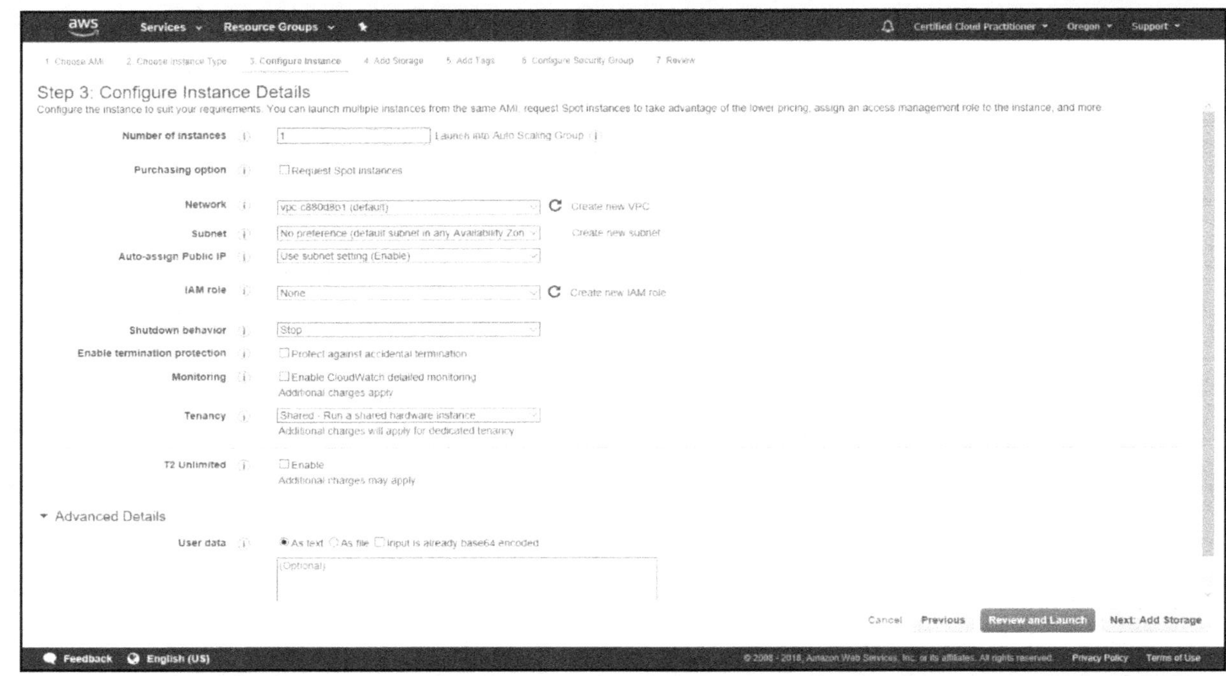

7. Configure instance details according to your requirements by defining the number of instances; request any spot instances; selecting a VPC; selecting a particular availability zone for your subnet; enabling the Auto-assign Public IP for remote instance access; assigning an IAM role; defining shutdown behavior and termination protection; enabling monitoring and running your instance on a shared or dedicated host. For now, keep all settings as default and click "Next: Add Storage".

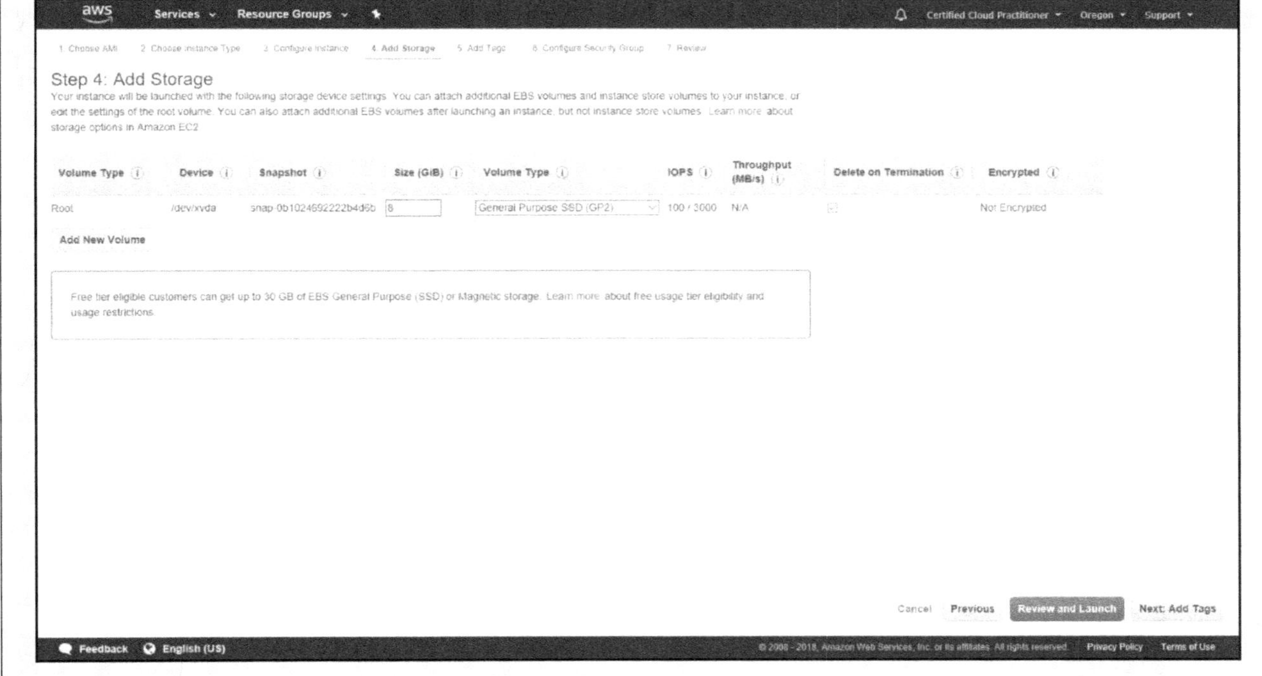

8. You now need to define the EBS volume details such as size and type. This EBS volume will be attached to our EC2 instance. Keep everything as default and click "Next: Add Tags". For more details see Amazon Elastic Block Store (Amazon EBS).

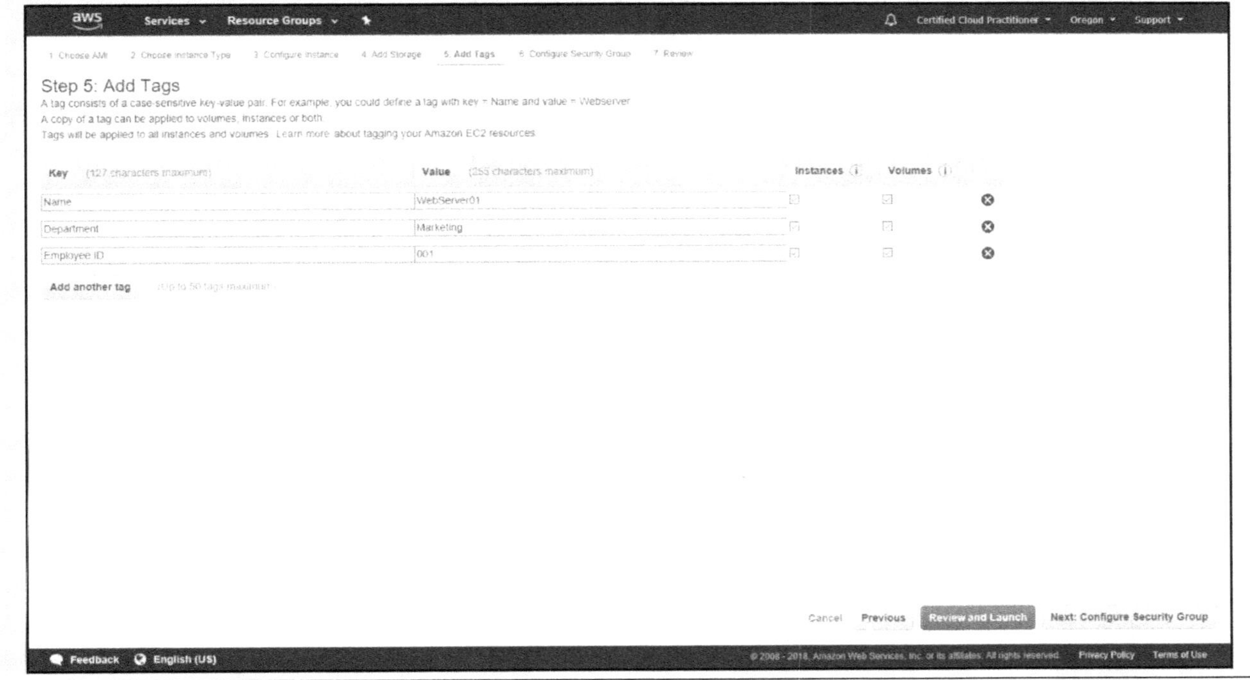

9. Tags are labels you assign to AWS Resources. Add tags to this EC2 instances by defining a key-value pair. Here tags are added to Name, Department and Employee ID with their key values. Click "Next: Configure Security Group". For more details see Tags.

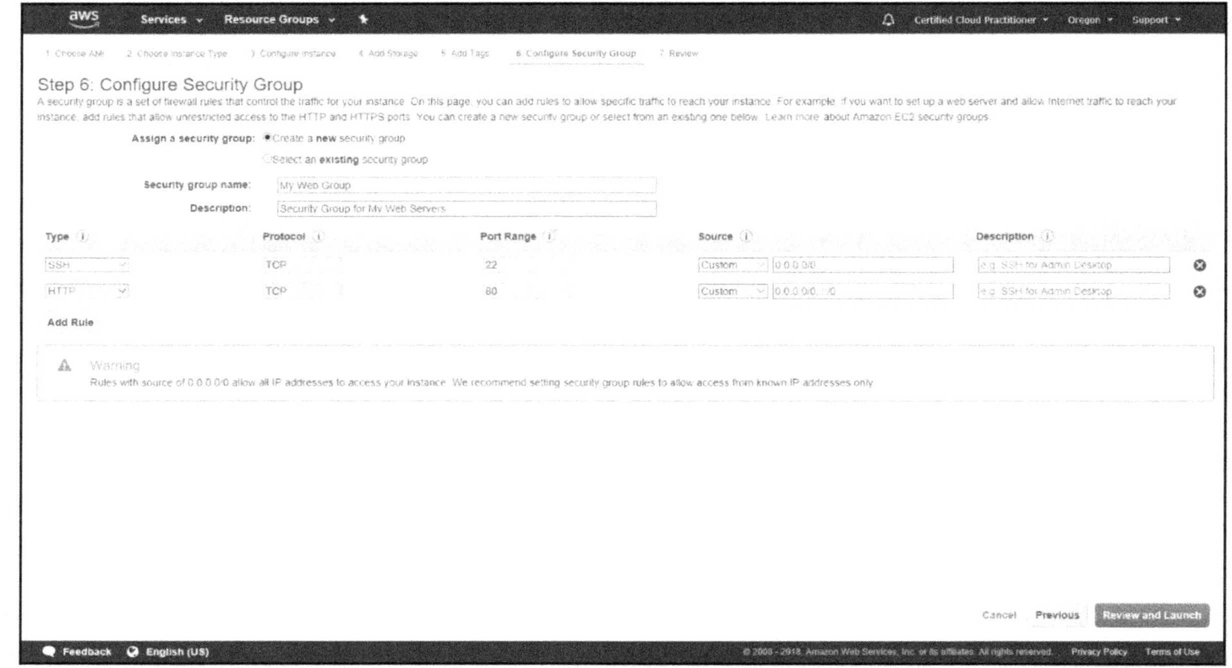

10. Security groups are like the virtual firewall in the cloud. Create a new security group and enter a name. For example, we have named our group as 'My Web Group'. Since we are using a Linux machine, we will need SSH protocol to log in our EC2 instance. We will use this EC2 instance as a webserver, so we need to allow web traffic to the server. Click "Add Rule" to add HTTP. After that, click "Review and Launch".

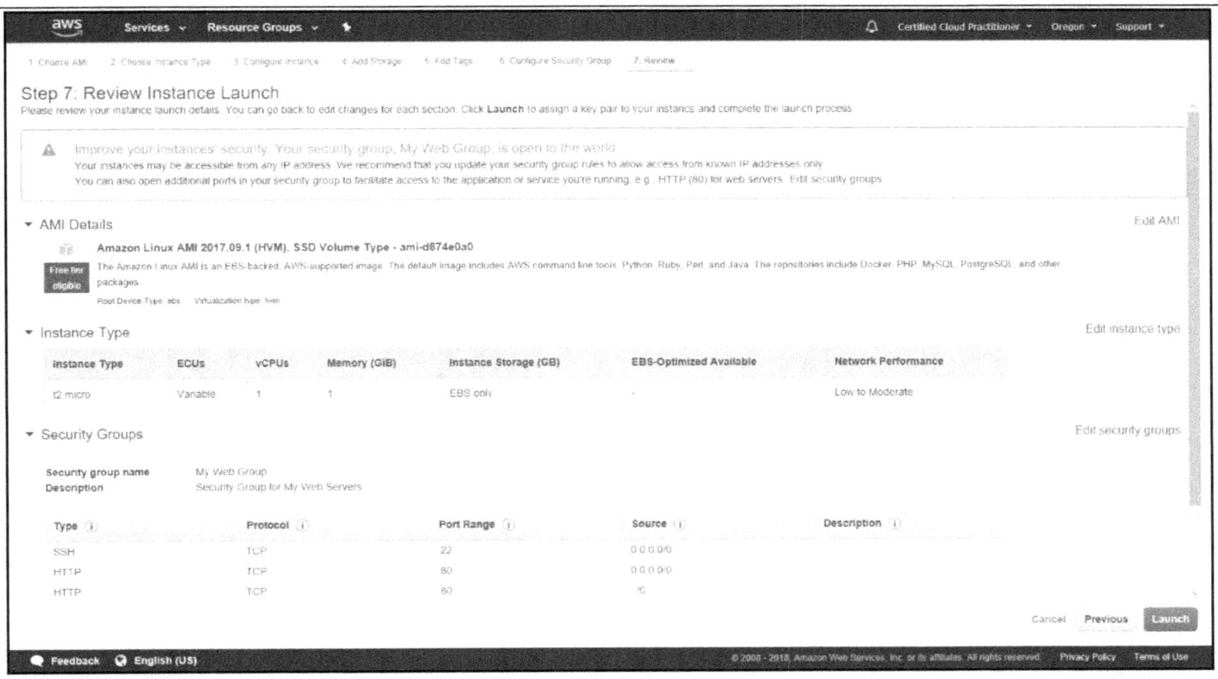

11. Review the details and click “Launch”.

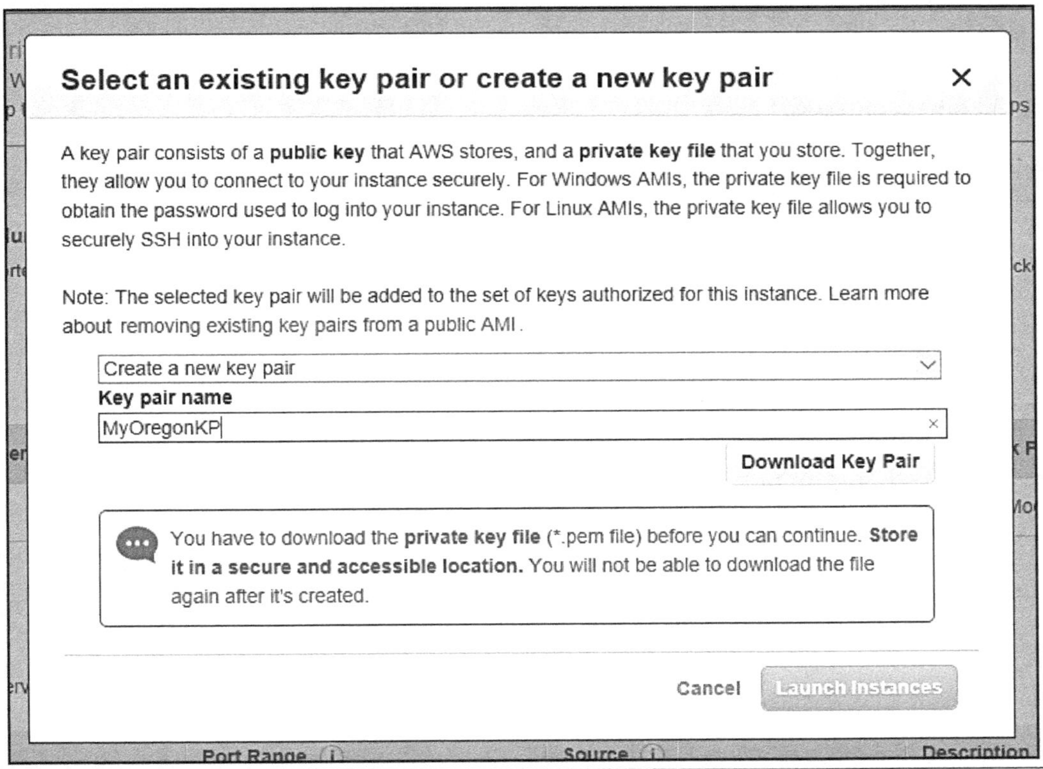

12. You will need a key pair to SSH for your instance. Select "Create a new key pair" and give it the name "MyOregonKP". Click "Download Key Pair" to download it to your PC. Once downloaded, click "Launch Instances".

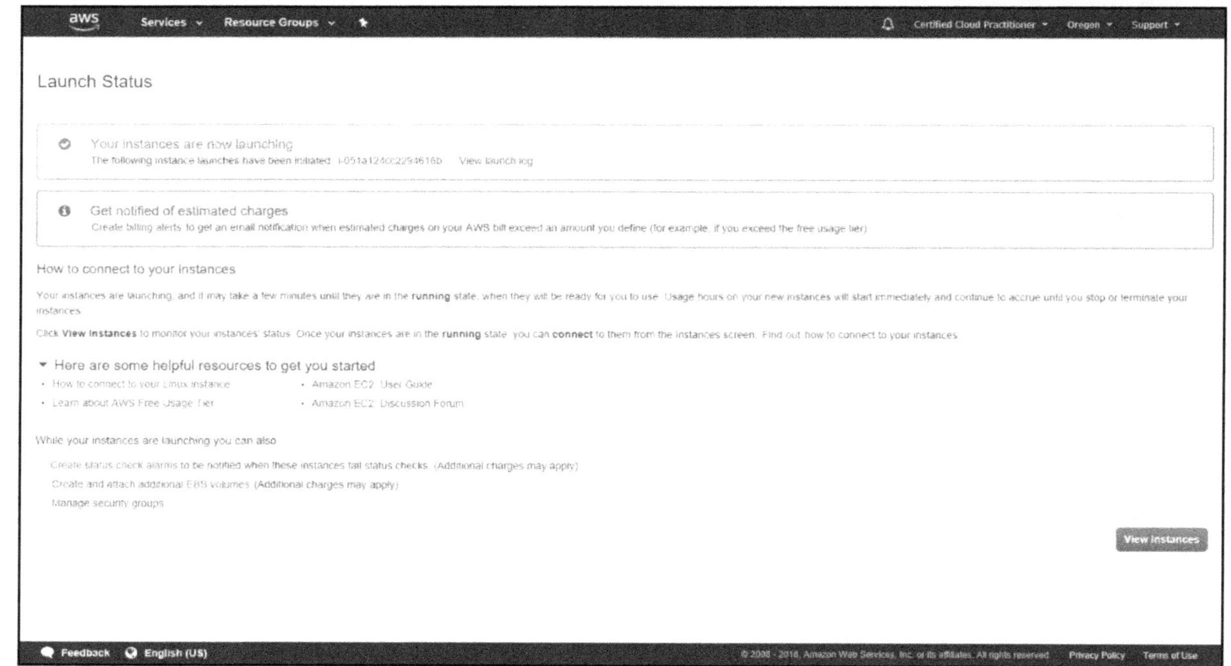

13. Click "View instances".

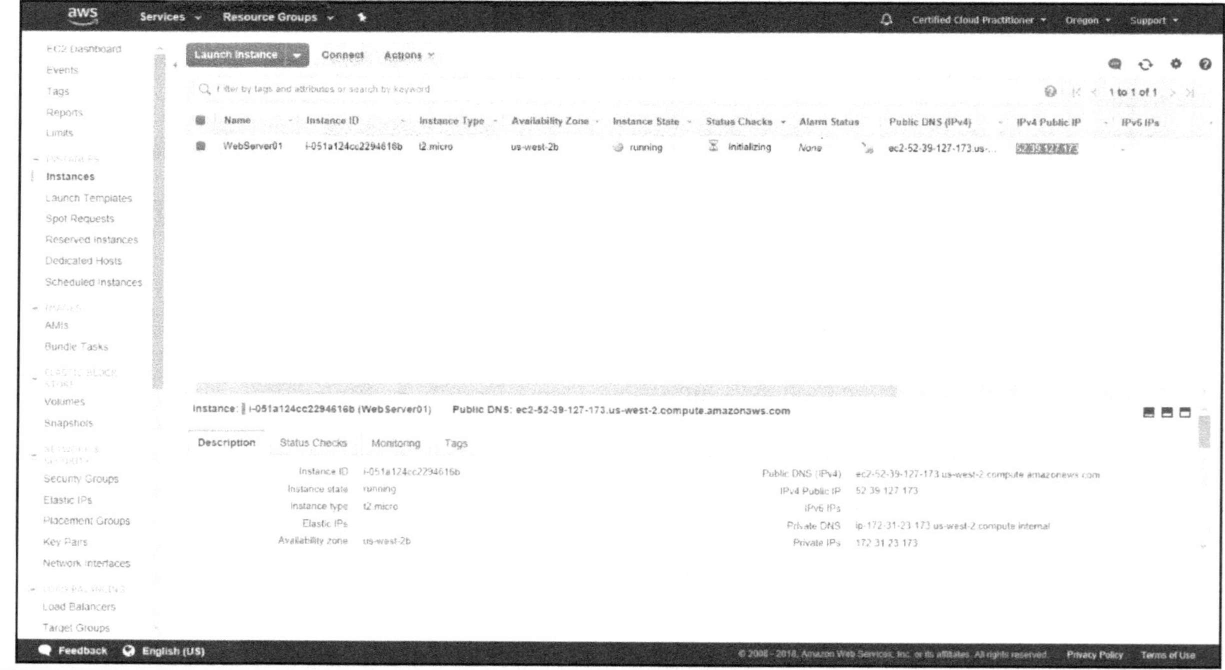

14. Once the instance is up and running, copy the public IP address of the instance onto a notepad. You will need this in the future to log in to the instance.
15. Using the key pair that you created, SSH into your EC2 instance. If you are using a Mac platform, follow the instructions on this link:

"https://docs.aws.amazon.com/quickstarts/latest/vmlaunch/step-2-connect-to-instance.html"

16. On a Windows platform, open "PuTTYgen".

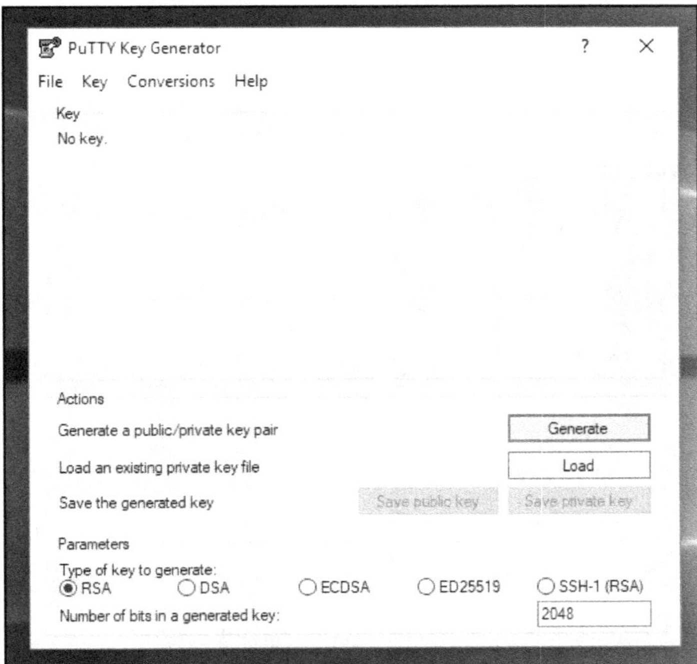

17. Click "Load" to load the existing private key file 'MyOregonKP.pem' that you downloaded when creating the EC2 instance. With PuTTYgen, convert the '.pem.' file to a '.ppk.' file.

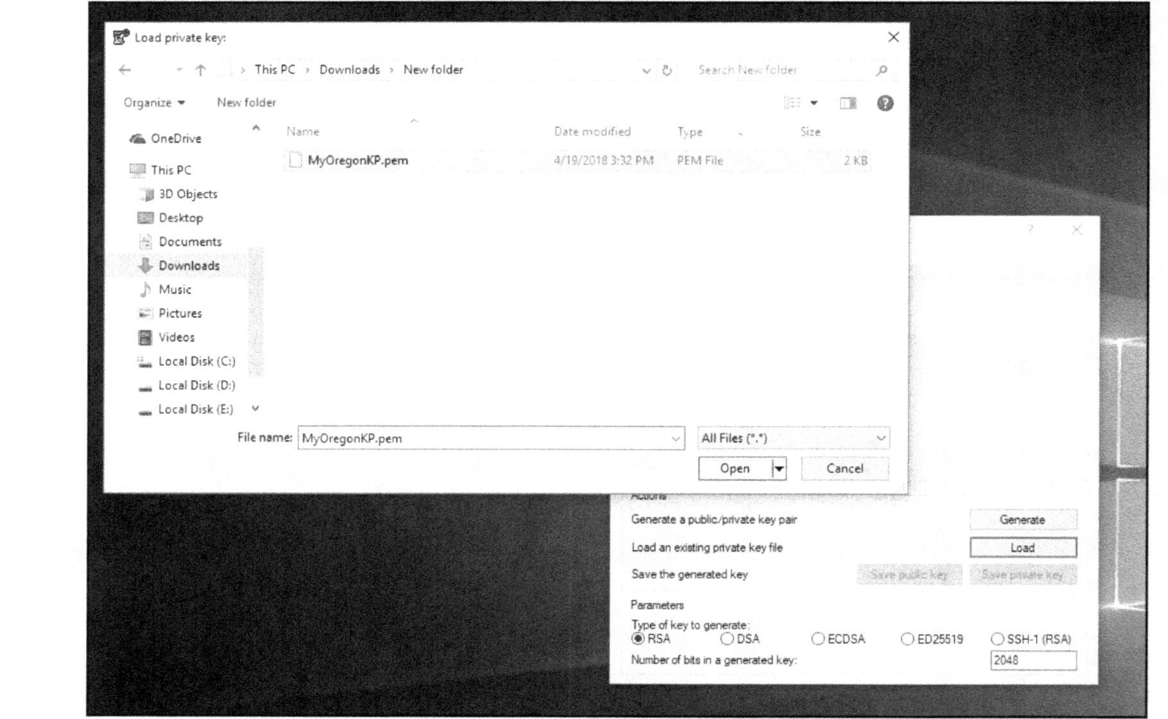

18. Navigate to the folder where your key is, select it and click "Open".

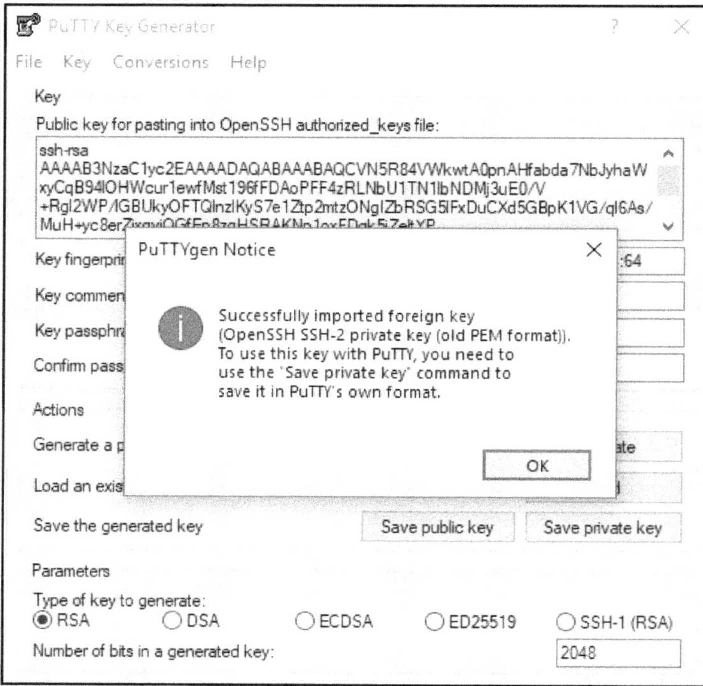

19. A dialogue box will be displayed that will say "Successfully imported foreign key". Click "OK".

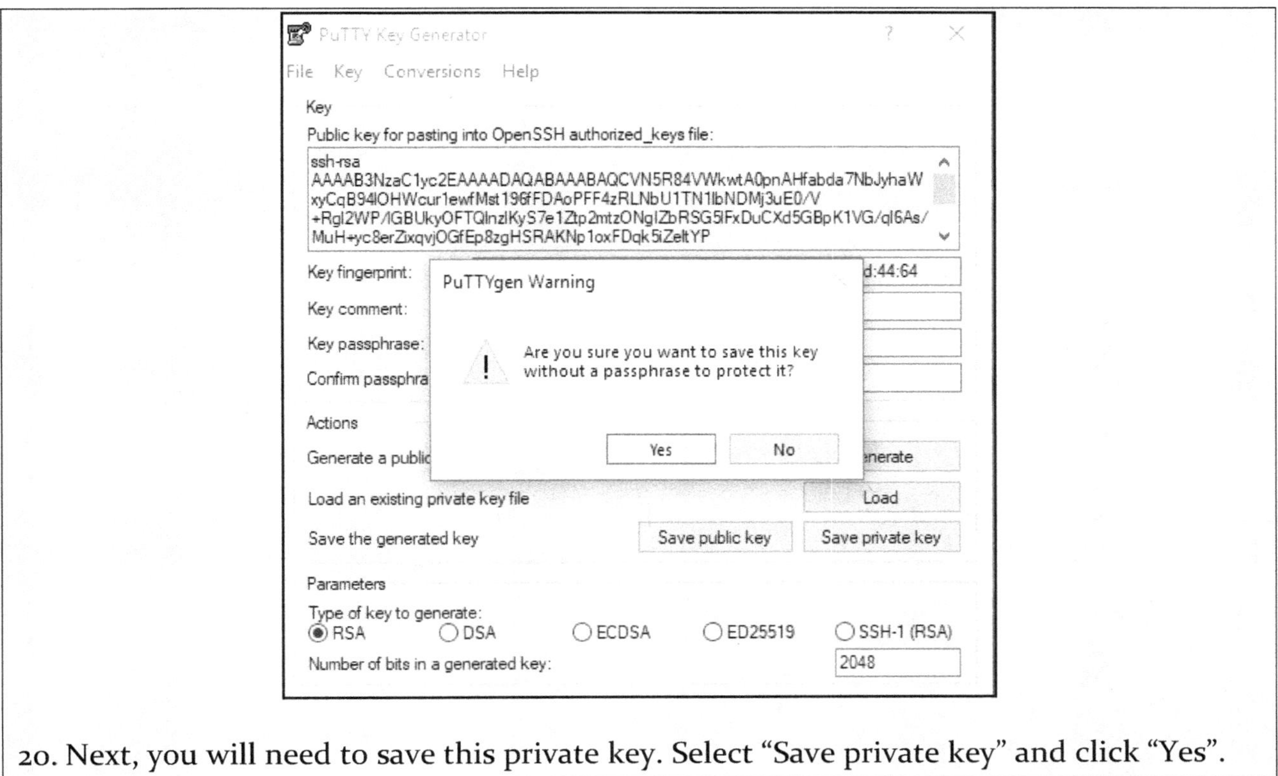

20. Next, you will need to save this private key. Select "Save private key" and click "Yes".

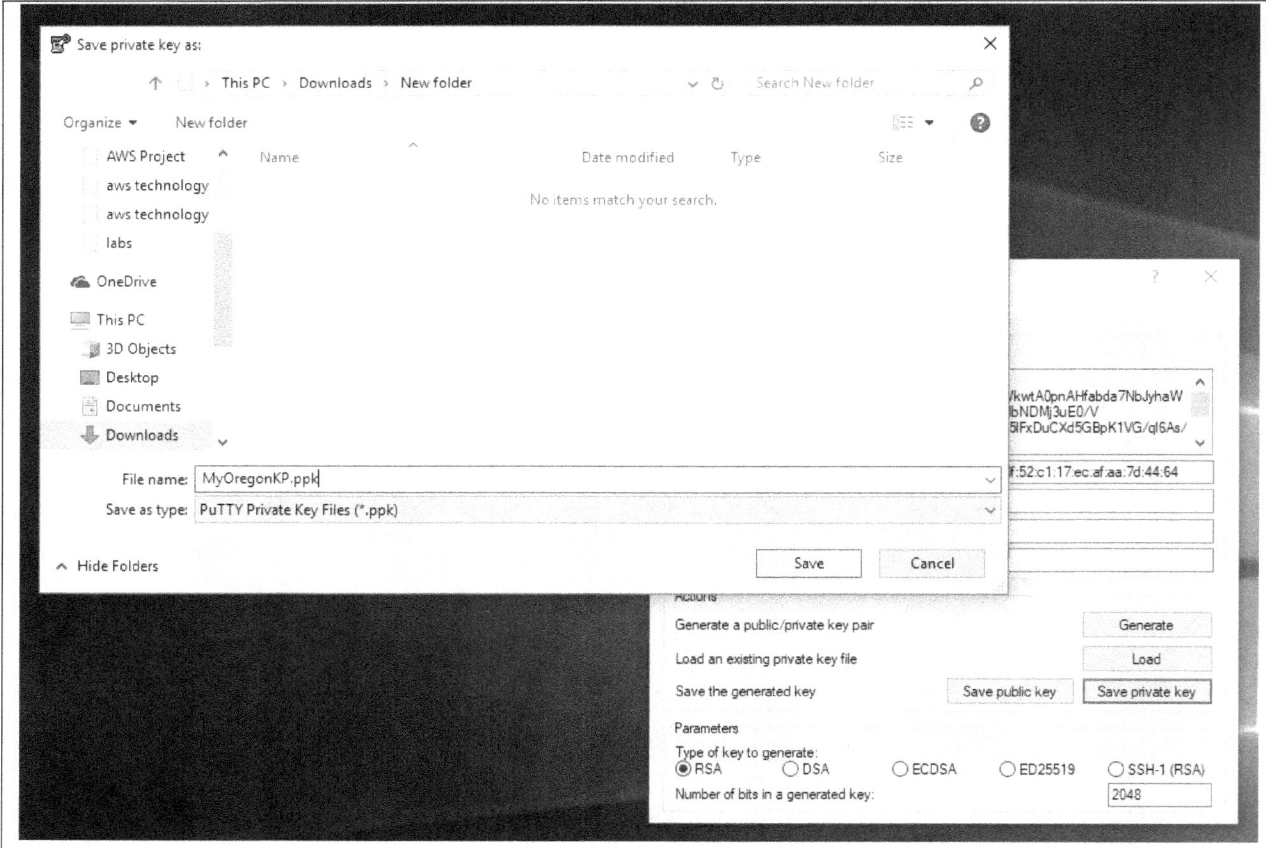

21. Enter the private key name and save it as 'MyOregonKP.ppk' file. Once you are done, close PuTTYgen and open "PuTTY".

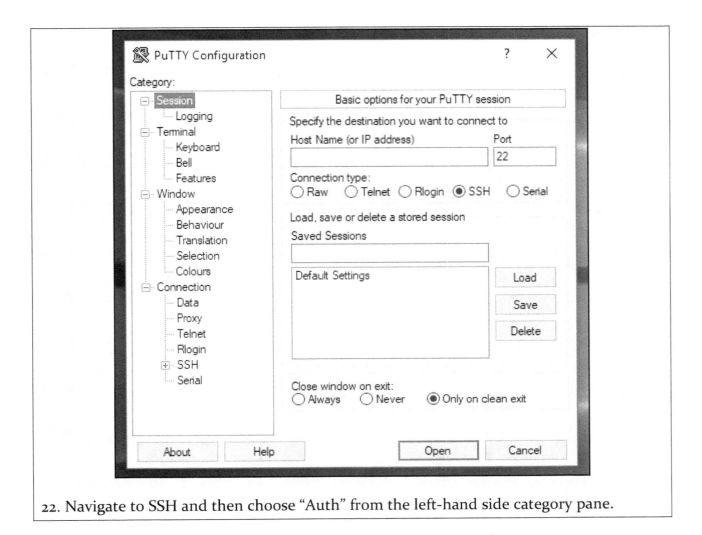

22. Navigate to SSH and then choose “Auth” from the left-hand side category pane.

PuTTY Configuration

Category:

Features
Window
Appearance
Behaviour
Translation
Selection
Colours
Connection
Data
Proxy
Telnet
Rlogin
SSH
Kex
Host keys
Cipher
Auth
TTY
X11
Tunnels
Bugs
More bugs

Options controlling SSH authentication

Display pre-authentication banner (SSH-2 only)
Bypass authentication entirely (SSH-2 only)

Authentication methods
Attempt authentication using Pageant
Attempt TIS or CryptoCard auth (SSH-1)
Attempt "keyboard-interactive" auth (SSH-2)

Authentication parameters
Allow agent forwarding
Allow attempted changes of username in SSH-2
Private key file for authentication:
Browse...

About | Help | Open | Cancel

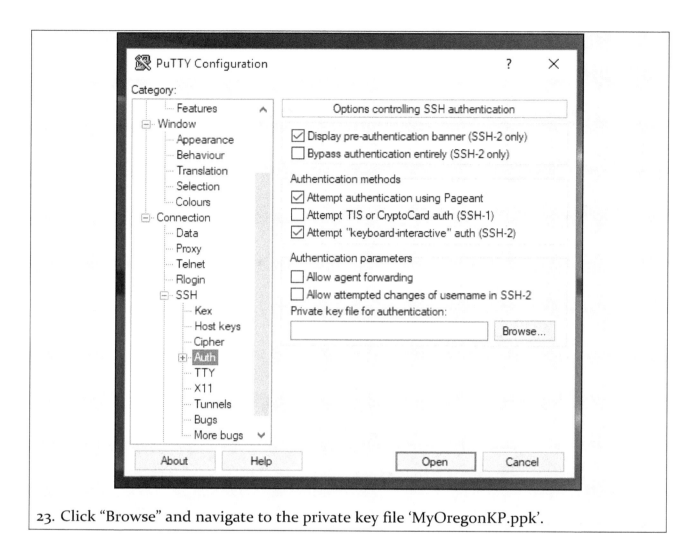

23. Click “Browse” and navigate to the private key file ‘MyOregonKP.ppk’.

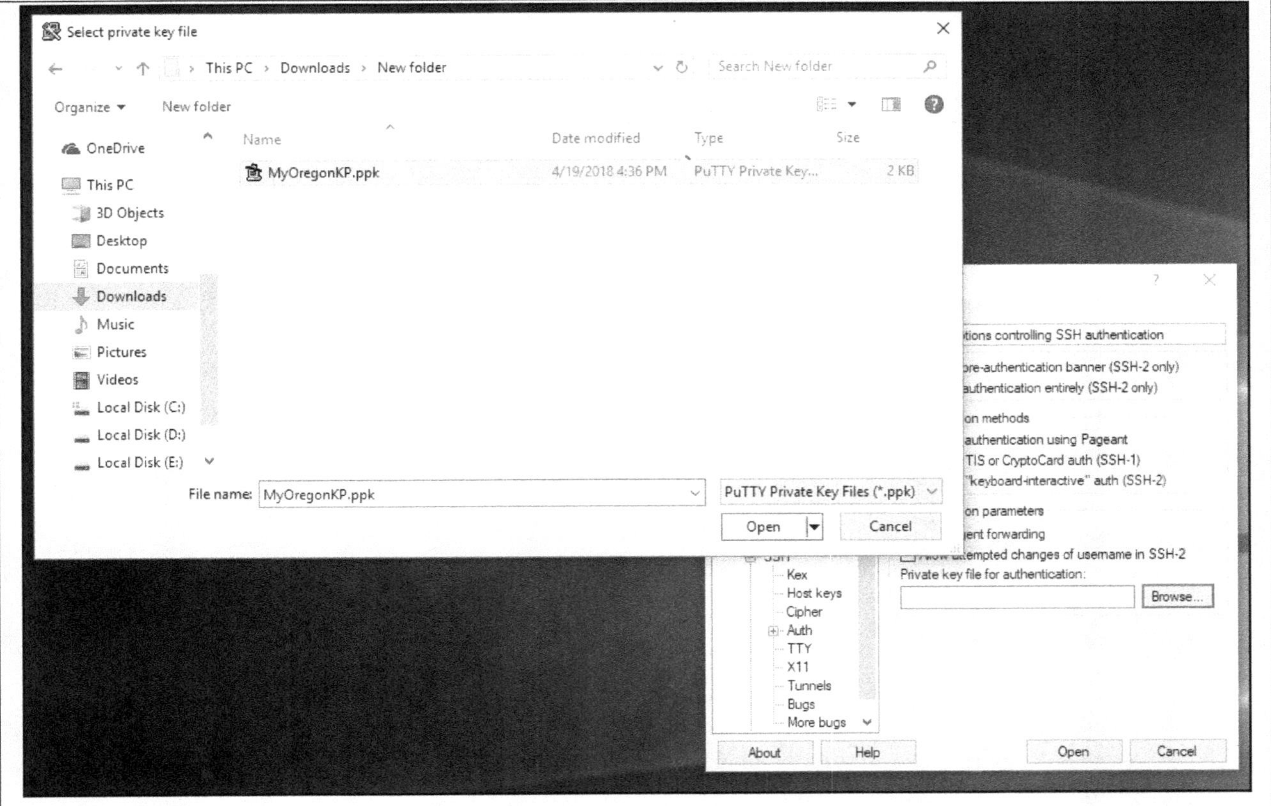

24. Select the key 'MyOregonKP.ppk' and click "Open". Now, select "Session" from the left-hand side of the category pane.

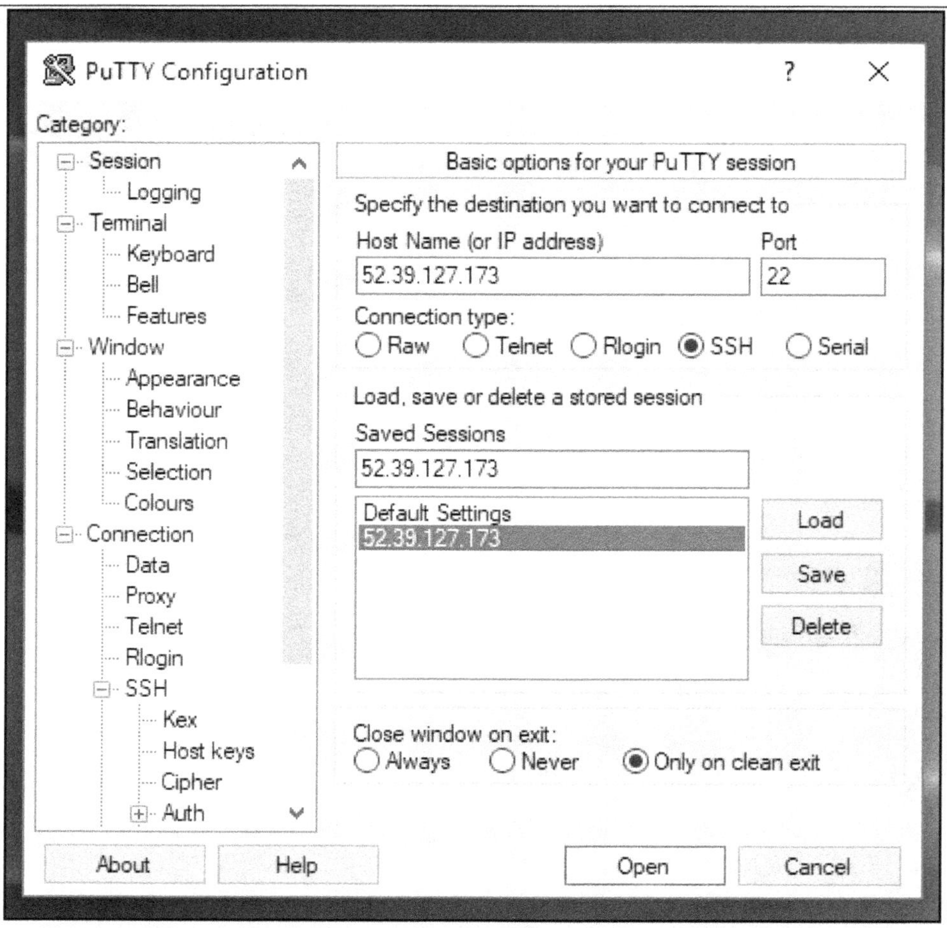

25. Copy the public IP address of the EC2 instance you previously saved in Notepad and paste it into the "Host Name (or IP address)" and "Saved Sessions" fields. Click the "Save" button, select the IP address and click "Open".

```
ec2-user@ip-172-31-23-173:~
login as: ec2-user
Authenticating with public key "imported-openssh-key"

       __|  __|_  )
       _|  (     /   Amazon Linux AMI
      ___|\___|___|

https://aws.amazon.com/amazon-linux-ami/2017.09-release-notes/
8 package(s) needed for security, out of 13 available
Run "sudo yum update" to apply all updates.
[ec2-user@ip-172-31-23-173 ~]$
```

26. It may prompt you for a username. If it does, type in "ec2-user" and hit enter. You will be logged in to your Amazon Linux AMI on a Windows machine.

EXAM TIPS:

- Use a private key to connect to an EC2 instance
- Security groups are virtual firewalls in the cloud
- You need to open ports in order to use them. Popular ports are SSH(22), which is required for Linux instances, and RDP(3389) for Windows
- HTTP(80) and HTTPS(443) are used when using the EC2 instance as a webserver

AWS Storage

Cloud Storage is a critical part of cloud computing as it is where all the data used by the applications is stored. All applications including databases, data warehouses, big data analytics, Internet of Things, backup and archive depend heavily on some form of data storage architecture. Amazon Web Services provides a variety of low-cost cloud storage services with high durability and availability. It offers object, file and block storage choices to support application and archival requirements as well as for use in disaster recovery.

Amazon Simple Storage Service (Amazon S3)duuysdiaisifdi

Amazon Simple Storage Service (Amazon S3) is an object storage service designed to store, access and retrieve any type and amount of data over the internet through a simple web service interface. S3 provides a secure and highly durable and scalable platform for user-generated content like photos, videos, music, and files, as well as active archive, backup and recovery, and data lakes for Big Data analytics and data warehouse platforms. It can also act as a foundation for serverless computing.

Amazon S3 Features

- **Simple:** Simple to use with a web-based management console and mobile app
- **Durable:** Provides durable infrastructure to store important data. Data is redundantly stored across multiple facilities with multiple devices in each facility
- **Scalable:** Store as much data as you want and access it when needed while being able to scale storage up or down as required. It allows for concurrent read and write access to data by many separate clients or application threads
- **Secure:** Supports data transfer over SSL and automatic encryption of data once it has been uploaded. You can also configure bucket policies to manage object permissions, and use access control lists to control access to your data
- **Available:** Amazon S3 Standard is designed for up to 99.99% availability of objects over a given year and is backed by the Amazon S3 Service Level Agreement
- **Low Cost:** Allows you to store large amounts of data at a very low cost. You can set policies to automatically migrate your data to Standard - Infrequent Access orAmazon Glacier for archiving to further reduce costs
- **Simple Data Transfer:** Provides multiple options for cloud data migration, and makes it simple and cost-effective to move large volumes of data into or out of Amazon S3
- **Integrated:** Amazon S3 is deeply integrated with other AWS services to make it easier to build solutions that use a range of AWS services
- **Easy to Manage:** Amazon S3 Storage Management features allow you to take a data-driven approach to storage optimization, data security and management efficiency by giving you information about your data. This means you can manage your storage based on the personalized metadata that you receive

Amazon S3 Basics

Amazon S3 is an object-based storage system where objects are simply files such as text files, images and videos. It provides safe and secure storage as the data is spread across at least two or three availability zones, depending upon how many availability zones are present within that particular region.

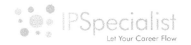

Buckets:

A bucket is a container for objects stored in Amazon S3. To upload your data, whether it is photos, videos or documents, you first need to create a bucket in one of the AWS Regions. You can then upload any number of objects to the bucket. Each object can contain up to 5 TB of data. Amazon S3 bucket names are globally unique, regardless of the AWS Region in which you create the bucket. Amazon S3 creates buckets in the region that you specify. You can choose any AWS Region that is geographically close to you to optimize latency, minimize costs or address regulatory requirements.

This is an example of an S3 Bucket URL:

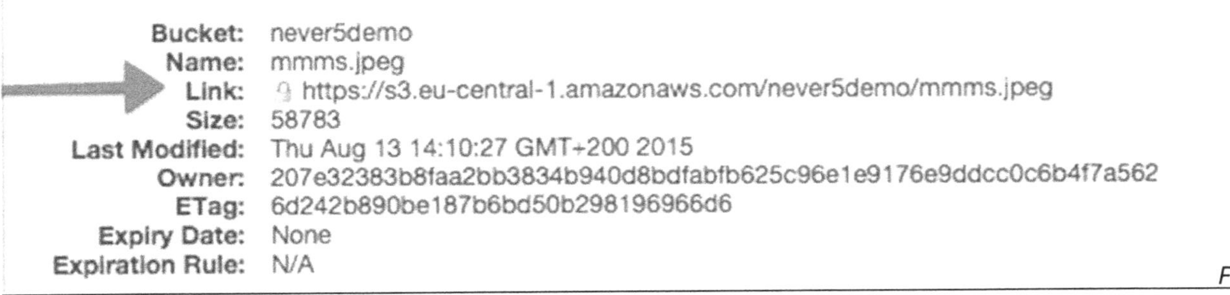

Figure 3-07. S3 Bucket URL

Whenever you view your buckets, you will view them all irrespective of which region they are in. The actual console interface is similar at the global level to the Identity Access Management (IAM). You have to specify a particular region to deploy your buckets.

You can use Amazon S3 to host Static websites (such as .html). Deploying static websites on S3 is ideal if there are large numbers of requests to the site. Websites that are dynamic or require database connection, such as WordPress, cannot be hosted on S3. By default, all buckets are private with no public read access, however you can use bucket policies to make entire S3 buckets public. This enables you to host a static website on S3.

Objects:

Objects are the fundamental entities stored in Amazon S3. Objects consist of object data and metadata. The metadata is a set of name-value pairs that describe the object. These include default metadata, such as the date last modified, together with standard HTTP metadata, such as Content-Type. An object is uniquely identified within a bucket by a key

and a version ID. You can change the storage class and encryption of your objects without notice.

Keys:

A key is a unique identifier for an object within a bucket, like a name. Every object in a bucket has only one key. The combination of a bucket, key, and version ID uniquely identifies each object.

Amazon S3 Data Consistency Model:

Amazon S3 achieves high availability by replicating data across multiple servers within Amazon data centers. If a PUT request is successful, your data will be safely stored. When you upload a file to S3, you will receive an HTTP 200 code if the upload was successful. However, information about the changes must be replicated across Amazon S3, which can take some time. Amazon S3 provides:

- Read after Write consistency for PUTS of new objects

Eventual consistency across facilities for overwrite PUTS and DELETES may take some time. For example, if you upload a new object to S3 for the first time and immediately attempt to open it, you will be able to read it immediately. However, if the object is replaced or updated then accessed immediately, Amazon S3 may return the prior data until the change is fully propagated. This is because S3 is spread across multiple devices across multiple facilities, so if you try to read an object you just updated, it can take some time for the changes to synchronize across those devices and facilities.

Amazon S3 Storage Classes

1. ***Storage Classes for Frequently Accessed Objects:***
   - ***Standard S3:*** This is the best storage option for data that you frequently access. Amazon S3 delivers low latency and high throughput and is ideal for use cases such as cloud applications, dynamic websites, content distribution, gaming and data analytics
   - ***Reduced Redundancy Storage:*** This storage class is designed for noncritical, reproducible data that can be stored with less redundancy than the standard storage class
2. ***Storage Classes for Infrequently Accessed Objects:***
   - ***S3 Standard*** – Infrequent Access: This is ideal for data that is accessed infrequently but requires rapid access when needed, such as long-term backups

and disaster recovery. It is a lower cost than S3 Standard but incurs higher charges to retrieve or transfer data

- **S3 One Zone** – Infrequent Access: This stores data in only one Availability Zone, making it less expensive than Standard- IA. However, the data is not resilient to the physical loss of the availability zone. Only use this type of storage if you can recreate the data if the availability zone fails.

	S3 Standard	S3 Standard-Infrequent Access	Reduced Redundancy Storage
Durability	99.999999999%	99.999999999%	99.99%
Availability	99.99%	99.99%	99.99%
Concurrent Facility Fault Tolerance	2	2	1
SSL Support	Yes	Yes	Yes
First Byte Latency	Milliseconds	Milliseconds	Milliseconds
Lifecycle Management Policies	Yes	Yes	Yes

Table 3-1: Comparison S3 Standard, S3 Standard-IA, and Reduced Redundancy Storage

	S3 Standard	S3 Standard- IA	S3 One Zone - IA
Durability	99.999999999%	99.999999999%	99.999999999%
Availability	99.99%	99.9%	99.5%
Availability SLA	99.9%	99%	99%
Availability Zones	≥ 3	≥ 3	1
Min. Object Size	N/A	128 KB	128 KB
Min. Storage Duration	N/A	30 days	30 days
Retrieval Fee	N/A	per GB retrieved	per GB retrieved
First Byte Latency	milliseconds	milliseconds	milliseconds
Storage Type	Object level	Object level	Object level
Lifecycle Transitions	Yes	Yes	Yes

Table 3-2: Comparison S3 Standard, S3 Standard-IA, and S3 One Zone-IA

Amazon S3 Fundamental Characteristics

Security & Access Management:

A. *Flexible Access Control Mechanism*

Amazon S3 supports several mechanisms that give you the flexibility to control who can access your data, as well as how, when and where they can access it. Amazon S3 provides four different access control mechanisms:

1. **AWS Identity and Access Management (IAM) Policies:** IAM enables organizations to create and manage multiple users under a single AWS

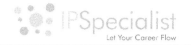

account. With IAM policies, you can grant IAM users fine-grained control to any Amazon S3 bucket or object.

2. **Access Control Lists (ACLs):** Allows you to control objects from an individual object level. You can use ACLs to selectively grant certain permissions to individual objects.
3. **Bucket Policies:** Secure your data at a bucket level. Amazon S3 bucket policies can be used to add or deny permissions across some or all of the objects within a single bucket.
4. **Query String Authentication:** With Query String Authentication, you can share Amazon S3 objects through URLs that are only valid for a specified and limited period.

B. Encryption

You can securely upload or download your data to Amazon S3 via the SSL-encrypted endpoints using the HTTPS protocol. You can also choose to have your data encrypted at rest by Amazon S3 with server-side encryption (SSE). Amazon S3 will automatically encrypt your data on write and decrypt your data on retrieval.

C. Versioning

Amazon S3 provides protection with versioning capability. You can use versioning to preserve, retrieve and restore every version of each object stored in your Amazon S3 bucket. This backup mechanism allows you to easily recover from unintended user actions and application failures.

Storage Management

A. Object Tagging

S3 object tags are key-value pairs applied to S3 objects that can be created, updated or deleted at any time during the lifetime of the object. With these, you can create Identity and Access Management (IAM) policies, setup S3 Lifecycle policies, and customize storage metrics.

A. Data Lifecycle Management

You can create lifecycle policies for your objects within S3. For example, you can set S3 Lifecycle policies that will command Amazon S3 to automatically migrate your data to lower cost storage as your data ages.

B. *Cross Region Replication*

You can automatically replicate the contents of one bucket to another bucket by using cross-region replication. Cross-Region Replication (CRR) makes it simple to replicate new objects into another AWS Region for reasons of reduced latency, compliance, security, disaster recovery and a number of other use cases.

Data Transfer

Amazon S3 charges for the following:

Figure 3-08: AWS S3 Charges

S3 Transfer Acceleration

Amazon S3 Transfer Acceleration enables fast, easy and secure transfer of files over long distances between end users and an S3 bucket. Transfer acceleration takes advantage of Amazon CloudFront's globally distributed edge locations. When the data arrives at an edge location, it is routed to Amazon S3 over an optimized network path.

For example, with S3 transfer acceleration enabled, if users want to upload an object to a bucket at a particular location, they can upload it to the edge location nearest to them. Once the edge location has received the object, it will upload it to the particular storage location using Amazon's internal backbone network. This can dramatically increase the speed of uploads because users no longer need to upload objects directly to the storage location. Instead, they are uploading them to a server much closer to them.

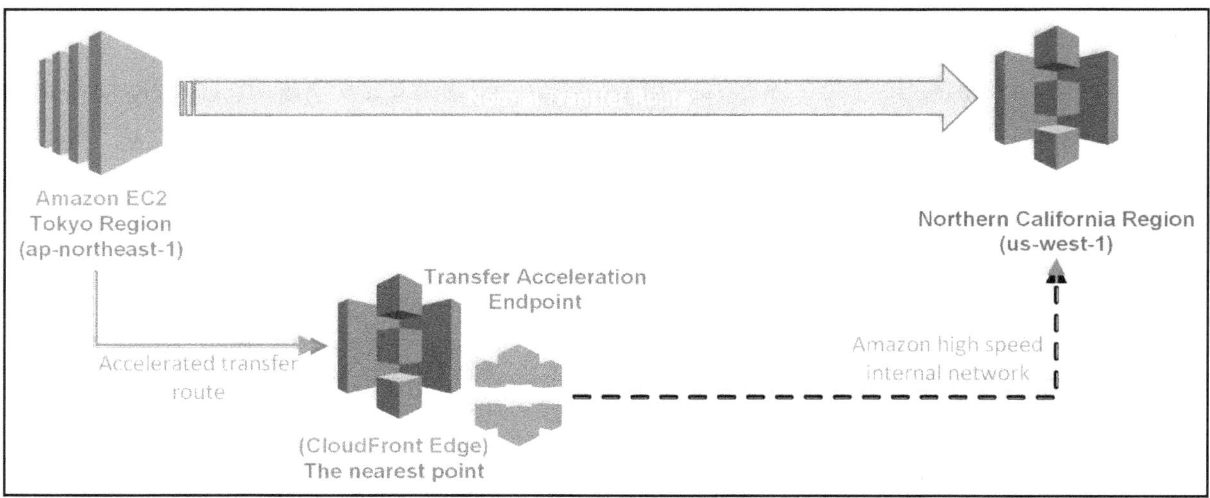

Figure 3-09: Amazon S3 Transfer Acceleration

EXAM TIPS:

- A bucket is simply a place to store your objects. Think of it as a directory on your computer, except that it can be accessed from anywhere in the world using the AWS Console or the command line
- Amazon S3 is a unique namespace: you cannot have the same bucket name as anyone else
- When you view your buckets, you view them globally, but you can have buckets in individual regions
- S3 is object-based storage only for files and is not suitable to install on an operating system
- Successful uploads will generate an HTTP 200 status code
- You can encrypt objects in transit to S3 using SSL. You can also encrypt objects at rest on S3 using different encryption methods
- To restrict access to an entire bucket, use Bucket Policies. To restrict access to an individual object, use Access Control Lists
- You can automatically replicate the contents of one bucket to another bucket using cross-region replication
- You can change the storage class and encryption of your objects without prior notice
- Understand what S3 transfer accelerator is

Lab 3-5: AWS S3 Transfer Acceleration

1. Log in to the “AWS Console”.
2. Click on “Services”.
3. Select “S3” from the storage list.

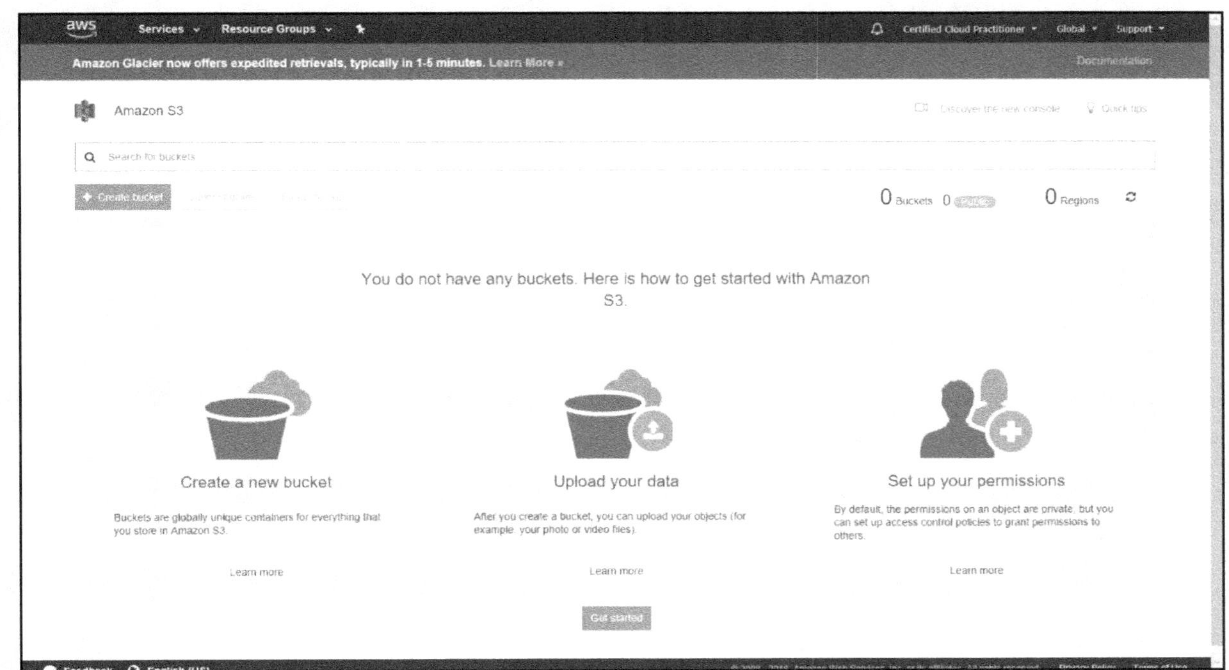

4. Similar to Identity Access Management, Amazon S3 interface is also global. You can see this in the top right corner. You can select the region in which you want to deploy your S3 bucket while creating it. Click on “Create bucket”.

Create bucket

1 Name and region | 2 Set properties | 3 Set permissions | 4 Review

Name and region

Bucket name

Enter DNS-compliant bucket name

Bucket name must not be empty

Region

US West (Oregon)

Copy settings from an existing bucket

You have no buckets | 0 Buckets

Cancel | Next

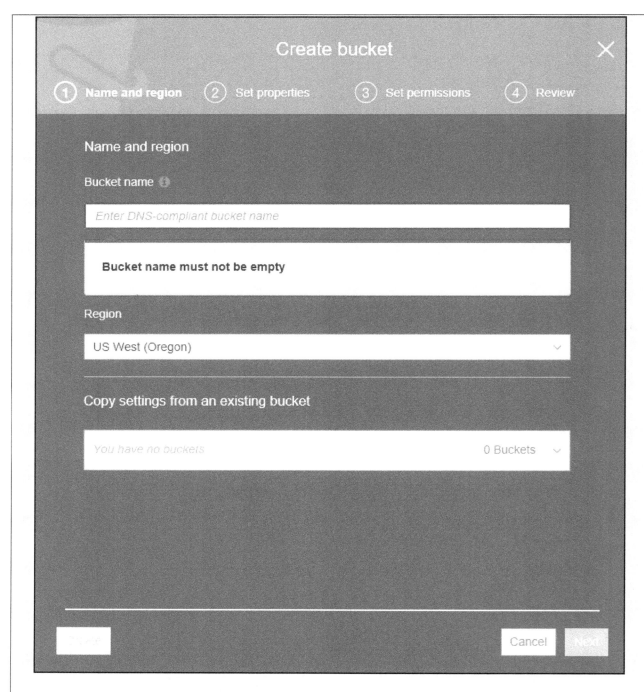

5. Enter a DNS-compliant bucket name. It should not contain uppercase characters and must start with a lowercase letter or number. The bucket name must be between 3 and 63 characters long with no invalid characters.

6. Select a region where you want to deploy your bucket from the list of "Regions".

Create bucket

1 Name and region 2 Set properties 3 Set permissions 4 Review

Name and region

Bucket name

ccp.bucket

Region

US West (Oregon)

Copy settings from an existing bucket

You have no buckets 0 Buckets

Create Cancel Next

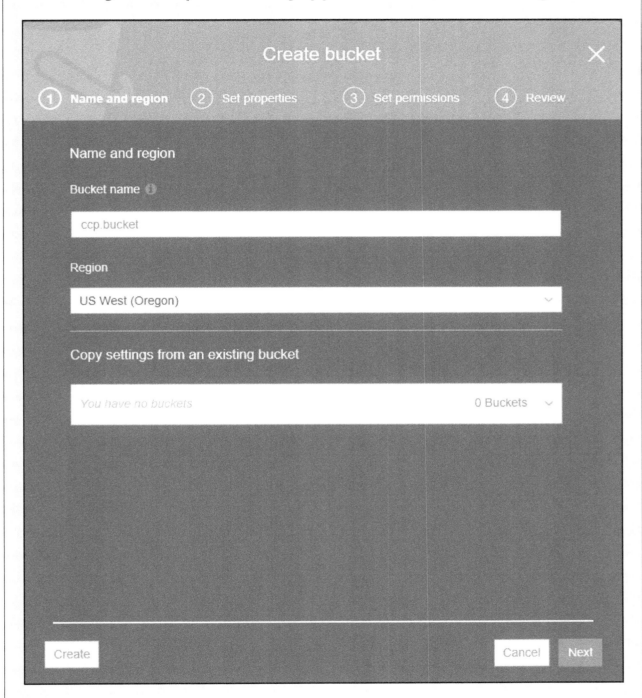

7. Click "Next" to proceed to the properties section. This is where you can enable Versioning, Server access logging, Object-level logging and automatic Encryption and add Tags.

Create bucket

Name and region
2 Set properties
3 Set permissions
4 Review

Versioning

Keep multiple versions of an object in the same bucket

Learn more

Server access logging

Set up access log records that provide details about access requests.

Learn more

Tags

Use tags to track your cost against projects or other criteria.

Learn more

Object-level logging

Record object-level API activity using the CloudTrail data events feature (additional cost).

Learn more

Default encryption

Previous Next

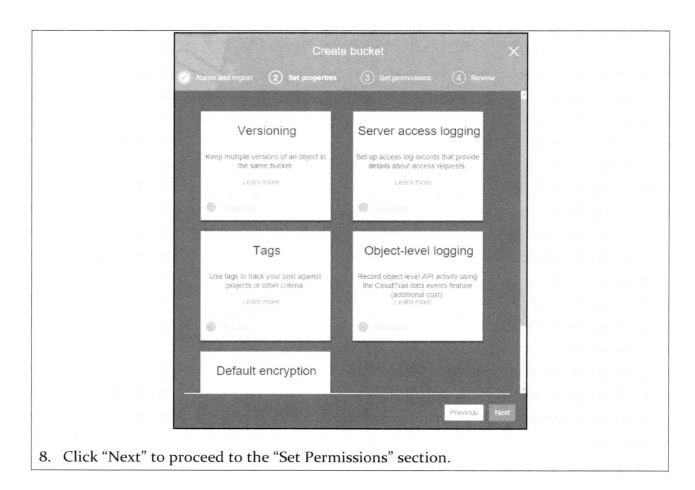

8. Click "Next" to proceed to the "Set Permissions" section.

Create bucket

Name and region | Set properties | 3 Set permissions | 4 Review

Manage users

User ID	Objects	Object permissions
saima(Owner)	Read Write	Read Write

Access for other AWS account + Add account

Account	Objects	Object permissions

Manage public permissions

Do not grant public read access to this bucket (Recommended)

Manage system permissions

Do not grant Amazon S3 Log Delivery group write access to this bucket

Previous Next

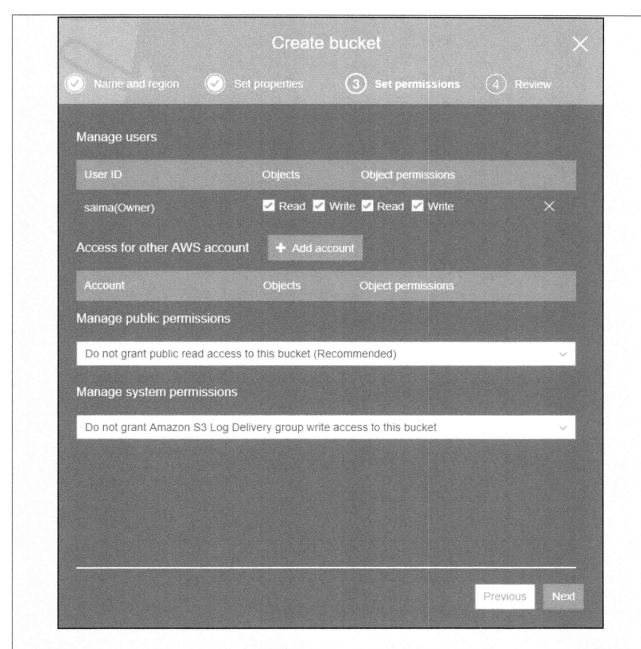

9. Here, you can manage users and set permissions and allow public access to the bucket if necessary. By default, all buckets are private. For this example, leave everything as it is and click “Next”.

Create bucket

Name and region | Set properties | Set permissions | 4 Review

Name and region — Edit

Bucket name ccp.bucket **Region** US West (Oregon)

Properties — Edit

Versioning	Disabled
Server access logging	Disabled
Tagging	0 Tags
Object-level logging	Disabled
Default encryption	None

Permissions — Edit

Users	1
Public permissions	Disabled
System permissions	Disabled

Previous | Create bucket

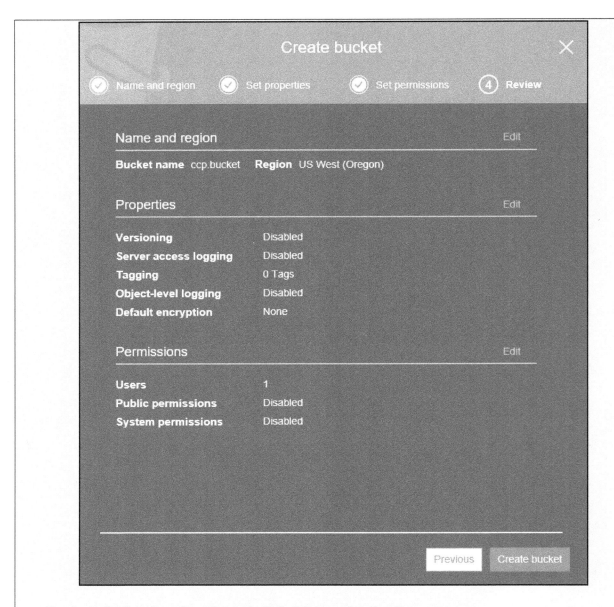

10. Review the bucket details and click "Create bucket".

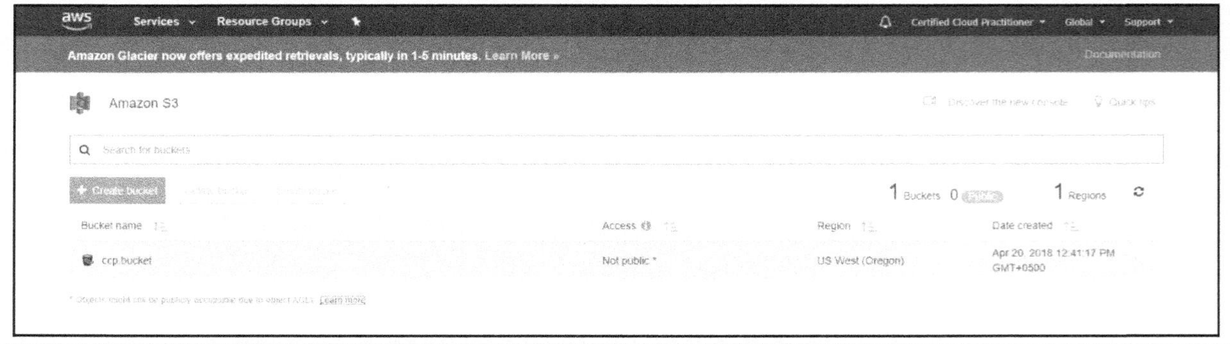

11. Click on the bucket named "ccp.bucket" to open it and start adding files.

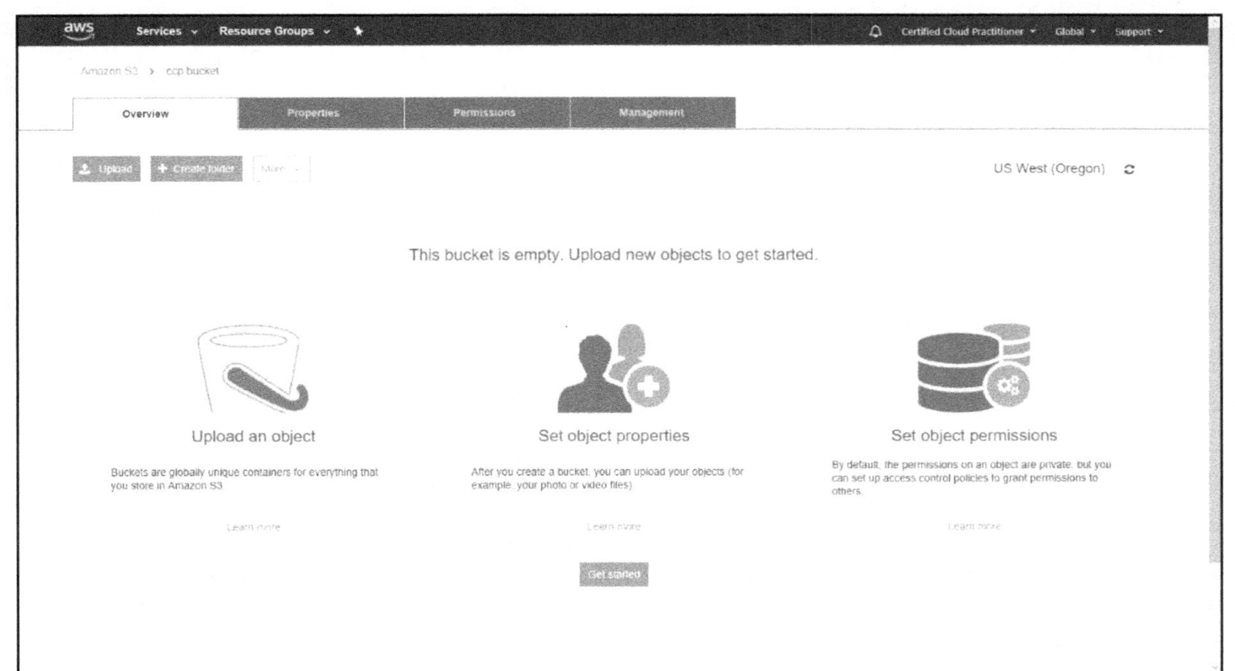

12. Click "Create folder" to add a new folder to the bucket.

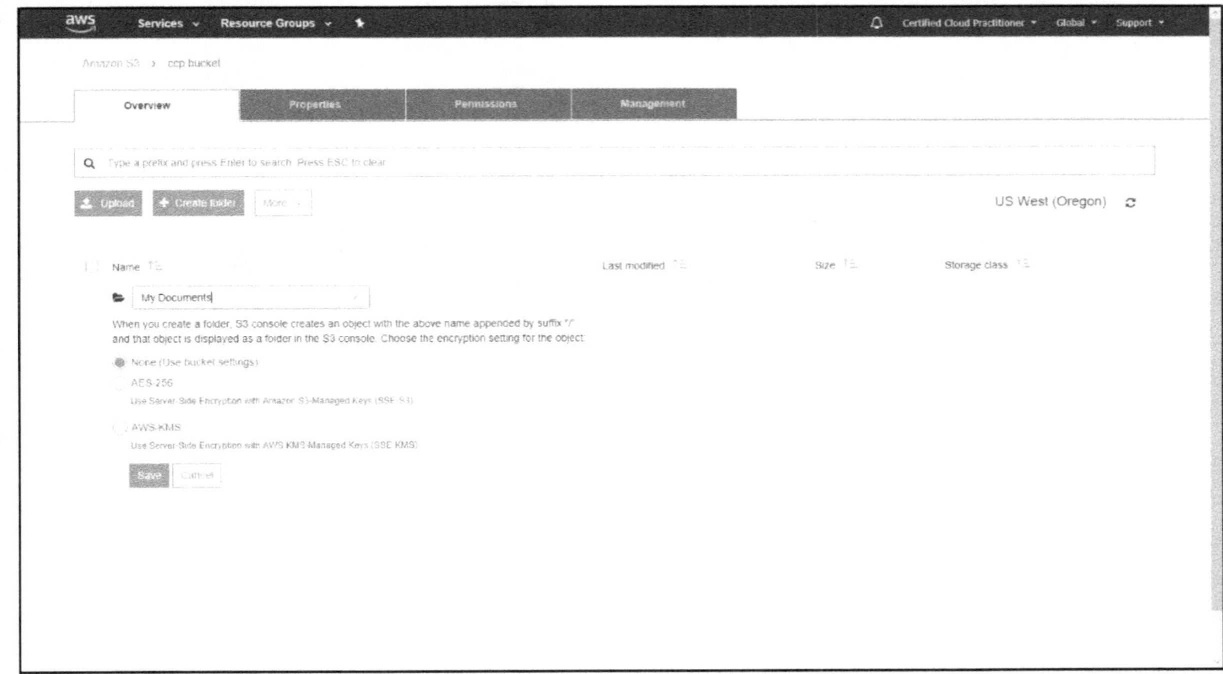

13. The folder will be added as an object in the bucket. Select the encryption type for the object and click "Save".

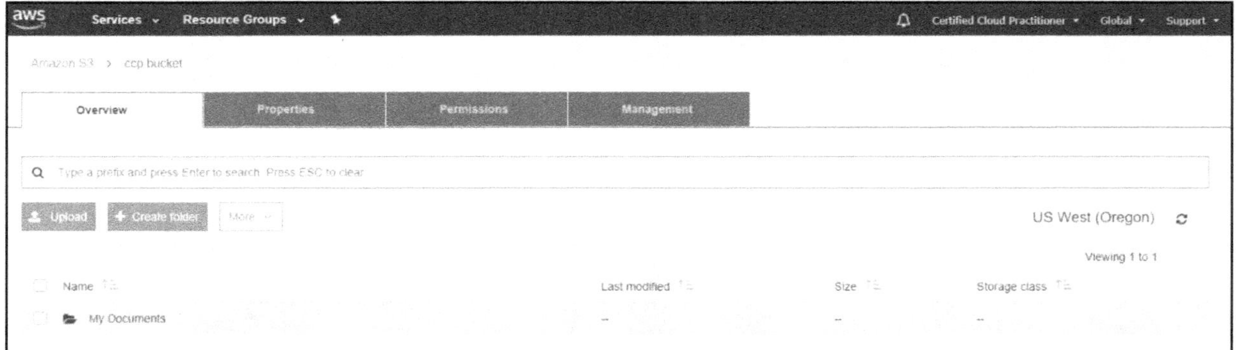

14. Add files to the bucket by clicking the "Upload" button.

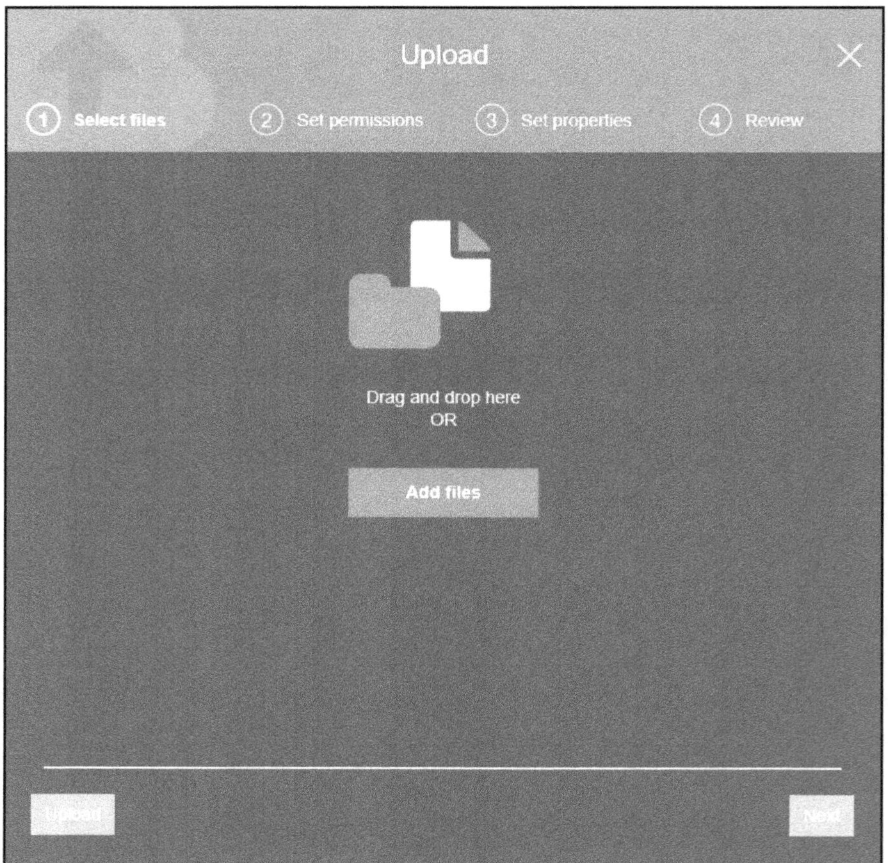

15. Click "Add files" and select any files to upload.

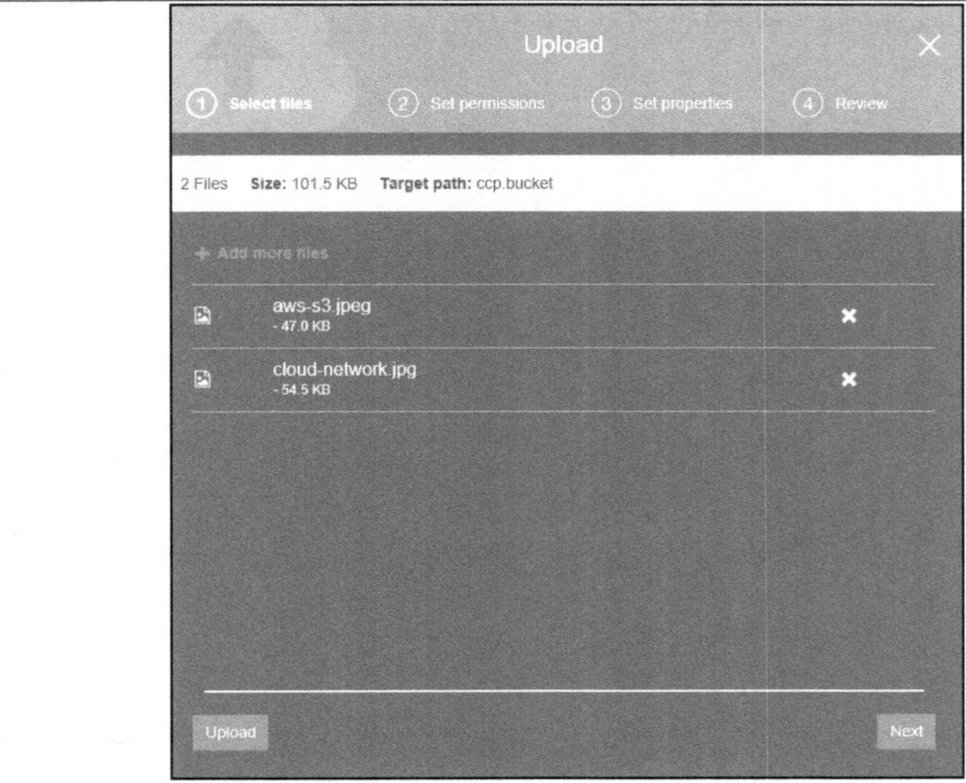

16. After selecting the files you would like to upload, you can click "Upload" to upload them directly or "Next" to set permissions and properties for the files.

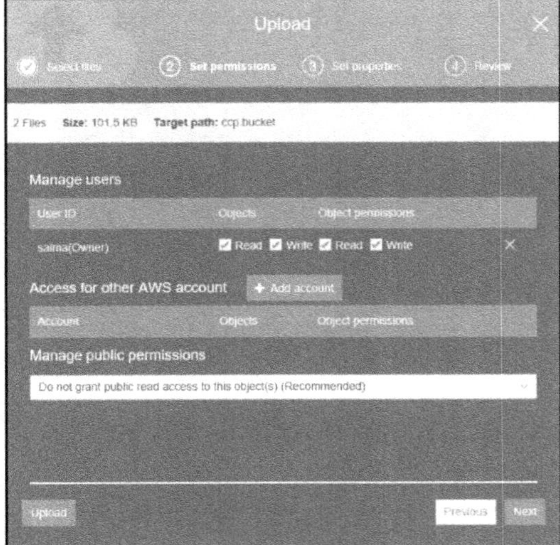

17. In the "Set permissions" section, you can manage users and their access permissions. You can also define whether you want to grant public access to the files. Once these permissions are selected, click "Next".

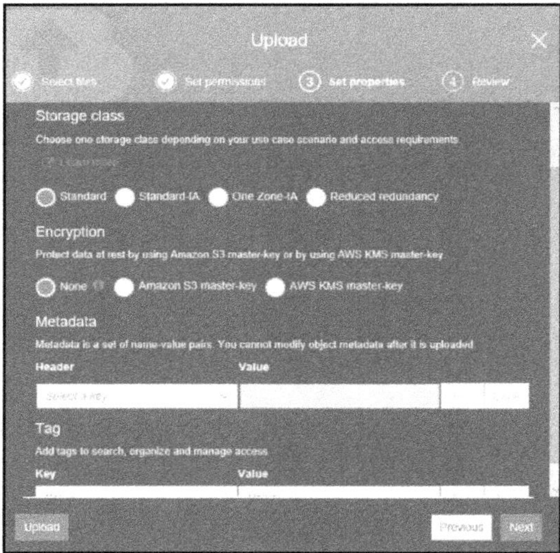

18. In the "Set properties" section, you can select the storage class, the encryption type for the files and add metadata and tags if necessary. Click "Next" when done.

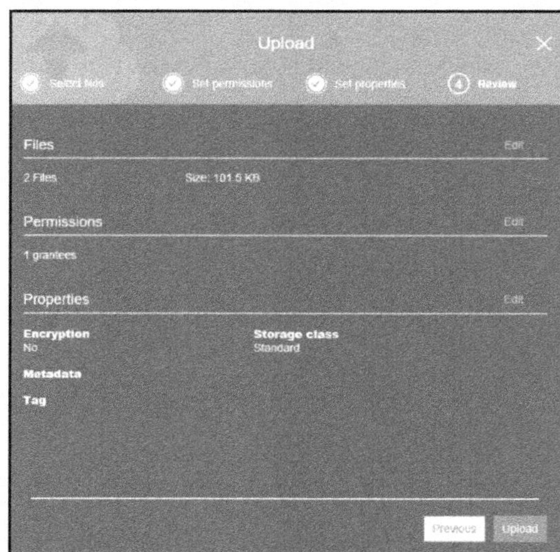

19. Review the details and click "Upload" to upload your selected files to the bucket.

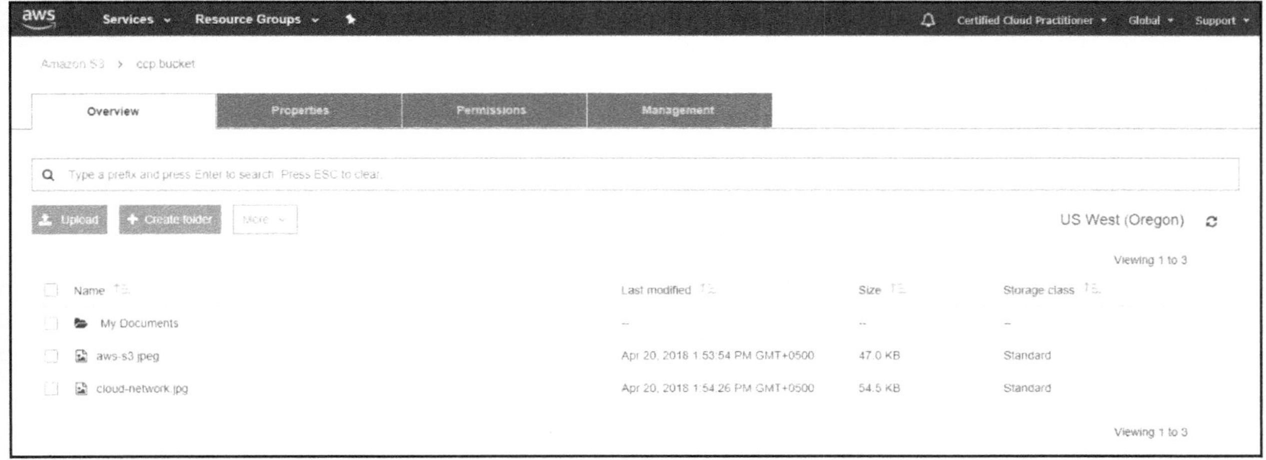

20. After the files are uploaded, you can continue to edit the properties and permissions of the files. To do this, click on any file to navigate to its overview tab.

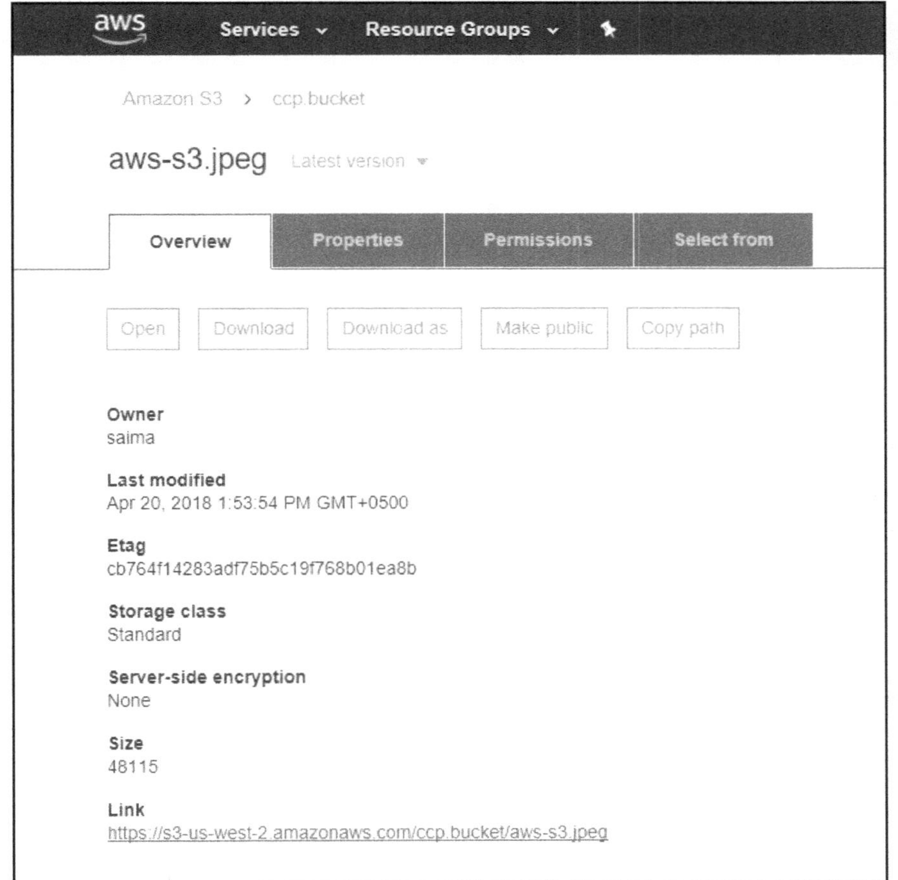

21. Here, you will see a URL link to the file. Since public access to the file is not granted, clicking the link will only result in an error page.


```
<?xml version="1.0" encoding="UTF-8"?>
- <Error>
    <Code>AccessDenied</Code>
    <Message>Access Denied</Message>
    <RequestId>BB25169CFEDA4D9D</RequestId>
    <HostId>pjeBY+CUvBNIJu6cJj1JhnTqzyIN3i9R6nzz6SfECIoZH81mQXiIpdG+lIxdD0LHWBeXzQcbOxs=</HostId>
  </Error>
```


22. The reason for the error is that you have not set public read permissions on the file. To make it publicly accessible, click the "Back" button in your browser and select the "Permissions" tab.

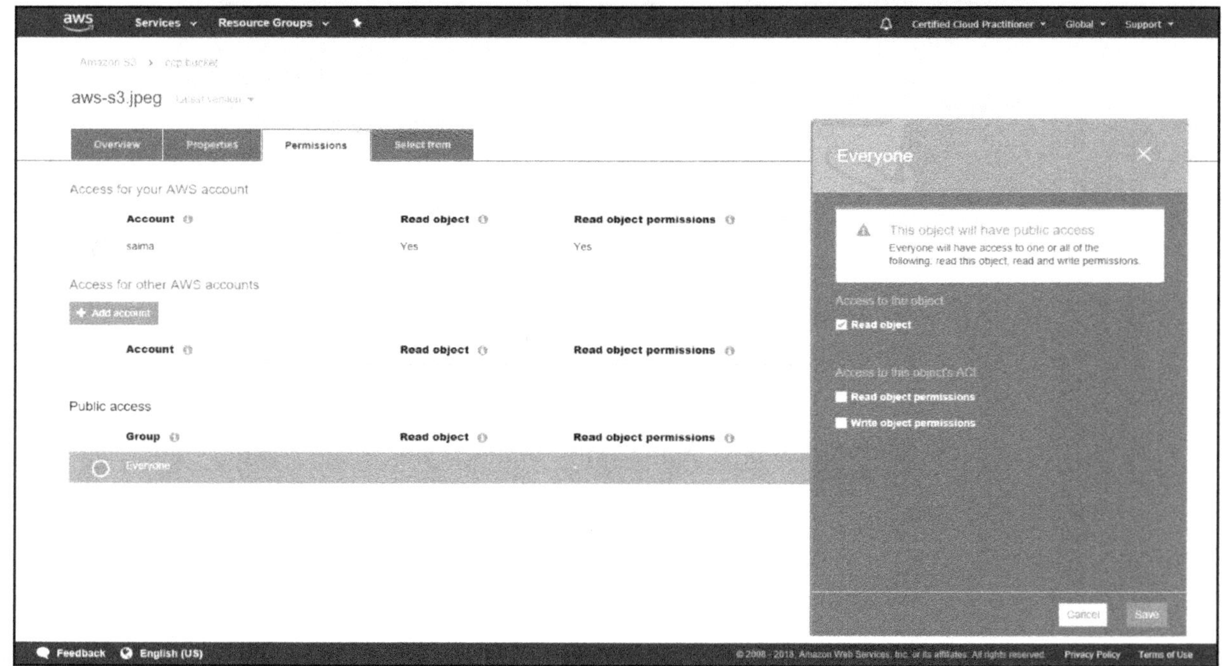

23. Under Public access, select "Everyone". This will open a pop-up window. Select "Read object" under the "Access to the object" section, then click "Save".

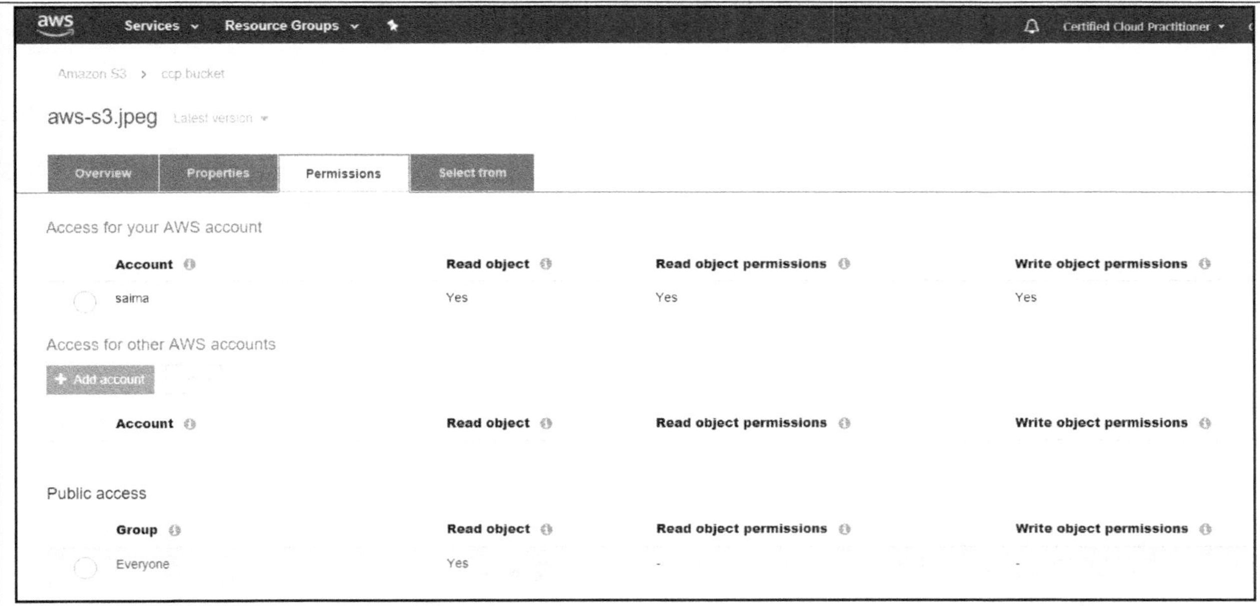

24. You will now be able to see that the "Read object permission" under the Public access is marked as "Yes".

25. Return to the overview tab and click on the URL again. You will now be able to see your file.
26. Another way of doing this is by enabling access from the bucket's main page.

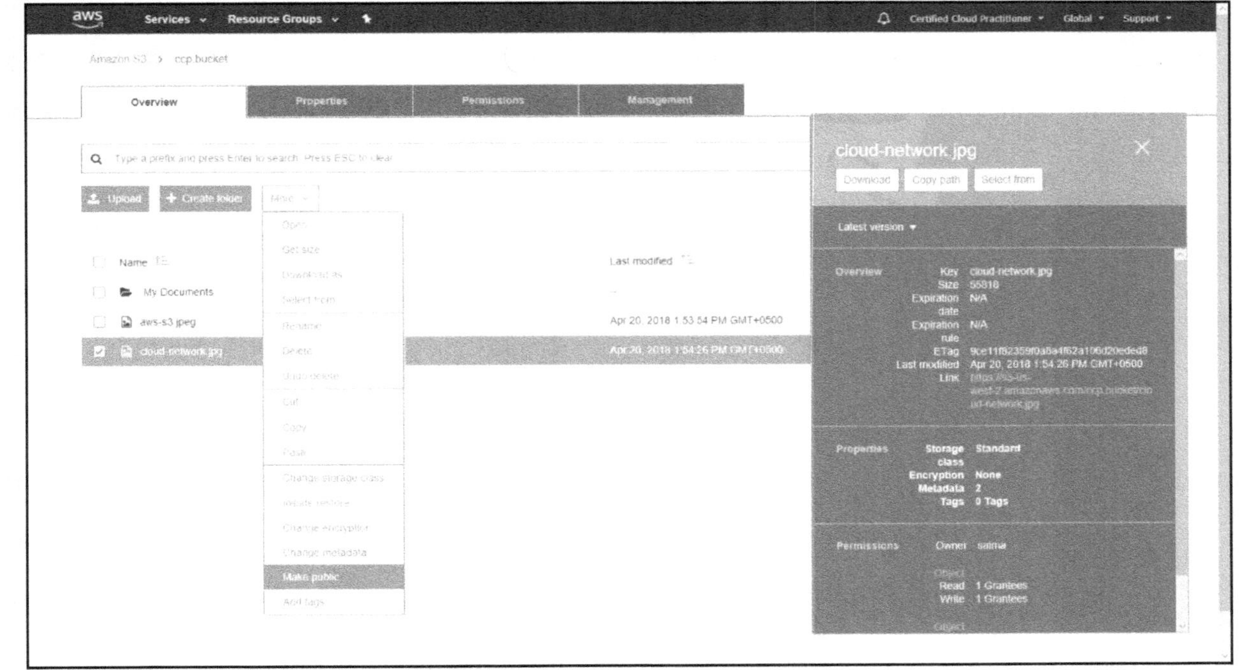

27. Select the file, click the “More” button and select “Make public” from the drop-down menu. This is an easier way of enabling public access to the file. If you now click on the URL of the file, you will be able to read it publicly via the browser.

The bucket’s main window contains Overview, Properties, Permissions, and Management tabs.

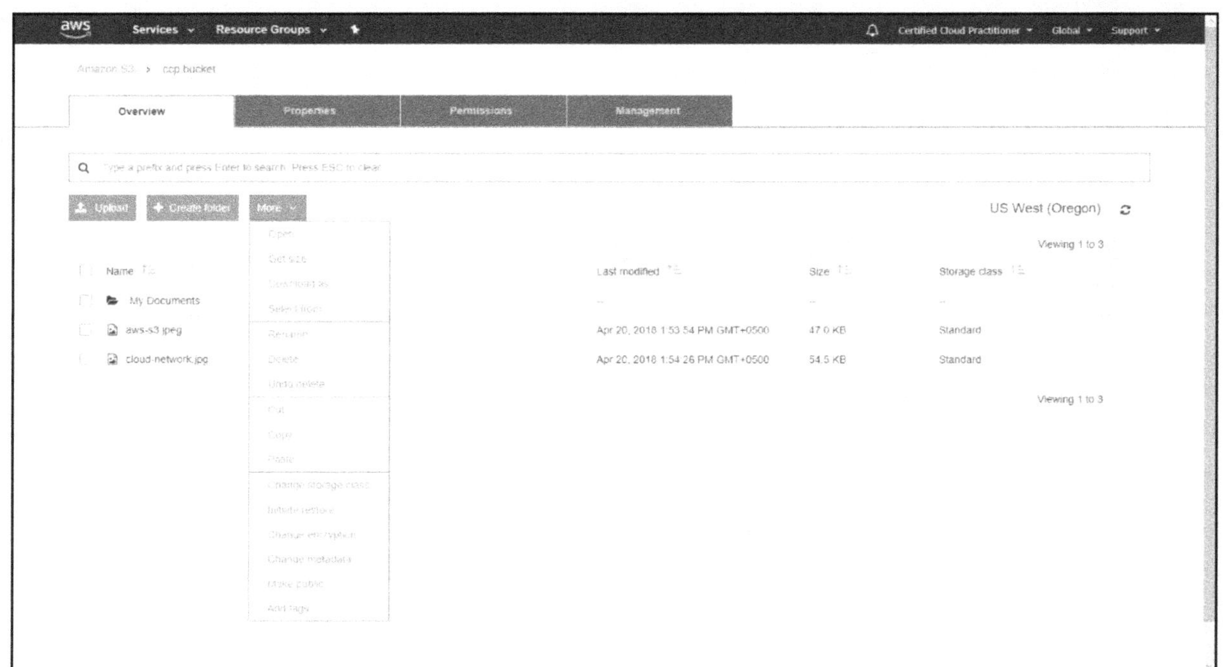

The Overview tab displays all the objects in the bucket and options to upload files and create folders as well as a drop-down menu of file-specific actions.

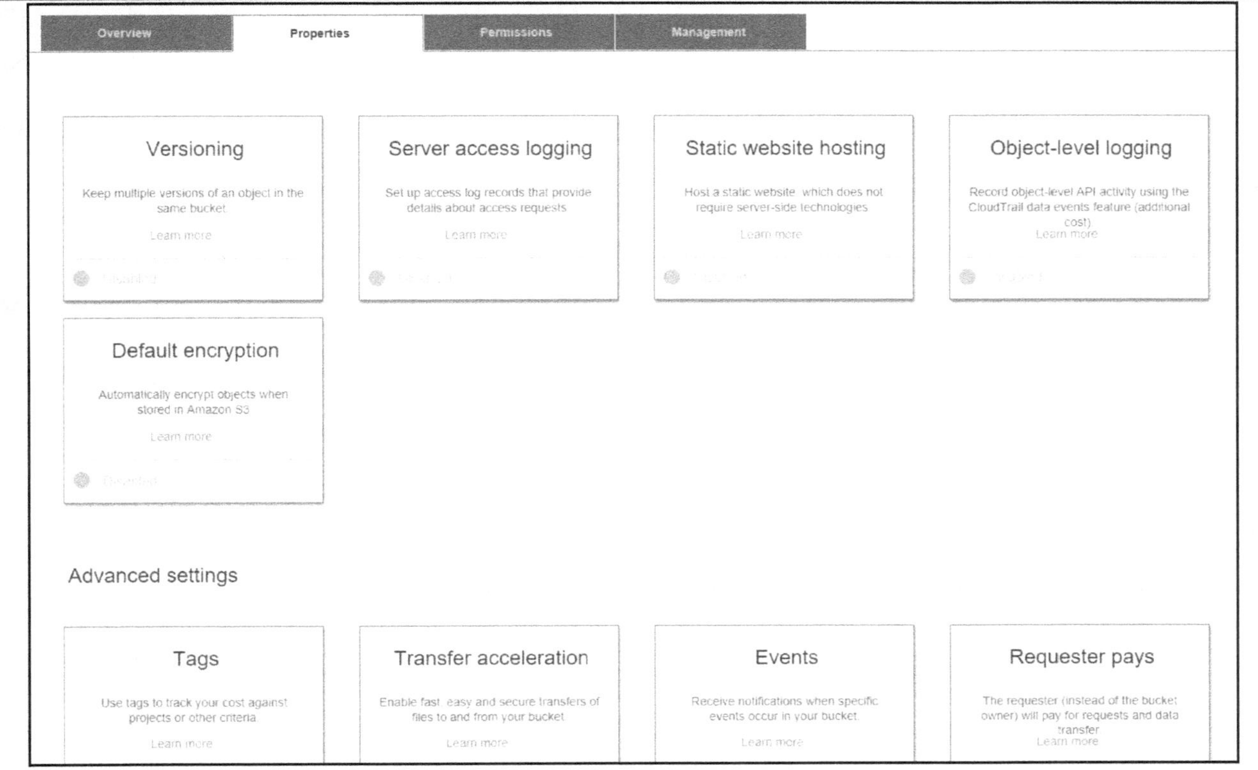

The Properties tab provides you with a range of options, such as Versioning, Static website hosting, Default encryption, Tags and Transfer acceleration.

28. Click on "Transfer acceleration" for a quick overview of this option.

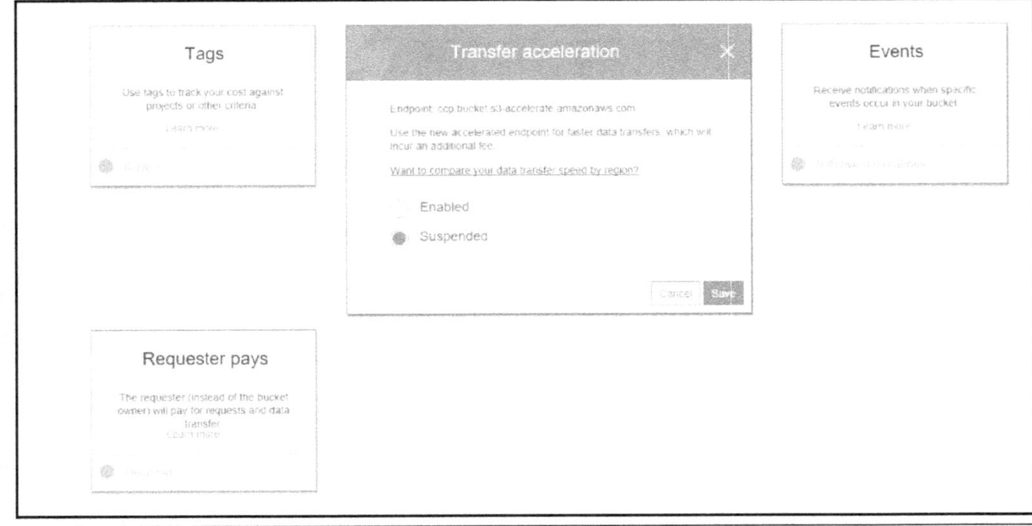

29. This will open up a window asking whether you would like to enable transfer acceleration. To get an idea of how transfer acceleration will affect your data transfers, click on the link 'Want to compare your data transfer speed by region?'

Amazon S3 Transfer Acceleration

Speed Comparison

Upload speed comparison in the selected region

(Based on the location of bucket: ccp.bucket)

Oregon

(US-WEST-2) 6% faster

S3 Direct Upload Speed

Upload complete

S3 Accelerated Transfer Upload Speed

Upload complete

This speed checker uses multipart uploads to transfer a file from your browser to various Amazon S3 regions with and without Amazon S3 Transfer Acceleration. It compares the speed results and shows the percentage difference for every region.

Note: In general, the farther away you are from an Amazon S3 region, the higher the speed improvement you can expect from using Amazon S3 Transfer Acceleration. If you see similar speed results with and without the acceleration, your upload bandwidth or a system constraint might be limiting your speed.

Upload speed comparison in other regions

San Francisco (US-WEST-1) 3% slower

S3 Direct Upload Speed – Upload complete

S3 Accelerated Transfer Upload Speed – Upload complete

Virginia (US-EAST-1) 6% slower

S3 Direct Upload Speed – Upload complete

S3 Accelerated Transfer Upload Speed – Upload complete

Dublin (EU-WEST-1) 3756% faster

S3 Direct Upload Speed – Upload complete

S3 Accelerated Transfer Upload Speed – Upload complete

Frankfurt (EU-CENTRAL-1) 400% faster

S3 Direct Upload Speed – Upload complete

S3 Accelerated Transfer Upload Speed – Upload complete

Tokyo (AP-NORTHEAST-1) 388% faster

S3 Direct Upload Speed – Upload complete

S3 Accelerated Transfer Upload Speed – Upload complete

Seoul (AP-NORTHEAST-2) 100% slower

S3 Direct Upload Speed – Upload complete

S3 Accelerated Transfer Upload Speed – Upload complete

Singapore
(AP-SOUTHEAST-1) 93% slower
S3 Direct Upload Speed
Upload complete
S3 Accelerated Transfer Upload Speed
Upload complete

Sydney
(AP-SOUTHEAST-2) 293% faster
S3 Direct Upload Speed
Upload complete
S3 Accelerated Transfer Upload Speed
Upload complete

São Paulo
(SA-EAST-1) 68% faster
S3 Direct Upload Speed
Upload complete
S3 Accelerated Transfer Upload Speed
Upload complete

Mumbai
(AP-SOUTH-1) 31% faster
S3 Direct Upload Speed
Upload complete
S3 Accelerated Transfer Upload Speed
Upload complete

Ohio
(US-EAST-2) 1% slower
S3 Direct Upload Speed
Upload complete
S3 Accelerated Transfer Upload Speed
Upload complete

Canada Central
(CA-CENTRAL-1) 9% faster
S3 Direct Upload Speed
Upload complete
S3 Accelerated Transfer Upload Speed
Upload complete

London
(EU-WEST-2) 7% faster
S3 Direct Upload Speed
Upload complete

This speed checker simulates the transfer of a file from your browser to various Amazon S3 regions with and without Amazon S3 Transfer Acceleration. It compares the results and shows the percentage difference for every region.

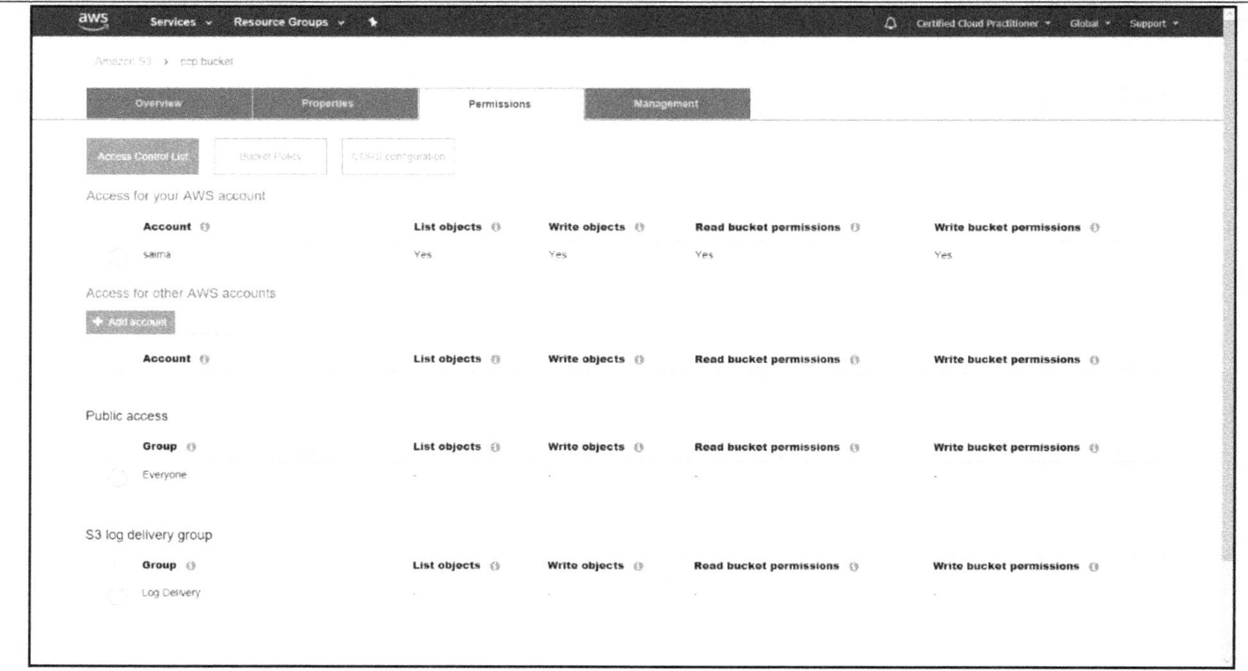

The Permissions tab provides access management options and allows you to write bucket policies.

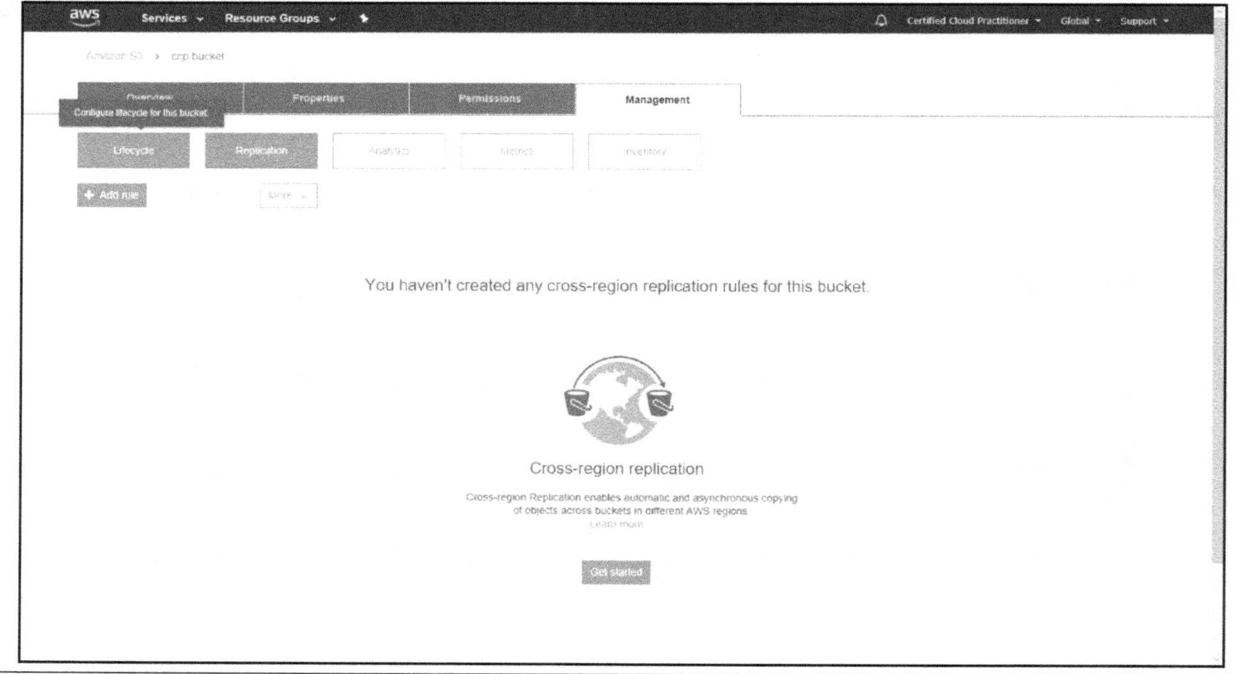

The management tab provides options for lifecycle configuration, analytics, metrics, inventory and replication. When configured, cross-region replication will replicate the contents of one bucket to another. This can be used for disaster recovery management.

Lab 3-6: Static Website hosting on S3

1. Log in to the “AWS Console”.
2. Click on “Services”.
3. Select “S3” from the Storage list.

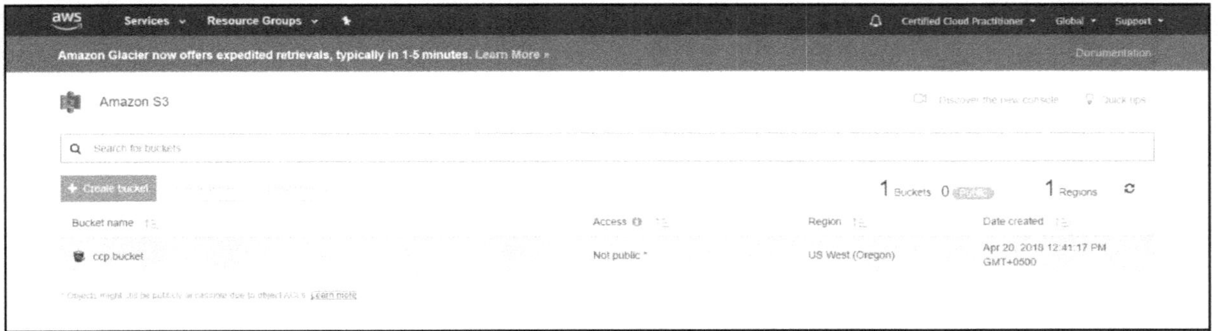

4. Click “Create bucket” to create a new bucket for the static website.

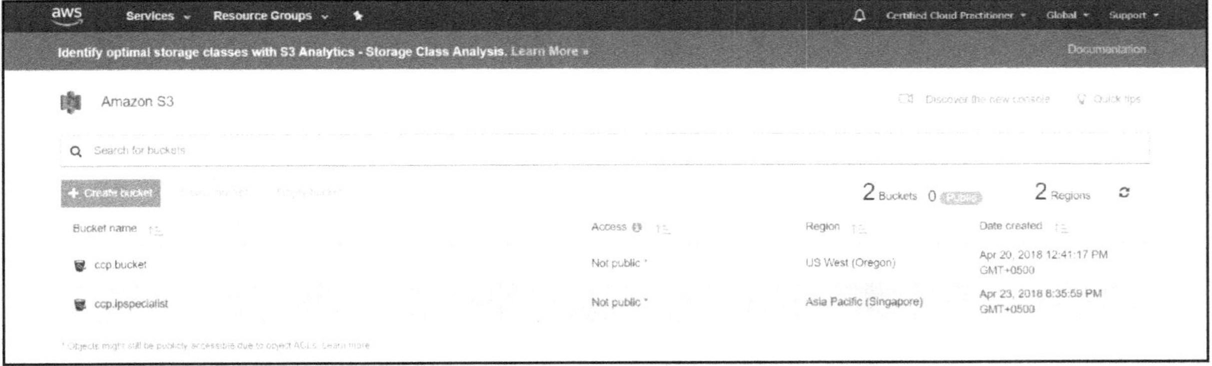

5. Create a bucket as we did in the previous lab.
6. Once the bucket is created, upload the .html files and other website content onto it. Click on the bucket to upload files.

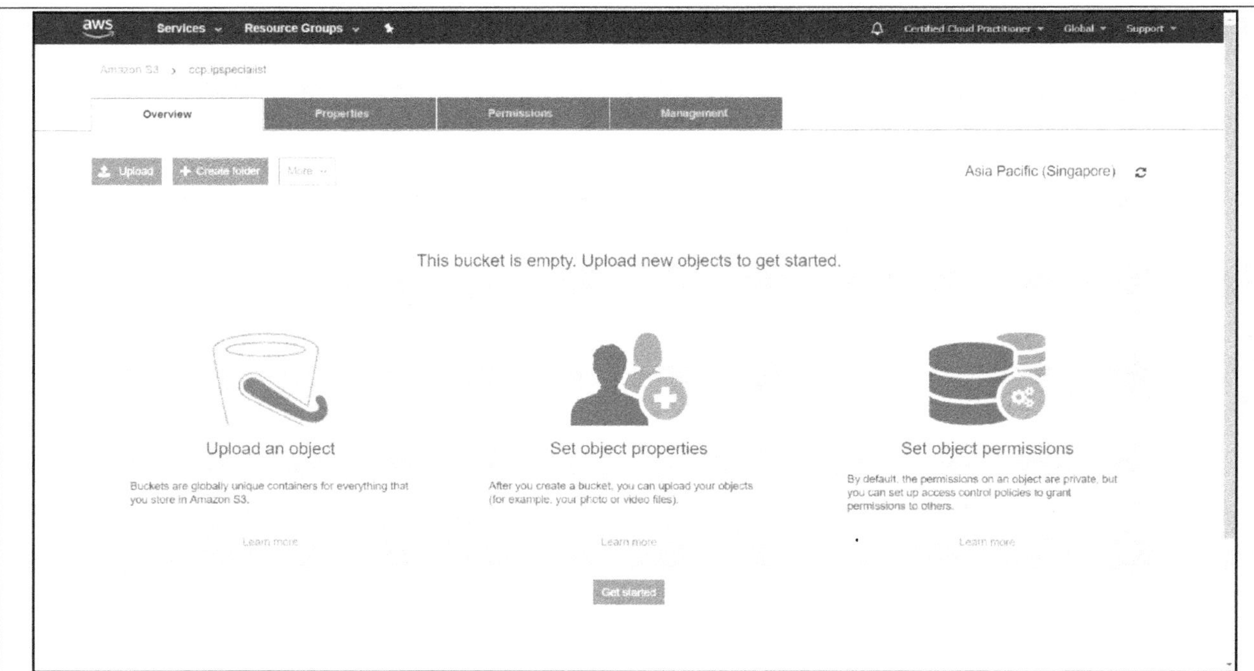

7. Click "Upload".

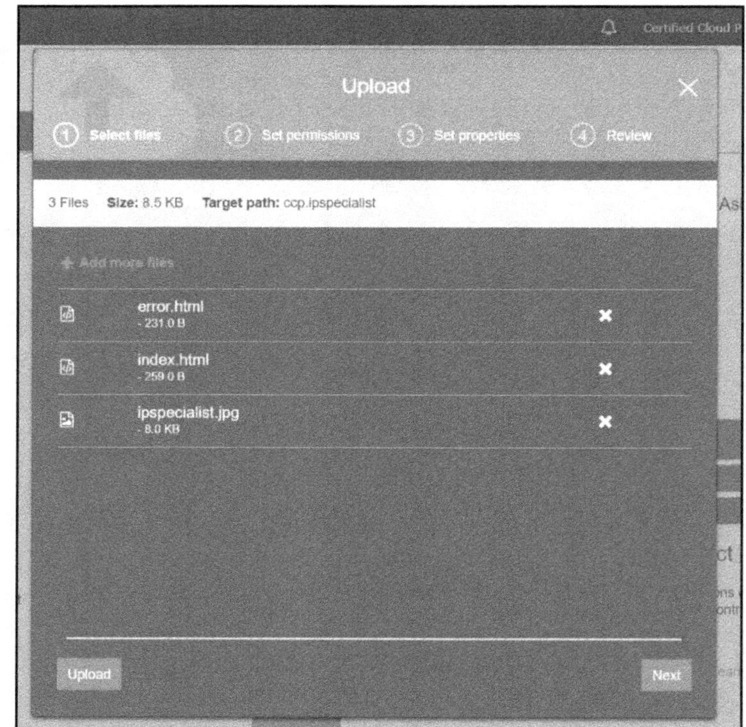

8. Here, you are uploading 'index.html' and 'error.html' files for the landing and error pages of your website respectively. 'ipspecialist.jpg' is an image file you will also be using on your website.

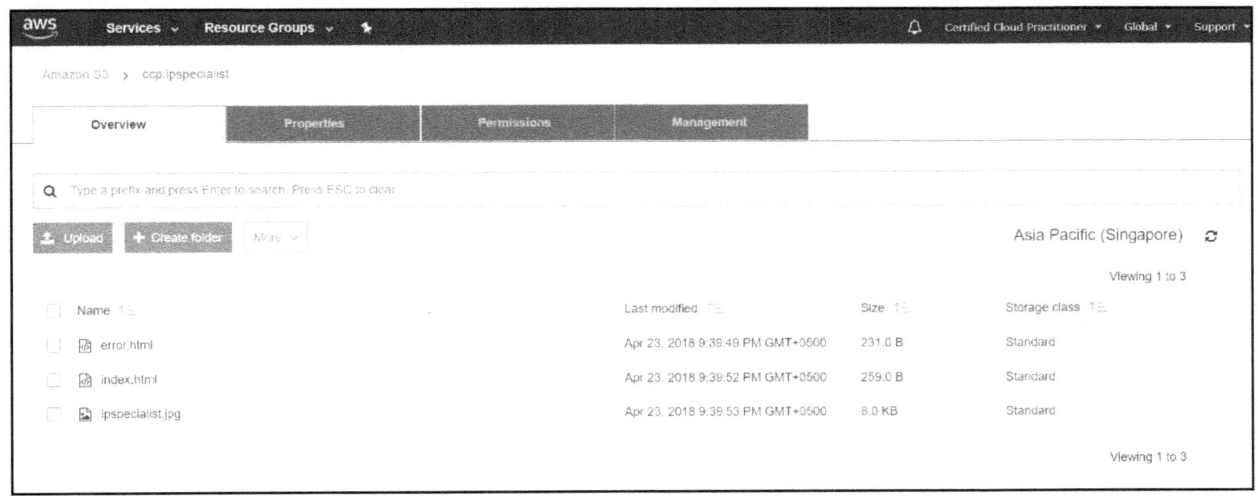

The 'index.html' and 'error.html' files contain simple code as follows:

index.html

```
<html>
    <title>
        Hello Cloud Specialists
    </title>
    <body>
        <div align="center">
            <h1>Welcome to IpSpecialist.net</h1>
            <h2>Let your career flow</h2>
            <img src="https://s3-us-west-2.amazonaws.com/ccp.bucket/ipspecialist.jpg">
        </div>
    </body>
</html>
```

error.html

```
<html>
    <title>
        Error
    </title>
    <body>
        <div align="center">
            <h1>Sorry Cloud Specialists, there has been an error!</h1>
            <img src="https://s3-us-west-2.amazonaws.com/ccp.bucket/ipspecialist.jpg"">
        </div>
    </body>
</html>
```

9. To make a website publicly accessible, all contents of the bucket must be granted public access. You can use a bucket policy to make the entire bucket public. Click on the "Permissions" tab.

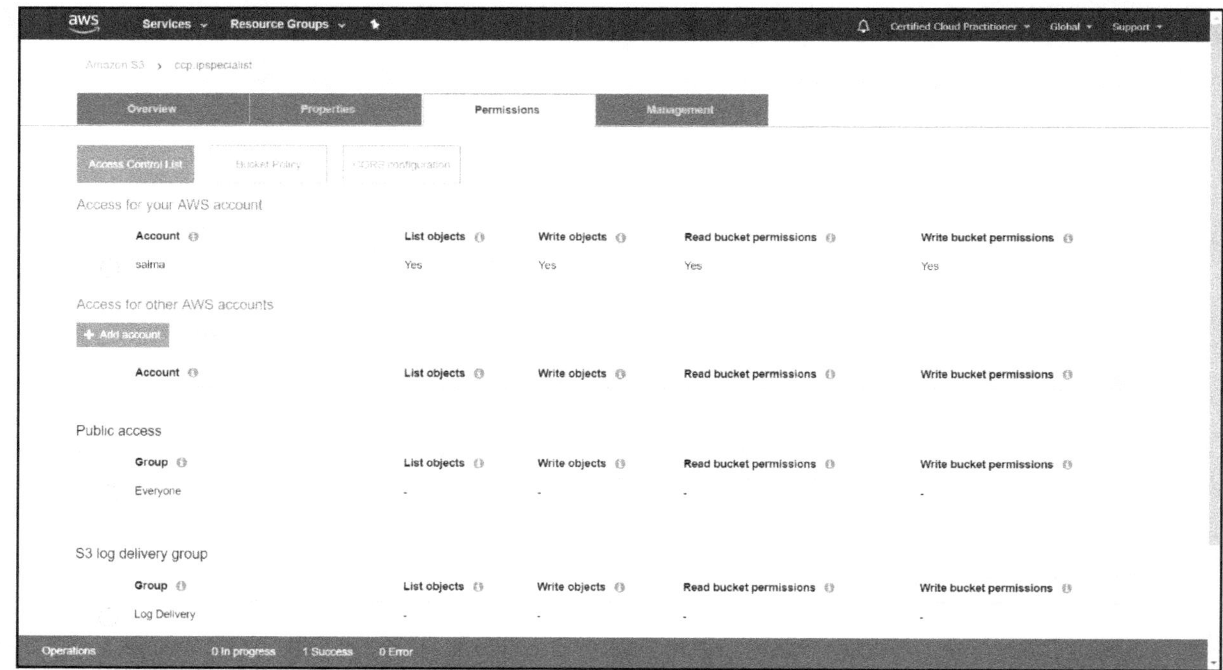

10. Click on "Bucket Policy" to open the tab.

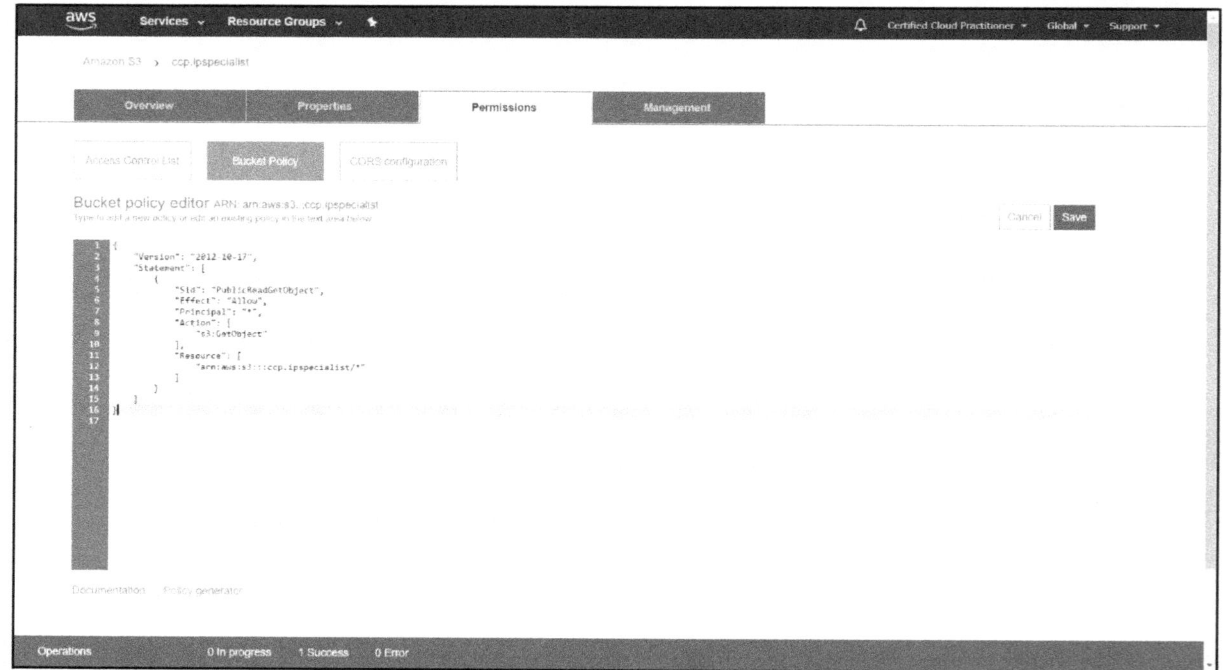

11. Copy and paste the above .json code into the bucket policy text area and click "Save". Make sure that line 12 of the code contains your bucket name.

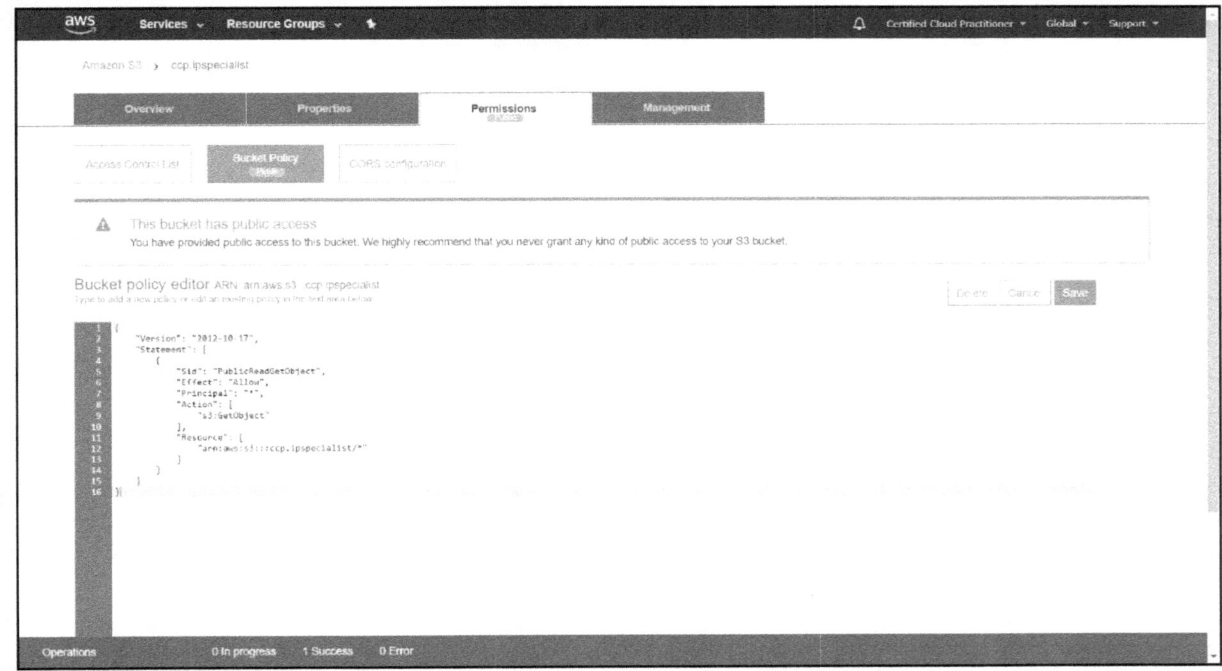

12. Once you click save, you will see a notification alert to tell you that the bucket now has public access. The above .json code grants public access to your bucket. Now click on the "Properties" tab.

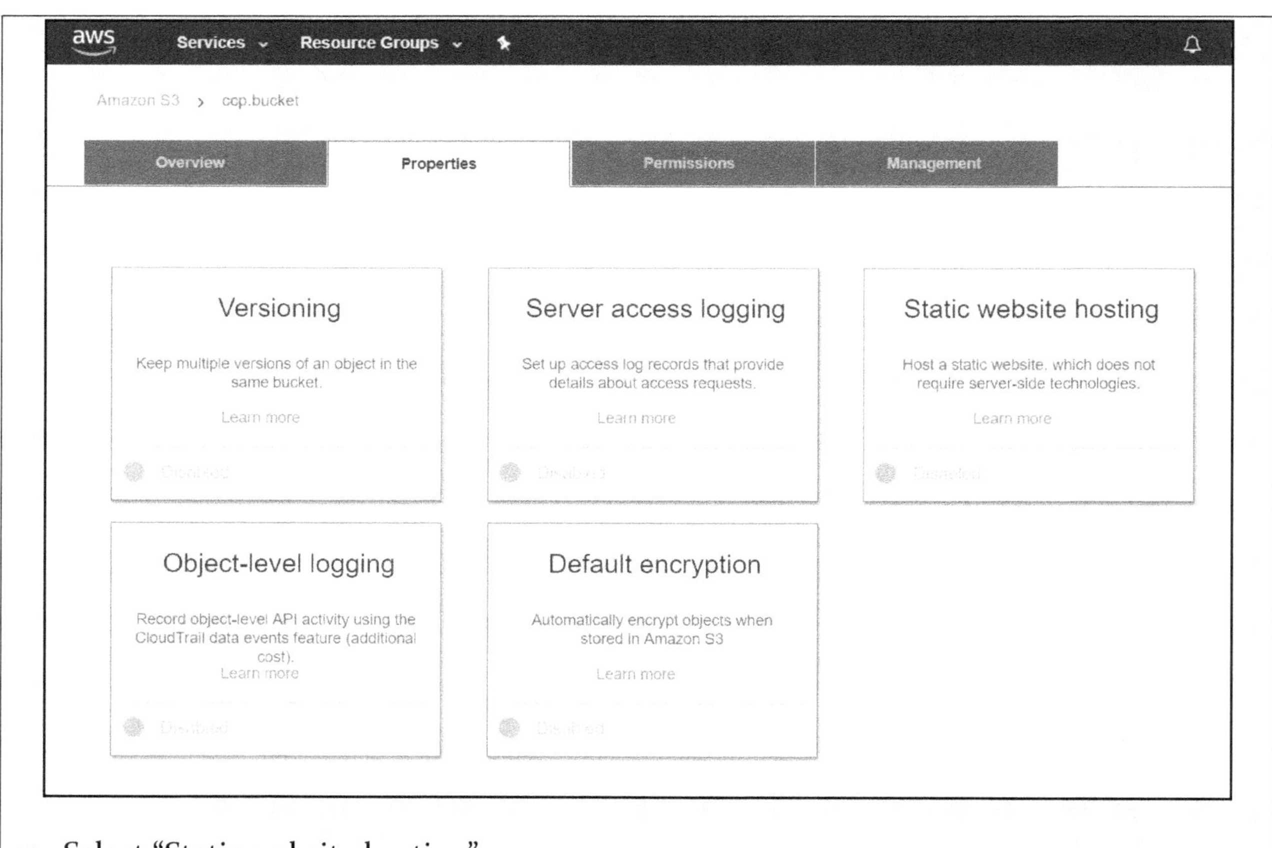

13. Select "Static website hosting".

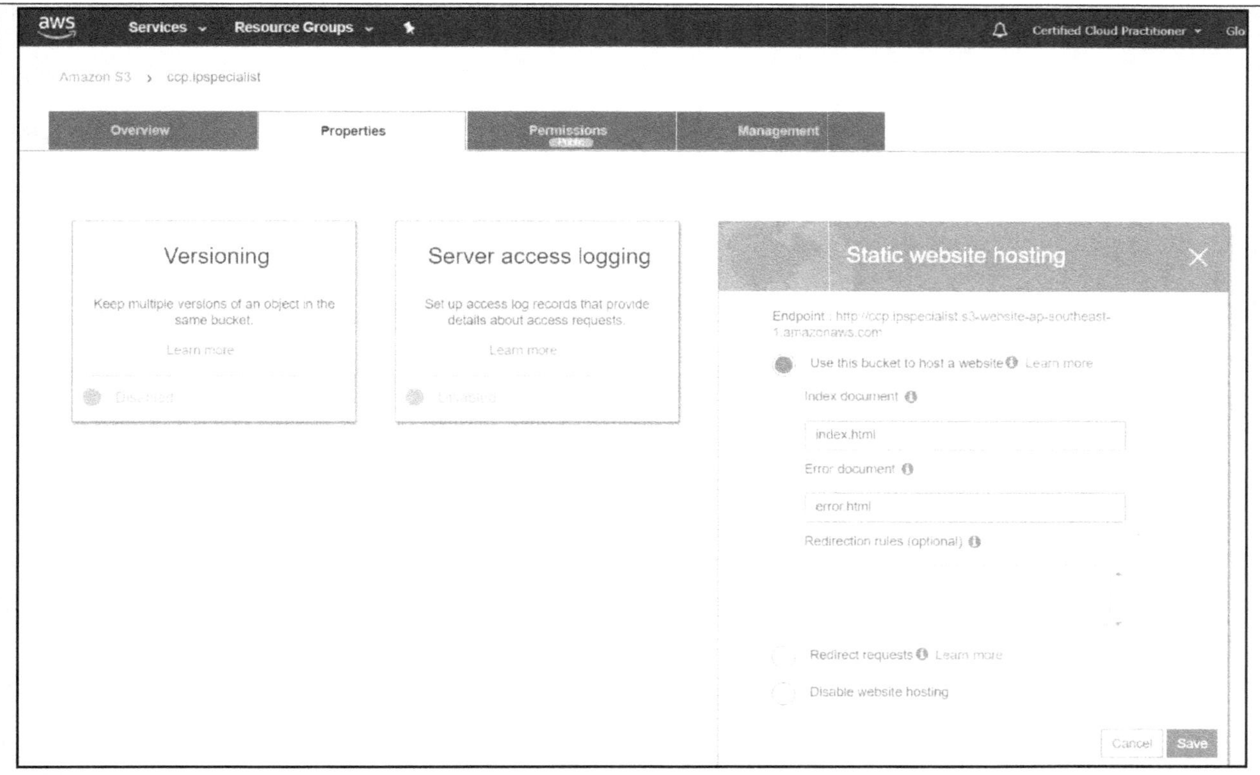

14. Select "Use this bucket to host a website" and enter the index and error document file names, which in your case are 'index.html' and 'error.html'. Click "Save".
15. Now click on the endpoint link given at the top, which is your website URL, to open your website.

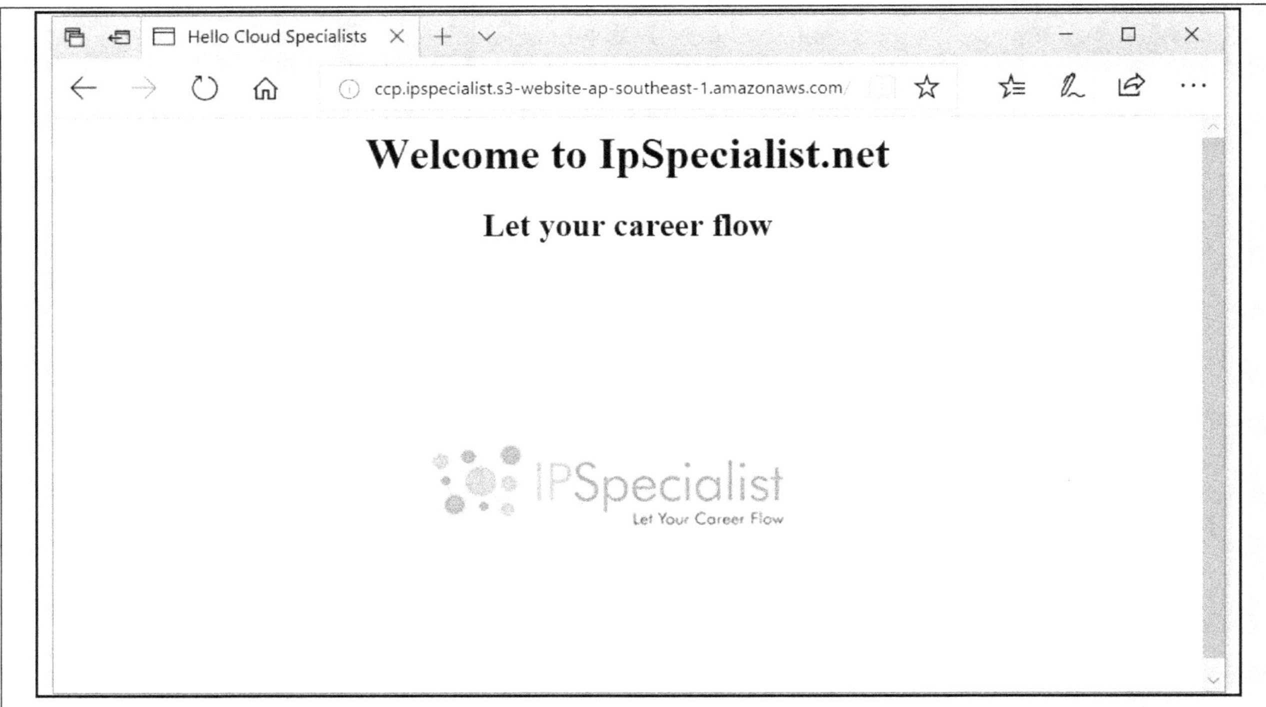

16. If the 'index.html' file is removed or renamed, the URL link will lead to the error page.

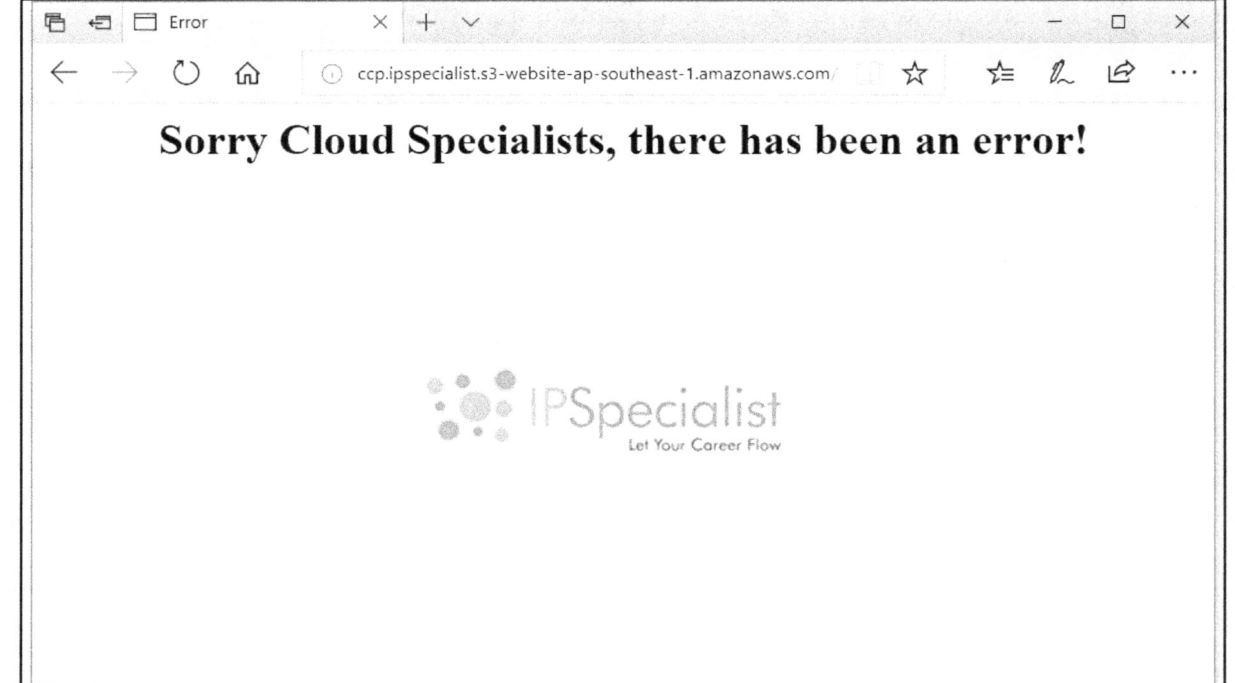

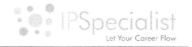

EXAM TIPS:

- Use S3 to host static websites only, such as .html. Websites that require database connections, such as WordPress, cannot be hosted on S3
- S3 scales automatically to meet your demands. Many businesses will put static websites onto S3 when they think there will be a large number of requests on the website

Amazon Glacier

Amazon Glacier is an exceptionally low-cost storage service, which offers durable, secure and flexible storage for data archival and long-term backup. Users can reliably store any amount of data for as little as $0.004 per gigabyte per month, which results in significant savings as compared to on-premises solutions. Amazon Glacier is optimized for data that is infrequently accessed and that does not require immediate availability. Glacier has retrieval times of 3 to 5 hours for bulk data. It can retain data easily and cost effectively for decades for future analysis or reference. It provides three options for accessing archives, from a few minutes to several hours, to cater to varying retrieval needs.

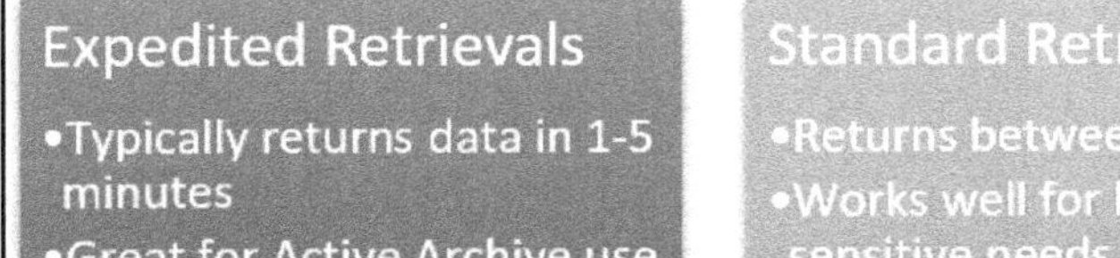

Expedited Retrievals
•Typically returns data in 1-5 minutes
•Great for Active Archive use cases
Standard Retrievals
•Returns between 3-5 hours
•Works well for less time-sensitive needs
Bulk Retrievals
•Returns large amounts of data within 5-12 hours
•Lowest-cost retrieval option

Figure 3-10: Amazon Glacier

Key Features:

- The extremely low-cost design is ideal for long-term archiving
- Designed for 99.999999999% durability of objects across multiple availability zones
- Redundantly stores data in multiple facilities and on multiple devices within each facility
- Data is resilient in the event of the destruction of one entire availability zone
- Supports SSL encryption of data in transit and at rest
- The Vault Lock feature enforces compliance via a lockable WORM policy

- Lifecycle management automates migration of objects between storage classes depending on data age
- Performs regular, systematic data integrity checks and is built to be automatically self-healing

> EXAM TIP: Understand the key differences between S3 and Glacier. S3 is for current data and Glacier is for archived data where a 3 to 5 hours retrieval time is acceptable. Use Amazon S3 if you need low latency or frequent access to your data. Use Amazon Glacier if low storage cost is vital and you do not require instant access to your data.

Comparison of Amazon S3 and Amazon Glacier

	S3 Standard - IA	S3 One Zone - IA	Glacier
Durability	99.999999999%	99.999999999%	99.999999999%
Availability	99.9%	99.5%	N/A
Availability SLA	99%	99%	N/A
Availability Zones	≥ 3	1	≥ 3
Min. Object Size	128 KB	128 KB	N/A
Min. Storage Duration	30 days	30 days	90 days
Retrieval Fee	per GB retrieved	per GB retrieved	per GB retrieved
First Byte Latency	milliseconds	milliseconds	minutes or hours
Storage Type	Object level	Object level	Object level
Lifecycle Transitions	Yes	Yes	Yes

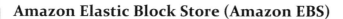

Table 3-3: S3 Vs. Glacier

Amazon Elastic Block Store (Amazon EBS)

Amazon Elastic Block Store (Amazon EBS) provides persistent block storage volumes to use with Amazon EC2 instances in the AWS Cloud. EBS allows you to create storage volumes and attach them to Amazon EC2 instances in the same availability zone. Once attached, the volumes appear as a mounted device similar to any hard drive or other block device. The instance can interact with the volume just as it would with a local drive. You can format the volume with a file system, run a database, install applications on it directly or use it in any other way you would use a block device.

Each Amazon EBS volume is replicated automatically within its availability zone to protect you from the failure of a single component. A volume can only be attached to one instance at a time, but many volumes can be attached to a single instance. This increases

I/O and throughput performance, as your data will be striped across multiple volumes. This is useful for database applications that are subject to frequent random reads and writes. If an instance fails or gets detached from an EBS volume, the volume can be attached to any other instance in the same availability zone.

Amazon EBS volumes provide the reliable, low-latency performance needed to run your workloads while allowing you to scale your usage up or down while paying for only what you use. Amazon EBS is intended for application workloads that benefit from fine-tuning for performance, cost and capacity. Typical use cases include: Big Data analytics engines, like the Hadoop/HDFS ecosystem and Amazon EMR clusters; relational and NoSQL databases, like Microsoft SQL Server and MySQL or Cassandra and MongoDB; stream and log processing applications, like Kafka and Splunk; and data warehousing applications, like Vertica and Teradata.

Amazon EBS volumes can also be used as boot partitions for Amazon EC2 instances, letting you preserve your boot partition data, irrespective of the life of your instance, and bundle your AMI in one-click. You can also stop and restart instances that boot from Amazon EBS volumes while preserving state, with very fast start-up times.

Amazon EBS Volume Types:

- General Purpose SSD(gp2)
    - General purpose SSD balances price and performance for a variety of transactional workloads
    - Use Cases: Boot-volumes, low-latency interactive apps, development & testing
    - Volume Size: 1 GB - 16 TB
    - Max IOPS: 10,000
    - Max throughput/volume: 160 MB/s
- Provisioned IOPS SSD (io1)
    - Highest performance SSD, designed for latency-sensitive transactional workloads
    - Use Cases: I/O-intensive applications, NoSQL and relational databases
    - Volume Size: 4 GB - 16 TB
    - Max IOPS: 32,000

- Max throughput/volume: 500 MB/s

- Throughput Optimized HDD (st1)
  - Low-cost HDD, designed for frequently accessed, throughput-intensive workloads
  - Use Cases: Big data, data warehouses and log processing
  - Volume Size: 500 GB - 16 TB
  - Max Volume: 500
  - Max throughput/volume: 500 MB/s
- Cold HDD (sc1)
  - Lowest cost HDD, designed for less frequently accessed workloads
  - Use Cases: Colder data requiring fewer scans per day, such as File Servers
  - Volume Size: 500 GB - 16 TB
  - Max Volume: 250
  - Max throughput/volume: 250 MB/s

Amazon EBS Magnetic Volumes

Amazon EBS Magnetic volumes are previous generation volumes backed by hard disk drives (HDDs). They are ideal for workloads with smaller data sets where data is infrequently accessed and where a low storage cost is more important than the consistency of performance. EBS Magnetic volumes offer approximately 100 IOPS on average, with an ability to burst to hundreds of IOPS, and support volumes from 1GB to 1TB in size. It offers the lowest cost per gigabyte of all bootable EBS volume types.

EXAM TIP: EBS is simply a virtual disk where you install your operating system and all relevant files. SSD-backed storage is for transactional workloads and HDD-backed storage is for throughput workloads.

Lab 3-7: Using AWS Command Line

```
login as: ec2-user
Authenticating with public key "imported-openssh-key"

       __|  __|_  )
       _|  (     /   Amazon Linux AMI
      ___|\___|___|

https://aws.amazon.com/amazon-linux-ami/2018.03-release-notes/
1 package(s) needed for security, out of 4 available
Run "sudo yum update" to apply all updates.
[ec2-user@ip-172-31-23-114 ~]$
```

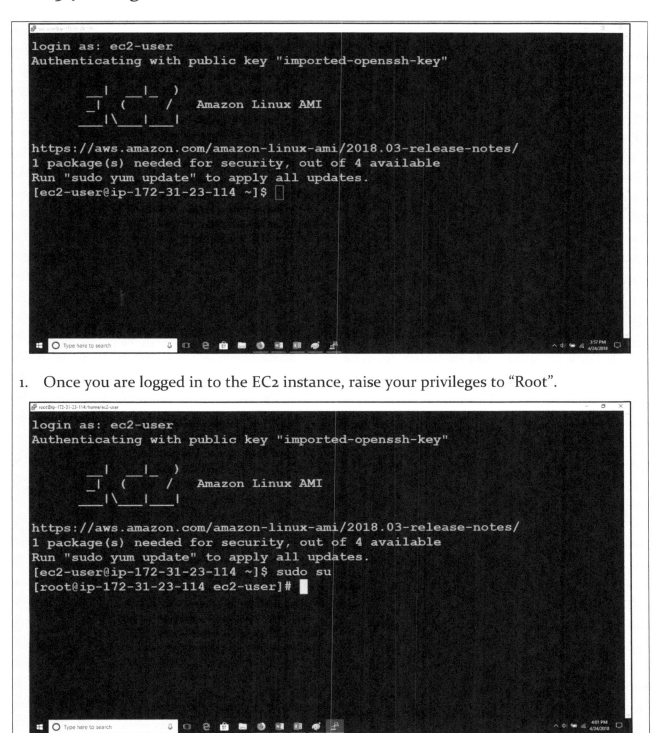

1. Once you are logged in to the EC2 instance, raise your privileges to "Root".

```
login as: ec2-user
Authenticating with public key "imported-openssh-key"

       __|  __|_  )
       _|  (     /   Amazon Linux AMI
      ___|\___|___|

https://aws.amazon.com/amazon-linux-ami/2018.03-release-notes/
1 package(s) needed for security, out of 4 available
Run "sudo yum update" to apply all updates.
[ec2-user@ip-172-31-23-114 ~]$ sudo su
[root@ip-172-31-23-114 ec2-user]#
```

2. You can raise your privileges by typing "**sudosu**". Now, use this command line to work with your EC2 instance.

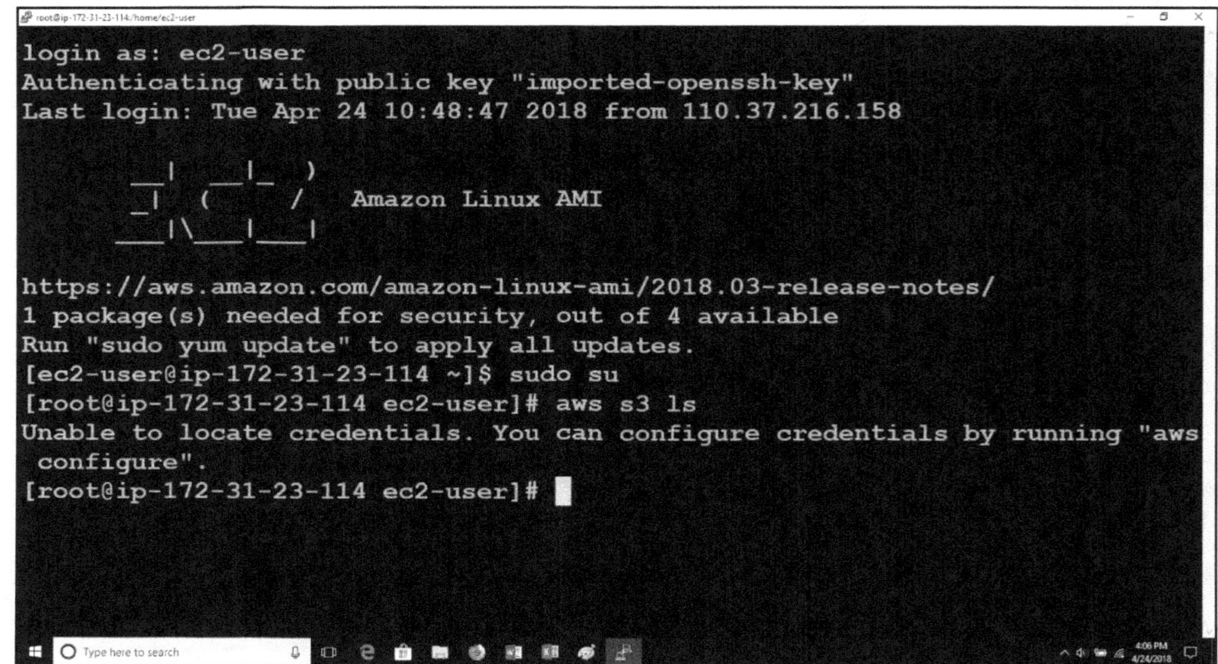

3. By typing "aws s3 ls", you can list all of the items in your Amazon S3 storage. However, here, it is unable to locate the credentials. You can configure credentials using the command "awsconfigure".

```
login as: ec2-user
Authenticating with public key "imported-openssh-key"
Last login: Tue Apr 24 10:48:47 2018 from 110.37.216.158

       __|  __|_  )
       _|  (     /   Amazon Linux AMI
      ___|\___|___|

https://aws.amazon.com/amazon-linux-ami/2018.03-release-notes/
1 package(s) needed for security, out of 4 available
Run "sudo yum update" to apply all updates.
[ec2-user@ip-172-31-23-114 ~]$ sudo su
[root@ip-172-31-23-114 ec2-user]# aws s3 ls
Unable to locate credentials. You can configure credentials by running "aws
 configure".
[root@ip-172-31-23-114 ec2-user]# aws configure
AWS Access Key ID [None]:
```

4. It will prompt you for the AWS Access Key ID. Open up the credentials file you downloaded when you created your IAM User (for example, Saima_Talat) and copy and paste the credentials here at the command line.

```
login as: ec2-user
Authenticating with public key "imported-openssh-key"
Last login: Tue Apr 24 11:21:43 2018 from 110.37.216.158

       __|  __|_  )
       _|  (     /   Amazon Linux AMI
      ___|\___|___|

https://aws.amazon.com/amazon-linux-ami/2018.03-release-notes/
1 package(s) needed for security, out of 4 available
Run "sudo yum update" to apply all updates.
[ec2-user@ip-172-31-23-114 ~]$ sudo su
[root@ip-172-31-23-114 ec2-user]# aws s3 ls
Unable to locate credentials. You can configure credentials by running "aws
 configure".
[root@ip-172-31-23-114 ec2-user]# aws configure
AWS Access Key ID [None]: AKIAJ3VFLC7IZDHEVHSQ
AWS Secret Access Key [None]: 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
Default region name [None]:
```

5. After entering the Access Key ID and Secret Access Key, you will be prompted for the default region name. Here, we will say that your EC2 server is in the region 'us-west-2b'.

```
root@ip-172-31-23-114:/home/ec2-user
Authenticating with public key "imported-openssh-key"
Last login: Tue Apr 24 11:21:43 2018 from 110.37.216.158

       __|  __|_  )
       _|  (     /   Amazon Linux AMI
      ___|\___|___|

https://aws.amazon.com/amazon-linux-ami/2018.03-release-notes/
1 package(s) needed for security, out of 4 available
Run "sudo yum update" to apply all updates.
[ec2-user@ip-172-31-23-114 ~]$ sudo su
[root@ip-172-31-23-114 ec2-user]# aws s3 ls
Unable to locate credentials. You can configure credentials by running "aws
 configure".
[root@ip-172-31-23-114 ec2-user]# aws configure
AWS Access Key ID [None]: AKIAJ3VFLC7IZDHEVHSQ
AWS Secret Access Key [None]: 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
Default region name [None]: us-west-2b
Default output format [None]:
[root@ip-172-31-23-114 ec2-user]# clear
```

6. Leave the default output format blank and clear the screen by typing "clear".

```
root@ip-172-31-23-114:/home/ec2-user
[root@ip-172-31-23-114 ec2-user]#
```

7. The IAM User 'Saima_Talat' you created in the IAM section had administrative access. This means you can now perform all the administrative actions.

```
root@ip-172-31-23-114:/home/ec2-user
[root@ip-172-31-23-114 ec2-user]# aws s3 ls
2018-04-20 07:41:18 ccp.bucket
2018-04-23 17:00:45 ccp.ipspecialist
[root@ip-172-31-23-114 ec2-user]#
```

8. If you retype "aws s3 ls" to list the content of Amazon S3 storage, you will see the two buckets 'ccp.bucket' and 'ccp.ipspecialist'. Now, let's create a bucket from the command line.

```
[root@ip-172-31-23-114 ec2-user]# aws s3 ls
2018-04-20 07:41:18 ccp.bucket
2018-04-23 17:00:45 ccp.ipspecialist
[root@ip-172-31-23-114 ec2-user]# aws s3 mb s3://ccp.commandline.bucket
make_bucket: ccp.commandline.bucket
[root@ip-172-31-23-114 ec2-user]# aws s3 ls
2018-04-20 07:41:18 ccp.bucket
2018-04-24 11:50:07 ccp.commandline.bucket
2018-04-23 17:00:45 ccp.ipspecialist
[root@ip-172-31-23-114 ec2-user]#
```

9. Here we have created a new bucket with the name 'ccp.commandline.bucket' using the command "aws s3 mb", where 'mb' stands for make bucket. If you run the list command again, you can see that the new bucket has been created.

```
[root@ip-172-31-23-114 ec2-user]# echo "Hello Cloud Practitioner" > hello.txt
[root@ip-172-31-23-114 ec2-user]# ls
hello.txt
[root@ip-172-31-23-114 ec2-user]# nano hello.txt
```

10. Here, we have created a text file named 'hello.txt' using the command 'echo' to display "Hello Cloud Practitioner". Run the list command again to ensure that the file has been created. To open it, use the text editor "nano".

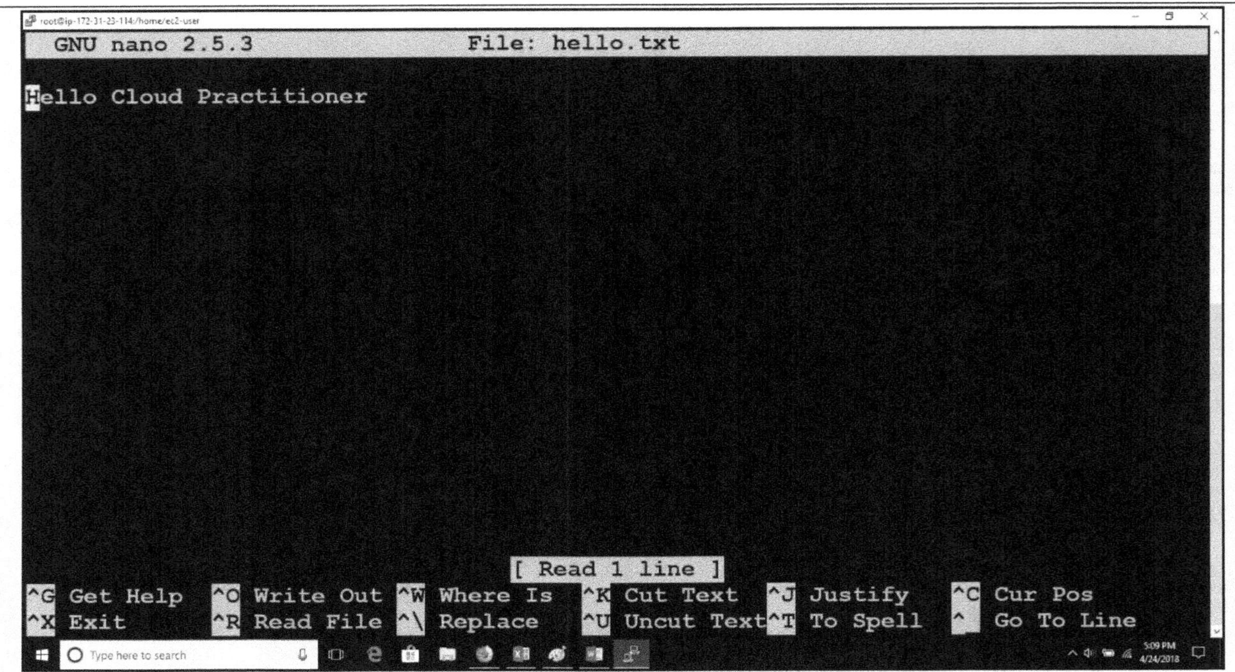

11. This is the text editor displaying the content "Hello Cloud Practitioner". Press ctrl+x to exit the editor.

```
[root@ip-172-31-23-114 ec2-user]# aws s3 ls
2018-04-20 07:41:18 ccp.bucket
2018-04-24 11:50:07 ccp.commandline.bucket
2018-04-23 17:00:45 ccp.ipspecialist
[root@ip-172-31-23-114 ec2-user]# aws s3 cp hello.txt s3://ccp.commandline.bucket
upload: ./hello.txt to s3://ccp.commandline.bucket/hello.txt
[root@ip-172-31-23-114 ec2-user]#
```

12. Copy the text file 'hello.txt' from the EC2 instance to the S3 bucket 'ccp.commandline.bucket' using the command "cp", which means copy.

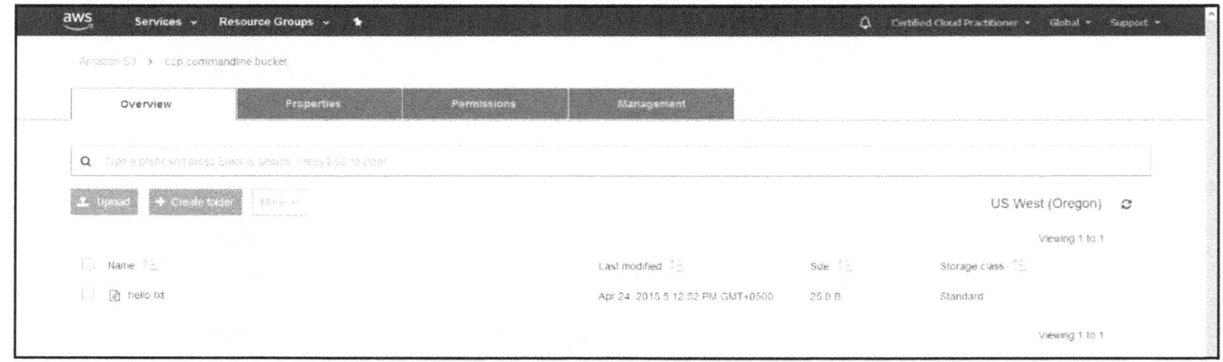

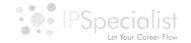

13. If you log in through the AWS console, you will be able to see that the 'hello.txt' file has now been copied into the S3 bucket 'ccp.commandline.bucket'.

Lab 3-8: Using Roles

1. Log in to the AWS command line as described previously.

```
root@ip-172-31-23-114:~/.aws
[root@ip-172-31-23-114 ec2-user]# cd ~/.aws
[root@ip-172-31-23-114 .aws]# ls
config  credentials
[root@ip-172-31-23-114 .aws]# nano credentials
```

2. The command 'cd ~/.aws' is used to change the directory to AWS root. The list command displays the files stored on it, including the 'credentials' file. If you open this file with the "nano" text editor, you will be able to see the credentials.

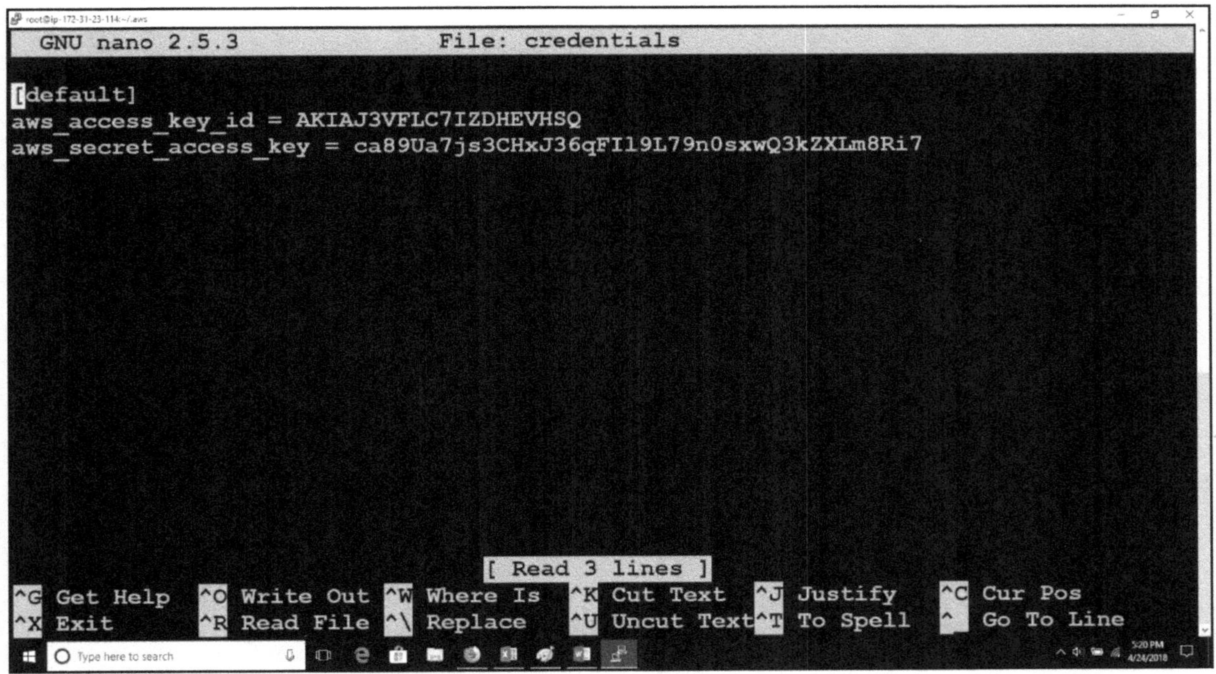

3. If someone hacks into the EC2 instance, they can easily get access to the Access Key ID and Secret Access Key which can compromise security. To avoid this breach, use Roles instead.

```
[root@ip-172-31-23-114 ec2-user]# cd ~/.aws
[root@ip-172-31-23-114 .aws]# ls
config  credentials
[root@ip-172-31-23-114 .aws]# nano credentials
[root@ip-172-31-23-114 .aws]# rm -rf credentials
[root@ip-172-31-23-114 .aws]# ls
config
[root@ip-172-31-23-114 .aws]# aws s3 ls
Unable to locate credentials. You can configure credentials by running "aws configu
re".
[root@ip-172-31-23-114 .aws]#
```

4. First, delete any credentials stored on your EC2 instance, as storing credentials on the EC2 instance is not safe. For this, use the "rm" command to remove the credentials. If you type in "ls", you will see that the credentials are now gone. To test this, if you run "aws s3 ls", it will publish the prompt 'unable to locate credentials'. Now, open up the AWS Console and select "IAM" from services.

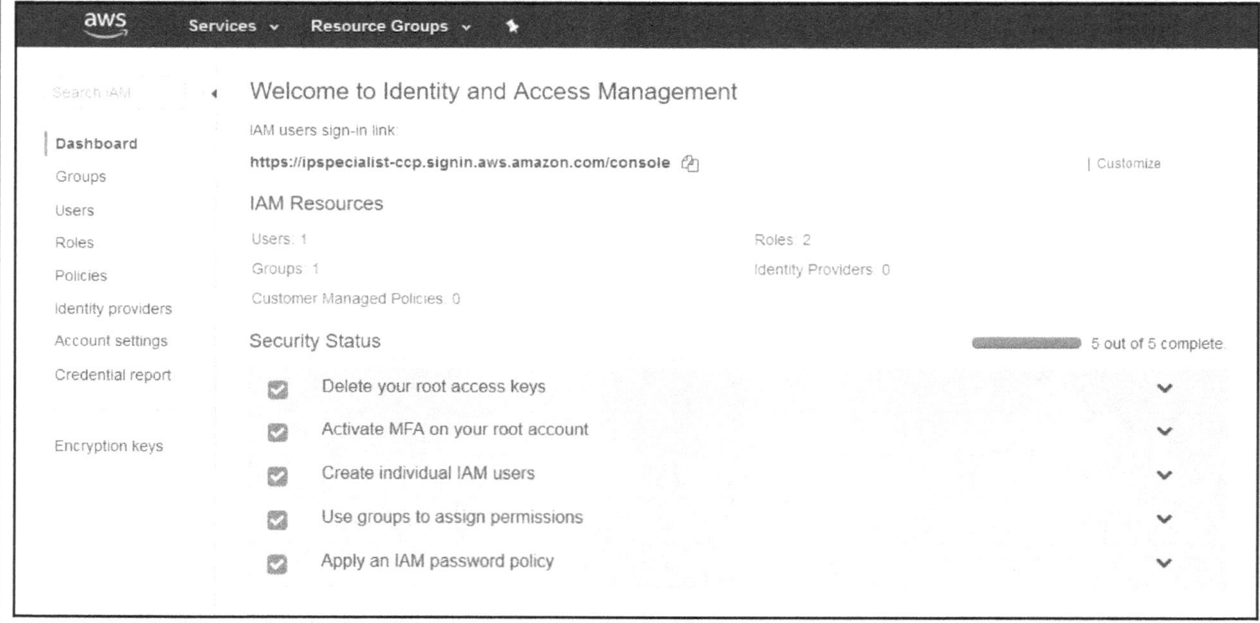

5. Select "Roles" from the left-hand pane.

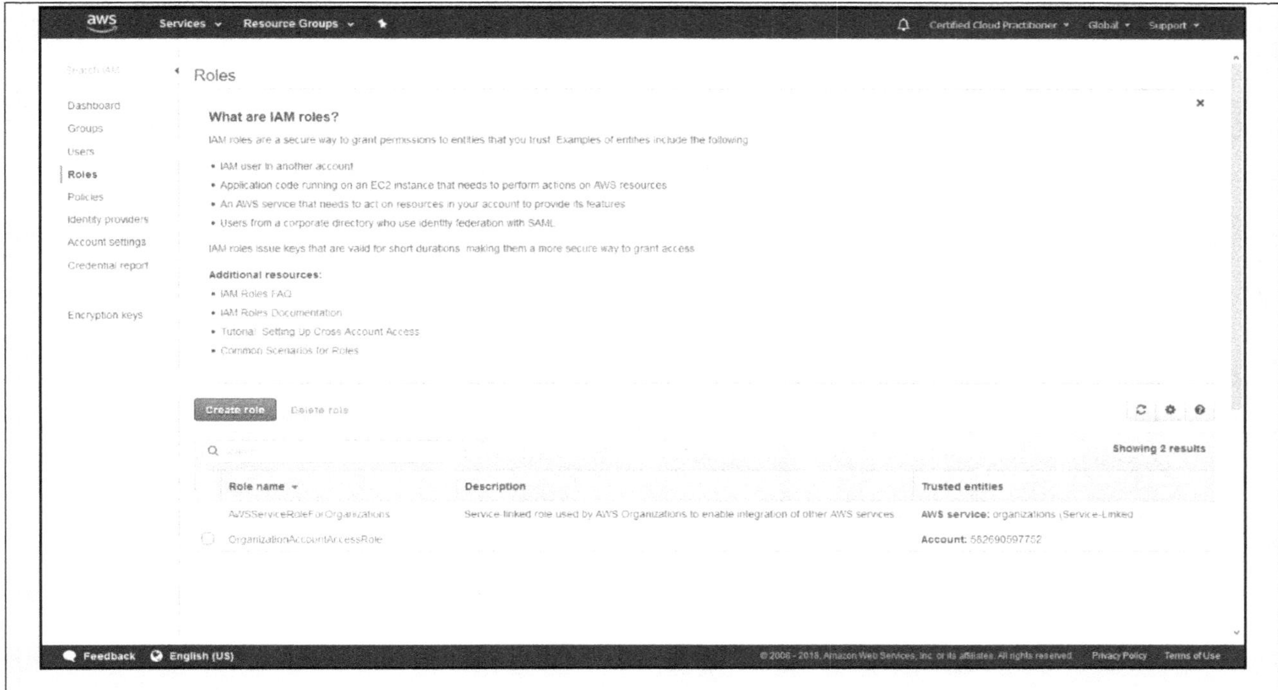

6. Here, we are going to create a new role. Roles are a secure way to grant permissions to entities. Click on “Create role”.

Create role

1 2 3

Select type of trusted entity

AWS service EC2, Lambda and others | **Another AWS account** Belonging to you or 3rd party | **Web identity** Cognito or any OpenID provider | **SAML 2.0 federation** Your corporate directory

Allows AWS services to perform actions on your behalf. Learn more

Choose the service that will use this role

EC2
Allows EC2 instances to call AWS services on your behalf.

Lambda
Allows Lambda functions to call AWS services on your behalf.

API Gateway	Config	Elastic Container Service	Lex	SWF
AppSync	DMS	Elastic Transcoder	Machine Learning	SageMaker
Application Auto Scaling	Data Pipeline	ElasticLoadBalancing	MediaConvert	Service Catalog
Auto Scaling	DeepLens	Glue	OpsWorks	Step Functions
Batch	Directory Service	Greengrass	RDS	Storage Gateway
CloudFormation	DynamoDB	GuardDuty	Redshift	
CloudHSM	**EC2**	Inspector	Rekognition	
CloudWatch Events	EMR	IoT	S3	
CodeBuild	ElastiCache	Kinesis	SMS	
CodeDeploy	Elastic Beanstalk	Lambda	SNS	

Select your use case

EC2

* **Required** **Cancel** **Next: Permissions**

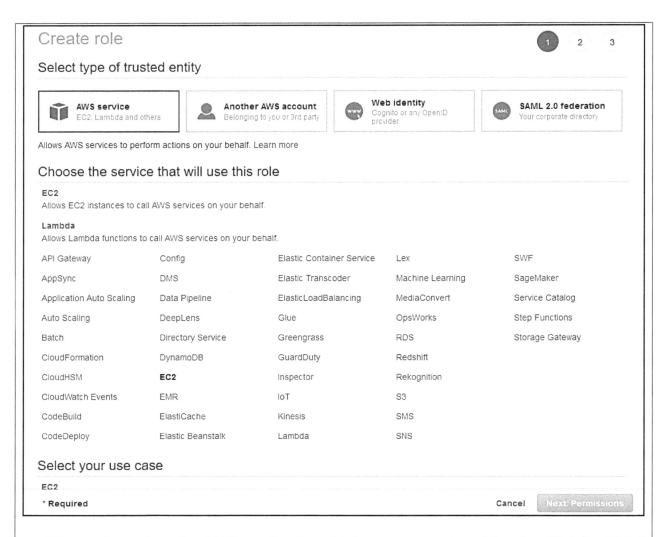

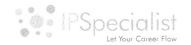

7. We need to select the AWS service for which we are creating this role. Click on "EC2" from the list of services.

Auto Scaling
Batch
CloudFormation
CloudHSM
CloudWatch Events
CodeBuild
CodeDeploy
DeepLens
Directory Service
DynamoDB
EC2
EMR
ElastiCache
Elastic Beanstalk
Glue
Greengrass
GuardDuty
Inspector
IoT
Kinesis
Lambda
OpsWorks
RDS
Redshift
Rekognition
S3
SMS
SNS
Step Functions
Storage Gateway

Select your use case

EC2
Allows EC2 instances to call AWS services on your behalf.

EC2 - Scheduled Instances
Allows EC2 Scheduled Instances to manage instances on your behalf.

EC2 - Spot Fleet
Allows EC2 Spot Fleet to launch and manage spot fleet instances on your behalf.

EC2 - Spot Fleet Auto Scaling
Allows Auto Scaling to access and update EC2 spot fleets on your behalf.

EC2 - Spot Fleet Tagging
Allows EC2 to launch spot instances and attach tags to the launched instances on your behalf.

EC2 - Spot Instances
Allows EC2 Spot Instances to launch and manage spot instances on your behalf.

EC2 Role for Simple Systems Manager
Allows EC2 instances to call AWS services like CloudWatch and SSM on your behalf.

EC2 Spot Fleet Role
Allows EC2 Spot Fleet to request and terminate Spot Instances on your behalf.

* **Required** Cancel **Next: Permissions**

8. Select your use case from the list. You need to allow the EC2 instance to call AWS services on your behalf, so select the first option and click "Next: Permissions".

Create role

1 2 3

Attach permissions policies

Choose one or more policies to attach to your new role.

Create policy | Refresh

Filter: Policy type | s3 | Showing 4 results

	Policy name	Attachments	Description
	AmazonDMSRedshiftS3Role	0	Provides access to manage S3 settings for Redshift endpoin...
✓	AmazonS3FullAccess	0	Provides full access to all buckets via the AWS Management...
	AmazonS3ReadOnlyAccess	0	Provides read only access to all buckets via the AWS Manag...
	QuickSightAccessForS3StorageManagement...	0	Policy used by QuickSight team to access customer data pro...

* Required

Cancel | Previous | Next: Review

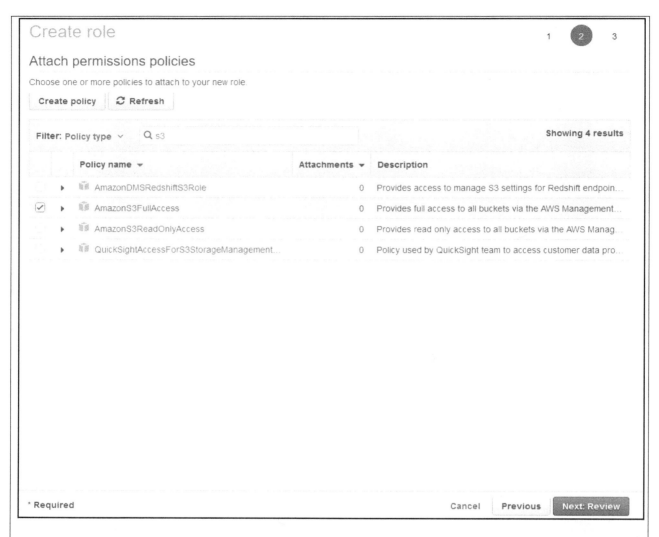

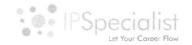

9. Type “S3” into the search bar to find S3 permission policies and select “AmazonS3FullAccess” to grant S3 administrative access. Click “Next: Review”.

Create role

Review

Provide the required information below and review this role before you create it.

Role name* MyS3AdminAccess

Use alphanumeric and '+=,.@-_' characters. Maximum 64 characters.

Role description Provides admin access to S3

Maximum 1000 characters. Use alphanumeric and '+=,.@-_' characters.

Trusted entities AWS service: ec2.amazonaws.com

Policies AmazonS3FullAccess

* Required Cancel Previous Create role

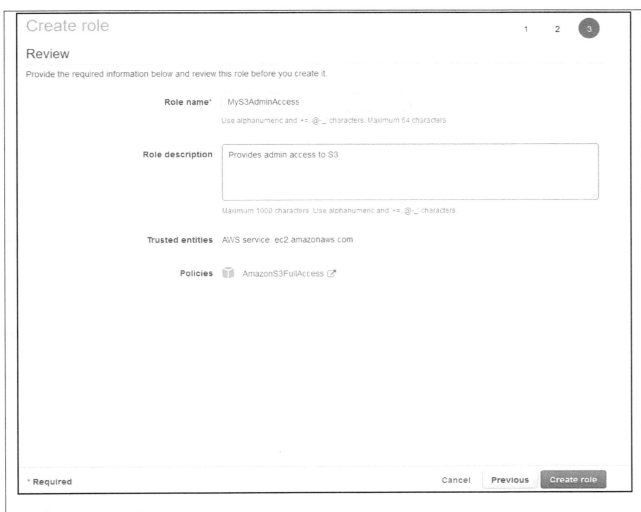

10. Enter a role name and its description. Here, we have named our role "MyS3AdminAccess". Click "Create role".

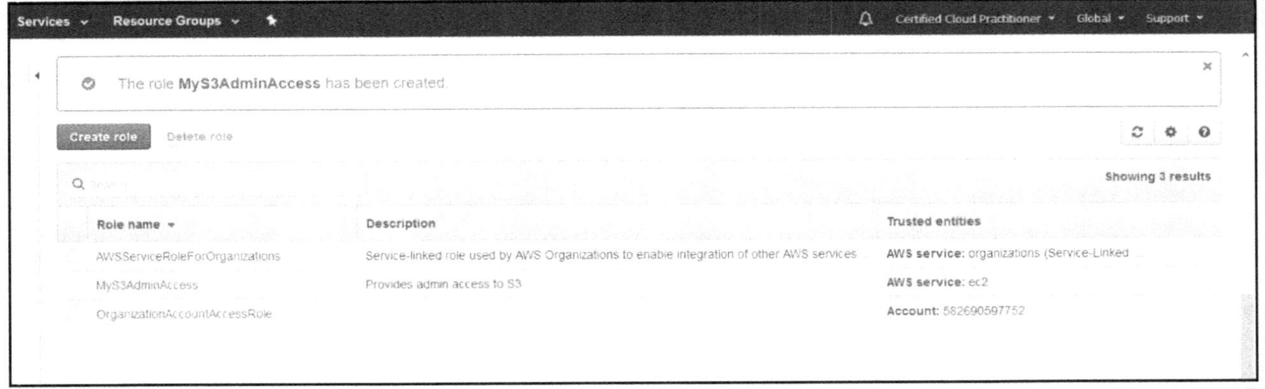

11. The role "MyS3AdminAccess" has been created. We now need to attach this role to the EC2 instance. Click on "Services" and select "EC2".

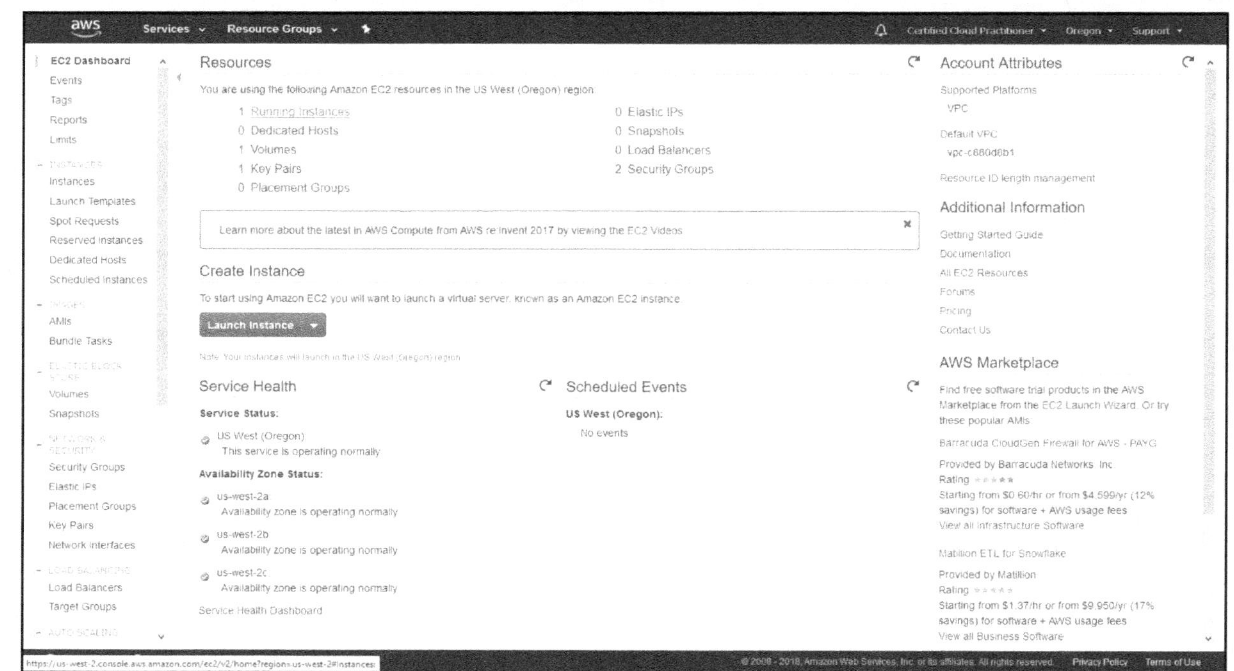

12. Click on "Running Instances".

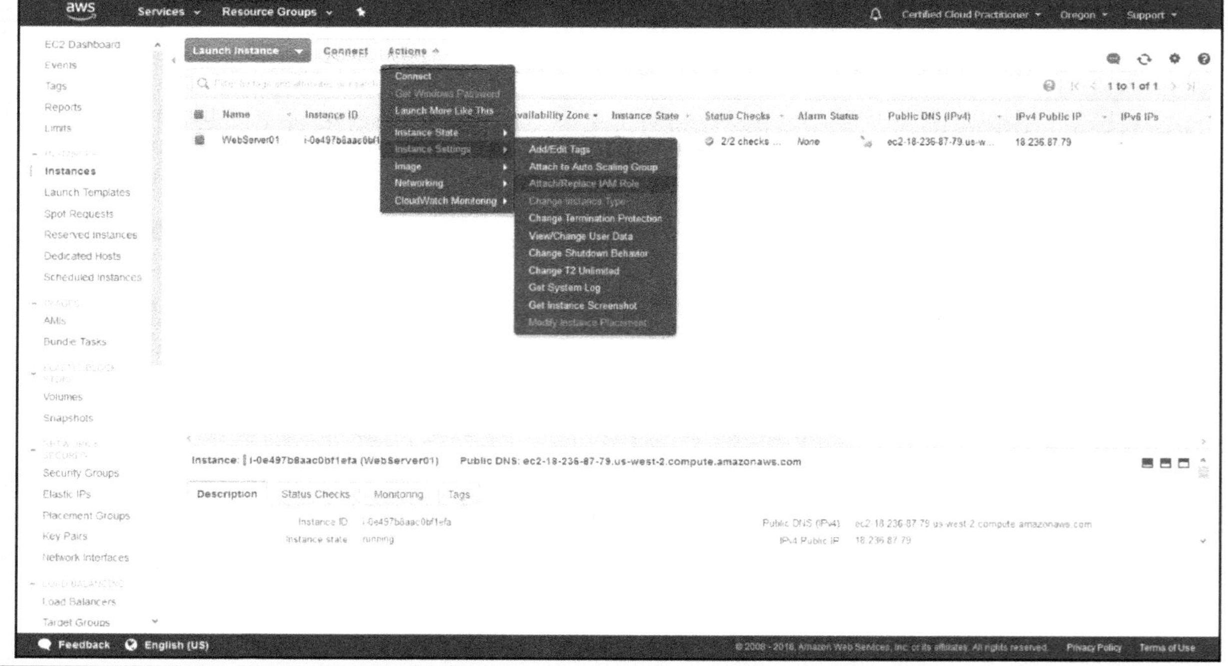

13. Select your EC2 instance and click on "Actions" to open a drop-down menu. Navigate to "Instance Settings" and select "Attach/Replace IAM Role".

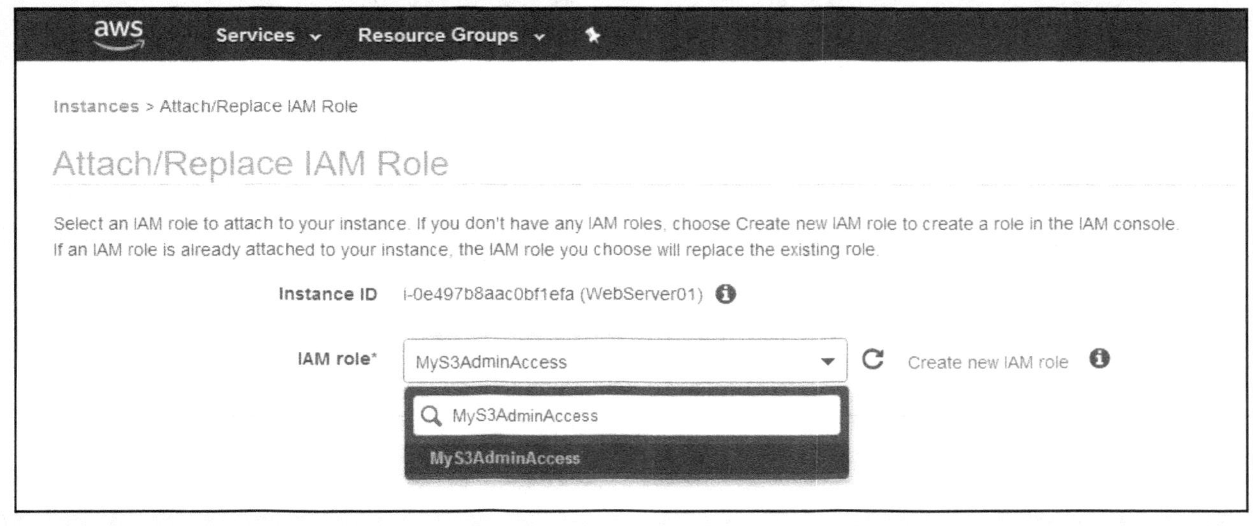

14. From the drop-down list, select the IAM Role you just created and click "Apply".

15. Click "close" and open up Terminal for Mac or PuTTY for Windows, where you left off.

```
[root@ip-172-31-23-114 ec2-user]# cd ~/.aws
[root@ip-172-31-23-114 .aws]# ls
config  credentials
[root@ip-172-31-23-114 .aws]# nano credentials
[root@ip-172-31-23-114 .aws]# rm -rf credentials
[root@ip-172-31-23-114 .aws]# ls
config
[root@ip-172-31-23-114 .aws]# aws s3 ls
Unable to locate credentials. You can configure credentials by running "aws configu
re".
[root@ip-172-31-23-114 .aws]# aws s3 ls
2018-04-20 07:41:18 ccp.bucket
2018-04-24 11:50:07 ccp.commandline.bucket
2018-04-23 17:00:45 ccp.ipspecialist
[root@ip-172-31-23-114 .aws]# ls
config
[root@ip-172-31-23-114 .aws]#
```

16. Now, if you run the same command "aws s3 ls" to list the objects within S3, you will be able to see the buckets however it does not show the credential files. Therefore, using roles means that your EC2 instance can communicate with S3 in a much more secure way.

EXAM TIPS:

- Roles are much more secure than using Access Key IDs and Secret Access Keys and are easier to manage
- You can apply roles to EC2 instances at any time; the change takes place immediately once applied
- Roles are universal. You do not need to specify regions for them, similar to creating users

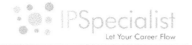

Lab 3-9: Building a Web Server

1. Log in to the “AWS Console”.
2. Click “Services”.
3. Select “EC2” from Compute.
4. Click “Running Instances”.

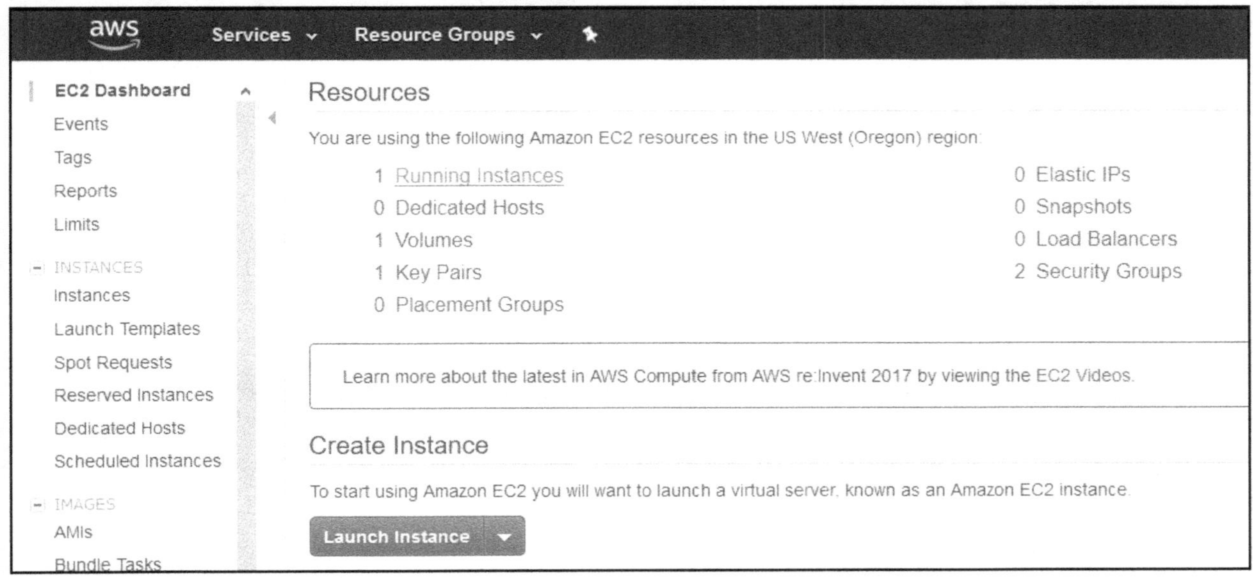

5. Copy the public IP address of the EC2 instance to log in through the AWS command line. Open up Terminal for Mac or PuTTY for Windows.

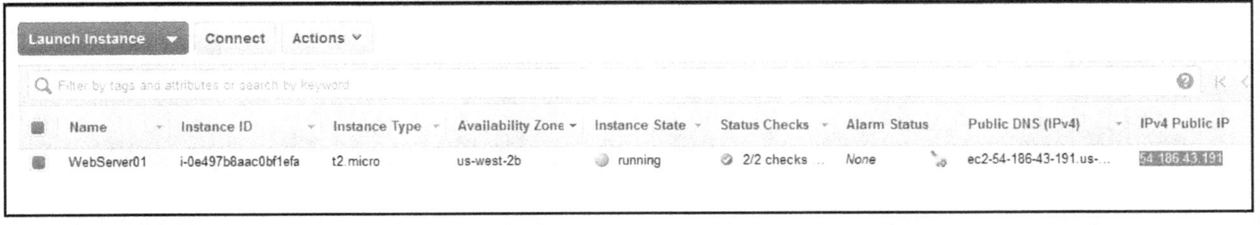

6. Type in “sudosu” to get super-user access, and clear the screen.

```
login as: ec2-user
Authenticating with public key "imported-openssh-key"
Last login: Tue Apr 24 12:08:16 2018 from 110.37.216.158

       __|  __|_  )
       _|  (     /   Amazon Linux AMI
      ___|\___|___|

https://aws.amazon.com/amazon-linux-ami/2018.03-release-notes/
1 package(s) needed for security, out of 4 available
Run "sudo yum update" to apply all updates.
[ec2-user@ip-172-31-23-114 ~]$ sudo su
[root@ip-172-31-23-114 ec2-user]# clear
```

7. All webservers need Apache or IIS to make them a webserver. Apache is for Linux and IIS (Internet Information Service) is the Windows version of a webserver .'httpd'. Here, you can install Apache.

```
[root@ip-172-31-23-114 ec2-user]# yum install httpd -y
```

8. Once Apache is installed, you need to start the Apache server.

```
  Installing : httpd-tools-2.2.34-1.16.amzn1.x86_64                3/5
  Installing : apr-util-ldap-1.5.4-6.18.amzn1.x86_64               4/5
  Installing : httpd-2.2.34-1.16.amzn1.x86_64                      5/5
  Verifying  : httpd-tools-2.2.34-1.16.amzn1.x86_64                1/5
  Verifying  : apr-util-1.5.4-6.18.amzn1.x86_64                    2/5
  Verifying  : httpd-2.2.34-1.16.amzn1.x86_64                      3/5
  Verifying  : apr-1.5.2-5.13.amzn1.x86_64                         4/5
  Verifying  : apr-util-ldap-1.5.4-6.18.amzn1.x86_64               5/5

Installed:
  httpd.x86_64 0:2.2.34-1.16.amzn1

Dependency Installed:
  apr.x86_64 0:1.5.2-5.13.amzn1
  apr-util.x86_64 0:1.5.4-6.18.amzn1
  apr-util-ldap.x86_64 0:1.5.4-6.18.amzn1
  httpd-tools.x86_64 0:2.2.34-1.16.amzn1

Complete!
[root@ip-172-31-23-114 ec2-user]#
```

9. Type in "service httpd start", to start the Apache server. Once again, clear the screen.

```
[root@ip-172-31-23-114 ec2-user]# service httpd start
Starting httpd:                                            [  OK  ]
[root@ip-172-31-23-114 ec2-user]#
```

10. Command 'cd' is used to change the directory. Type in the landing page path, which is "/var/www/html". Run the "ls" command and you will see that it is currently empty. Use the "echo" command to put up a sample text file 'welcome.txt'. Once done, open it up in "nano" editor to view the file.

```
[root@ip-172-31-23-114 ec2-user]# cd /var/www/html
[root@ip-172-31-23-114 html]# ls
[root@ip-172-31-23-114 html]# echo "Hello Cloud Practitioner" > welcome.txt
[root@ip-172-31-23-114 html]# ls
welcome.txt
[root@ip-172-31-23-114 html]# nano welcome.txt
```

11. Press ctrl+x to exit the editor, then open your browser to browse your landing page using the EC2 instance public IP address followed by the file name 'welcome.txt'.

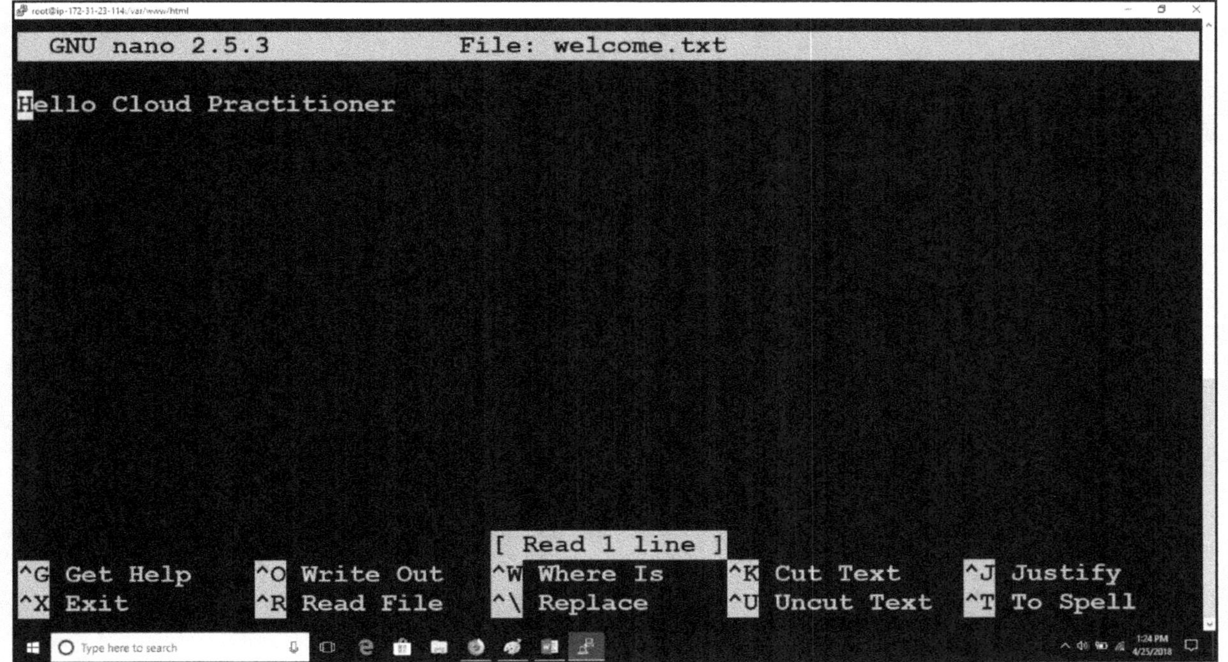

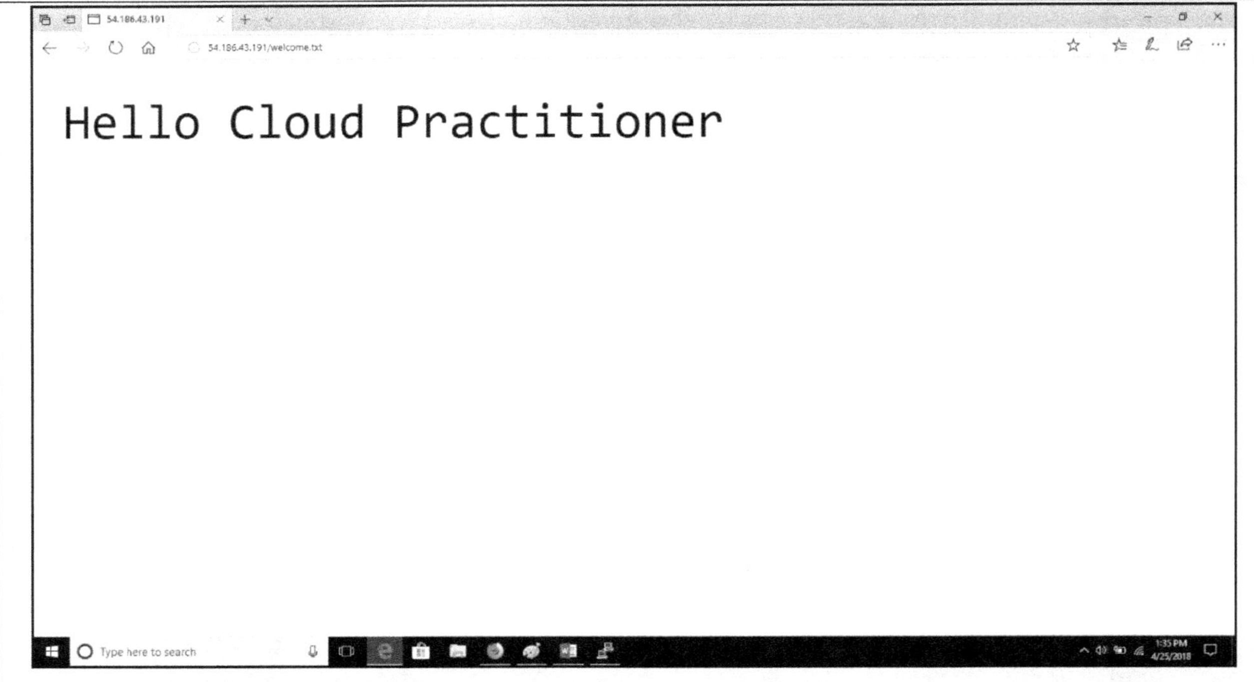

12. You now know that your webserver is working. Deploy the same "index.html" and "error.html" codes here that you previously used for static website hosting using the S3 buckets.
13. This is the S3 bucket 'ccp.ipspecialist' that contains the code that you previously used in static website hosting. It also contains your code files 'index.html' and 'error.html.' Copy these files to the landing page directory.

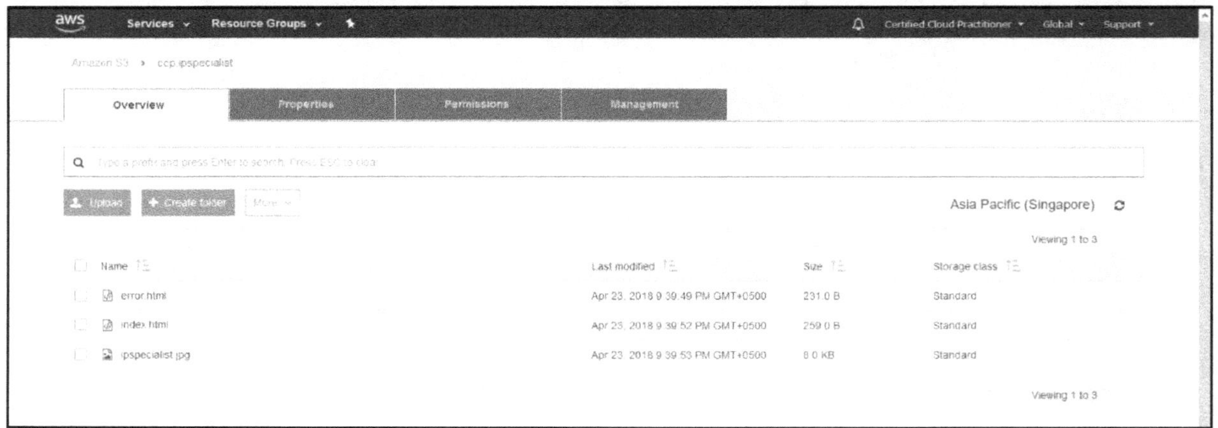

14. Use to "cp" command to copy the contents from the 'ccp.ipspecialist' bucket to the landing page directory '**/var/www/html**'.

```
[root@ip-172-31-23-114 html]# aws s3 ls
2018-04-20 07:41:18 ccp.bucket
2018-04-24 11:50:07 ccp.commandline.bucket
2018-04-23 17:00:45 ccp.ipspecialist
[root@ip-172-31-23-114 html]# aws s3 cp s3://ccp.ipspecialist /var/www/html
 --recursive
download: s3://ccp.ipspecialist/error.html to ./error.html
download: s3://ccp.ipspecialist/ipspecialist.jpg to ./ipspecialist.jpg
download: s3://ccp.ipspecialist/index.html to ./index.html
[root@ip-172-31-23-114 html]# ls
error.html  index.html  ipspecialist.jpg  welcome.txt
[root@ip-172-31-23-114 html]#
```

15. If your instance reboots, the Apache server will not restart automatically. To do start it up again, run the command "**chkconfighttpd on**".

```
[root@ip-172-31-23-114 html]# aws s3 ls
2018-04-20 07:41:18 ccp.bucket
2018-04-24 11:50:07 ccp.commandline.bucket
2018-04-23 17:00:45 ccp.ipspecialist
[root@ip-172-31-23-114 html]# aws s3 cp s3://ccp.ipspecialist /var/www/html
 --recursive
download: s3://ccp.ipspecialist/error.html to ./error.html
download: s3://ccp.ipspecialist/ipspecialist.jpg to ./ipspecialist.jpg
download: s3://ccp.ipspecialist/index.html to ./index.html
[root@ip-172-31-23-114 html]# ls
error.html  index.html  ipspecialist.jpg  welcome.txt
[root@ip-172-31-23-114 html]# chkconfig httpd on
[root@ip-172-31-23-114 html]#
```

16. Open up your browser and test your website.

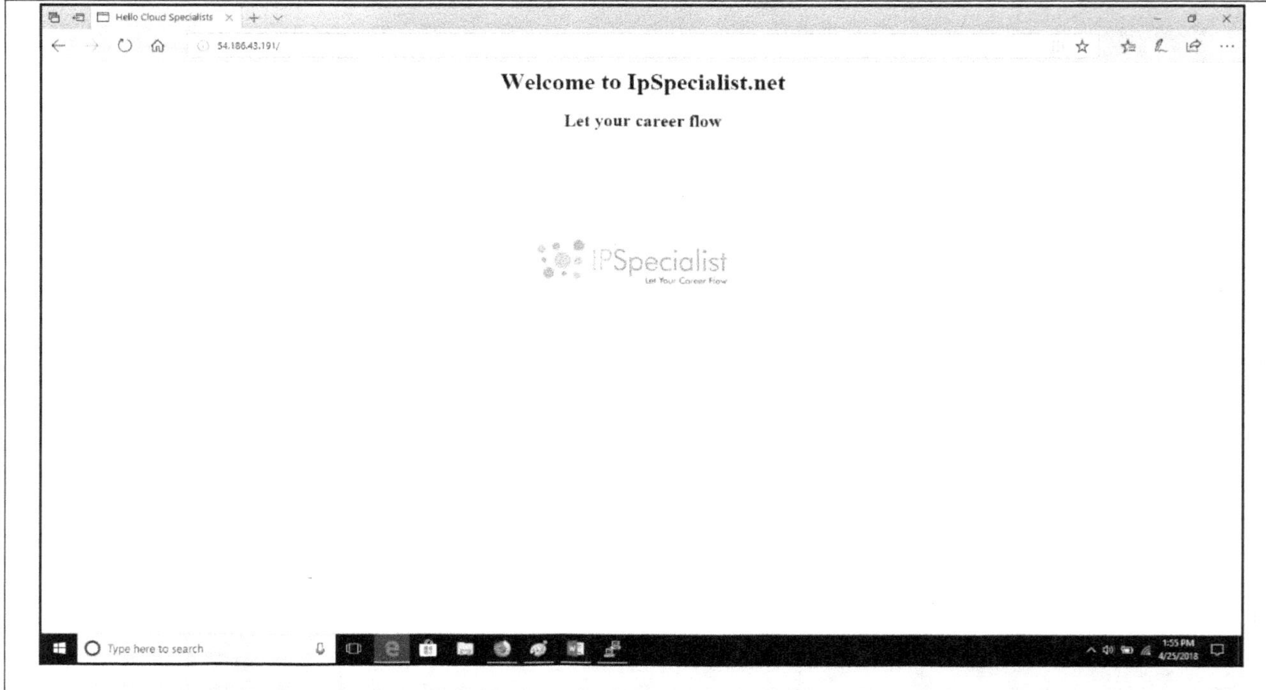

17. Enter the public IP address in the browser, and you should be able to see your webpage 'index.html'.

AWS Database

AWS offers a wide range of databases that are specifically designed to cater to the needs of specific application use cases. AWS fully managed database services include relational databases for transactional applications, non-relational databases for internet-scale applications and a data warehouse for analytical report and analysis.

EXAM TIP: You will be quizzed on which services and database technologies you should use, based on a given scenario. Make sure you thoroughly understand the different types of databases, their services, and typical use cases.

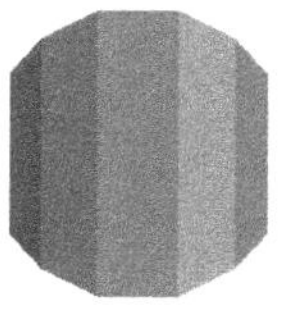

Amazon Relational Database Service (Amazon RDS)

Amazon Relational Database Service (Amazon RDS) is a managed relational database service that makes it easy to set up, operate and scale a relational database in the AWS cloud. It provides cost-efficient and resizable capacity while managing time-consuming database administration tasks.

Relational databases are similar to a traditional worksheet. A typical database includes tables made up of rows and fields (columns). A simple example of a table in a database is:

Employee ID	Employee Name	Department	Designation
001	John Smith	Finance	Manager
002	George Stanley	Human Resources	Senior Officer
003	Harry Walter	Human Resources	Clerk
004	David Anthony	IT	Network Engineer

Table 3-4: A Relational Database

Employee ID, Employee Name, Department, and Designation are different fields and each row represents an individual record. Relational databases are used for transactional applications like ERP, CRM and eCommerce to log transactions and store structured data.

Amazon RDS Supported Databases

Amazon RDS offers six familiar database engines to choose from, including Amazon Aurora, MySQL, MariaDB, Oracle, Microsoft SQL Server, and PostgreSQL. Amazon RDS handles routine database tasks such as provisioning, patching, backup, recovery, failure detection and repair. Amazon RDS will also automatically back up your database and keep the database software up to date.

Amazon RDS Key Features

Amazon RDS makes it easy to use replication to enhance database availability, improve data durability and scale beyond the capacity constraints of a single database instance for read-heavy database workloads. Amazon RDS provides two distinct replication options that serve different purposes:

- Multi-Availability Zones
- Read Replicas

Multi-Availability Zones:

In Multi-AZ mode, Amazon RDS automatically provisions and manages a standby replica in a different availability zone with an independent infrastructure in a physically separate location. In the event of planned database maintenance, DB instance failure or an availability zone failure, Amazon RDS will automatically failover to the standby replica so that database operations can resume quickly without administrative intervention.

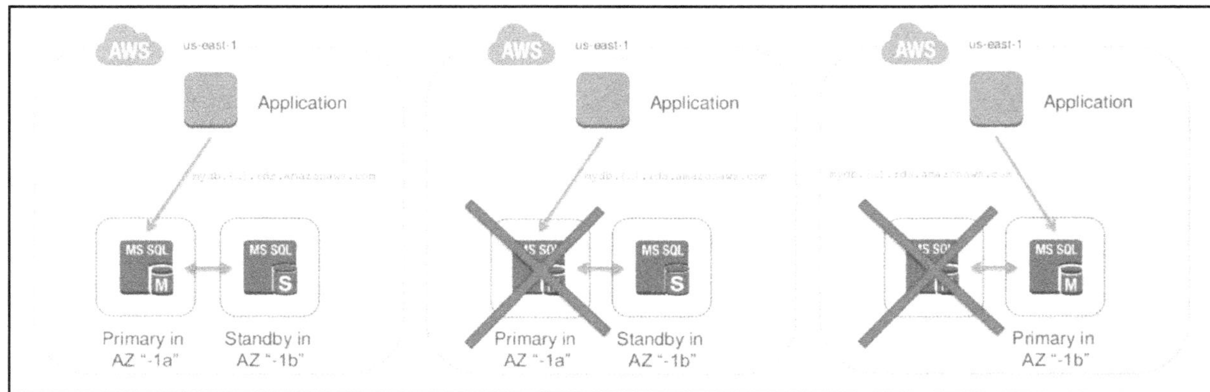

Figure 3-11: Multi-AZ Deployment

Multi-AZ deployments utilize synchronous replication, making the database write concurrently on both the primary and standby to ensure the standby will be up-to-date if a failover occurs. With Multi-AZ deployments, replication is transparent; that is, you do not interact directly with the standby and it cannot be used for reading operations.

***Read Replicas*:**

Amazon RDS offers Read Replicas to scale beyond the capacity constraints of a single DB Instance for read-heavy database workloads. A read replica of a given source DB Instance can be created using the AWS Management Console, the RDS API or the AWS Command Line Interface.

Once the read replica is created, database updates on the source DB instance are asynchronously replicated to the read replica. Replication lag can vary significantly as updates are applied to read replicas after they occur on the source DB Instance. This means database updates made to a standard (non-Multi-AZ) source DB instance may not be present on associated read replicas if the source DB instance fails.

Multiple read replicas can be created for a given source DB Instance to distribute read traffic for a single application. Typical reasons for deploying read replicas include: scaling beyond the capacity of a single DB instance, serving read traffic in the case of unavailability of the source DB instance, and running business-reporting queries.

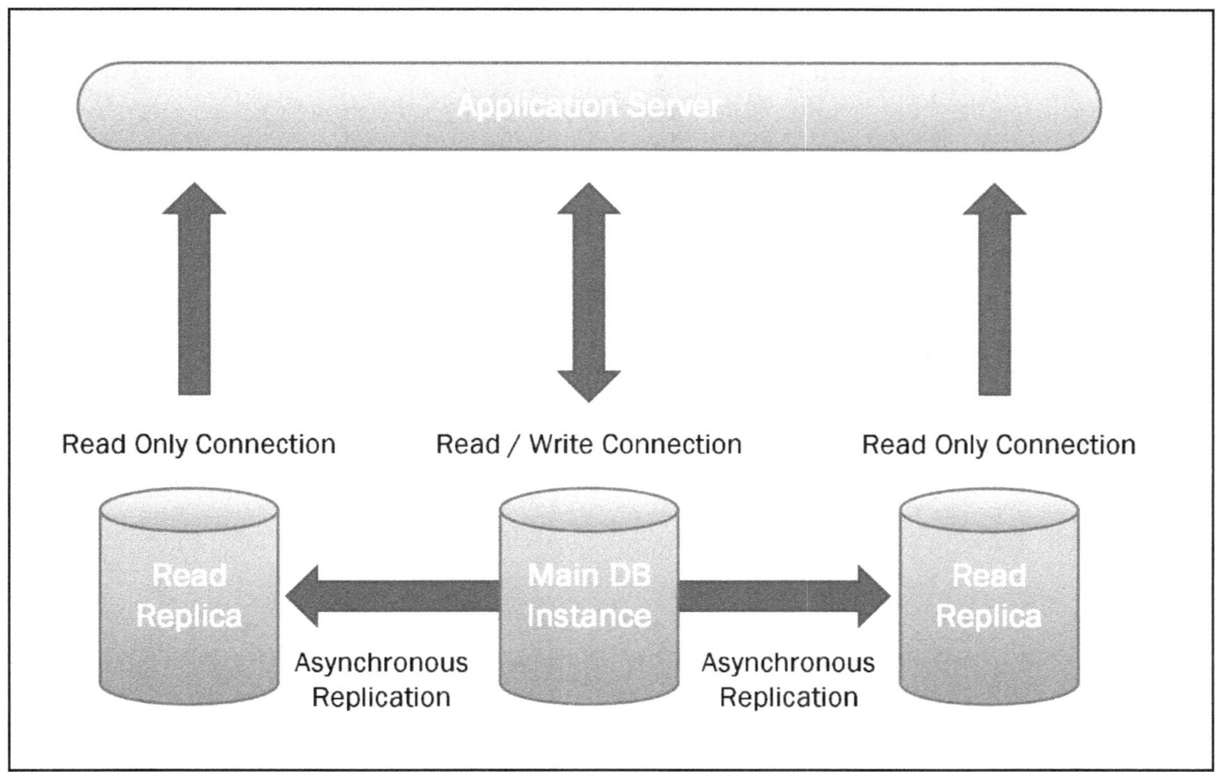

Figure 3-12: Read Replicas Deployment

When used together, multi-AZ deployments and read replicas in combination offer the benefits of both. By specifying a given Multi-AZ deployment as the source DB instance for the read replica, you achieve the data durability and availability benefits of Multi-AZ deployments and the read scaling benefits of read replicas.

EXAM TIP: RDS has two key features: Multi Availability Zones for disaster recovery and read replicas for performance improvement.

Amazon Aurora

Amazon Aurora is a MySQL and PostgreSQL-compatible relational database engine built for the cloud that combines the speed and availability of high-end commercial databases with the ease and cost-efficiency of open source databases. Amazon Aurora delivers up to five times better performance than MySQL and up to three times better performance than PostgreSQL. It provides the reliability, security and availability of commercial-grade databases at a tenth of the cost.

Amazon Aurora is entirely managed by Amazon Relational Database Service (RDS), which automates time-consuming administration tasks like hardware provisioning,

database setup, patching, backup, recovery, failure detection and repair. The Amazon Aurora database instance can be quickly launched from the RDS Management Console and is designed to be compatible with MySQL and PostgreSQL so that existing applications and tools can run without requiring any modification.

Amazon Aurora delivers high performance and availability with auto-scaling up to 64TB per database instance. Its storage is fault-tolerant and self-healing, which means that disk failures are repaired in the background without the loss of database availability. It is designed to detect database crashes automatically and start over without the need for crash recovery or rebuilding the database cache. If the entire instance fails, Amazon Aurora automatically fails over to one of up to 15 read replicas. It has a continuous backup to Amazon S3 and replication across three Availability Zones.

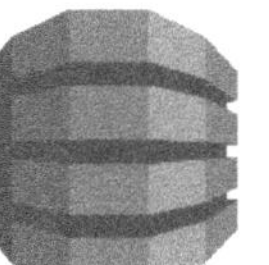

Amazon DynamoDB

Amazon DynamoDB is a fully managed, fast and flexible NoSQL database service for applications that require consistent and predictable performance with seamless scalability. DynamoDB offloads the administrative burden of operating and scaling distributed databases so that customers do not have to worry about hardware provisioning, setup or configuration, throughput capacity planning, replication, software patching or cluster scaling.

Non-Relational databases such as NoSQL consist of collection, documents, and key-value pairs. You can change the design of the database by adding extra fields. An example of a document within a collection could be:

JSON/NoSQL Code

```
• {
    "_id" : "5834",
    "firstname" : "John",
    "surname" : "Smith",
    "age" : "23",
    "address" : [
              {"street" : "21 jump street",
               "suburb" : "Richmond",}
              ]
  }
```

Figure 3-13: Example

Amazon DynamoDB supports both document and key-value store models. This flexible data model, with its reliable performance and automatic scaling of throughput capacity make it an appropriate choice for web, mobile, gaming, IoT, ad tech and many other

applications. Internet-scale applications like socializing, hospitality and ride sharing that serve content and store structured and unstructured data are good examples of applications, which would benefit from Amazon DynamoDB.

DynamoDB Accelerator (DAX)

The Amazon DynamoDB Accelerator (DAX) is a fully managed, highly available, in-memory cache that can reduce DynamoDB response times from milliseconds to microseconds, even at millions of requests per second.

DynamoDB scales automatically with your applications by turning on the DynamoDB accelerator.

EXAM TIP: The choice of data model depends on the type of database: Choose Amazon RDS (specifically Amazon Aurora) if you have a relational database, or choose Amazon DynamoDB if you have a non-relational database or need automatic scaling.

Amazon Redshift

Amazon Redshift is a fast and fully managed petabyte-scale data warehouse that is simple and cost-effective when analyzing large data sets using standard SQL and existing Business Intelligence (BI) tools. It runs complex analytic queries against petabytes of structured data by means of sophisticated query optimization, columnar storage on high-performance local disks and massively parallel query execution. Queries are distributed and parallelized across multiple physical resources, and most results are returned in seconds.

Data Warehousing is used for business intelligence activities such as reporting and data analysis, in which huge data queries are run on the database to pull in large and complex data sets. The use of big data queries and business intelligence tools on your production database may cause it to crash due to the amount and load of queries being made. Instead, a copy of the production database is maintained as a data warehouse where these reporting and querying operations can be performed.

Traditional data warehouses require time to build and large resources in order to manage large data sets. Furthermore, dealing with the financial cost of building, maintaining and growing any self-managed on-premises data warehouses is challenging. As the amount of data increases, you will need to compromise on what data to load into your data warehouse and what data to archive in storage so that you can manage costs, retain low

ETL complexity, and deliver good performance. Amazon Redshift greatly lowers the cost and operational overhead of a data warehouse.

The Amazon Redshift data warehouse can easily be scaled up or down, either using the AWS Management Console or with a single API call. Amazon Redshift automatically patches and backs up your data warehouse using replication and continuous backups to increase availability and enhance data durability. This means it can automatically recover from component and node failures.

Like other Amazon Web Services, Amazon Redshift follows a pay-as-you-go model, with no up-front investments or commitments. You only pay for the resources that you use.

EXAM TIP: You can use Amazon Redshift for the purposes of Business Intelligence and Data Warehousing.

AWS Networking & Content Delivery

AWS networking products offer you features and services that enable you to isolate your cloud infrastructure, scale your request handling capacity and connect your physical network to your private virtual network. The products include a content delivery network, virtual private cloud, direct connections, load balancing and DNS.

These AWS networking products work together to fulfill your application requirements. For example, Elastic Load Balancing works with Amazon Virtual Private Cloud (VPC) to provide robust networking and security features.

Amazon Virtual Private Cloud (Amazon VPC)

Amazon VPC lets you provision a logically isolated section of the AWS cloud from which you can launch AWS resources to a virtual network that you define. You have complete control over your virtual networking environment, including the selection of IP address ranges, the creation of subnets, and the configuration of route tables and network gateways.

A Virtual Private Cloud is a cloud computing model that offers an on-demand configurable pool of shared computing resources located within a public cloud environment while providing a certain level of isolation from other users of the public cloud. Since the cloud is only accessible to a single client in a VPC model, it offers privacy

with greater control and a secure environment in which only the specified client can operate.

You can easily customize the network configuration of your Amazon VPC. For example, you can create a public-facing subnet for your web servers that has access to the Internet, and place your backend systems, such as databases or application servers, in a private-facing subnet with no internet access. You can also leverage multiple layers of security, including security groups and network access control lists, to help control access to Amazon EC2 instances in each subnet. Additionally, it enables you to create a hardware Virtual Private Network (VPN) connection between your corporate datacenter and your VPC to leverage the AWS cloud as an extension to your corporate datacenter.

Features & Benefits

Multiple Connectivity Options:

- Connect directly to the Internet using public subnets
- Connect to the Internet using Network Address Translation using private subnets
- Connect securely to your corporate datacenter
- Connect privately to other VPCs
- Privately connect to AWS Services without using an Internet gateway, NAT or firewall proxy through a VPC Endpoint
- Privately connect to SaaS solutions supported by AWS PrivateLink
- Privately connect your internal services across different accounts and VPCs

Secure:

- Advanced security features such as security groups and network access control lists enable inbound and outbound filtering at the instance level and at the subnet level
- Store data in Amazon S3 and restrict access so that it is only accessible from instances in your VPC
- For additional isolation, launch dedicated instances which run on hardware dedicated to a single customer

Simple:

- Setup VPC quickly and easily using the AWS Management Console
- Easily select common network setups that best match your needs
- Subnets, IP ranges, route tables and security groups are automatically created using VPC Wizard

Scalability & Reliability:

- Amazon VPC provides all of the benefits of the AWS platform

Amazon VPC Functionality

With Amazon Virtual Private Cloud (Amazon VPC), you can:

- Create an Amazon VPC on AWS's scalable infrastructure and specify its private IP address range
- Expand your VPC by adding secondary IP ranges
- Divide your VPC's private IP address range into one or more public or private subnets to facilitate the running of applications and services in your VPC
- Assign multiple IP addresses and attach multiple elastic network interfaces to instances in your VPC
- Attach one or more Amazon Elastic IP addresses to any instance in your VPC so it can be reached directly from the internet
- Bridge the VPC and your onsite IT infrastructure with an encrypted VPN connection, extending your existing security and management policies to your VPC instances as if they were running within your infrastructure
- Enable EC2 instances in the EC2-Classic platform to communicate with instances in a VPC using private IP addresses
- Associate VPC Security Groups with instances on EC2-Classic
- Use VPC Flow Logs to log information about network traffic through the network interfaces in your VPC
- Enable both IPv4 and IPv6 in your VPC

Components of Amazon VPC

- ***A Virtual Private Cloud:*** A logically isolated virtual network in the AWS cloud. You define the IP address space for a VPC from ranges you select
- ***Subnet:*** A segment of a VPC's IP address range where you can place groups of isolated resources
- ***Internet Gateway:*** The Amazon VPC side of a connection to the public Internet
- ***NAT Gateway:*** A highly available, managed Network Address Translation (NAT) service for your resources in a private subnet to access the internet
- ***Hardware VPN Connection:*** A hardware-based VPN connection bridge between your Amazon VPC and your data center, home network or co-location facility
- ***Virtual Private Gateway:*** The Amazon VPC side of a VPN connection
- ***Customer Gateway:*** The customer's side of a VPN connection

- ***Router:*** Routers interconnect subnets and direct traffic between internet gateways, virtual private gateways, NAT gateways and subnets
- ***Peering Connection:*** A peering connection enables you to route traffic via private IP addresses between two peered VPCs.
- ***VPC Endpoints:*** Enables private connectivity to services hosted in AWS from within your VPC, without using an internet gateway, VPN, or any Network Address Translation (NAT) devices or firewall proxies.
- ***Egress-only Internet Gateway:*** A stateful gateway to provide egress-only access for IPv6 traffic from the VPC to the Internet

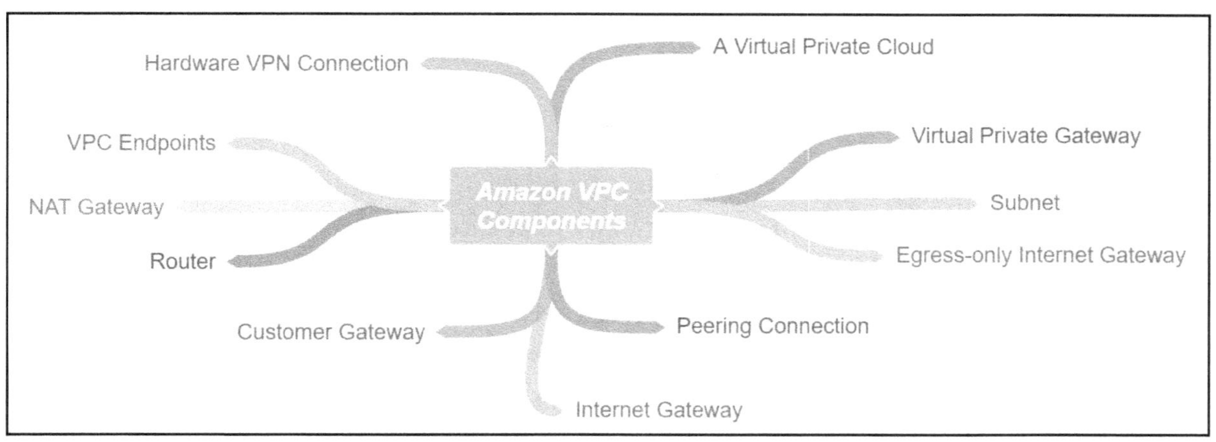

Figure 3-14: Mind Map of Amazon VPC Components

EXAM TIP: Use Amazon VPC to isolate cloud resources in a private virtual network.

Amazon CloudFront

Amazon CloudFront is a global Content Delivery Network (CDN) service that securely delivers data, videos, applications and APIs to end users with low latency and high transfer speeds. Amazon CloudFront can be used to deliver an entire website, including dynamic, static, streaming and interactive content, through a worldwide network of data centers called Edge Locations. When a user requests content, it is automatically routed to the nearest edge location with the lowest latency, so that content is delivered with the best possible performance.

- If the content is already in the edge location with the lowest latency, CloudFront delivers it immediately
- If the content is not currently in that edge location, CloudFront retrieves it from the Amazon S3 bucket or HTTP server, for example, a web server, that you have identified as the source for the definitive version of your content

A CDN is a network or system of distributed servers that deliver webpages and other web content to end users based on the geographic location of the user, the origin of the webpage and a content delivery server using edge locations.

- Origin: The source of the files that the CDN will distribute. This can be an S3 bucket, an EC2 instance, an Elastic load balancer, or Route53
- Distribution: The name given to the CDN, consisting of a collection of edge locations

Amazon CloudFront has several regional edge cache locations globally, at close proximity to the end users. These regional edge caches are located between the origin web server and the global edge locations that serve content directly to end users. As objects become less popular, individual edge locations remove them to make room for more popular content. Regional edge caches have a larger cache width than any individual edge location, so objects remain in the cache longer at the nearest regional edge caches. This helps keep more of the content closer to its viewers, reducing the need for CloudFront to go back to the origin webserver and improving overall viewing performance. For example, CloudFront edge locations in Europe will now attempt to go to the regional edge cache in Frankfurt to fetch an object, before going back to your origin webserver.

> EXAM TIP: Amazon CloudFront is a way of caching very big objects, such as image files and video files in the cloud.

How Does CloudFront Deliver Content?

1. A user accesses your website or application and requests one or more objects, such as an image file and an HTML file.
2. DNS routes the request to the CloudFront edge location that can best serve the request in terms of latency, typically the nearest CloudFront edge location.
3. At the edge location, CloudFront checks its cache for the requested files. If the files are in the cache, CloudFront returns them to the user. If the files are not in the cache, it does the following:

a. CloudFront compares the request with the specifications in the distribution and forwards the request to the applicable origin server for the corresponding file type. For example: to your Amazon S3 bucket for image files or to your HTTP server for the HTML files.

b. The origin servers send the files back to the CloudFront edge location.

c. As soon as the first byte arrives from the origin, CloudFront begins to forward the files to the user. CloudFront also adds the files to the cache in the edge location for the next time anyone requests those files.

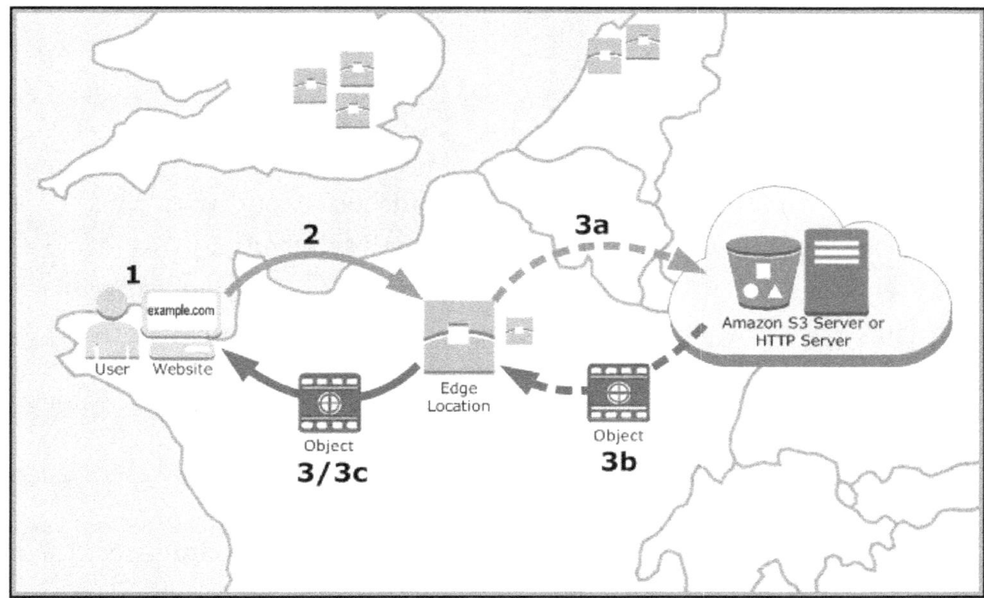

Figure 3-15: Delivering Content through CloudFront

Amazon CloudFront Benefits:

- **Global, Growing Content Delivery Network**

  The Amazon CloudFront content delivery network is built on the expanding global AWS infrastructure that currently includes 54 Availability Zones in 18 geographic regions.

- **Secure Content at the Edge**

  Amazon CloudFront provides both network- and application-level protection. It is seamlessly integrated with AWS WAF and AWS Shield Advanced to protect your applications from sophisticated

threats and DDoS attacks with the automatic protection of AWS Shield Standard provided at no additional cost.

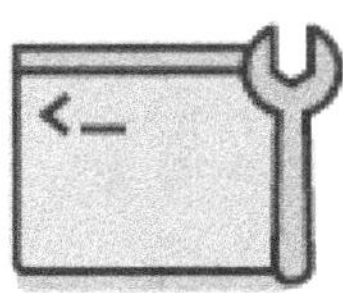

- **Programmable CDN**

  All Amazon CloudFront features can be programmatically configured using APIs or the AWS Management Console. With Lambda@Edge you can easily run your code across AWS locations worldwide, allowing you to respond to your end users with the lowest latency.

- **High Performance**

  CloudFront is directly connected with hundreds of end-user ISPs and uses the AWS backbone network to accelerate the delivery of content end-to-end. CloudFront also offers regional edge cache locations as part of their standard offering, to ensure consistently high cache hit ratios across the globe.

- **Cost Effective**

  Like other AWS products, there are no long-term contracts or minimum monthly usage commitments when using Amazon CloudFront. You pay only for as much or as little content you actually deliver through the content delivery service.

- **Deep Integration with Key AWS Services**

  Amazon CloudFront is optimized to work with other services in AWS, such as Amazon S3, Amazon EC2, Elastic Load Balancing and Amazon Route 53. Amazon CloudFront also works seamlessly with any non-AWS origin server that stores the original and definitive versions of your files.

Lab 3-10: Create CloudFront Distribution for Large Files

1. Log in to the "AWS Console".
2. Click on "Services".
3. Select "S3" from Storage.

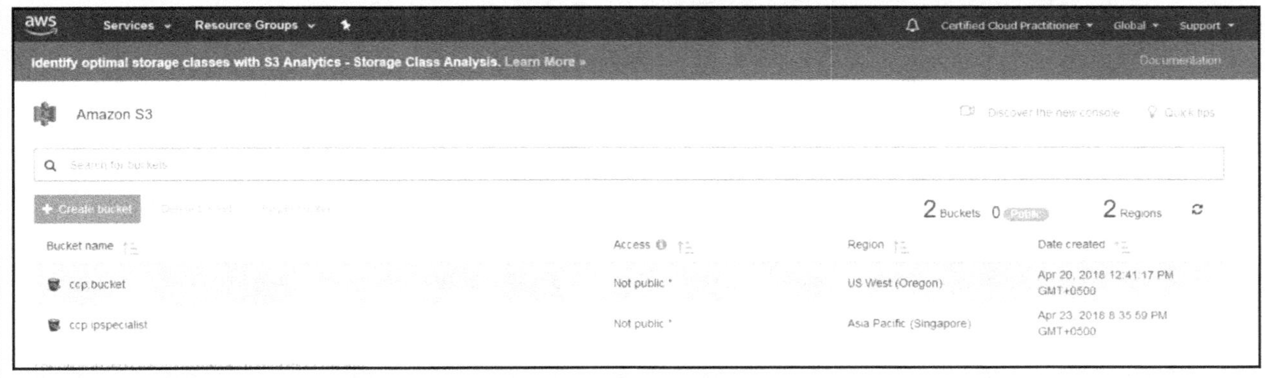

4. We will now upload a large image file to our bucket. Select the bucket "ccp.bucket" to upload your image file.

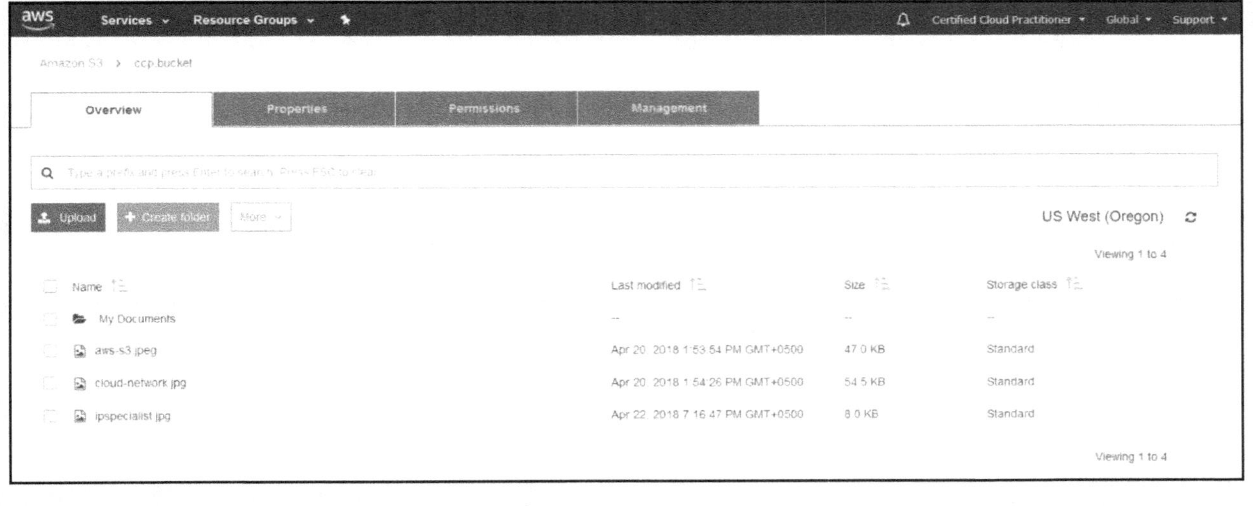

5. Click on "Upload".

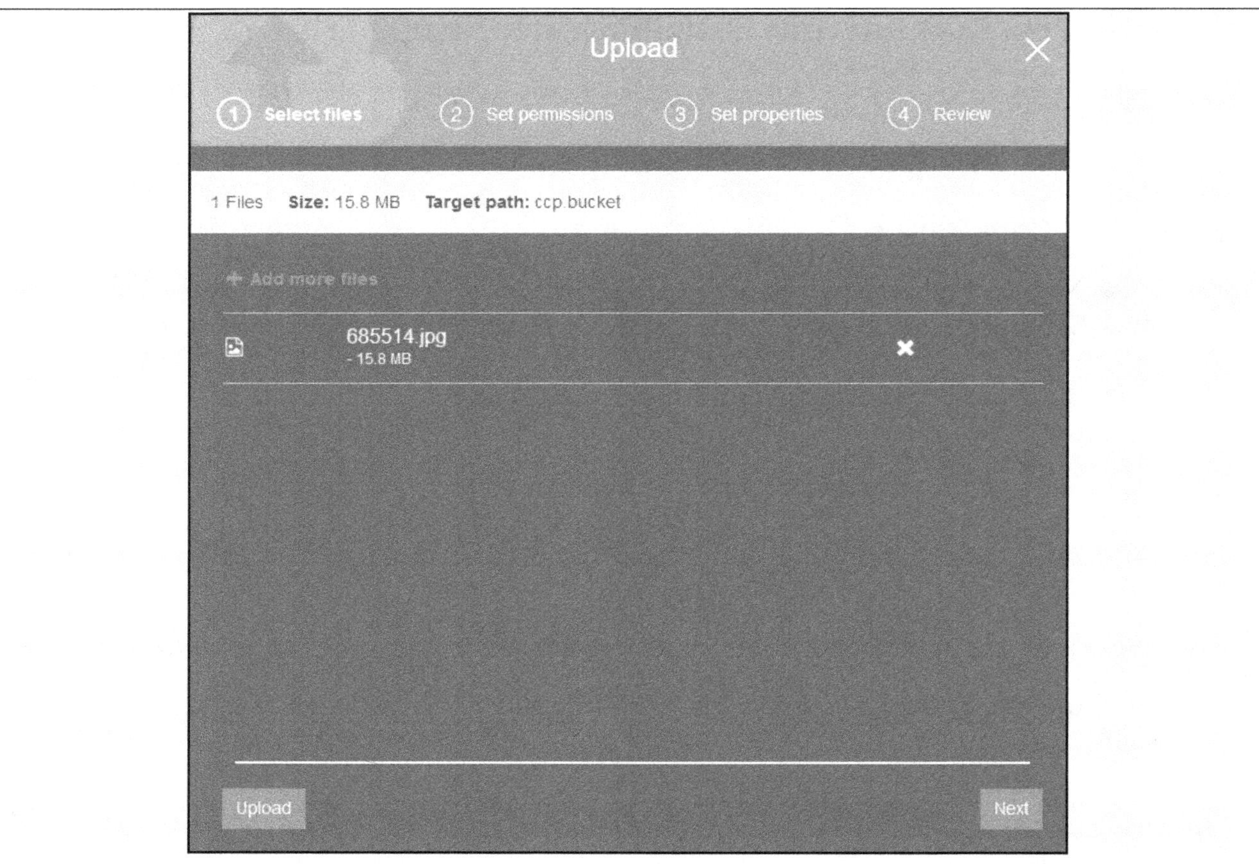

6. Add a large file and click "Upload". It may take some time to upload, depending on the region and size of the file.

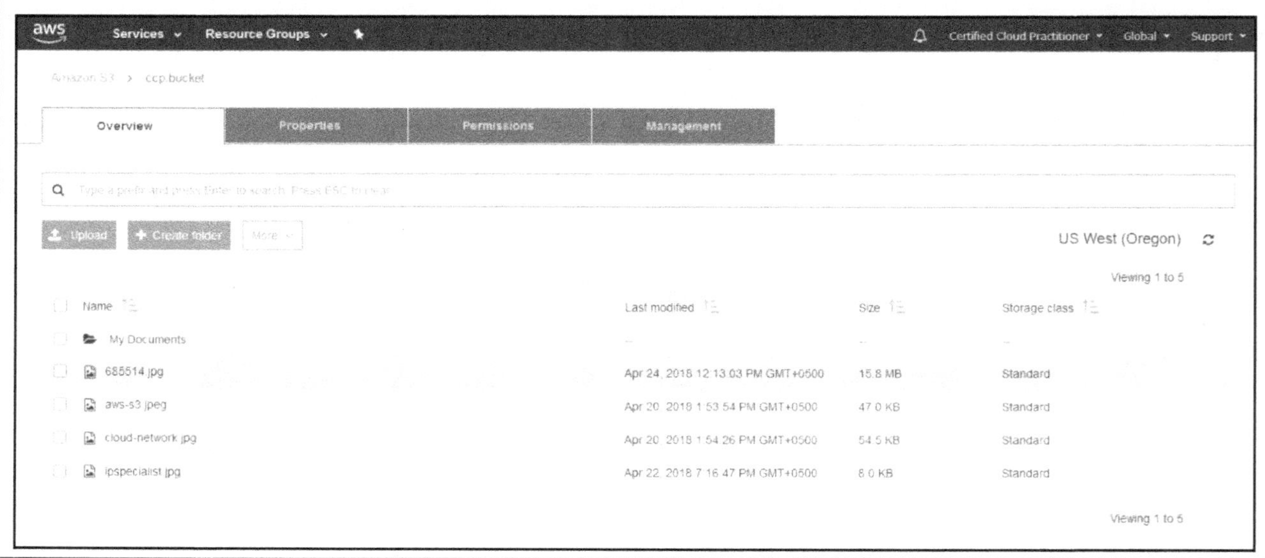

7. Once the file '685514.jpg' is uploaded, you need to make it public so that it can be accessed.

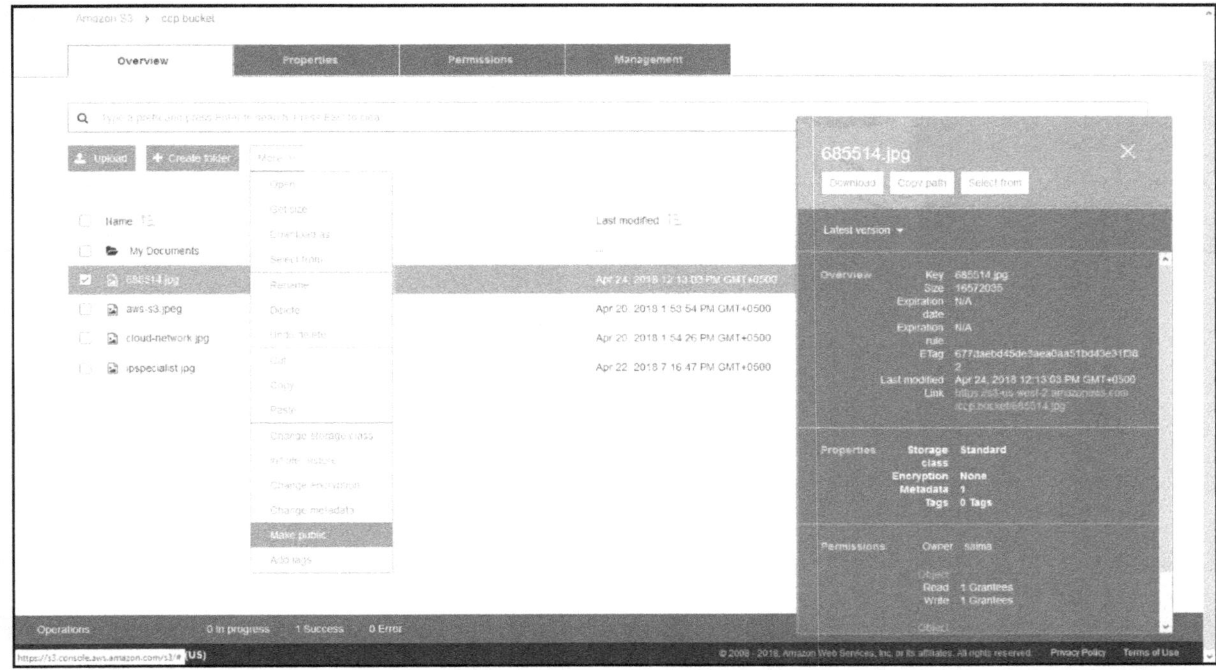

8. Select the image file, click "More" and then select "Make public".
9. Once done, return to the main AWS console and select "Services".
10. Scroll down to "Network & Content Delivery" and select "CloudFront".

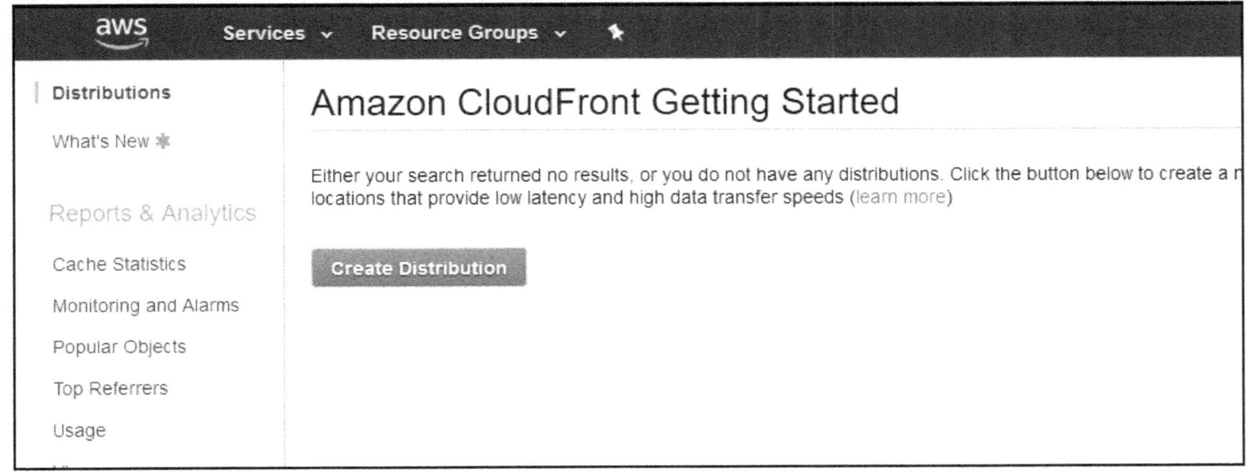

11. Click "Create Distribution".

Select a delivery method for your content.

Web

Create a web distribution if you want to:

- Speed up distribution of static and dynamic content, for example, .html, .css, .php, and graphics files.
- Distribute media files using HTTP or HTTPS.
- Add, update, or delete objects, and submit data from web forms.
- Use live streaming to stream an event in real time.

You store your files in an origin - either an Amazon S3 bucket or a web server. After you create the distribution, you can add more origins to the distribution.

Get Started

RTMP

Create an RTMP distribution to speed up distribution of your streaming media files using Adobe Flash Media Server's RTMP protocol. An RTMP distribution allows an end user to begin playing a media file before the file has finished downloading from a CloudFront edge location. Note the following:

- To create an RTMP distribution, you must store the media files in an Amazon S3 bucket.
- To use CloudFront live streaming, create a web distribution.

Get Started

Cancel

12. You will be given two options: Web distribution, and RTMP distribution. We want to distribute an image file, therefore we will be using Web distribution. Select "Get Started".

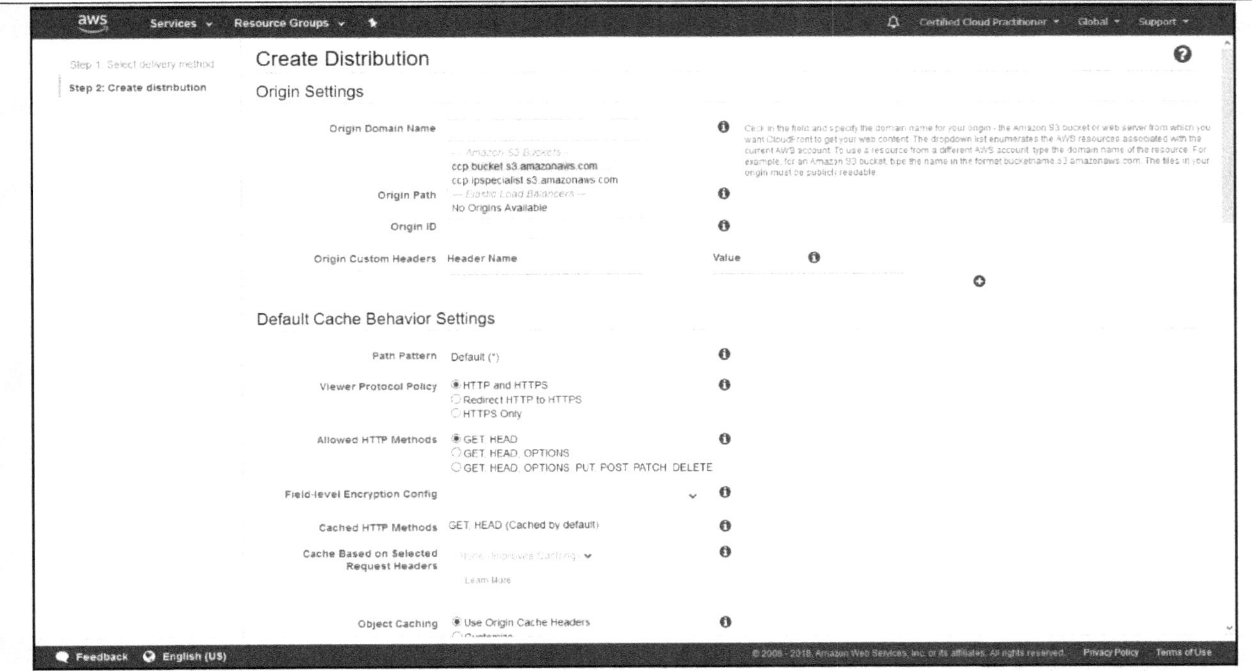

13. First, you need to select the Origin Domain Name. The origin of your image file is the S3 bucket "ccp.bucket".

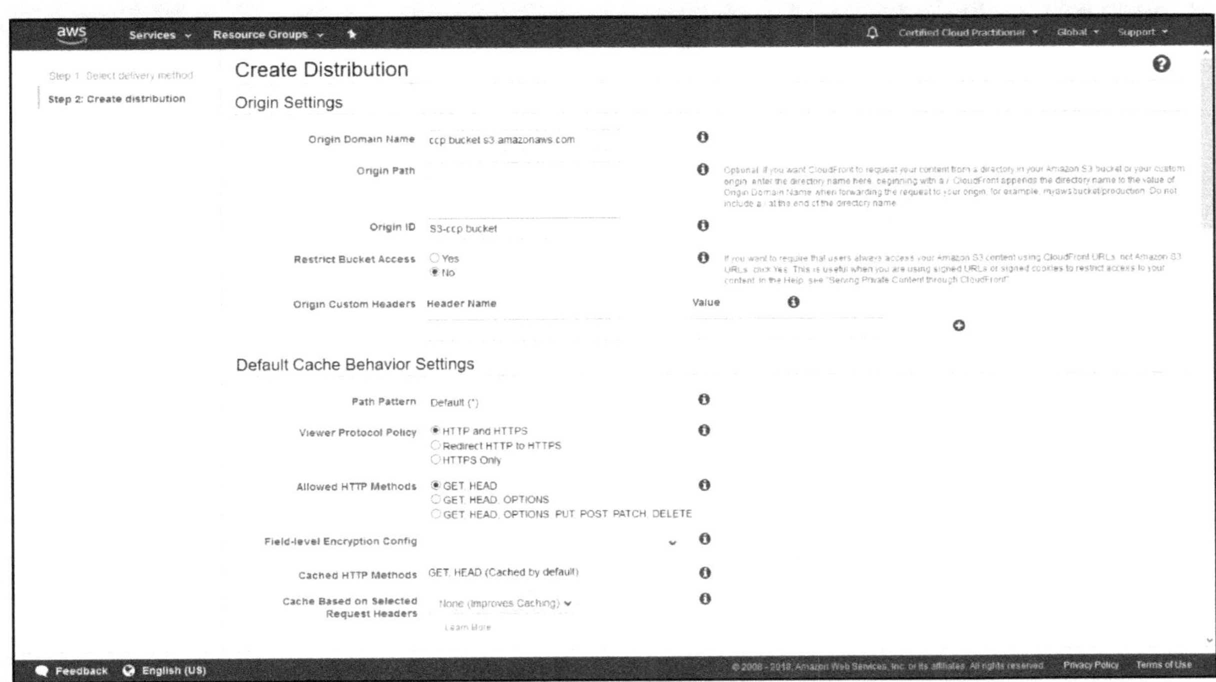

14. If you have any sub-directories or folders in your bucket, you can define the path of your file in the Origin Path field.

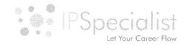

15. You can also restrict access to the content using the Amazon S3 URL and only allow access to CloudFront URL.
16. Scroll down to the end of the distribution settings.

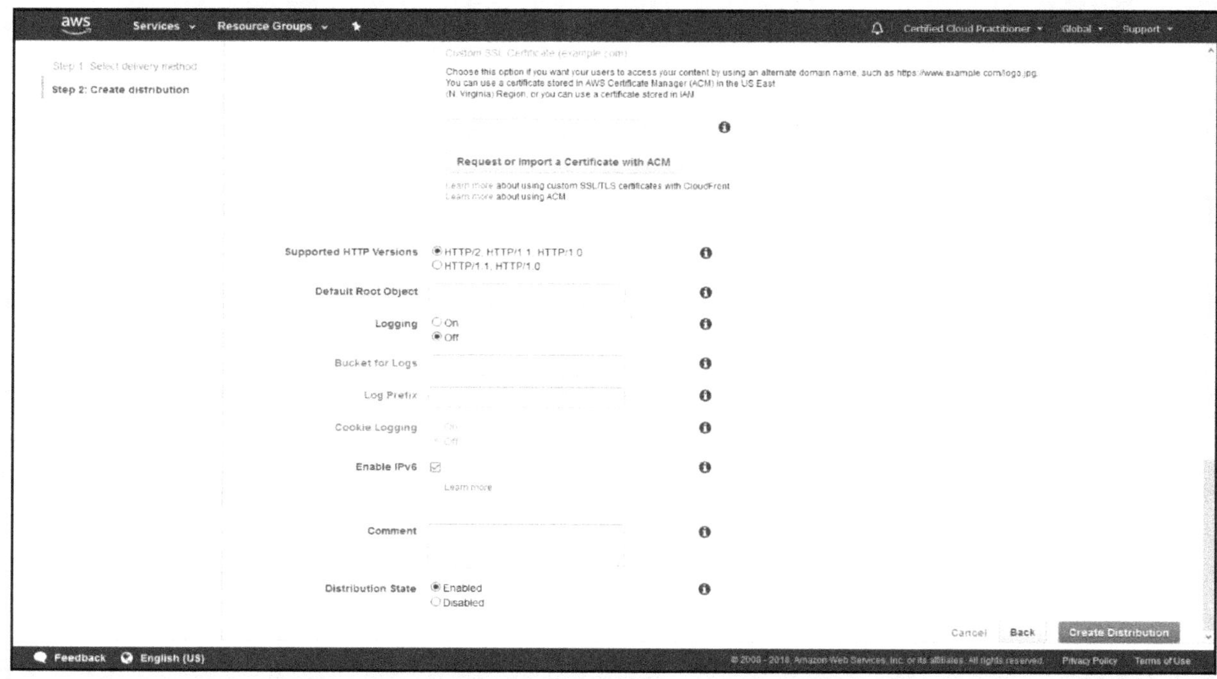

17. For now, leave everything as it is and click "Create Distribution". CloudFront Distribution will take some time to deploy.

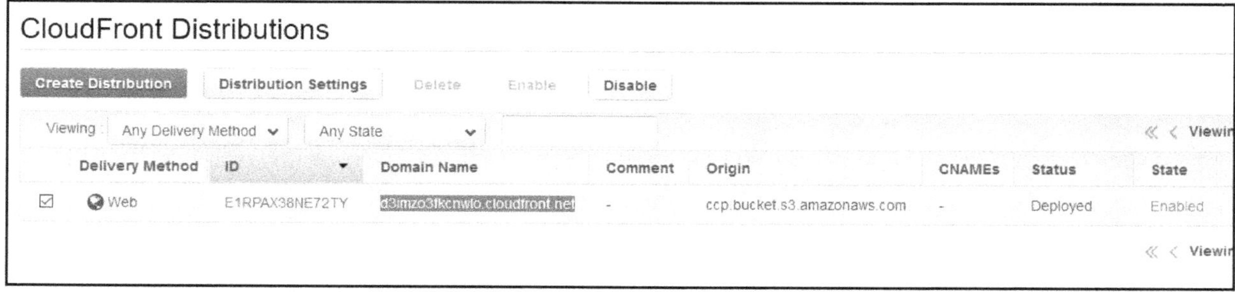

18. Once the distribution is deployed, copy the domain name and paste it into your browser followed by the image file name '685514.jpg'.

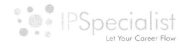

19. As soon as you hit enter to browse your file, the CloudDistribution will contact your nearest edge location to check whether the file is present there. Since you are accessing the file for the first time, the file will not be available at the edge location and ultimately will have to be fetched from the origin bucket location. You will see that the image file took some time to load on your browser.
20. Since the image file has now been requested once, it will now be present at the nearest edge location. If you refresh your page, you will notice how much fast your image file loads the second time.

EXAM TIPS:

- A CDN Edge Location is where content is cached. This is separate from an AWS Region or Availability Zone
- Web Distribution is typically used with websites

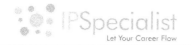

Elastic Load Balancing

Elastic Load Balancing (ELB) automatically distributes incoming application traffic across multiple EC2 instances. It seamlessly provides the necessary load balancing capacity required for the distribution of application traffic so that you can achieve greater levels of fault tolerance in your applications.

Elastic Load Balancing supports three types of load balancers: Application Load Balancers, Network Load Balancers, and Classic Load Balancers. You can select a load balancer based on your application needs. These load balancers feature high availability, automatic scaling and robust security.

Application Load Balancer	Network Load Balancer	Classic Load Balancer
• Makes routing decisions at the application layer (layer 7) and is best suited for load balancing of HTTP and HTTPS traffic. • Application Load Balancer routes traffic to targets - EC2 instances, containers and IP addresses within Amazon Virtual Private Cloud (Amazon VPC) based on the content of the request. • Ideal for applications requiring advanced routing capabilities, micro-services, and container-based architectures.	• Makes routing decisions at the transport layer (Layer 4) and is best suited for load balancing of TCP traffic where extreme performance is required. • Network Load Balancer routes connections to targets - Amazon EC2 instances, containers and IP addresses based on IP protocol data. • Optimized to handle sudden and volatile traffic patterns and is capable of handling millions of requests per second while maintaining ultra-low latencies.	• Makes routing decisions at the transport layer (TCP/SSL) or the application layer (HTTP/HTTPS) and supports either EC2 Classic or a VPC. However, it is recommended to use Application Load Balancer for Layer 7 and Network Load Balancer for Layer 4 when using Virtual Private Cloud (VPC). • Classic Load Balancer routes traffic based on either application or network level information. • Ideal for simple load balancing of traffic across multiple EC2 instances.

Figure 3-16: Elastic Load Balancing

Use an Application Load Balancer for flexible application management and TLS termination. If your application needs extreme performance and static IP, then use the Network Load Balancer. Use the Classic Load Balancer if your application is built within the EC2 Classic network.

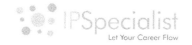

Lab 3-11: Using a Load Balancer

1. Log in to the "AWS Console".
2. Click on "Services".
3. Select "EC2" from Compute.

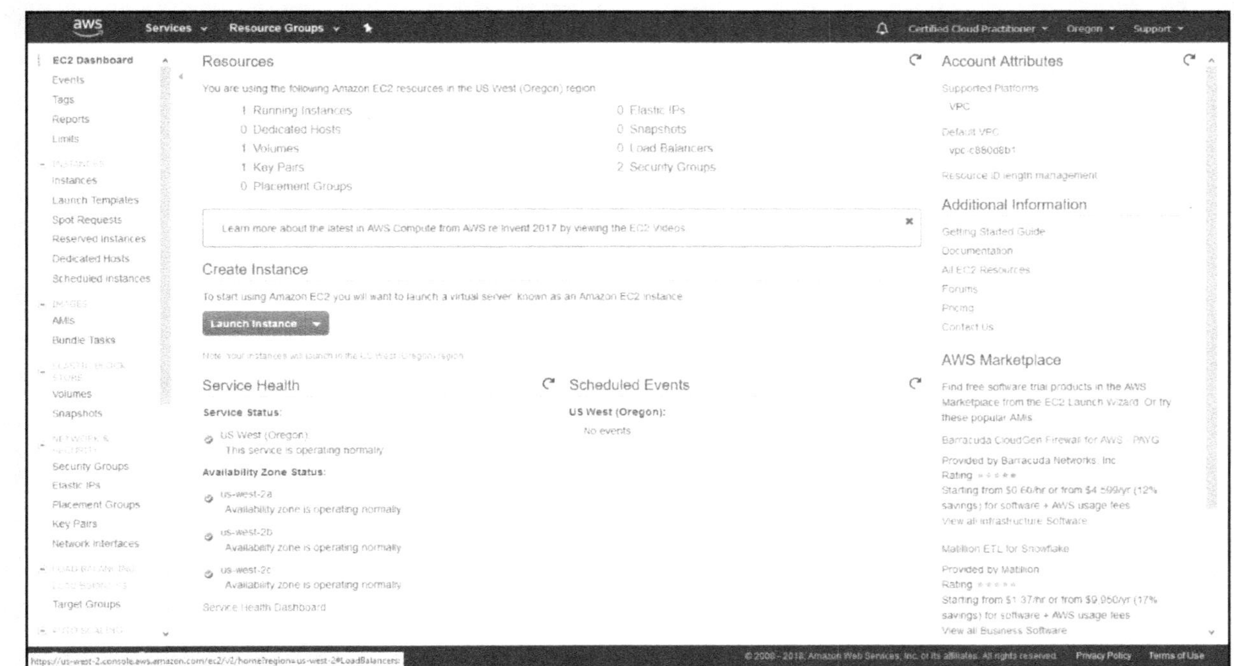

4. Scroll down the left-hand pane and select "Load Balancers" under the "Load Balancing" tab.
5. Click "Create Load Balancer".

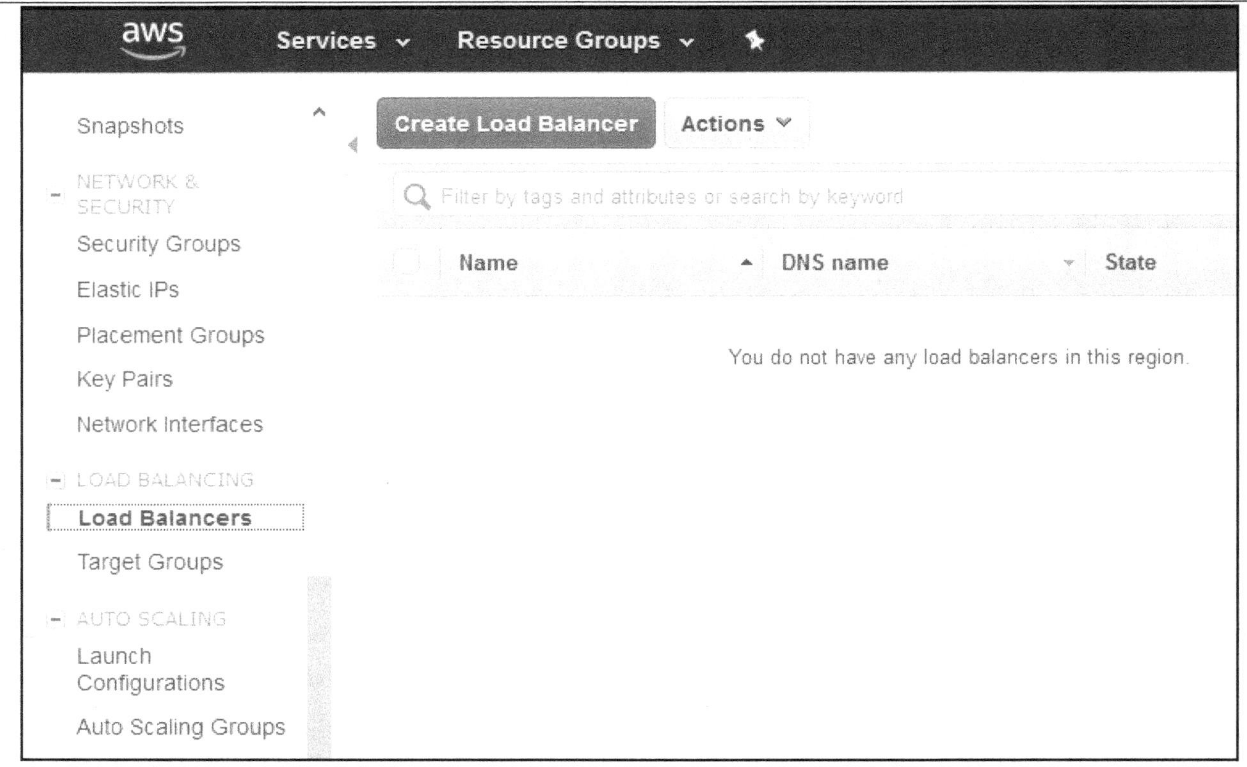

6. Select the type of load balancer. For example, let's use the Application Load Balancer. Click "Create" on the Application Load Balancer.

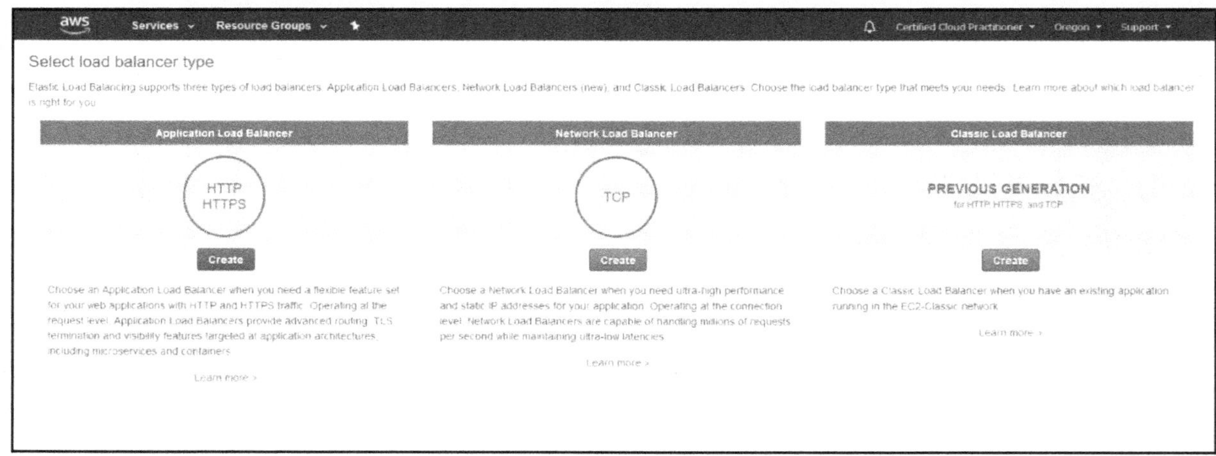

7. Enter a name for your load balancer. You will be using this load balancer as internet facing, and the address type is IPv4. Its open to http port 80. Select all the availability zones for the load balancer. Click "Next: Configure Security Settings".

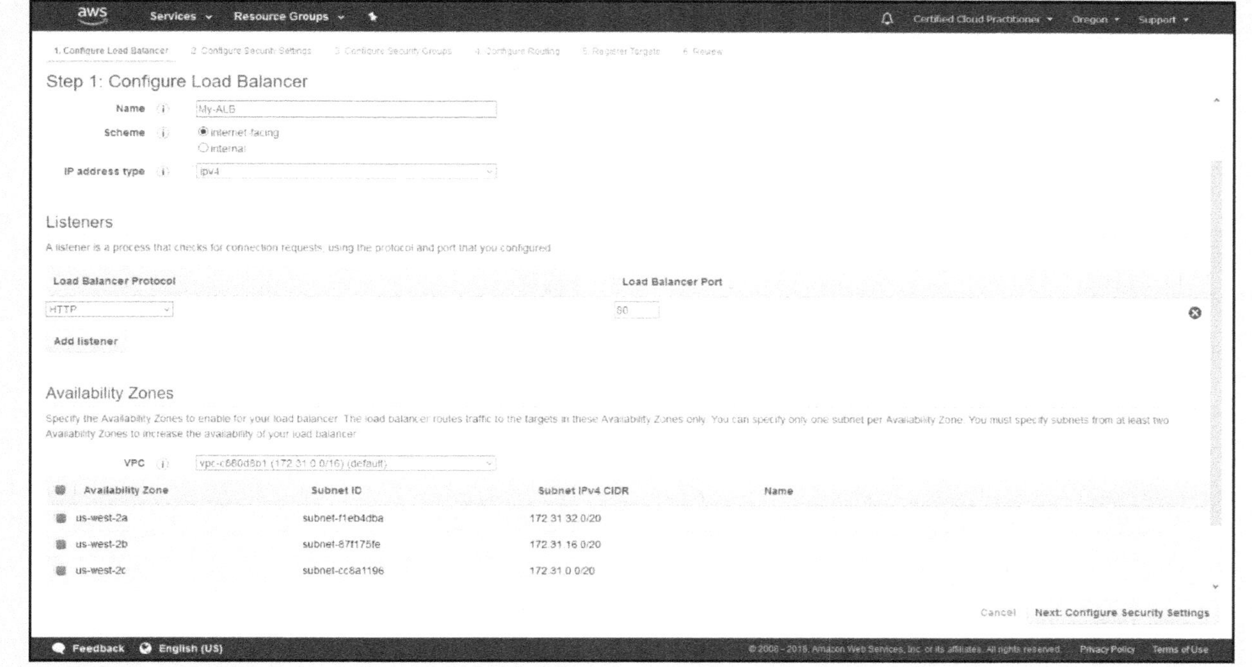

8. This notification prompt is advising the user to use HTTPS. For now, we will not be using it, so click "Next: Configure Security Groups".

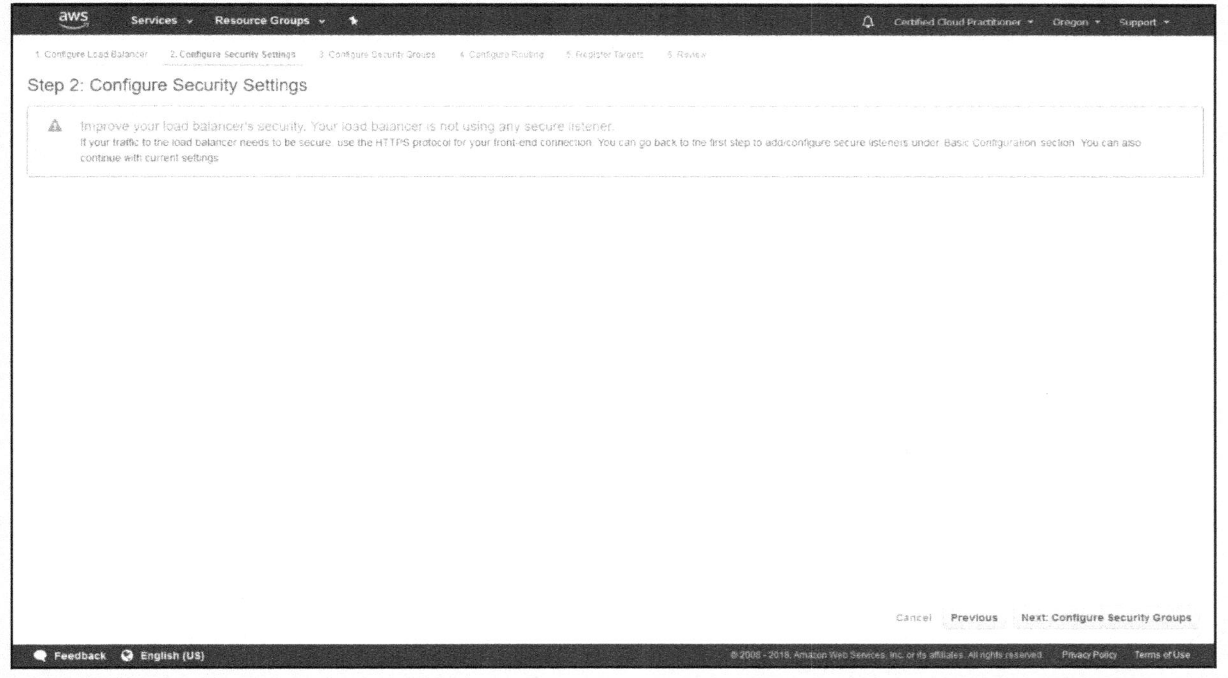

9. Select the security group "My Web Group" that you have already created for your web servers and click "Next: Configure Routing".

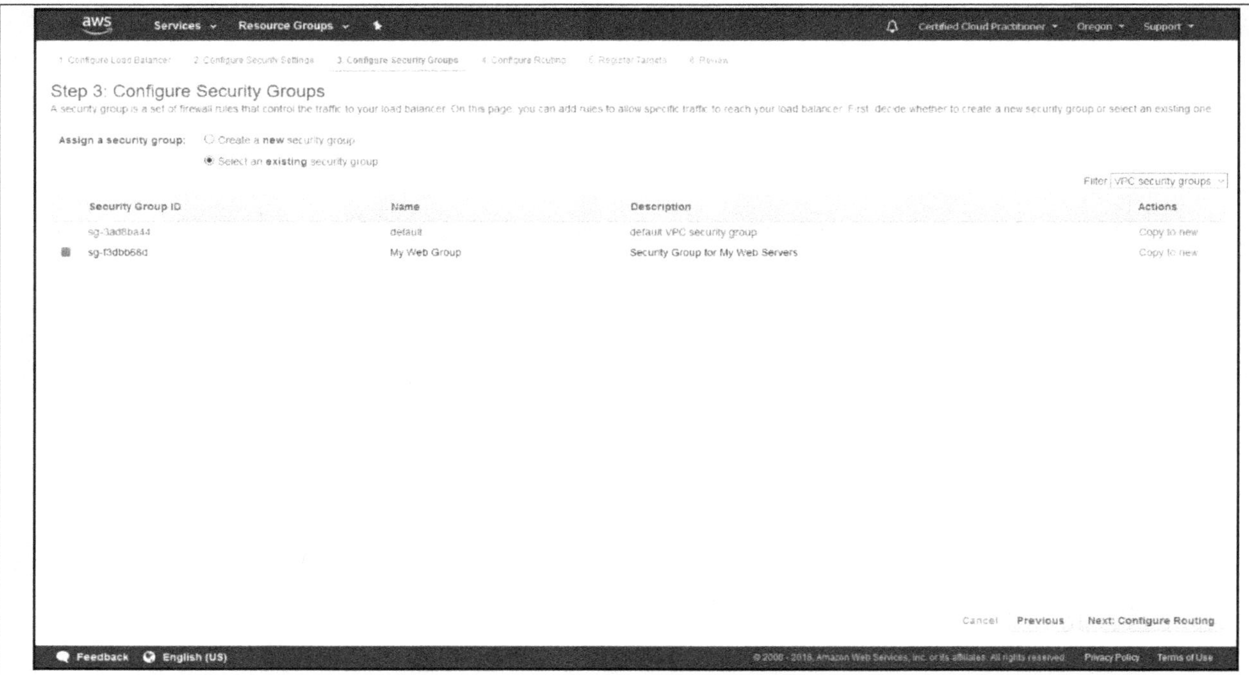

10. Here, you will create a new target group for the load balancer. Enter a name for the target group. Select “HTTP port 80” and “instance” as the target type. For now, you do not need to define any specific path for health checks such as index.html or error.html. Keep it as the default directory. Click “Next: Register Targets”.

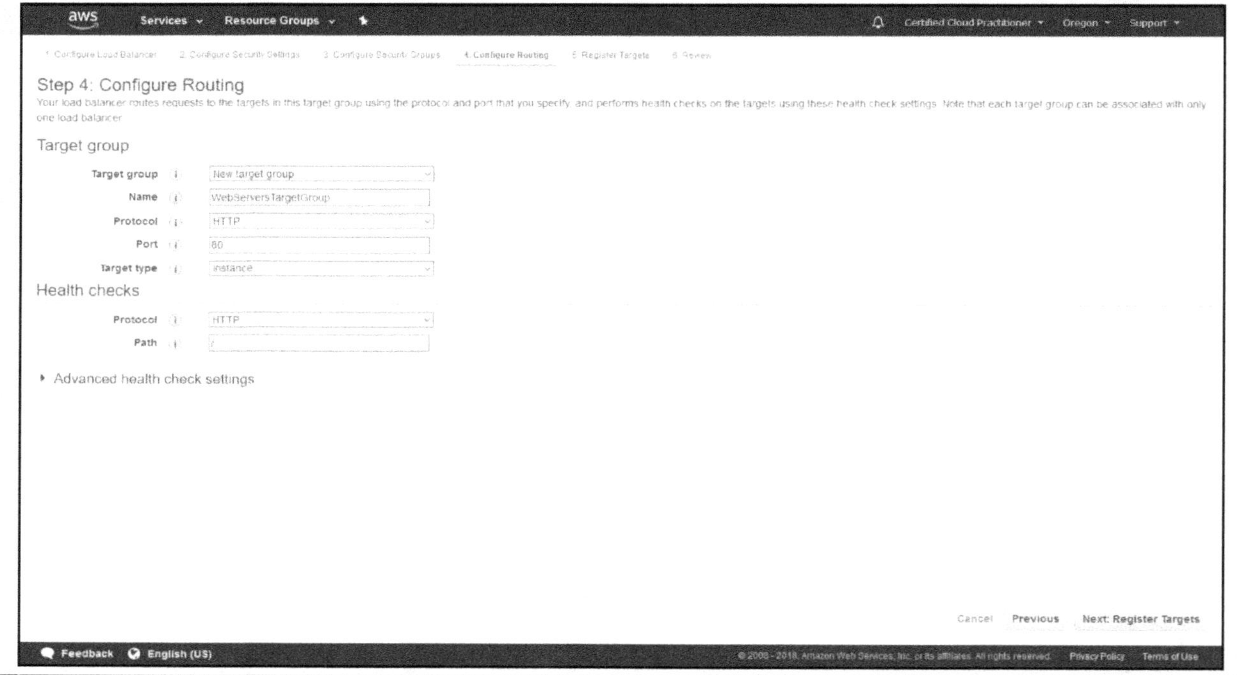

11. Select your EC2 instance and click "Add to registered". This will add the instance to the registered targets list at the top of the screen. Click "Next: Review".

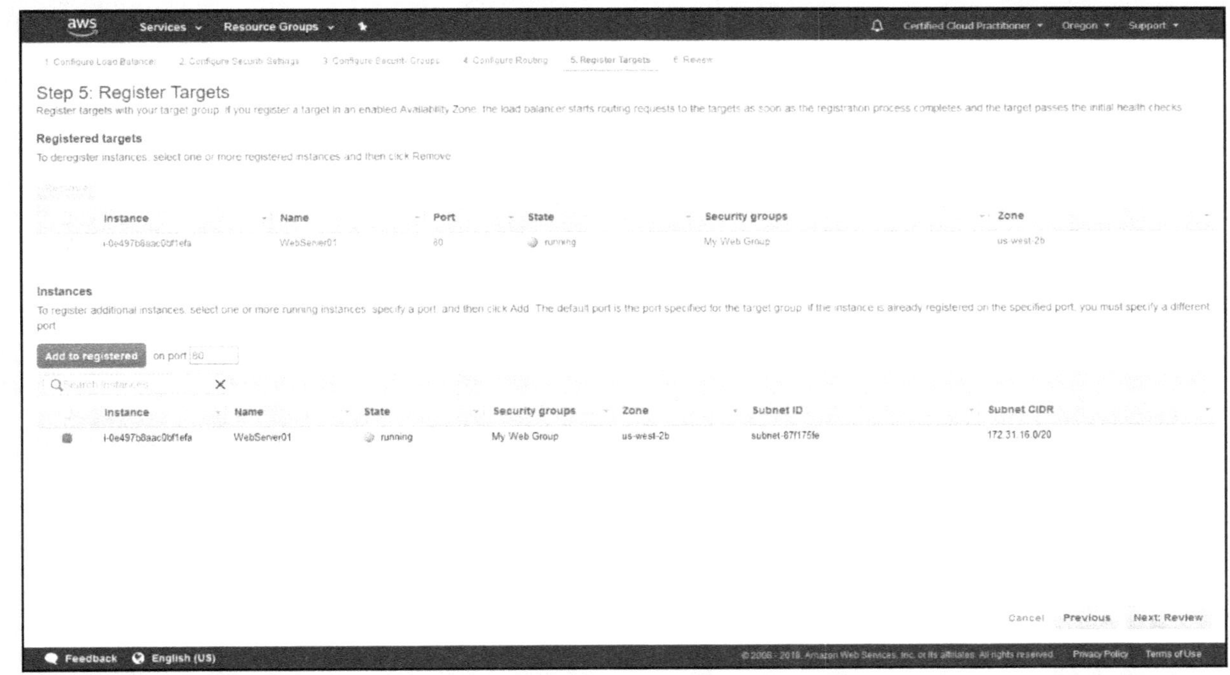

12. Review the details and click "Create".

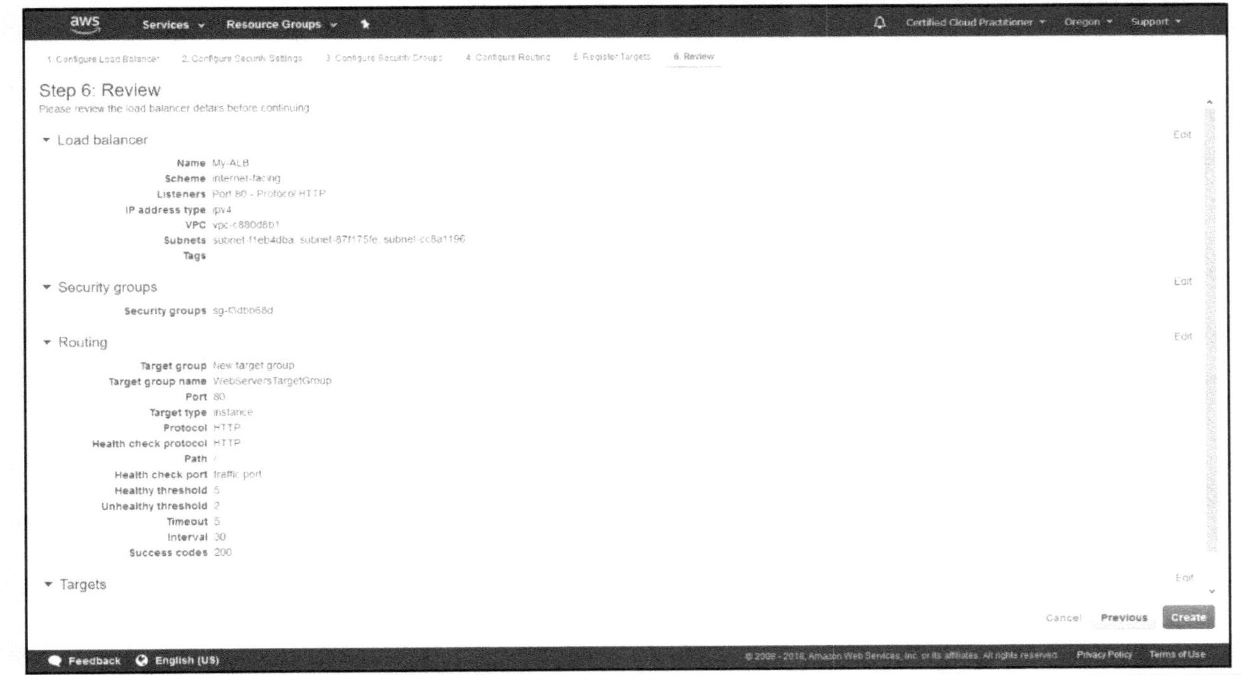

13. Click "Close" to return to the load balancer's main page.

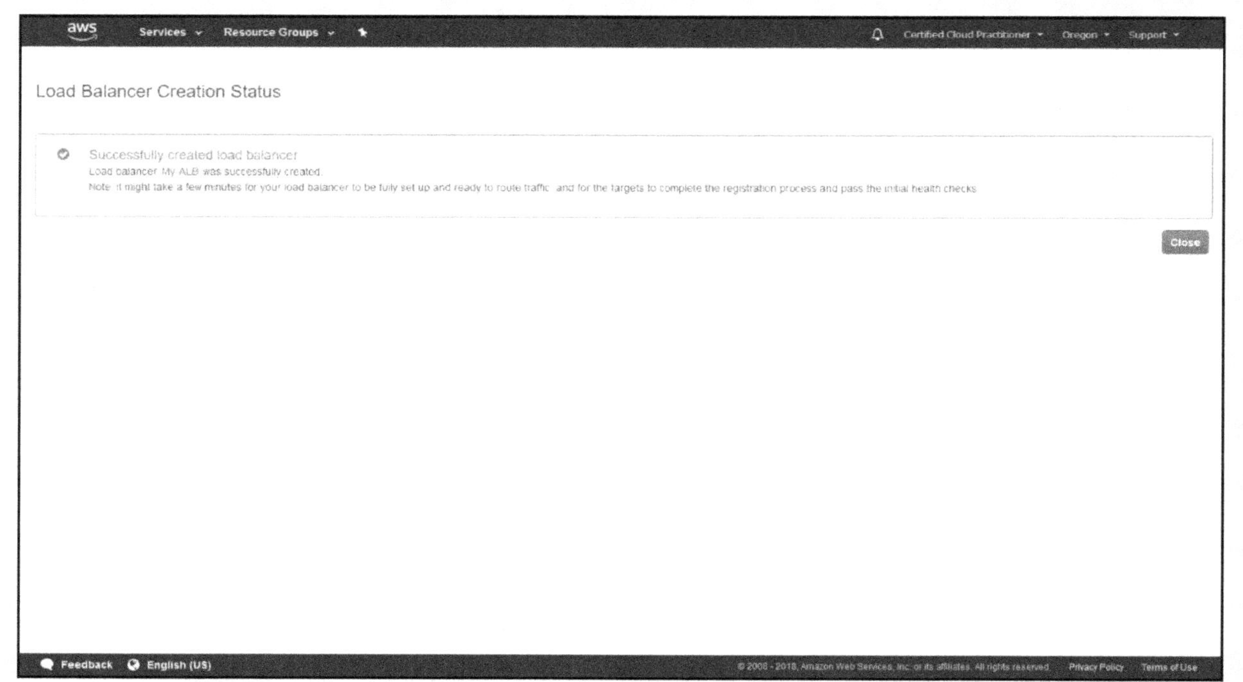

14. The load balancer is now active. Create another webserver to add behind this load balancer. Go to EC2 to launch another instance, following the same steps you used previously.

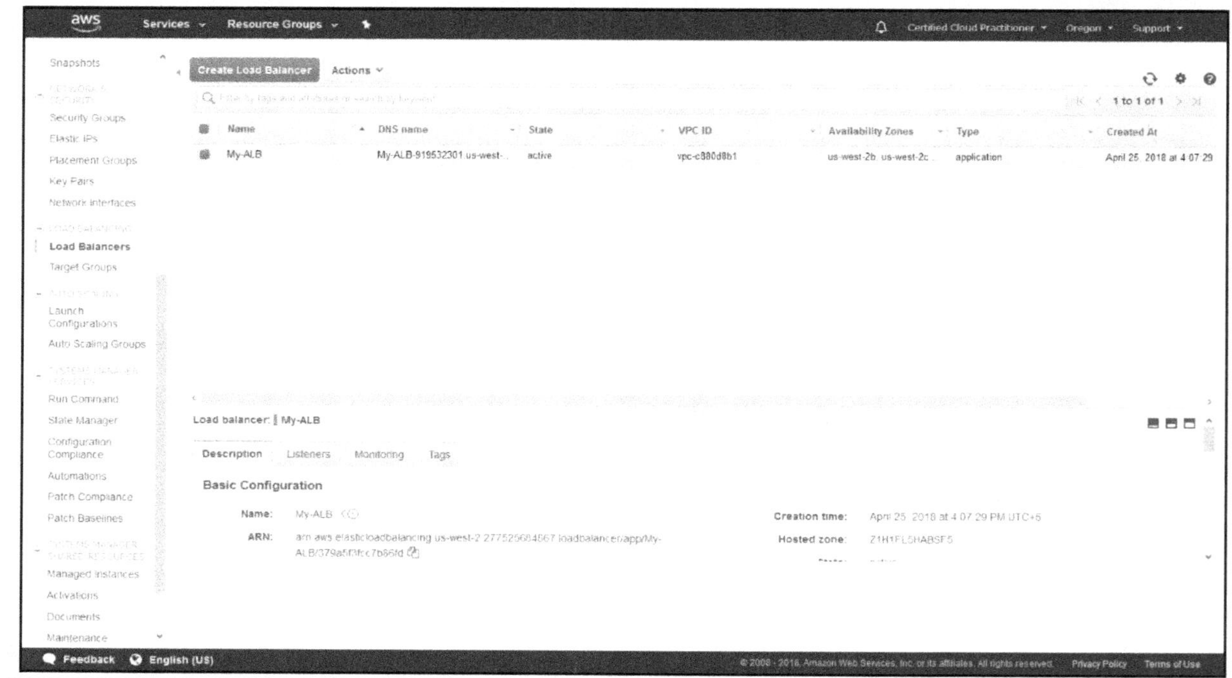

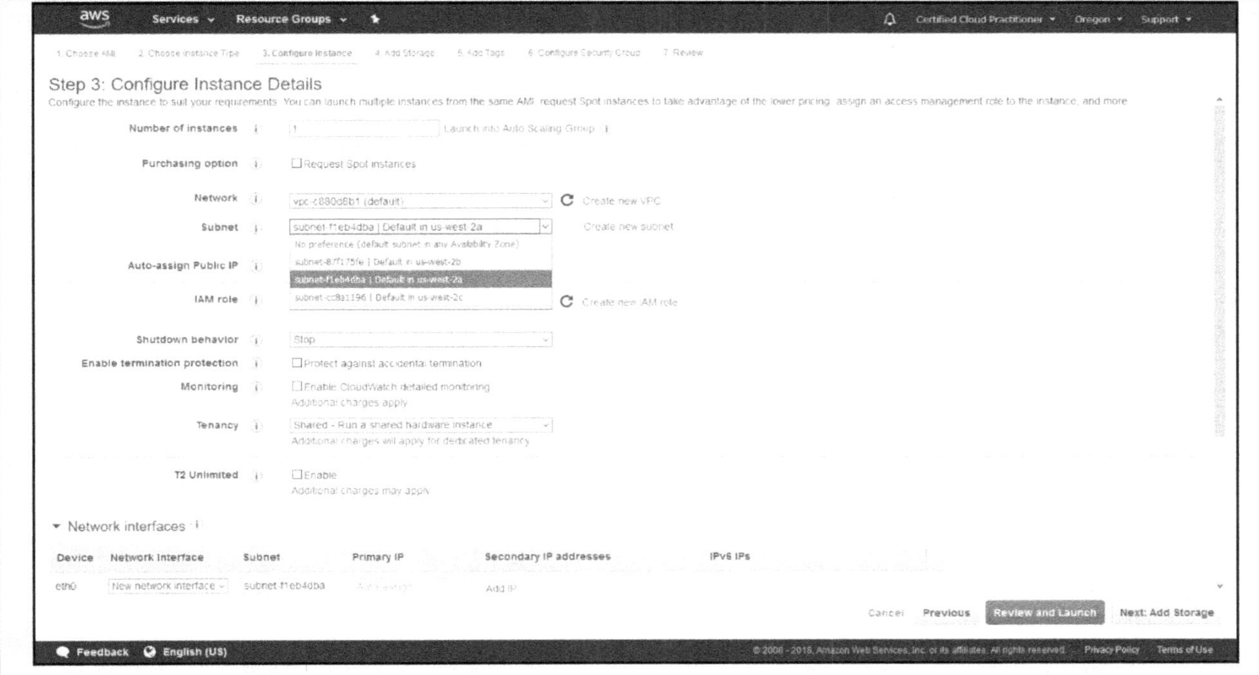

15. When you reach the "Configuring Instance Details" screen, make sure you select a different availability zone for this instance. Your previous EC2 instance is in the availability zone 'us-west-2b'. Therefore, select "us-west-2a" for this instance. Scroll down to "Advanced Details" section.
16. In this section, you can pass user data to the instances and configure commands that you want to run when this instance is booting up. Click "Next: Add Storage" after adding the following code:

- #!/bin/bash
- yum update -y
- yum install httpd -y
- service httpd start
- chkconfighttpd on
- echo "Welcome to IPSpecialist" >> /var/www/html/index.html

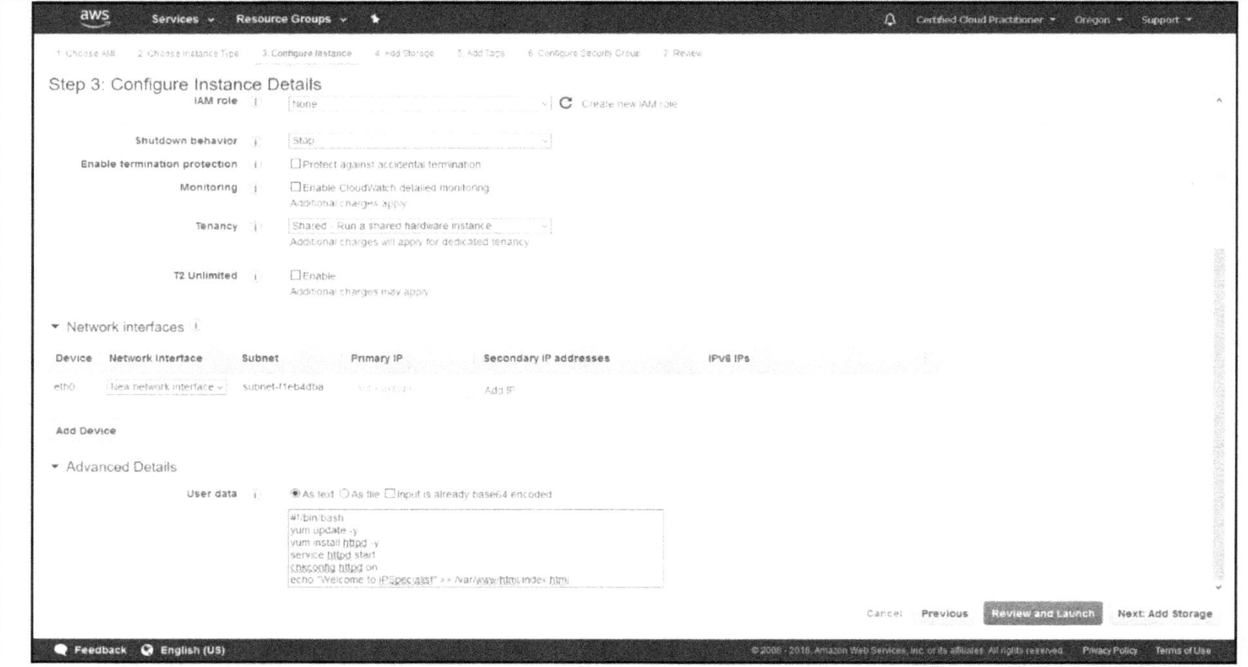

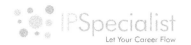

17. Leave this section as it is and click "Next: Add Tags".

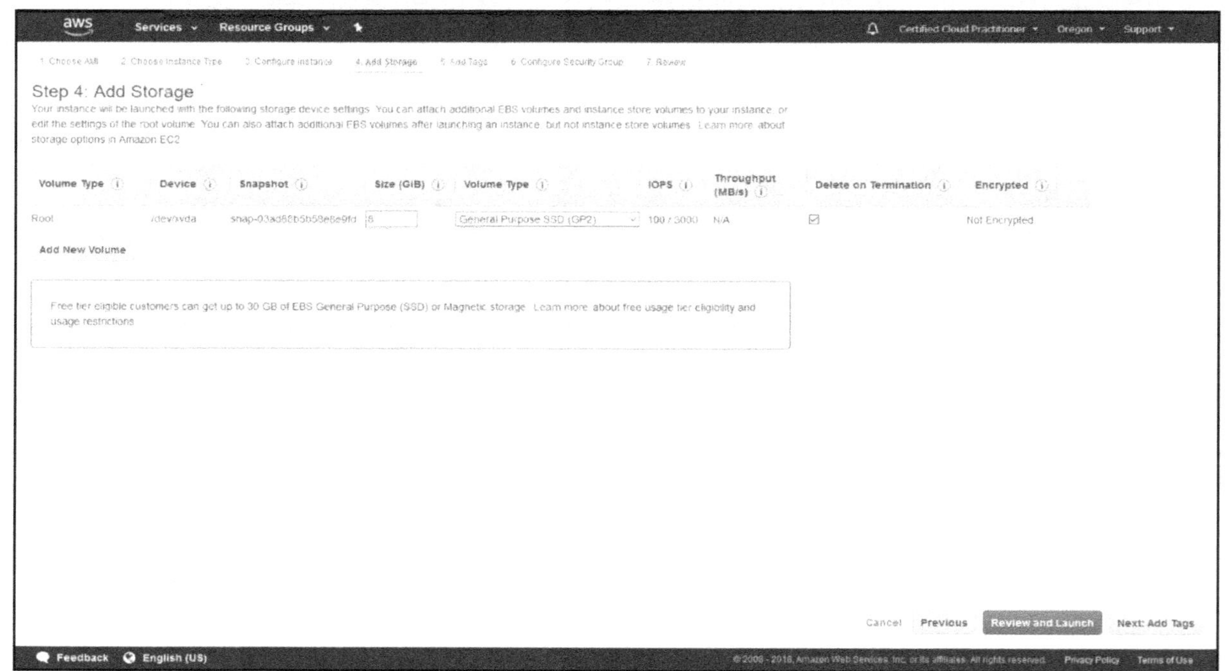

18. Add tags as you did before and click "Next: Configure Security Group".

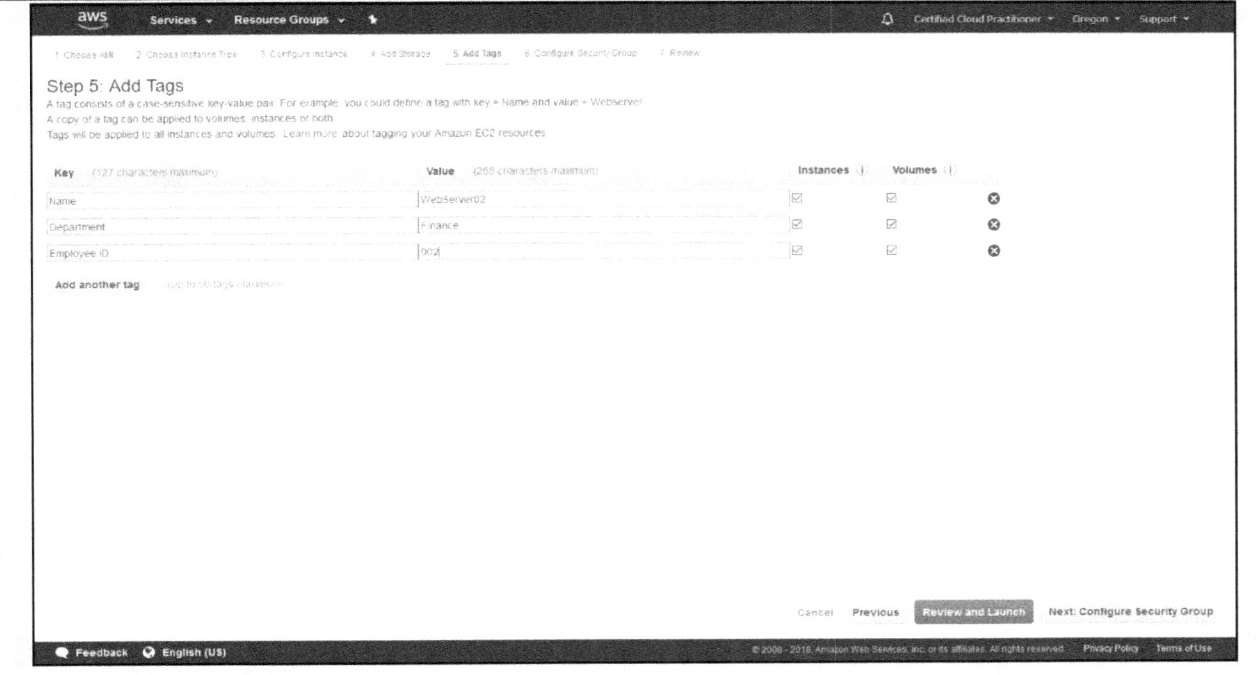

19. Here you will select the existing security group, "My Web Group", that you have already made. Click "Review and Launch".

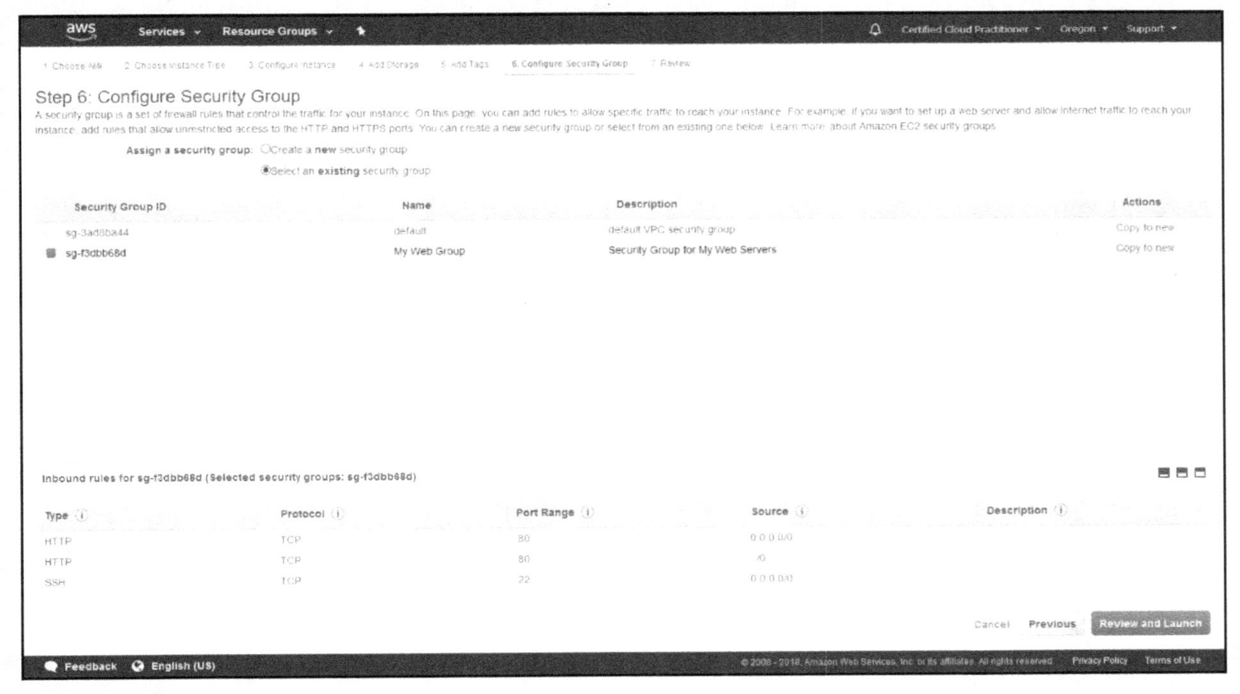

20. Select the existing key pair and click "Launch Instance".

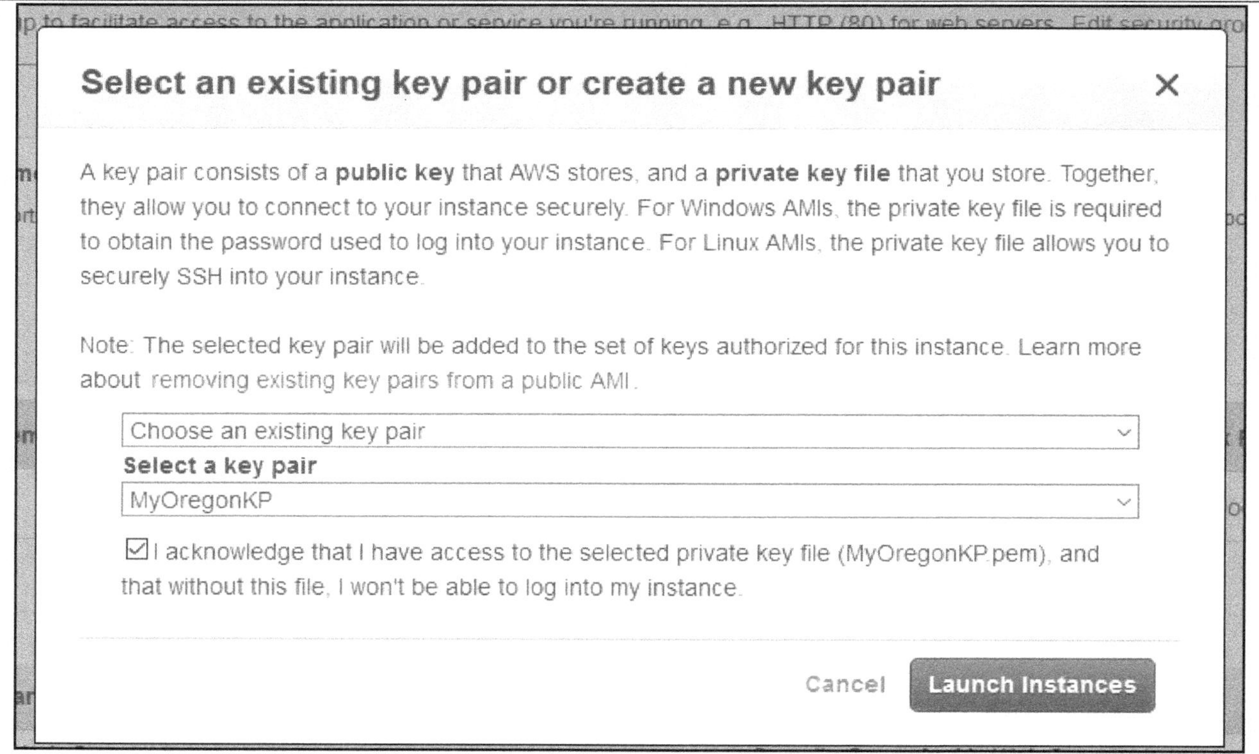

21. You can now see that both instances are up and running in different availability zones. You have already added one instance to the load balancer; you now also need to add the new instance to the load balancer's target group. Select "Target Groups" from under the "Load Balancing" tab.

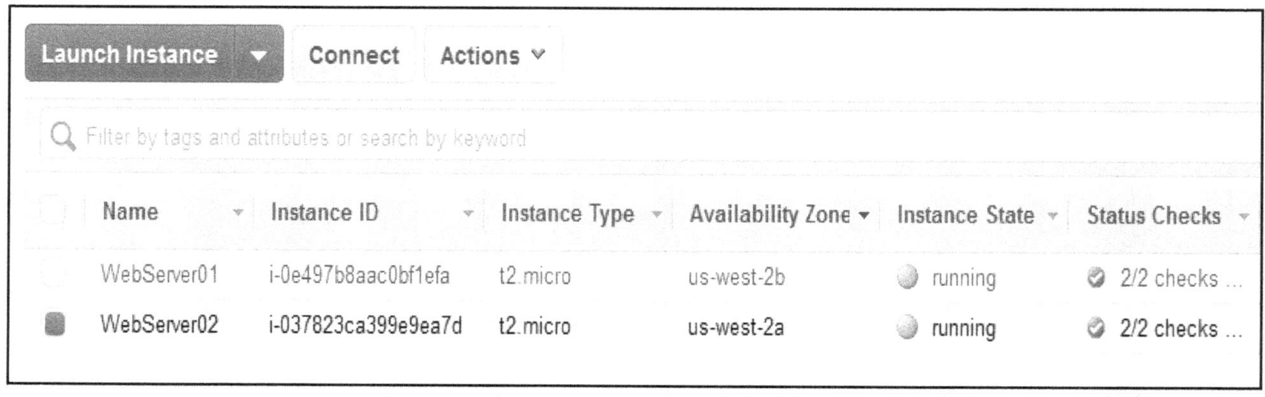

22. Select the "Targets" tab from the list of tabs and click "Edit" to edit the target group.

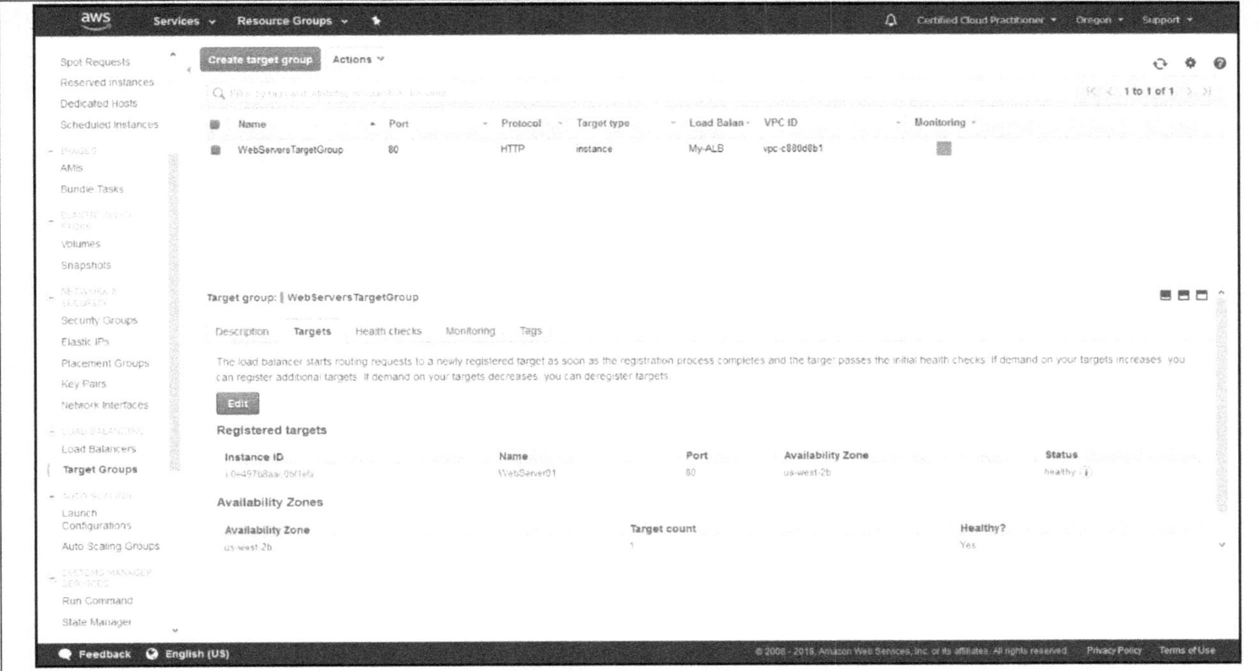

23. Select the instance that needs to be added and click "Add to registered" to register the instance in the registered targets list. Click "Save".

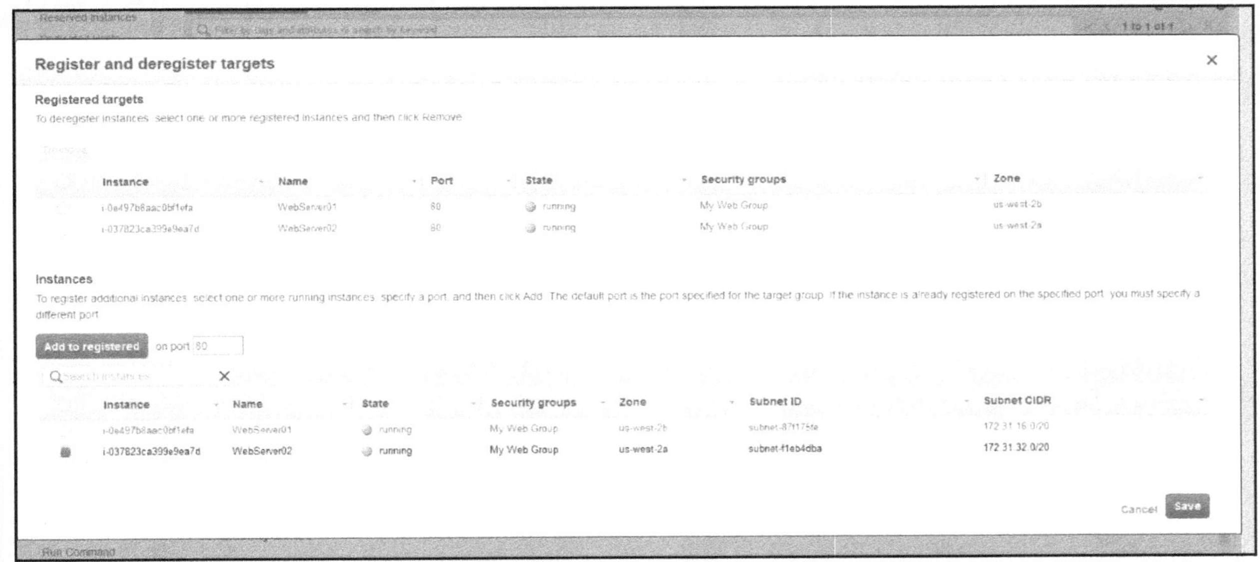

24. Now, both webservers are behind your load balancer. Click "Load Balancers" from under the "Load Balancing" tab.

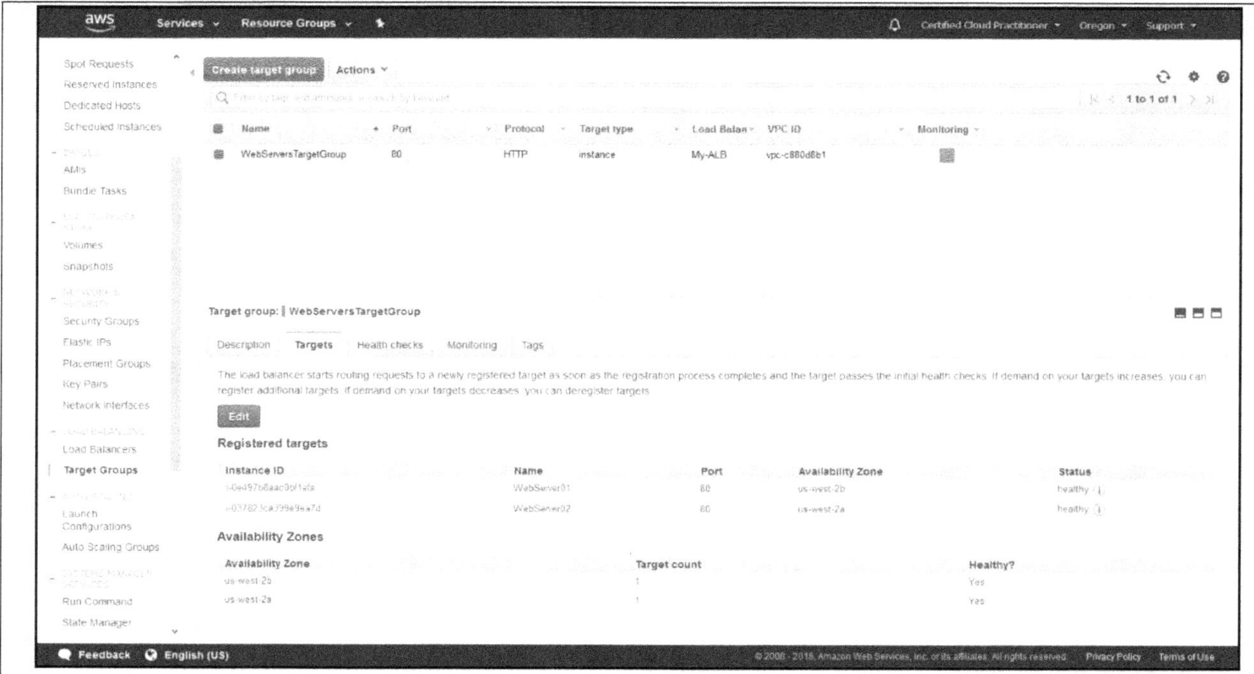

25. Copy the DNS name and open it in your browser.

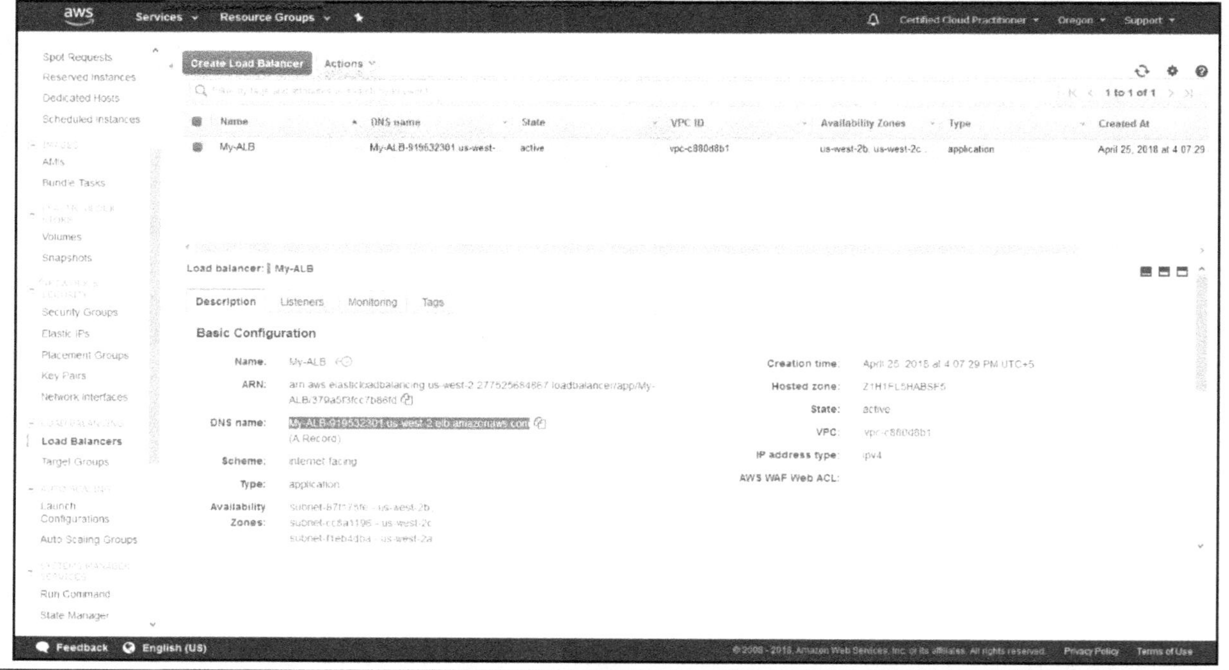

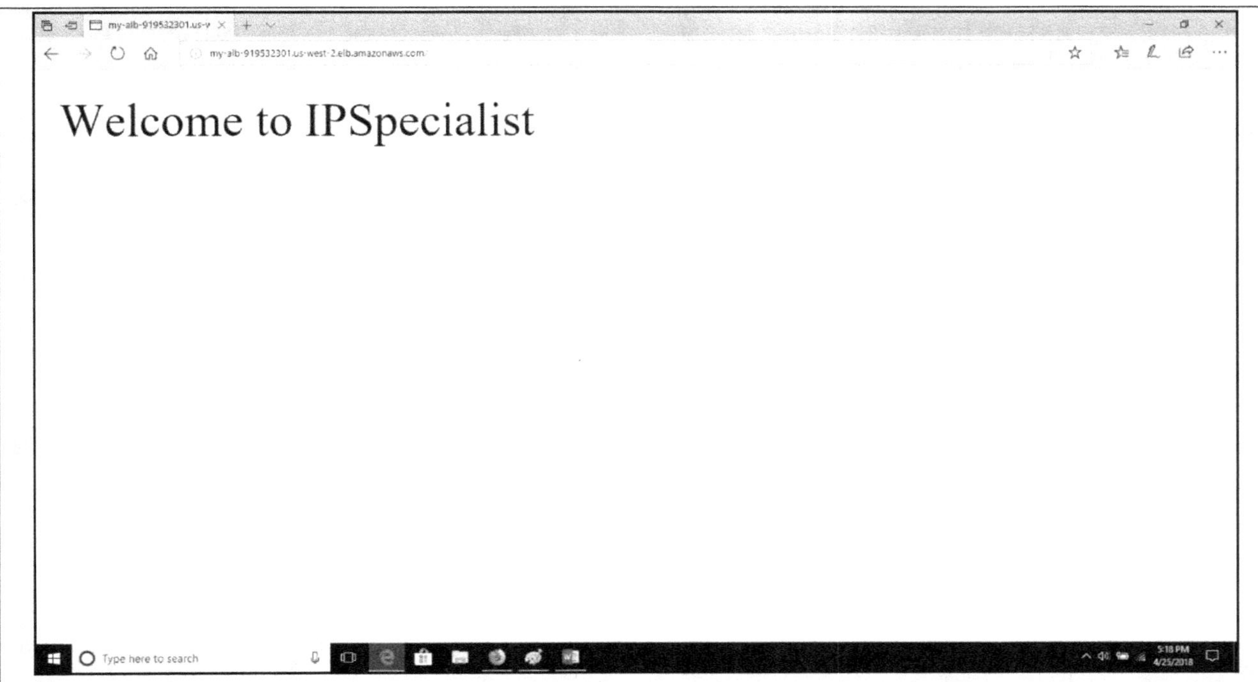

26. For now, this DNS name leads to the new webserver we just created. If you terminate this instance and then use the same DNS name, the load balancer will detect that one of the webservers is down and will redirect traffic to the other webserver. Go back to the EC2 instances and stop one instance.

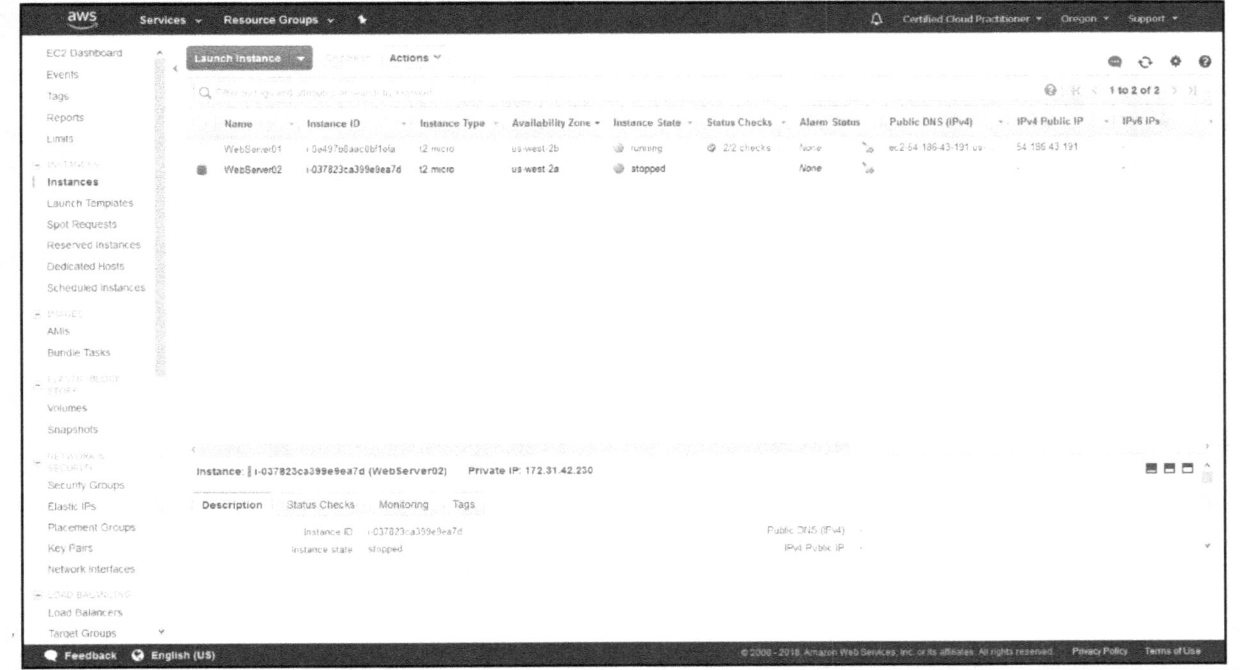

27. Here, we have stopped the new instance we created. Go back to the browser and use the same DNS name.

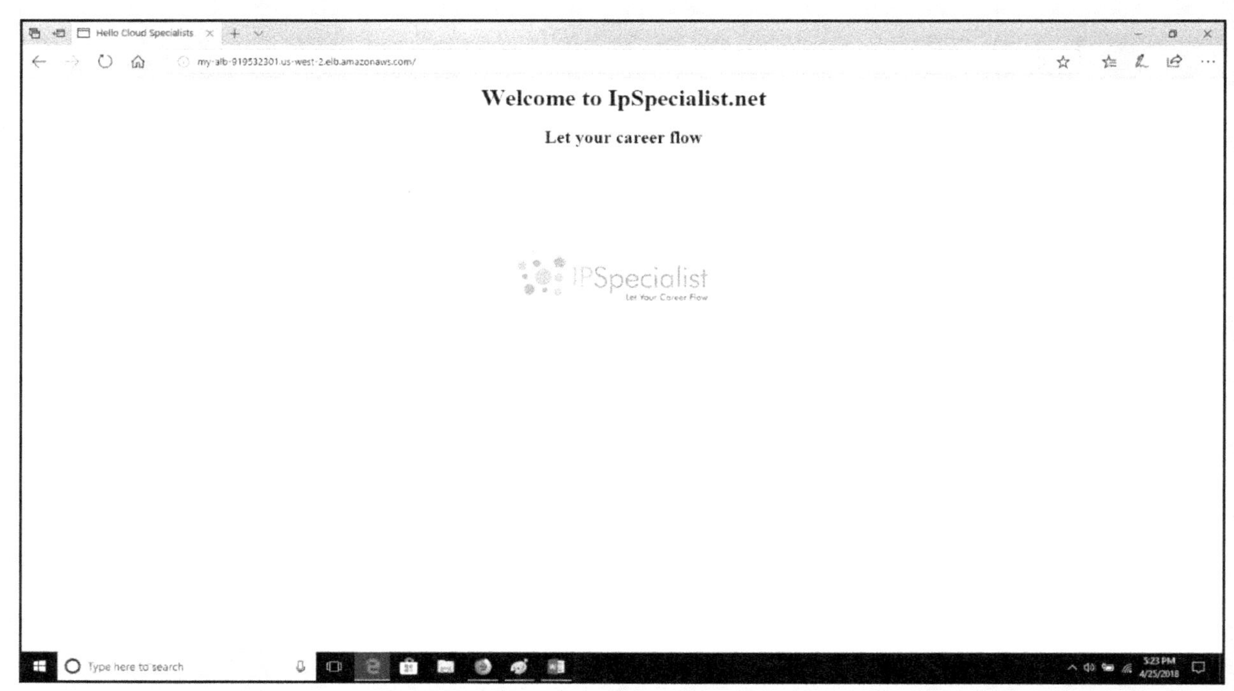

28. This time it leads to the other webserver, as the load balancer detects that one of them is down and redirects to the active webserver.

Amazon Route 53

Amazon Route 53 provides a highly available and scalable cloud DNS web service that effectively connects user requests to infrastructure running in AWS, such as EC2 instances, Elastic Load Balancers or Amazon S3 buckets. It can also be used to route users to infrastructure outside of AWS. DNS (Domain Name System) is a globally distributed service that translates human-readable domain names like www.example.com to numeric machine-readable IP addresses like 192.0.2.1 used by computers to connect to each other.

Amazon Route 53 traffic flow makes it easy for users to manage traffic globally through a variety of routing types, including latency-based routing, Geo DNS and weighted round robin, all of which can be combined with DNS Failover to enable a variety of low-latency and fault-tolerant architectures.

You can use Amazon Route 53 to register new domains, transfer existing domains, route traffic for your domains to your AWS and external resources and monitor the health of your resources.

- **DNS Management:**

  If you already have a domain name, such as example.com, Route 53 can tell the Domain Name System (DNS) where on the internet it can find web servers, mail servers and other resources for your domain.

- **Traffic Management:**

  Route 53 traffic flow provides a visual tool that you can use to create and update sophisticated routing policies in order to route end users to multiple endpoints for your application, whether they are in a single AWS Region or distributed around the globe.

- **Availability Monitoring:**

  Route 53 can monitor the health and performance of your application as well as that of your web servers and other resources. Route 53 can also redirect traffic to healthy resources and independently monitor the health of your application and its endpoints.

- **Domain Registration:**

  If you need a domain name, you can find an available name and register it using Route 53. Amazon Route 53 will automatically configure DNS settings for your domains. You can also make Route 53 the registrar for existing domains that you have registered with other registrars.

EXAM TIP: Route 53 is Amazon's DNS service. If you own a domain name and want to host a website on it using Amazon S3, you need to have the exact same bucket name as the domain name for it to work.

Resource Groups and Tagging

Resource Groups

Resource Groups allow you to easily create, maintain and view a collection of resources that share one or more common tags or portions of tags. You can use resource groups to organize your AWS resources by marking resources from multiple services and regions

with a common tag. You can then view those resources together in a customizable pane of the AWS Management Console.

To create a resource group, you can simply identify the tags that contain the items that members of the group should have in common. Resource groups can display metrics, alarms and configuration details, making it easier to manage and automate tasks on large numbers of resources at one time. Examples of these bulk actions include:

- Applying updates or security patches
- Upgrading applications
- Opening or closing ports to network traffic
- Collecting specific logs and monitoring data from your fleet of instances

Lab 3-12: Creating Resource Groups

1. Log in to the "AWS Console".
2. Click on "Resource Groups".

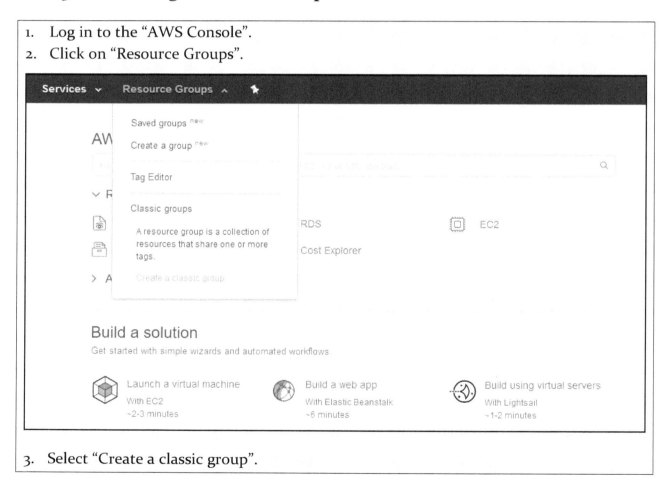

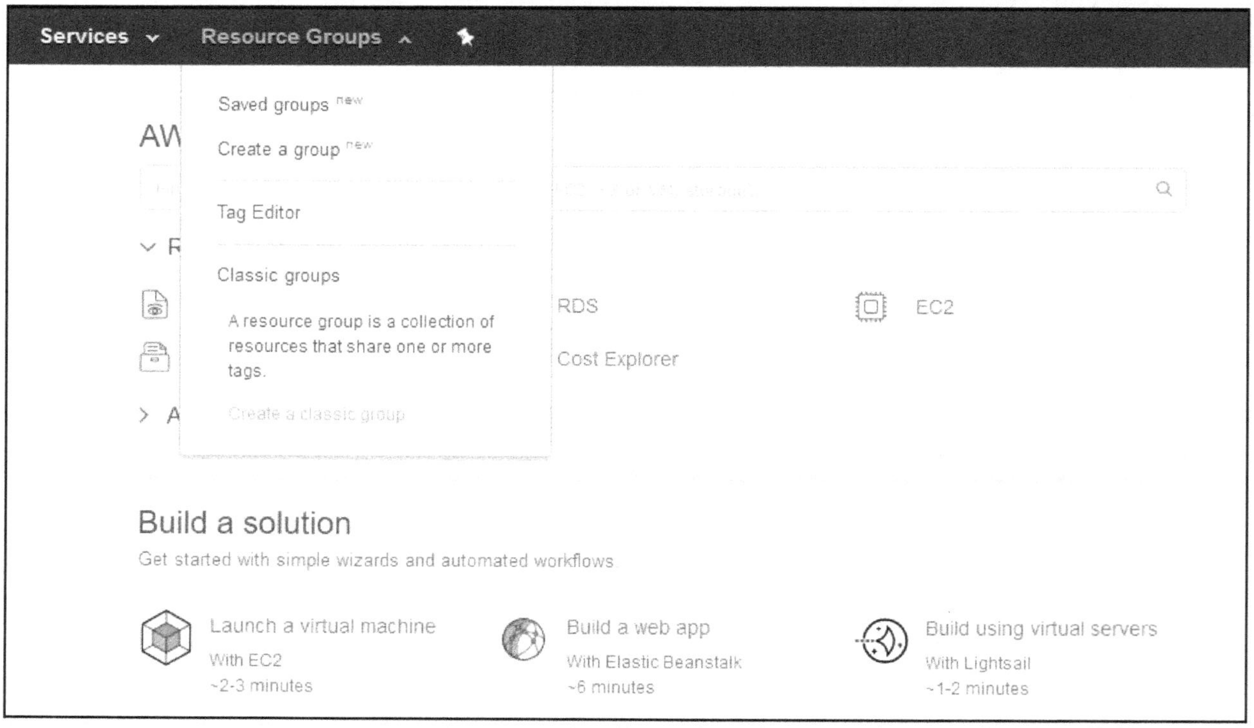

3. Select "Create a classic group".

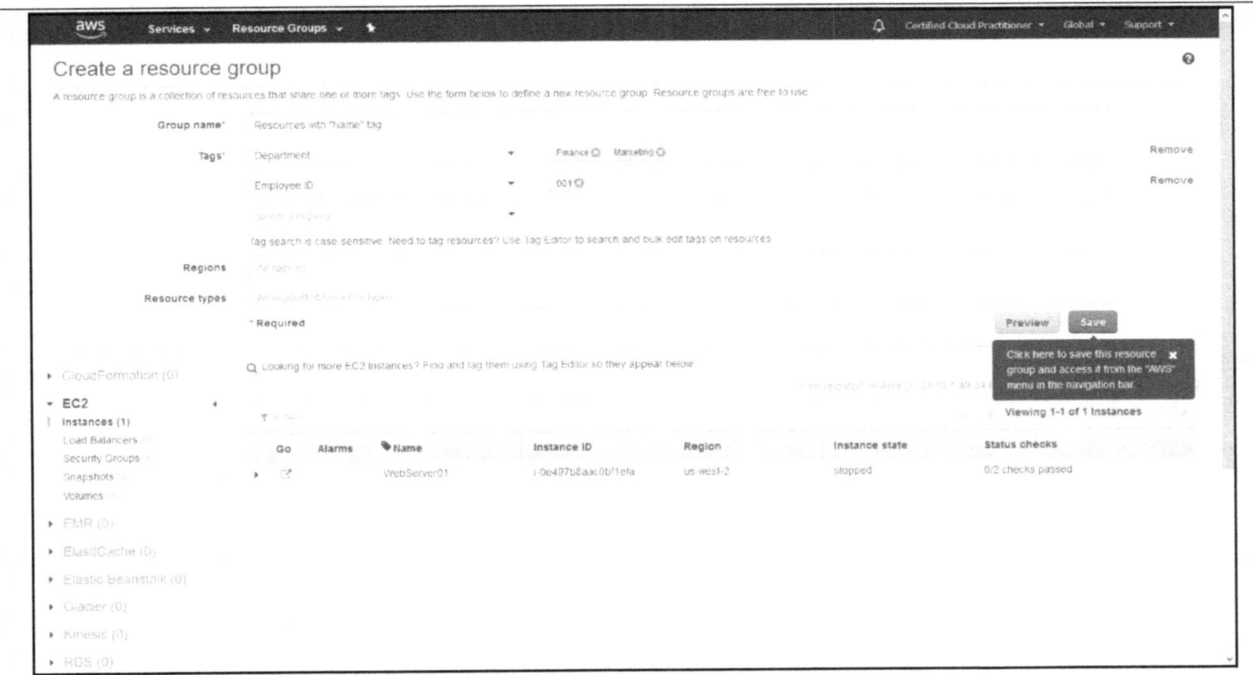

4. Here, we will make a resource group using the tags we created while provisioning resources. Enter a resource group name and the tags you want to include in this group. For example, we have selected the "Department" tag with the values 'Finance' and 'Marketing' and also another tag of 'Employee ID' with only the value '001'. Click "Preview" to view the resources that fall into the above criteria, then click "Save".

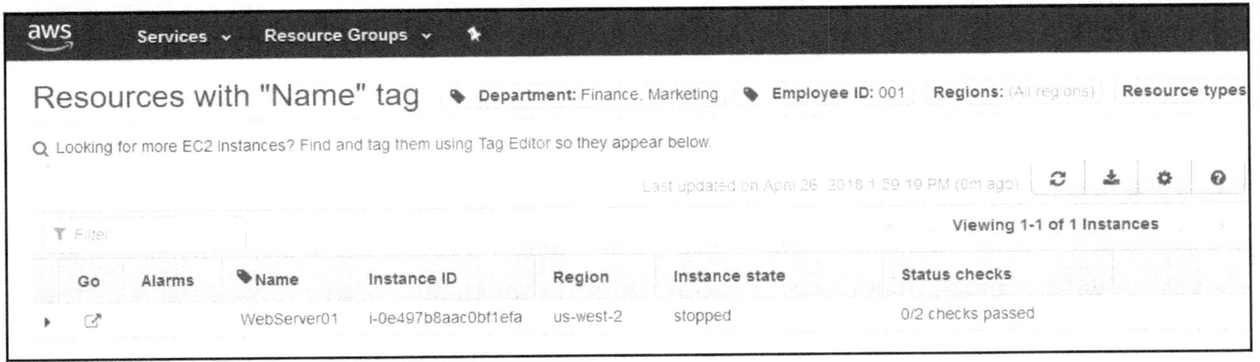

5. Your Resource Group has been created displaying all the resources with the tags and values you requested.

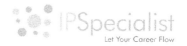

Tags

Tags are words or phrases that act as metadata for identifying and organizing your AWS resources. Each tag is a label that you assign to an AWS resource, consisting of a key and a value, both of which you define. The tag limit varies with the resource, but most can have up to 50 tags.

With most AWS resources, you have the option of adding tags when you create the resource, whether it is an Amazon EC2 instance, an Amazon S3 bucket or another resource. You can also add, change or remove these tags one resource at a time within the console of each resource. Adding tags to multiple resources at once can be done by using Tag Editor.

Tags can sometimes be inherited. When we use services such as Auto-scaling, CloudFormation, and Elastic Beanstalk, they can provide other resources with inherited tags. If you delete a resource, any tags for the resource are also deleted. You can edit tag keys and values, and you can remove tags from a resource at any time. With Tag Editor, you can search for the resources that you want to tag, then add, remove or edit tags for the resources shown in your search results. Tag Editor provides a central and unified way to easily create and manage user-defined tags across services and regions.

The tags function like properties of a resource, so they are shared across the entire account. It enables you to categorize your AWS resources in different ways, for example, by purpose, owner or environment. This is useful when you have many resources of the same type; you can quickly identify a specific resource based on the tags you have assigned to it. Tagging can help you to organize your resources and enables you to simplify resource and access management and cost allocation.

Assigning tags to resources allows for higher levels of automation and greater ease of management. You can execute management tasks at scale by listing resources with specific tags, then executing the appropriate actions. For example, you can list all resources with a particular tag and value, then either delete or terminate each of them. This is useful to automate the shutdown or removal of a set of resources at the end of the working day. Creating and implementing an AWS tagging standard across the accounts of your organization will enable you to manage and govern your AWS environments in a consistent manner.

Lab 3-13: Using Tag Editor

1. Log in to the "AWS Console" and click on "Resource Groups".

2. Select "Tag Editor".

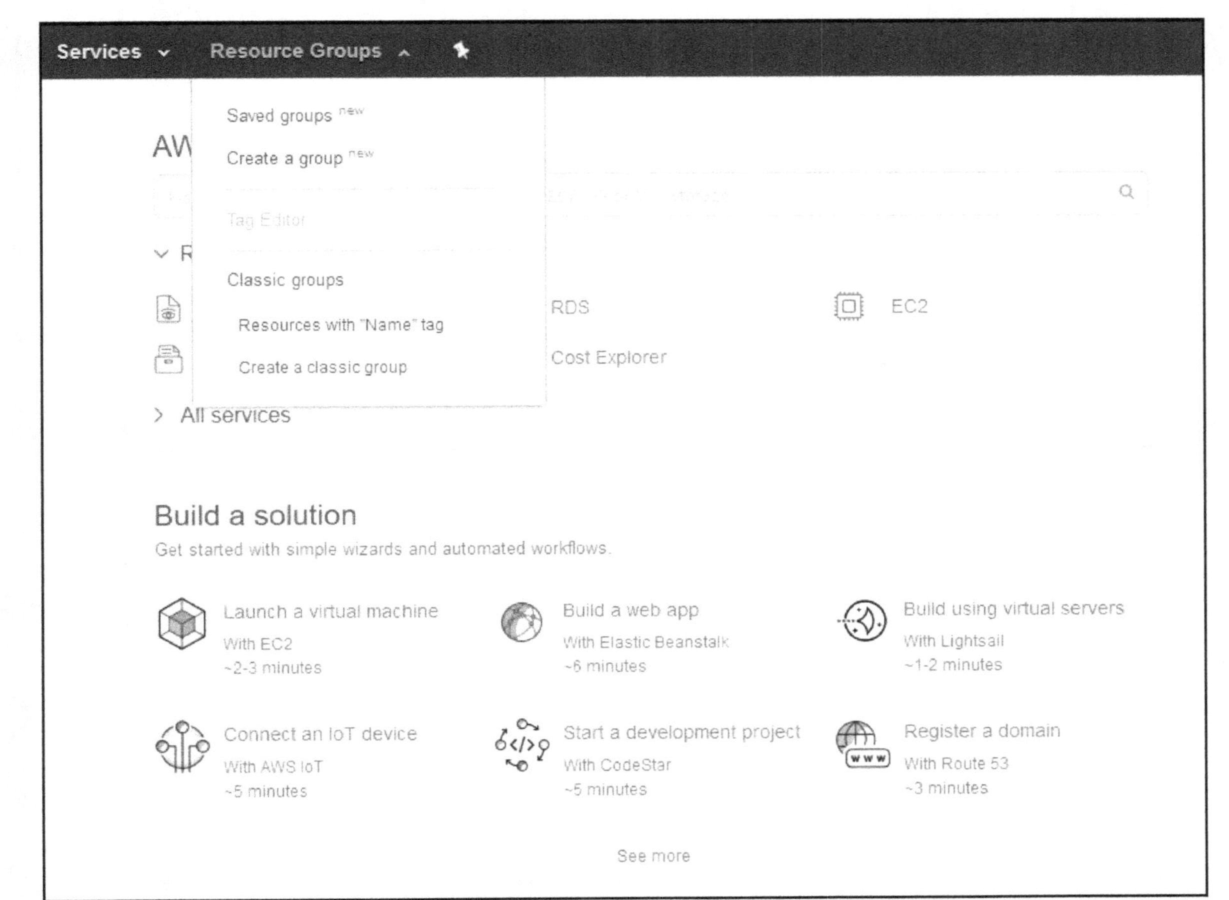

3. You can use the tag editor to find resources easily by the tags created at the time of provisioning resources. The editor allows you to add, edit and delete tags. Click "Create a new tag key" to add a new tag field.

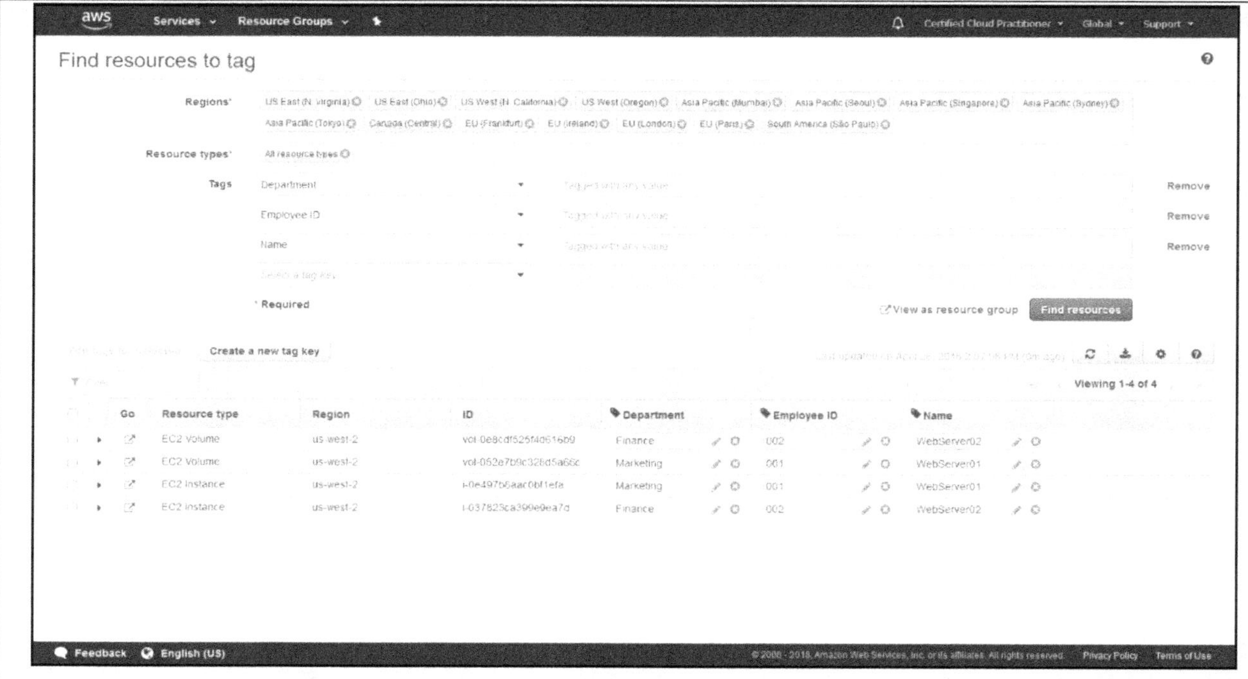

4. Enter a new key name and click "Add key".

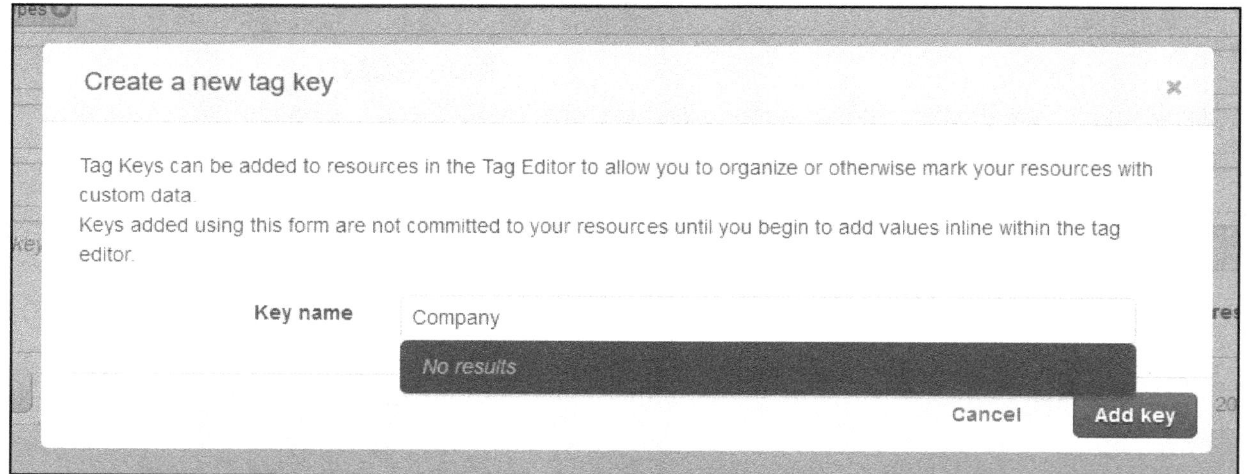

5. The new tag "Company" has been added. You can click on the "+" button to add values to the tag.

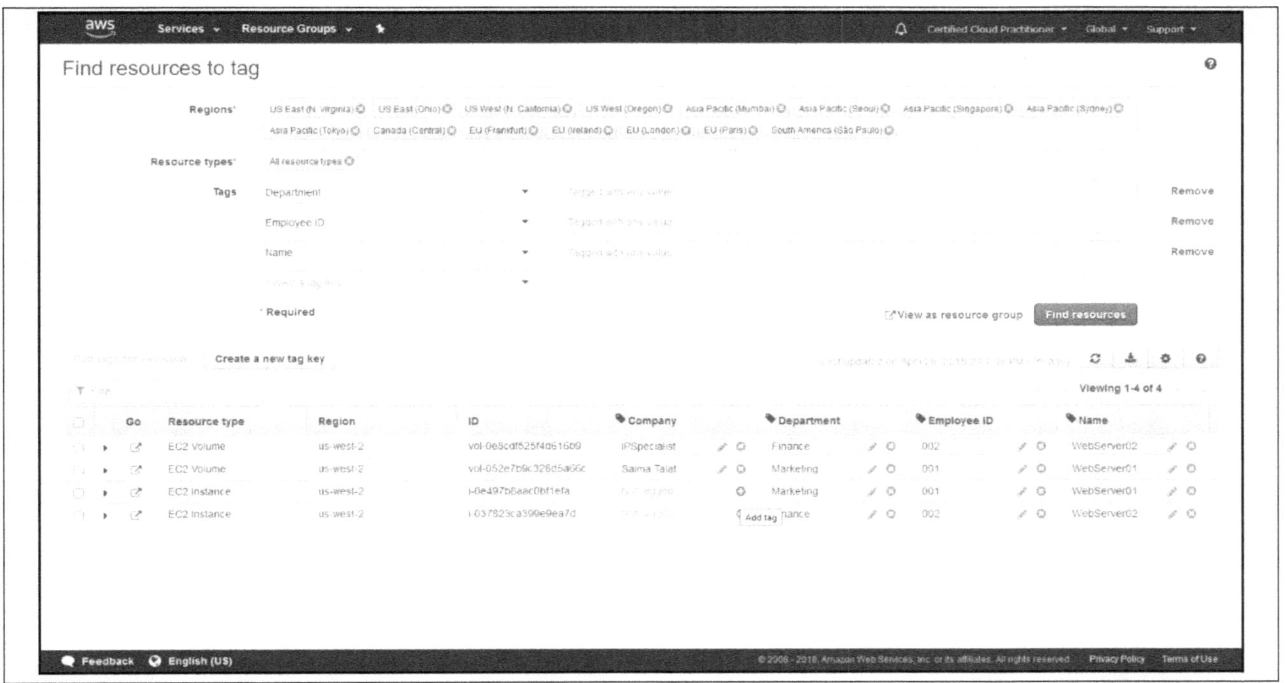

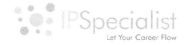

Chapter 4: Billing and Pricing

Introduction

AWS runs with a pay-as-you-go pricing approach for over 70 cloud services. While the number and types of services offered by AWS have increased dramatically, the philosophy of pricing has not changed. At the end of each month, you only pay for what you used in the previous billing period, and you can start or stop using a product at any time. No long-term contracts are required.

AWS is based on the strategy of pricing each service independently to provide customers with remarkable flexibility. This allows them to choose exactly which services they need for their project and to pay only for what they use. AWS pricing is comparable to how you pay for utilities like water or electricity. You only pay for the services consumed with no additional costs or termination fees once you stop using them.

AWS Pricing Policy

Amazon Web Services (AWS) provides a variety of cloud computing services with a utility-style pricing model. For every service, you pay for exactly the amount of resources needed. The following pricing policies apply across AWS for all of the different services it offers:

- **Pay as you go**

  With AWS, you replace upfront capital investment with low variable cost and pay only for what you use. Charges are based on the underlying infrastructure and services consumed, allowing you to adapt to changing business needs without paying upfront for excess capacity. This improves your responsiveness to changes. No minimum commitments or long-term contracts are required with no complex licensing dependencies. For compute resources, you pay on an hourly basis from the time you launch a resource until the time you terminate it. For data storage and transfer, you pay on a per gigabyte basis.

- **Pay less when you reserve**

You can access volume-based discounts for certain products by investing in reserved capacity. This results in overall savings up to 60% over equivalent On-demand capacity, depending on the type of instance you reserve and whether you do upfront or partial payments. To optimize savings, choose the right combinations of storage solutions to help reduce costs while preserving performance, security and durability. As a result, you will benefit from the economies of scale and keeping costs under control.

- **Pay even less per unit by using more**

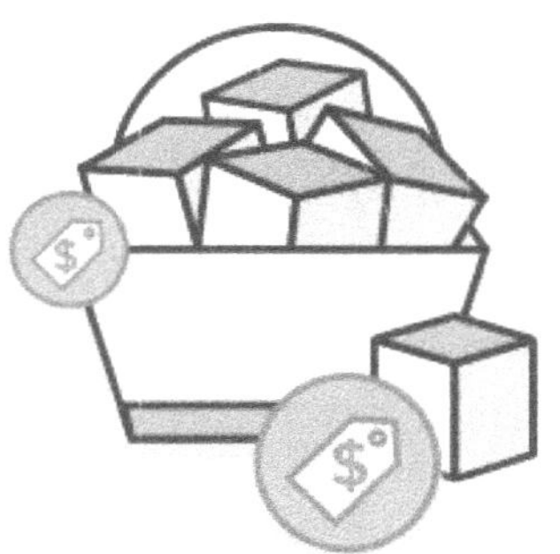

Save more as you grow bigger. While data transfer IN is always free of charge, there is a tiered pricing system for storage and data transfer OUT, meaning that the more you use, the less you pay per gigabyte. For compute, you get up to 10% volume discount if you reserve more. If you buy Reserved Instances, the larger the upfront payment, the greater the discount. Paying everything up-front will maximize discounts. Partial up-front RI's offer lower discounts, but you will also have to spend less up front. Although choosing to spend nothing up front gives you a smaller discount, it does free up capital to spend on other projects.

- **Pay even less as AWS grows**

AWS concentrates on decreasing data center hardware expenses, improving operational efficiencies, reducing power consumption, and generally lowering the cost of doing business. These optimizations and AWS's extensive and increasing economies of scale result in the transfer of savings back to the customer in the form of lower price. AWS has reduced pricing 44 times since 2006.

- **Custom pricing**
  If none of the pricing models suits your needs, AWS also offers custom pricing for high volume projects with more distinctive requirements. If you are using AWS in an enterprise environment, you can also acquire custom pricing.

EXAM TIP: Follow the pricing policy of AWS if you are faced with any scenario-based question; i.e., you only pay for what you use at the end of each month with no long-term contracts and you can start or stop using a product anytime. However, if you do enter into a long-term contract and pay for everything upfront, you will access the maximum amount of savings.

AWS Free Tier

AWS offers a free usage tier to enable new AWS customers to get familiarized with the cloud. A Free Tier account offers the benefit of getting free, hands-on experience with the AWS platform, products and services. Some of the AWS services are free only for the first 12 months while some remain free forever. For example, a new AWS customer can run a free Amazon EC2 Micro Instance for a year while also accessing the free usage tier for Amazon S3, Amazon Elastic Block Store, Amazon Elastic Load Balancing, AWS data transfer and other AWS services.

Free Services

AWS also provides a variety of services that are free with no additional charge:

- ***Amazon VPC***

  Amazon Virtual Private Cloud (Amazon VPC) enables you to provision a private logically isolated section of the AWS Cloud for launching AWS resources in a virtual network that you define.

- ***AWS Elastic Beanstalk***

  AWS Elastic Beanstalk enables you to quickly deploy and manage applications in the AWS cloud. The actual service itself is free; the resources it provisions, like EC2 instances or RDS instances, are not.

- ***AWS CloudFormation***

  The AWS CloudFormation service can be used by developers and system administrators. It allows you to create a group of related AWS resources and provision them in an arranged and predictable manner. AWS CloudFormation service is free; the resources that it provisions are not.

- ***AWS Identity and Access Management (IAM)***

  AWS IAM securely control user access to AWS services and resources by allowing access to those who are authenticated (signed in) and authorized (has permissions) to use selected resources.

- ***Auto-Scaling***

  Auto-Scaling adds (scales up) or removes (scales down) Amazon Elastic Compute Cloud (EC2) instances automatically, according to your defined conditions. Auto-Scaling seamlessly increases the number of Amazon EC2 instances during demand spikes to maintain performance, and decreases the number automatically when demand subsides to minimize costs.

- ***AWS OpsWorks***

  AWS OpsWorks is an application management service that simplifies the deployment and operation of applications of all forms and sizes.

- ***Consolidated Billing***

  Consolidated Billing can be used to combine all of the billing from your accounts into one single bill to obtain tiering benefits.

EXAM TIP: It is essential to remember all the free services offered by Amazon while preparing for the exam. The services themselves are free, but the resources they provision are not.

Fundamental Pricing Characteristics

When using the AWS Cloud platform, there are three fundamental characteristics you will be charged for:

- Compute
- Storage
- Data Transfer Out

These characteristics vary to some extent depending on the AWS product being used., however these core characteristics have the greatest influence on cost. The outbound data transfer is combined across Amazon EC2, Amazon S3, Amazon RDS, Amazon SimpleDB, Amazon SQS, Amazon SNS and Amazon VPC to be charged at the total outbound data transfer rate. This charge will appear on the monthly statement as AWS Data Transfer Out.

Free Inbound Data Transfer

While Data Transfer Out comes at a price, there is no charge for inbound data transfer across all Amazon Web Services in all regions. Additionally, there are no outbound data transfer charges between Amazon Web Services within the same region.

EXAM TIP: If you get a scenario-based question, think through the fundamental charges: whether it involves compute service, requires storage or if data is being transferred out to the internet. If yes, then you are going to be charged. If it only concerns data transfer in, it will be free.

Amazon Elastic Compute Cloud (Amazon EC2)

Amazon EC2 is a web service that enables you to obtain and configure resizable compute capacity in the cloud. Amazon only charges for the computing capacity you actually use. The following factors need to be considered when estimating the cost of using Amazon EC2:

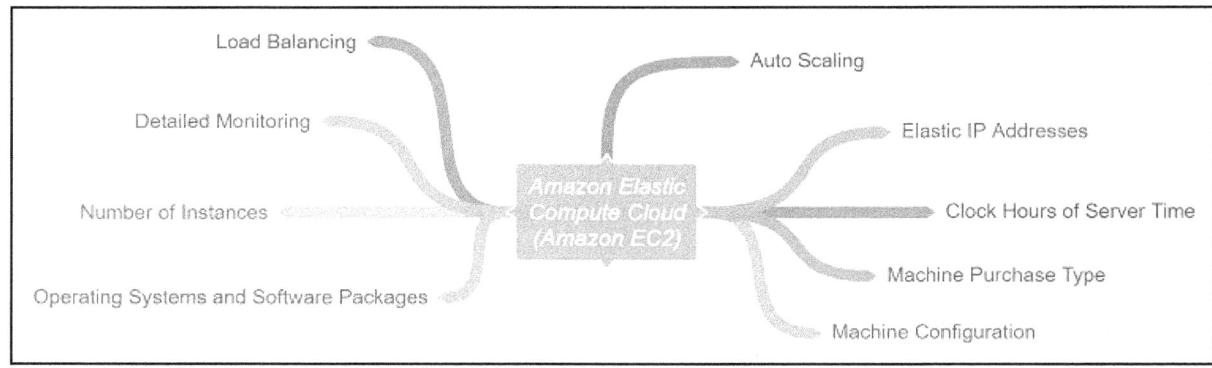

Figure 3-01: Mind Map of EC2 Cost Factors

- ***Clock Hours of Server Time*** – Running resources incurs charges. For example: the time between Amazon EC2 instances being launched until they are terminated; or from the time Elastic IPs are allocated until the time they are de-allocated

- ***Machine Configuration*** – Instance pricing varies depending upon the physical configuration of the Amazon EC2 instances, such as the operating system, number of cores, memory and the AWS region
- ***Machine Purchase Type*** – Purchase types can be On-Demand Instances, Reserved Instances or Spot Instances. With On-Demand Instances, you pay by the hour with no commitments. With Reserved Instances, you receive a significant discount on the hourly usage price either by paying a low one-off payment or no payment at all for each instance of the compute capacity you reserve. With Spot Instances, you can bid for unused Amazon EC2 capacity
- ***Number of Instances*** – Multiple resources of Amazon EC2 and Amazon EBS can be provisioned for managing and handling peak loads
- ***Load Balancing*** – Using an Elastic Load Balancer for distributing traffic among the Amazon EC2 instances can contribute to the monthly cost, determined by the number of hours the Elastic Load Balancer runs and the volume of data it processes
- ***Detailed Monitoring*** – Amazon CloudWatch can be used to monitor your EC2 instances. Basic monitoring is supported by default without any additional cost, however you can subscribe for detailed monitoring at a fixed monthly rate, which contains seven preselected metrics logged once a minute. Partial months are charged on an hourly pro rata basis, at a per instance-hour rate.
- ***Auto-Scaling*** – Auto-Scaling scales the number of Amazon EC2 instances up or down automatically to adjust to pre-defined deployment needs. This service is accessible at no additional cost except for the Amazon CloudWatch fees.
- ***Elastic IP Addresses*** – One Elastic IP (EIP) address linked to a running instance is free of charge
- ***Operating Systems and Software Packages*** – Operating Systems prices are included in the instance prices

Amazon Simple Storage Service (Amazon S3)

Amazon S3 is a web service that provides storage in the cloud. The simple web services interface can be used to store and retrieve any volume of data, at any time, from anywhere on the web. The following factors should be considered when estimating the cost of Amazon S3:

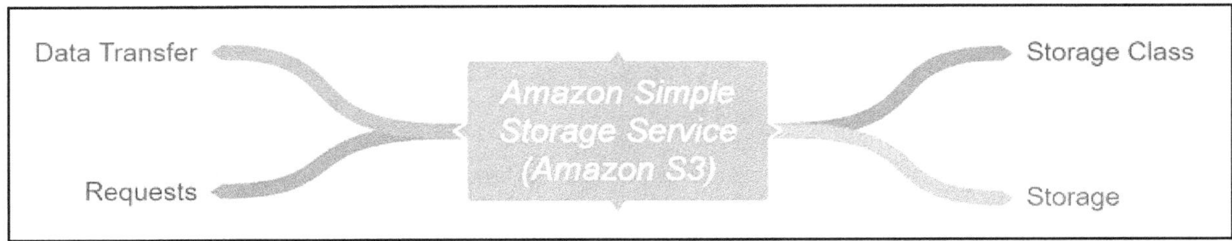

Figure 4-02: Mind Map of S3 Cost Factors

- ***Storage Class*** – Different storage classes have different rates:
  - *Standard Storage* is best for frequently accessed data, designed to provide 99.999999999% durability and 99.99% availability
  - *Standard – Infrequent Access* is used for storing less frequently accessed data with lower levels of redundancy than standard storage. It offers cheaper storage over time, but incurs higher charges when retrieving or transferring data
- ***Storage*** - The number and size of objects stored in your Amazon S3 buckets, plus the type of storage used
- ***Requests***- The number and type of requests. For Example, GET requests charge different rates to other requests, such as PUT and COPY requests
- ***Data Transfer*** - The amount of data transferred Out of the Amazon S3 buckets incurs a tiered fee per GB, whereas Data Transfer In is free of charge.

Amazon Relational Database Service (Amazon RDS)

Amazon RDS is a relational database web service in the cloud that allows you to set up, operate, and scale applications according to your needs. It lets you concentrate on applications and your business by offering cost-efficient and resizable capacity while also handling the database administration tasks. When estimating the cost of Amazon RDS, the following factors need to be considered:

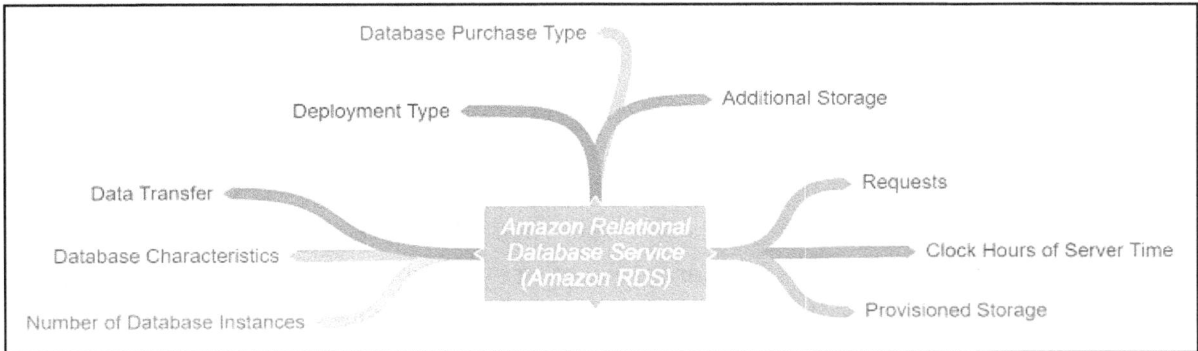

Figure 4-03: Mind Map of RDS Cost Factors

- ***Clock Hours of Server Time*** – Resources incur charges when they are running. For example, from the time you launch a DB instance until the moment you terminate it
- ***Database Characteristics*** – The physical characteristics of the database such as database engine, size and memory class affect how much you are charged
- ***Database Purchase Type*** – With On-Demand DB Instances, you pay for compute capacity for each hour your DB Instance runs, with no minimum commitments. With Reserved DB Instances, you receive a significant discount on the hourly usage charge by paying a low one-time, up-front payment for each DB Instance you reserve for a 1- or 3-year term
- ***A Number of Database Instances*** – Multiple DB instances can be provisioned with Amazon RDS to handle peak loads
- ***Provisioned Storage*** – For each active DB instance, there is no extra charge for backup storage of up to 100% of your provisioned database storage. Backup storage incurs charges calculated per gigabyte per month after the DB Instance is terminated
- ***Additional Storage*** – Along with the provisioned storage amount, the amount of backup storage also incurs charges calculated per gigabyte per month
- ***Requests*** – The number of input and output requests to the database
- ***Deployment Type*** – DB instances can be deployed in a single availability zone that is similar to a stand-alone data center or in multiple availability zones, which work like a secondary data center for increased availability and durability. The charges for storage and I/O differ depending upon the number of availability zones used for deployment

- ***Data Transfer*** – Inbound data transfer is free, whereas outbound data transfer costs are tiered

Amazon CloudFront

Amazon CloudFront is a web service for content delivery. It works with other Amazon Web Services to distribute content to end users with low latency and high data transfer speeds, with no minimum commitments. For a cost estimation of Amazon CloudFront, the following factors need to be considered:

Figure 4-04: Mind Map of CloudFront Cost Factors

- ***Traffic Distribution*** – The data transfer and request pricing differ across geographic regions and depend upon the edge location through which the content is served
- ***Requests*** – The number and type of requests (HTTP or HTTPS) made, and the geographic region in which the requests are made
- ***Data Transfer Out*** – The amount of data transferred out of your Amazon CloudFront edge locations

Amazon Elastic Block Store (Amazon EBS)

Amazon EBS offers block level storage volumes to be used with Amazon EC2 instances. These EBS volumes carry on independently, irrespective of the EC2 instance lifespan. They are off-instance storage, similar to virtual disks in the cloud. Amazon EBS offers three types of volume: General Purpose (SSD), Provisioned IOPS (SSD), and Magnetic, all with different costs and performance characteristics.

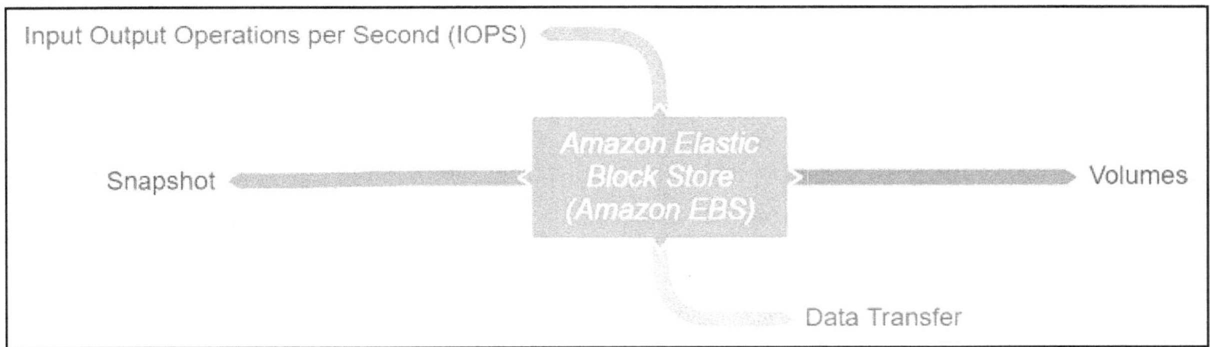

Figure 4-05: Mind Map of EBS Cost Factors

- ***Volumes*** – The amount of storage volume you use is charged in GB per month for all EBS volume types, until you release the storage
- ***Input Output Operations per Second (IOPS)*** – When using EBS Magnetic volumes, I/O is charged according to the number of requests made to your volume. For Provisioned IOPS (SSD) volumes, you will be charged for the amount you provision in IOPS (multiplied by the percentage of days you provision for the month). For General Purpose (SSD) volumes, I/O is included in the price
- ***Snapshot*** – Amazon EBS offers the ability to back up snapshots of your data to Amazon S3 for a durable recovery, with an added cost calculated per GB-month of data stored
- ***Data Transfer*** – Inbound data transfer is free, while outbound data transfer charges are tiered

Saving Further Costs

Many large enterprise organizations customize their contracts with AWS to optimize their costs and meet their unique needs. Different pricing models are available for some AWS products, offering you the flexibility to access services according to your requirements.

On-Demand Instance

With On-Demand Instances, you pay for computing capacity by the hour with no minimum commitment required.

Reserved Instance

Reserved Instances allow you to reserve compute capacity in advance for long-term savings. It provides significant discounts of up to 60 percent compared to On-Demand Instance pricing.

The following table compares one-year and three-year savings between the use of reserved instances versus on-demand instances. The figures are based on pricing as of January 2015 on an m3.large Linux instance type in the US East (N. Virginia) region.

	No Upfront	Partial Upfront	All Upfront	On-Demand
1 Year	$876.00	$767.12	$751.00	$1226.40
3 Years		$1461.40	$1373.00	$3679.20
Savings 1 Year	29%	37%	39%	
Savings 3 Years		60%	63%	

Table 4-1 Reduced Instances Vs. On-Demand Instances

Spot Instance

You can bid for unused Amazon Elastic Compute Cloud (Amazon EC2) capacity. Instances are charged at a Spot Price, which is set by Amazon EC2, which fluctuates depending on supply and demand. If your bid exceeds the current Spot Price, your requested instances will run iter until you terminate them or the Spot Price increases above your bid.

Pricing is tiered for storage and data transfer. The more you use, the less you pay per gigabyte (GB). Volume discounts are also available.

AWS Support Plans

AWS provides access to tools and expertise under a range of support plans that support the operational health and success of your AWS solutions. You can opt for a support plan according to your organizational requirements; whether you need technical support or additional resources to assist you in planning, deploying and optimizing your AWS environment. AWS offers four support plans to its customers: Basic, Developer, Business and Enterprise.

Basic — Get familiar with AWS

The Basic plan is the account you get on Free Tier. It offers its customers support for account and billing queries and service limit increases as well as:

Receiving basic support with access to support forums

Developer Experimenting with AWS

The Developer Support plan offers resources for customers testing or doing early development on AWS, as well as any customer who:

Wants access to guidance and technical support

Business Production use of AWS

The Business Support plan offers resources for customers running production workloads on AWS as well as any customer who:

Runs one or more applications in production environments

Enterprise Mission-critical use of AWS

The Enterprise Support plan offers resources for customers running business & mission critical workloads on AWS, as well as any customer who wants to:

Focus on proactive management to increase efficiency and availability

Features of AWS Support Plans

Different AWS Support plans have different features which they offer to their customers. The Basic plan is free whereas other plans offer pay-per-month pricing with no long-term contracts and an unlimited number of technical support cases to provide you with the level of support that you require.

All AWS customers inherently have anytime access to these Basic support plan features:

- Customer Service: one-on-one responses to account and billing queries
- AWS Community Support forums
- Service health checks
- Documentation, whitepapers and best-practice guides

Additionally, Developer support plan customers have access to these features:

- Best-practice guidance
- Client-side diagnostic tools
- Building-block architecture support: Guidance on using AWS products, features, and services

Business and Enterprise support plan customers also get these features:

- Use-case guidance: Which AWS products, features and services to use to best support your particular needs
- Identity and Access Management (IAM) to control user access to AWS Support
- AWS Trusted Advisor, for inspecting the user environments, identifying cost-saving prospects, closing security gaps and optimizing your infrastructure.

- AWS Support API for automating support cases and Trusted Advisor operations
- Third-party software support: help with Amazon EC2 instance operating systems, configurations and performance of third-party software components

In addition to all the above features, enterprise support plan customers enjoy the benefits of the following features:

- Application architecture guidance: Consultative partnership supporting specific use cases and applications
- Infrastructure event management: Support for product launches, architectural and scaling guidance for seasonal promotions and events and migrations depending on each use case
- AWS Concierge, for billing and account analysis and assistance
- Technical Account Manager, providing dedicated customer service personnel
- White-glove case routing
- Management business reviews

Comparison of Support Plans

The following table lists the key comparison factors between the four support plans offered by AWS:

	Basic	Developer	Business	Enterprise
Pricing	Free	From $29 per month	From $100 per month	From $15k per month
Technical Support		Business hours access to Cloud Support Associates via email	24x7 access to Cloud Support Engineers via email, chat & phone	24x7 access to Sr.Cloud Support Engineers via email, chat & phone
Technical Account Manager	No	No	No	Yes
Who Can Open Cases?	None	One prime contact/ Unlimited cases	Unlimited contacts/ Unlimited cases	Unlimited contacts/ Unlimited cases
Trusted Adviser	Access to 6 core Trusted Advisor checks	Access to 6 core Trusted Advisor checks	Access to full set of Trusted Advisor checks	Access to full set of Trusted Advisor checks
Programmatic Case Management			AWS Support API	AWS Support API

Table 4-2: AWS Support Plans

The table below describes the different tiers of case severity and their respective response times under different support plans:

Case Severity	Response Time	Support Plan	Description
General Guidance	< 24 business hours	Developer, Business, and Enterprise	General development question, or request a feature
System Impaired	< 12 business hours	Developer, Business, and Enterprise	Non-critical functions of the application behaving abnormally, or having a time-sensitive development question
Production System Impaired	< 4 hours	Business and Enterprise	Important functions of the application are impaired or degraded
Production System Down	< 1 hour	Business and Enterprise	Business is significantly impacted. Important functions of the application are unavailable
Business-Critical System Down	< 15 minutes	Enterprise Only	Business is at risk. Critical functions of the application are unavailable

Table 4-3: Case Severity and Response Times

EXAM TIP: Remember the different response times for the corresponding case severity for any particular plan. Also, keep in mind that the Technical Account Manager (TAM) is only available for the Enterprise Support Plan.

AWS Organizations

AWS Organizations is an account management service that allows you to consolidate multiple AWS accounts into a single organization, enabling you to create a hierarchical structure that can be managed centrally.

With AWS Organizations, you can create multiple groups of AWS accounts known as Organizational Units and then apply policies to those Organizational Units, commonly referred to as Service Control Policies (SCPs). These policies centrally control the use of AWS services across multiple AWS accounts, without the need for custom scripts or manual processes. Entities within the AWS accounts can only use the AWS services allowed by both the SCP and the AWS IAM Policy for the account.

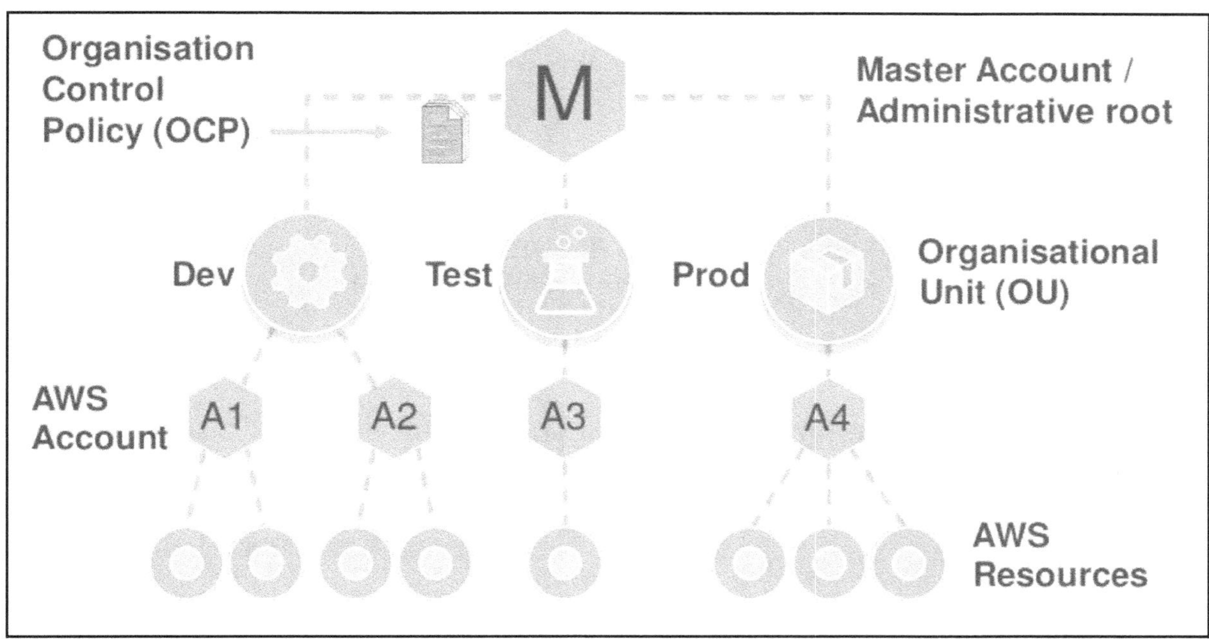

Figure 4-06: AWS Organization

AWS Organizations is available to all AWS customers at no additional charge for two feature sets:

- **Only consolidated billing features:** This mode only provides the consolidated billing features and does not include the other advanced features of AWS Organizations, such as the use of policies to restrict what can be accessed by users and roles in different accounts

- **All features:** This mode is the complete feature set that includes all the functionality of consolidated billing, in addition to the advanced features that provides more control over the accounts in your organization

Key Features of AWS Organizations

- ***Group-based account management:***
Create separate groups of AWS accounts to use with development and production resources, and then apply different policies to each group

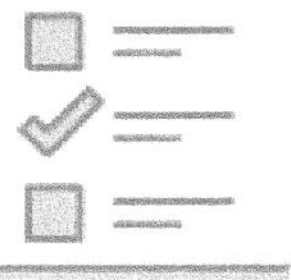

- ***Policy framework for multiple AWS accounts:***
AWS Organizations provides a policy framework for multiple AWS accounts. Apply policies to a group of accounts or to all the accounts in your organization

- ***API level control of AWS services:***
Use service control policies (SCPs) to manage and centrally control access to AWS services at an API level across multiple AWS accounts

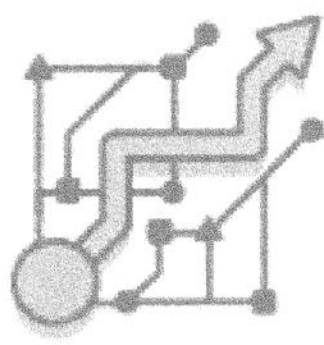

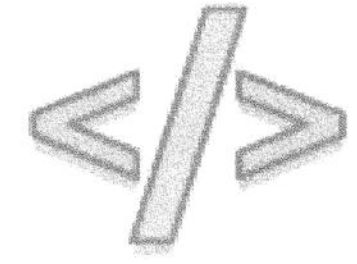

- ***Account creation and management APIs:***
Automate the creation and management of new AWS accounts through APIs. APIs create new accounts programmatically

- ***Consolidated billing:***
Set up a single payment method for all the AWS accounts in your organization through consolidated billing. It provides a combined view of charges incurred by all of your accounts

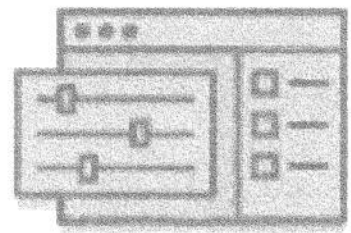

- ***Enable only consolidated billing features:***
Create new organizations with only consolidated billing features enabled. Advanced policy controls such as Service Control Policies (SCPs) are not enabled

Consolidated Billing

One of the key features of AWS Organizations is the consolidation of the billing of all the AWS accounts within your organization. A single AWS account acts as the paying master account linked with all other AWS accounts to form a simple one-level hierarchy. At the end of the month, the master account obtains a combined view of charges incurred by all of your AWS accounts, as well as a cost report for each member account that is associated with the master paying account. Consolidated billing is available at no additional cost.

Consolidated billing has the following key benefits:

- One Bill – Get one bill for multiple accounts
- Easy Tracking – Easily track the charges incurred by each account.
- Combined Usage – Combined usage from all accounts in the organization results in volume discounts

> EXAM TIP: The Paying Account should be used for billing purposes only. Do not deploy resources to the Paying Account. When monitoring is enabled on the Paying Account, billing data for all linked accounts are included. You can also separately create billing alerts for individual accounts.

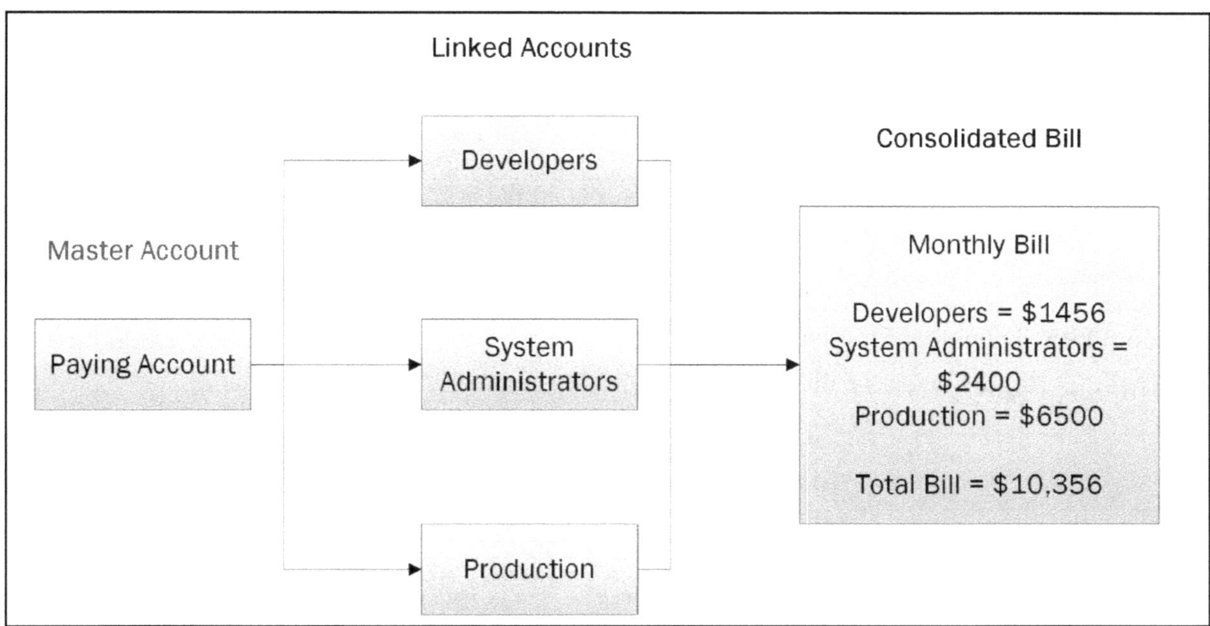

Figure 4-07: Consolidated Billing

With consolidated billing as the only feature enabled, each member account is independent of other member accounts. Unless the master account explicitly restricts

linked accounts through the use of policies, the owner of each member account can independently access resources, sign up for AWS services and use AWS Premium Support. Account owners use their own IAM username and password with independently assigned account permissions within the organization.

Currently, there is a soft limit of 20 accounts per organization and a hard limit of one level of billing hierarchy; that is to say that a master (paying) account cannot be part of the same organization as another master (paying) account.

EXAM TIP: AWS CloudTrail is a service used to monitor account activity and deliver generated event logs to the associated account's S3 Bucket. You can aggregate Log Files from multiple regions within a single S3 bucket of the Paying Account.

Consolidated Billing Examples

1. **Volume Discounts**

Services such as Amazon EC2 and Amazon S3 have tiered volume pricing that offers lower prices the more you use the service. In consolidated billing, AWS determines, which volume pricing tiers to apply by combining the total usage of all accounts. Consider the following scenario:

Account Name	Data Transfer OUT
Developers	8 TB
System Administrators	5 TB
Production	3 TB

The Data Transfer OUT rates from Amazon S3 to the internet for USA East (N. Virginia) Region are as follows:

Data Transfer Volume	Pricing
Up to 1 GB / Month	$0.00 per GB
Next 10 TB / Month	$0.09 per GB
Next 40 TB / Month	$0.085 per GB

Without consolidated billing, the cost would be calculated as:

- 8 TB will be charged as (8 * 1024) * $0.09 = $ 737.28
- 5 TB will be charged as (5 * 1024) * $0.09 = $ 460.80
- 3 TB will be charged as (3 * 1024) * $0.09 = $ 276.48
- Total Bill = $ 1474.56 for 16 TB of data transfer

With consolidated billing, data transfer charges for a total of 16 TB would be:

- Tier 1: First 10 TB would be charged as (10 * 1024) * $0.09 = $ 921.60
- Tier 2: Next 6 TB would be charged as (6 * 1024) * $0.085 = $ 522.24
- Total Consolidated Bill = $ 1443.84 for 16 TB of data transfer
- Therefore, there would be a saving of $30.72 using consolidated billing

2. **Reserved Instances:**

As AWS Organizations considers all the linked accounts in an organization as a single account, every member account will receive the hourly cost-benefit of any Reserved Instances purchased by any other member account within the organization. Consider the following scenario with two linked accounts:

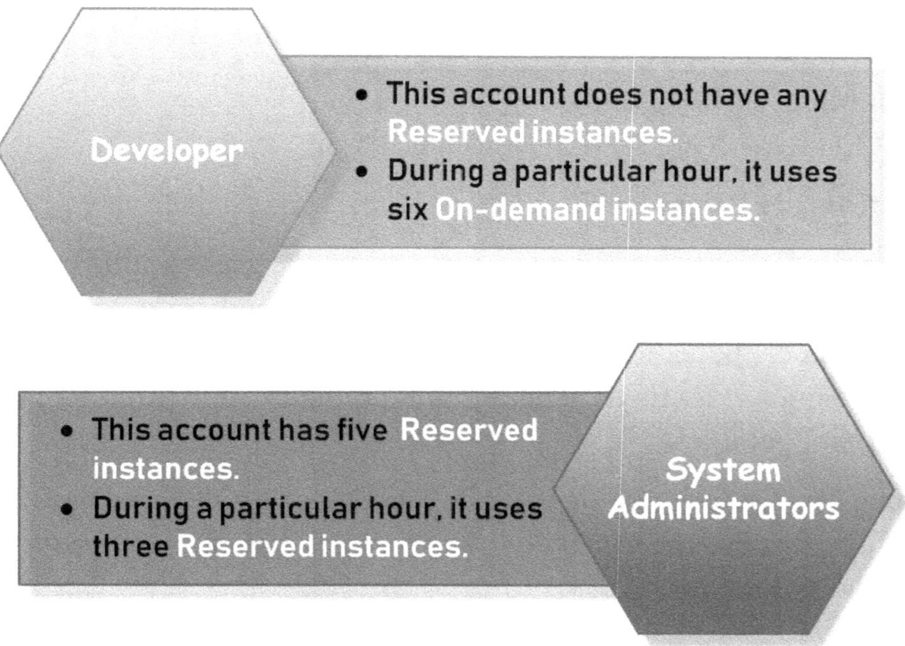

Figure 4-08: Linked Accounts with Reserved Instances

On the organization's consolidated bill, only nine instances would be charged. Five of these would be charged as Reserved Instances and the remaining four as regular

On-Demand Instances. If the accounts were not linked to a single consolidated bill, six On-Demand Instances and five Reserved Instances would have been charged.

The linked accounts will only receive the cost-benefit from each other's Reserved Instances if the launched instances are in the same availability zone, have the same instance size and belong to the same family of instance types.

> EXAM TIP: Consolidated Billing allows you to get volume discounts on all your accounts. When consolidated billing is enabled, unused reserved instances for EC2 are applied across the group.

> EXAM TIP: During the exam, you are going to get scenario-based questions asking about how you can save costs as a business. An answer to this is 'Consolidated Billing'.

AWS Cost Calculators

AWS offers calculators to help you to calculate your costs. There are two calculators available for this:

- AWS Simple Monthly Calculator
- AWS TCO (Total Cost of Ownership) Calculator

AWS Simple Monthly Calculator

The AWS Simple Monthly Calculator provides an estimation of your monthly bill depending on your unique configuration of resources. Whether you are running a single instance or dozens of individual services, you can organize your planned resources by service, and the Simple Monthly Calculator will provide you with an estimated cost per month for that configuration.

The calculator provides a per service cost breakdown, as well as an aggregate monthly estimate. You can also use the calculator to see an estimation of and breakdown of costs for common cloud solutions.

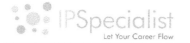

Lab 4-1: AWS Simple Monthly Calculator

1. Open "AWS Simply Monthly Calculator" in your browser by using the URL "https://calculator.s3.amazonaws.com/index.html".

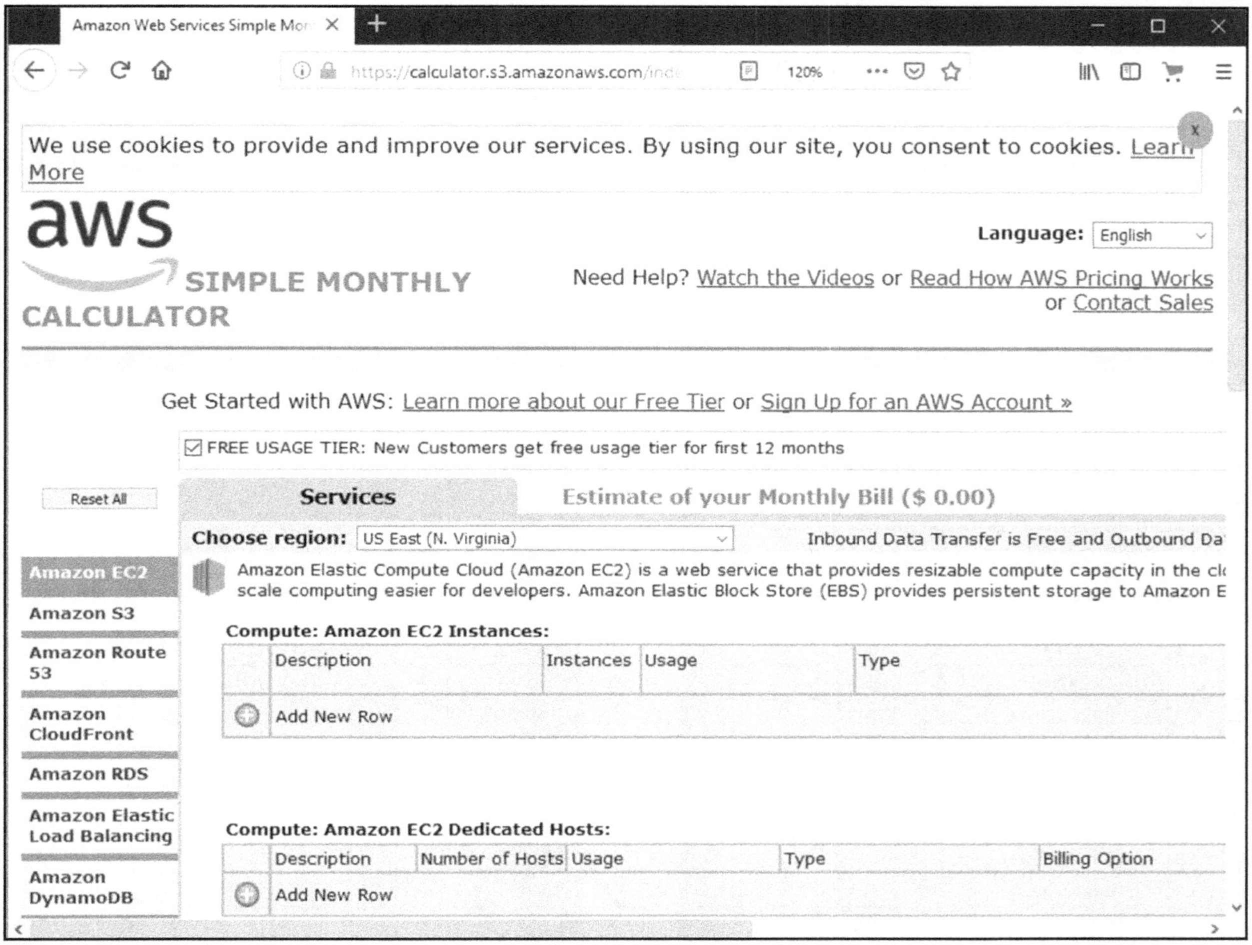

2. Select the Amazon Services you need and add configuration details such as the number of instances, instance types, billing options etc., depending on the type of service selected.

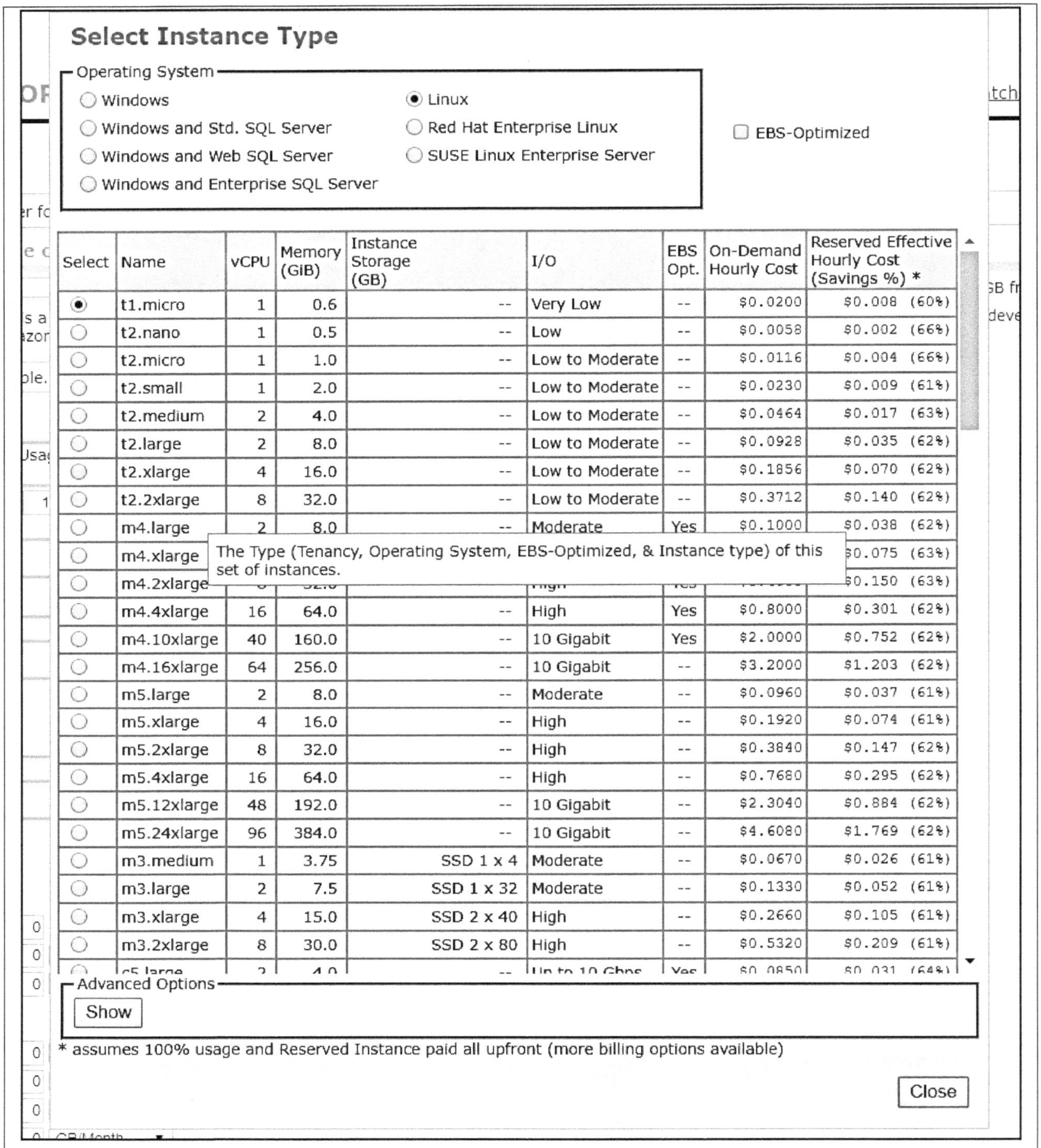

Select Instance Type

Operating System

- ○ Windows
- ○ Windows and Std. SQL Server
- ○ Windows and Web SQL Server
- ○ Windows and Enterprise SQL Server
- ◉ Linux
- ○ Red Hat Enterprise Linux
- ○ SUSE Linux Enterprise Server

☐ EBS-Optimized

Select	Name	vCPU	Memory (GiB)	Instance Storage (GB)	I/O	EBS Opt.	On-Demand Hourly Cost	Reserved Effective Hourly Cost (Savings %) *
◉	t1.micro	1	0.6	--	Very Low	--	$0.0200	$0.008 (60%)
○	t2.nano	1	0.5	--	Low	--	$0.0058	$0.002 (66%)
○	t2.micro	1	1.0	--	Low to Moderate	--	$0.0116	$0.004 (66%)
○	t2.small	1	2.0	--	Low to Moderate	--	$0.0230	$0.009 (61%)
○	t2.medium	2	4.0	--	Low to Moderate	--	$0.0464	$0.017 (63%)
○	t2.large	2	8.0	--	Low to Moderate	--	$0.0928	$0.035 (62%)
○	t2.xlarge	4	16.0	--	Low to Moderate	--	$0.1856	$0.070 (62%)
○	t2.2xlarge	8	32.0	--	Low to Moderate	--	$0.3712	$0.140 (62%)
○	m4.large	2	8.0	--	Moderate	Yes	$0.1000	$0.038 (62%)
○	m4.xlarge							$0.075 (63%)
○	m4.2xlarge							$0.150 (63%)
○	m4.4xlarge	16	64.0	--	High	Yes	$0.8000	$0.301 (62%)
○	m4.10xlarge	40	160.0	--	10 Gigabit	Yes	$2.0000	$0.752 (62%)
○	m4.16xlarge	64	256.0	--	10 Gigabit	--	$3.2000	$1.203 (62%)
○	m5.large	2	8.0	--	Moderate	--	$0.0960	$0.037 (61%)
○	m5.xlarge	4	16.0	--	High	--	$0.1920	$0.074 (61%)
○	m5.2xlarge	8	32.0	--	High	--	$0.3840	$0.147 (62%)
○	m5.4xlarge	16	64.0	--	High	--	$0.7680	$0.295 (62%)
○	m5.12xlarge	48	192.0	--	10 Gigabit	--	$2.3040	$0.884 (62%)
○	m5.24xlarge	96	384.0	--	10 Gigabit	--	$4.6080	$1.769 (62%)
○	m3.medium	1	3.75	SSD 1 x 4	Moderate	--	$0.0670	$0.026 (61%)
○	m3.large	2	7.5	SSD 1 x 32	Moderate	--	$0.1330	$0.052 (61%)
○	m3.xlarge	4	15.0	SSD 2 x 40	High	--	$0.2660	$0.105 (61%)
○	m3.2xlarge	8	30.0	SSD 2 x 80	High	--	$0.5320	$0.209 (61%)

The Type (Tenancy, Operating System, EBS-Optimized, & Instance type) of this set of instances.

Advanced Options

Show

* assumes 100% usage and Reserved Instance paid all upfront (more billing options available)

Close

3. Once you are finished selecting all the required resources and their configuration specifications, select the 'Estimate of your monthly bill" tab at the top to see your estimated monthly cost calculation.

Get Started with AWS: Learn more about our Free Tier or Sign Up for an AWS Account »

FREE USAGE TIER: New Customers get free usage tier for first 12 months

Services | **Estimate of your Monthly Bill ($ 9678.39)**

Estimate of Your Monthly Bill

☑ Show First Month's Bill (include all one-time fees, if any)

Below you will see an estimate of your monthly bill. Expand each line item to see cost breakout of each service. To save this bill and input values, click on 'Save and Share' button. To remove the service from the estimate, jump back to the service and clear the specific service's form.

Export to CSV | **Save and Share**

Item		
Amazon EC2 Service (US East (N. Virginia))		$ 43.92
Compute:	$ 43.92	
Amazon S3 Service (US East (N. Virginia))		$ 1.15
Standard Storage:	$ 1.15	
Amazon S3 Service (EU (London))		$ 2.82
Standard Storage:	$ 2.16	
Standard - IA Storage:	$ 0.66	
Amazon RDS Service (Asia Pacific (Sydney))		$ 8765.76
DB instances:	$ 8754.72	
Storage:	$ 11.04	
AWS Support (Business)		$ 879.86
Support for all AWS services:	$ 879.86	
Free Tier **Discount:**		**$** -15.12
Total Monthly Payment:		**$** 9678.39

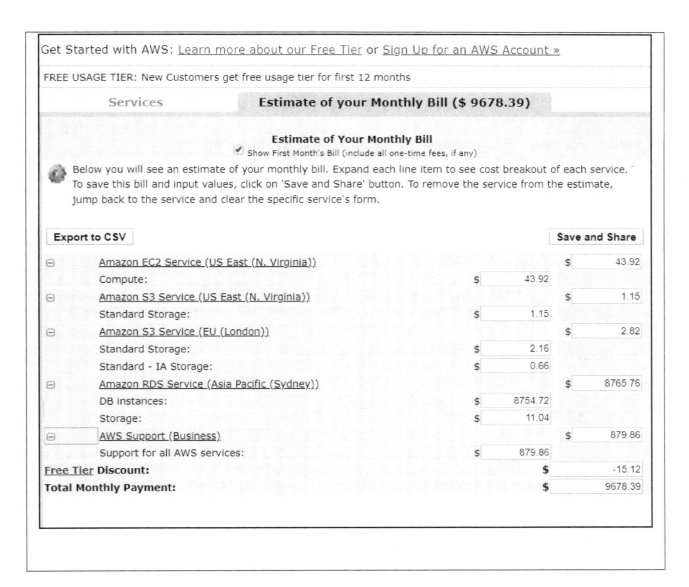

AWS TCO (Total Cost of Ownership) Calculator

AWS Total Cost of Ownership (TCO) Calculator provides a comparative analysis of the cost estimation by comparing on-premises and co-location environments to AWS.

It estimates the costs of migrating on-premises infrastructure to AWS and gives you the option to evaluate the savings you would receive if the infrastructure was running on AWS.

The TCO calculator matches your existing or planned infrastructure to the most cost-effective AWS offering. This tool considers all the costs of running a solution, including physical facilities, power and cooling, providing a realistic end-to-end comparison of your

costs in the form of a detailed set of reports. The calculator also gives you the option to modify assumptions that best meet your business needs.

Lab 4-2: AWS Total Cost of Ownership Calculator

1. Open the "AWS TCO Calculator" in your browser by using the URL "https://awstcocalculator.com/".

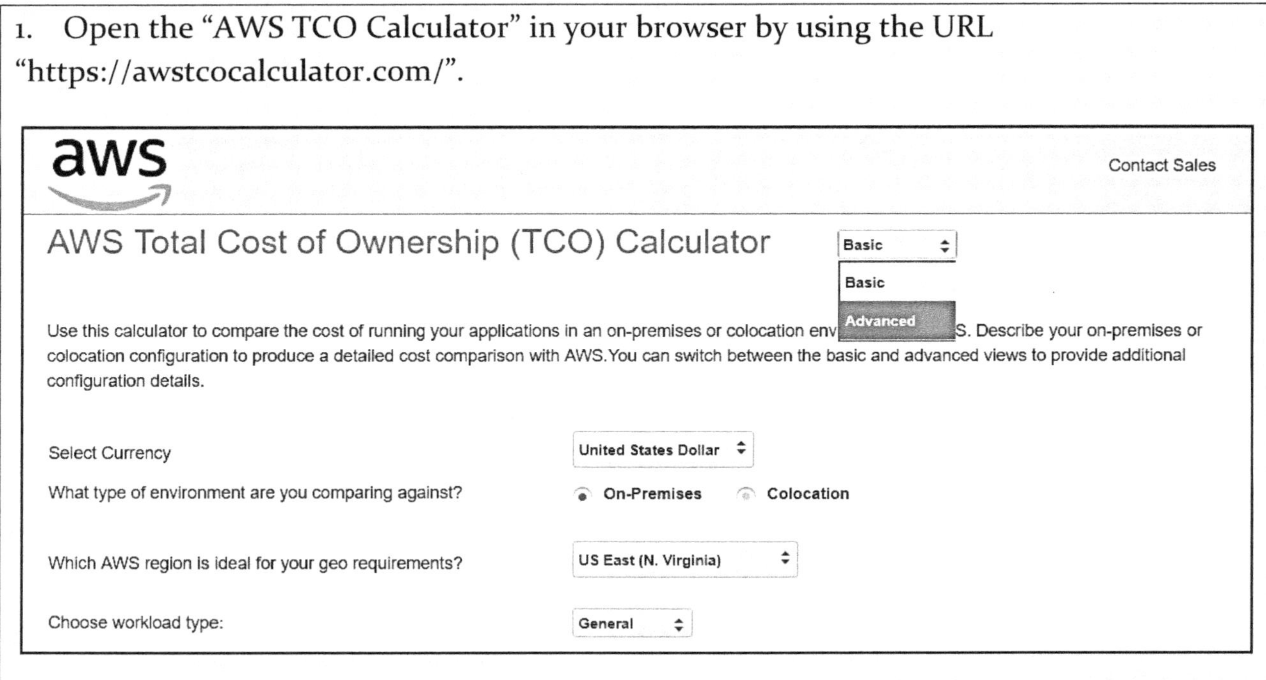

2. Select the Basic or Advanced Calculator type, depending on your requirements. Describe your existing On-Premises or Co-location environment and click "Calculate".

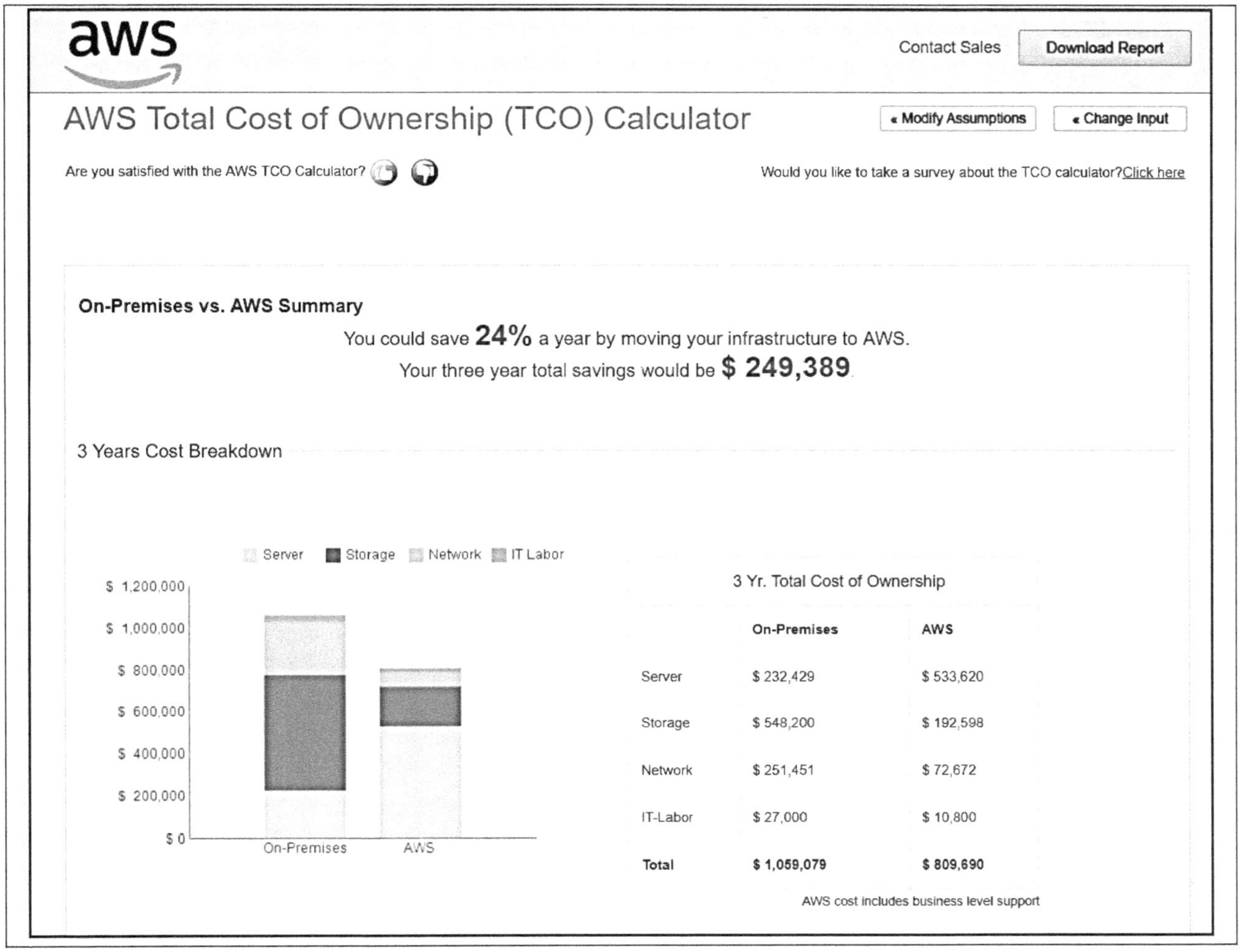

aws

Contact Sales | Download Report

AWS Total Cost of Ownership (TCO) Calculator

« Modify Assumptions | « Change Input

Are you satisfied with the AWS TCO Calculator?

Would you like to take a survey about the TCO calculator?Click here

On-Premises vs. AWS Summary

You could save **24%** a year by moving your infrastructure to AWS.
Your three year total savings would be **$ 249,389**

3 Years Cost Breakdown

Server | Storage | Network | IT Labor

$ 1,200,000
$ 1,000,000
$ 800,000
$ 600,000
$ 400,000
$ 200,000
$ 0

On-Premises | AWS

3 Yr. Total Cost of Ownership

	On-Premises	AWS
Server	$ 232,429	$ 533,620
Storage	$ 548,200	$ 192,598
Network	$ 251,451	$ 72,672
IT-Labor	$ 27,000	$ 10,800
Total	**$ 1,059,079**	**$ 809,690**

AWS cost includes business level support

aws

Contact Sales | Download Report

AWS cost includes business level support

Environment Details

Your On-Premises environment

Environment : Physical

# Servers	# Cores	RAM (GB)	OS	Avg.Util.	Optimize by
3	8	100	Linux	100%	RAM

Your AWS environment : US East (N. Virginia)

Closest AWS Instances

# Instances	Instance	vCPU	RAM (GiB)	Optimize by	Instance type
3	db.r3.4xlarge	16	122	RAM	3 Yr. Partial Upfront RI

Storage (TB)		
SAN	NAS	Object
100	0	0

Bandwidth (Mbps)	
Pipe Size	Peak/Avg. Ratio
2,000	3

EC2 Instance Mapping Criteria

Optimize by	Description
CPU	Option matches by VCPU count and then finds the lowest priced EC2 instance from the available choices
RAM	Option matches by RAM size and then finds the lowest priced EC2 instance from the available choices
Storage IO	Option matches by I/O requirements and then finds the lowest priced EC2 instance from the available choices

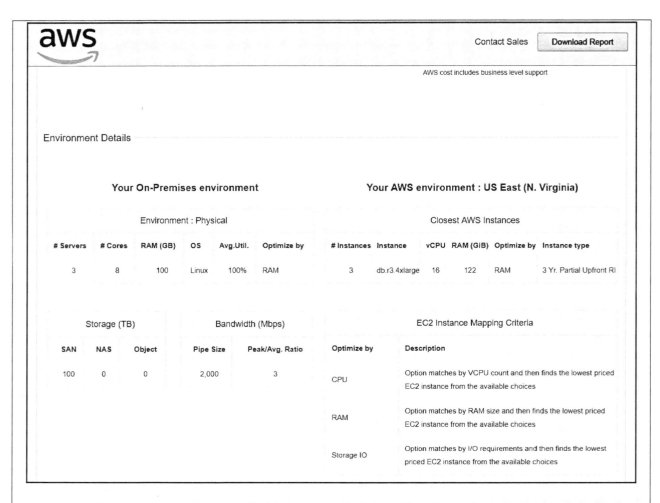

3. You will receive an instant summary report of the three-year TCO comparison broken down by cost categories that you can download. The report will also include detailed cost breakdowns, Methodology, Assumptions, and FAQs.

aws

Contact Sales | Download Report

Cost Breakdown

Your On-Premises Cost Breakdown

Server

Hardware : $ 39,485 [17%] Software : $ 133,812 [58%]
Overhead : $ 59,132 [25%]

Storage

Raw Capacity : $ 409,600 [75%] Backup : $ 48,600 [9%]
Overhead : $ 54,000 [10%] Admin : $ 36,000 [7%]

Network

Your AWS Cost Breakdown

Compute EC2

3 Yr Partial Upfront RI : $ 525,378 [100%]
On Demand : $ 0 [0%]

EBS

IOPS : $ 0 [0%] EBS Volumes : $ 171,418 [97%]
Snapshot : $ 4,524 [3%]

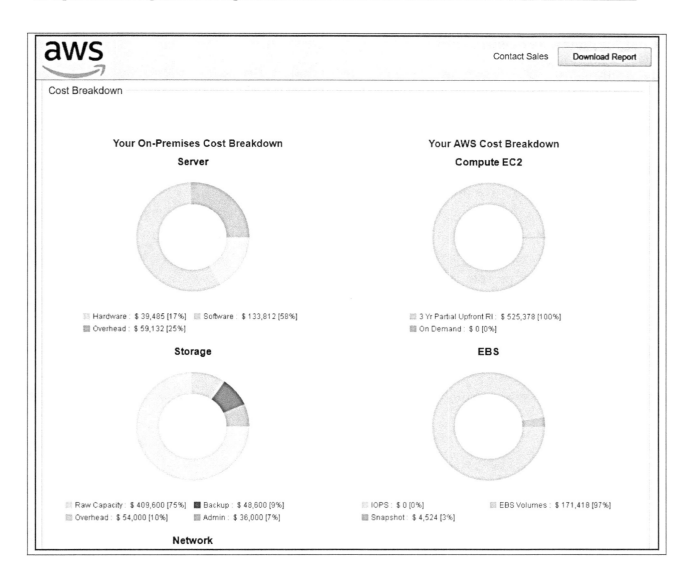

EXAM TIP: Do not get confused between the two calculators. TCO is a cost comparison tool to compare the on-premises cost of a solution with the cloud cost and to calculate how much you would save by moving to the cloud. The simple monthly calculator allows you to calculate your monthly AWS bill based on the resources consumed.

Cost Management Using Tags

Tags allow you to add business and organizational statistics to your billing and usage data. This helps in categorizing and tracking costs through significant, relevant business information. Tags may represent business categories (such as cost centers, application names, projects or owners) as a way to organize costs across various services and teams.

AWS provides two types of cost allocation tags: an AWS-generated tag and a user-defined tag. AWS defines, creates and applies the AWS-generated a tag for you, whereas User-defined tags are tags that you define, create, and apply to resources yourself. After creating and applying the tags to the resources, you can activate them on the Billing and Cost Management console for cost allocation tracking. You must activate both types of tags separately before they will appear in the Cost Explorer or on a Cost Allocation Report.

The Cost Allocation Report contains all of your AWS costs for each billing period. The report includes both tagged and untagged resources so that you can clearly organize the charges for your resources. For example, if you tag resources with an application name, you can track the total cost of a single application that runs on the AWS resources.

Practice Questions

1. What is the pricing model that allows AWS customers to pay for resources on an as needed basis?
   A. Pay as you go
   B. Pay as you own
   C. Pay as you reserve
   D. Pay as you use
   E. Pay as you buy

2. Which of the following are NOT benefits of AWS Cloud Computing? (Choose 2)
   A. Fault tolerant databases
   B. High latency
   C. Multiple procurement cycles
   D. Temporary and disposable resources
   E. High availability

3. Which of the following is NOT an advantage of cloud computing over on-premises computing?
   A. Benefit from massive economies of scale
   B. Trade capital expense for variable expense
   C. Pay for racking, stacking, and powering servers
   D. Eliminate guessing on your infrastructure capacity needs
   E. Increase speed and agility

4. What is the one main reason customers are switching to cloud computing?
   A. Finite Infrastructure
   B. Automation
   C. Overprovisioning
   D. Instant Configuration
   E. Agility

5. Which of the following are advantages of cloud computing? (Choose 4)
   A. The ability to 'go global' in minutes
   B. Increased speed and agility
   C. Variable expense
   D. Requires large amounts of capital
   E. Elasticity

6. Which of the following are characteristics of cloud computing? (Choose 3)
   A. Cloud charges are capital expenditures

B. Pay-as-you-go pricing
C. On-demand delivery
D. Services are delivered via Internet

7. Which of the following are types of cloud computing deployments? (Choose 3)
   A. Public Cloud
   B. Hybrid Cloud
   C. Mixed Cloud
   D. Private Cloud

8. Amazon Lightsail is an example of which of the following?
   A. Software-as-a-Service
   B. Platform-as-a-Service
   C. Functions-as-a-Service
   D. Infrastructure-as-a-Service

9. Which of the following are principles of sound cloud design? (Choose 4)
   A. Disposable resources
   B. Infrastructure as code
   C. Assume *everything* will fail
   D. Limit the number of 3rd-party services
   E. Scalability
   F. Tightly-coupled components
   G. Treat your servers like pets, not cattle

10. Which AWS service allows you to run code without having to worry about provisioning any underlying resources (such as virtual machines, databases etc.)
    A. EC2
    B. DynamoDB
    C. EC2 Container Service
    D. Lambda

11. When considering cost optimization, what model allows you to pay only for what computing resources you actually use?
    A. Economies of scale model
    B. Expenditure model
    C. Economies of scope model
    D. Consumption model

12. What is defined as the ability for a system to remain operational even if some of the components of that system fail?
    A. High Durability

B. DNS Failovers
C. High Availability
D. Fault Tolerance

13. What tool helps avoid limitations of being able to create new resources on-demand or scheduled?
   A. CloudWatch
   B. Route 53
   C. Auto Scaling
   D. Elastic Load Balancer

14. Which of the following is NOT one of the four areas of the performance efficiency pillar?
   A. Selection
   B. Tradeoffs
   C. Traceability
   D. Monitoring

15. Which design principles are recommended when considering performance efficiency? (Choose 2)
   A. Serverless architecture
   B. Expenditure awareness
   C. Matching supply with demand
   D. Enabling traceability
   E. Democratize advanced technologies

16. Why is AWS more economical than traditional data centers for applications with varying compute workloads?
   A. Amazon Elastic Compute Cloud (Amazon EC2) costs are billed on a monthly basis
   B. Customers retain full administrative access to their Amazon EC2 instances
   C. Amazon EC2 instances can be launched on-demand when needed
   D. Customers can permanently run enough instances to handle peak workloads

17. Which of the following are advantages of AWS cloud security? (Choose 2)
   A. AWS uses single-factor access control systems
   B. AWS retains complete control and ownership of your data region
   C. AWS infrastructure security auditing is periodic and manual
   D. AWS uses multi-factor access control systems
   E. You retain complete control and ownership of your data region

18. Which of the following are steps you should take in securing your Root AWS

account? (Choose 3)
A. Create a Root IAM role
B. Create individual IAM users
C. Activate Multifactor Authentication (MFA) on your root account
D. Use roles to assign permissions to IAM users

19. Which of the following is the document used to grant permissions to users, groups, and roles?
A. Policy
B. Passbook
C. Protocol
D. Paradigm

20. IAM policies are written using ________.
A. XML
B. SAML
C. JSON
D. SGML

21. Which of the following are valid access types for an IAM user? (Choose 3)
A. Using the AWS Software Developers Kit
B. Emergency access via Identity Access Management (IAM)
C. AWS Management Console access
D. Programmatic access via the command line
E. Security Group access via the AWS command line

22. Which of the following Compliance certifications attests to the security of the AWS platform regarding credit card transactions?
A. ISO 27001
B. SOC 2
C. SOC 1
D. PCI DSS Level 1

23. Which of the following is AWS' managed DDoS protection service?
A. AWS Shield
B. Security Groups
C. AWS WAF
D. Access Control Lists

24. Which of the following AWS services can help you assess the fault-tolerance of your AWS environment?
A. AWS WAF

B. AWS Trusted Advisor
C. AWS Shield
D. AWS Inspector

25. The AWS Web Application Firewall can go down to which of the following OSI layers?
A. 4
B. 5
C. 6
D. 7

26. You need to use an AWS service to assess the security and compliance of your EC2 instances. Which of the following services should you use?
A. AWS WAF
B. AWS Inspector
C. AWS Shield
D. AWS Trusted Advisor

27. Which of the following Compliance Guarantees attests to the fact that the AWS Platform has met the standard required for the secured storage of medical records in the US?
A. HIPPA
B. FERPA
C. GLBA
D. HITECH

28. Which of the following services will help you optimize your entire AWS environment in real time following AWS best practices?
A. AWS WAF
B. AWS Trusted Advisor
C. AWS Shield
D. AWS Inspector

29. You need to implement an automated service that will scan your AWS environment with the goal of both improving security and reducing costs. Which service should you use?
A. Service Catalog
B. CloudTrail
C. Trusted Advisor
D. Config Rules

30. Which of the following AWS services can assist you with cost optimization?

A. AWS WAF
B. AWS Trusted Advisor
C. AWS Inspector
D. AWS Shield

31. Under the Shared Responsibility model, for which of the following does AWS not assume responsibility?
A. Physical security of AWS facilities
B. Networking
C. Customer data
D. Hypervisors

32. Which of the following is true about security groups? (Choose 2)
A. Acts as a virtual firewall to control outbound traffic only
B. All inbound traffic is denied and outbound traffic is allowed by default
C. Acts as a virtual firewall to control inbound and outbound traffic
D. Acts as a virtual firewall to control inbound traffic only
E. All inbound traffic is allowed and outbound traffic is denied by default

33. Which of the following is NOT a feature of AWS Identity and Access Management?
A. Manage roles and their permissions
B. Manage users and their access
C. Manage federated users and their permissions
D. Manage services and their capacities

34. What is AWS Trusted Advisor?
A. Partner program that helps you validate your application deployment
B. Online tool that helps you configure resources to follow best practices
C. Professional Services offering that helps you migrate to cloud
D. AWS service that helps you manage access to your account

35. When creating an IAM policy, what are the two types of access that can be granted to a user? (Choose 2)
A. Authorized Access
B. AWS Management Console Access
C. Institutional Access
D. Programmatic Access
E. Administrative Root Access

36. Which of the following are the security benefits that AWS offers? (Choose 2)
A. Secure Global Infrastructure
B. Meet Compliance Requirements

C. Shared Collaboration Model
D. Data Storage
E. Inventory and Application Management

37. The AWS Risk and Compliance Program is made up of which of the following components? (Choose 3)
    A. Security Principles
    B. Risk Management
    C. Control Environment
    D. Information Security
    E. Physical Security
    F. Automation Environment
    G. Identity Management

38. What does AWS recommend as the best practice for the AWS Account Root User after initial login?
    A. Delete root user account
    B. Delete root user access keys
    C. Revoke all permissions on root user account
    D. Restrict permissions on root user account

39. In the Shared Responsibility Model, which of the following are examples of "Security in the cloud"? (Choose 2)
    A. Compliance with computer security standards and regulations
    B. Physical security of the facilities in which the services operate
    C. Which AWS services are used with the content
    D. Protecting the global infrastructure
    E. In which country the content is stored

40. Which of the following are included in AWS Assurance Programs? (Choose 2)
    A. Laws, Regulations, and Privacy
    B. Customer Testimonials
    C. Partner Validations
    D. Industry Best Practices
    E. Certification/Attestations

41. In the Shared Responsibility Model, for which aspect of securing the cloud is AWS responsible?
    A. Security of the cloud
    B. Security to the cloud
    C. Security for the cloud
    D. Security in the cloud

42. Which of the following are the resources that AWS provides to customers as guidance to secure their data in the cloud? (Choose 2)
    A. Customer Testimonials
    B. AWS Security Learning Path
    C. AWS Enterprise Support
    D. AWS Trusted Advisor
    E. Certified Partner Solutions

43. In a physical data center, security is typically considered in what area?
    A. Only in the perimeter
    B. In an edge location
    C. In the closest region
    D. In the closest availability zones

44. Which of the following is NOT considered a fault tolerant tool?
    A. S3
    B. SQS
    C. WAF
    D. RD

45. Which of the following cloud security controls ensures that only authorized and authenticated users are able to access your resources?
    A. Detective Controls
    B. Identity and Access Management
    C. Infrastructure Protection
    D. Incident Response

46. Which of the following is AWS's responsibility under the AWS Shared Responsibility model?
    A. Configuring third-party applications
    B. Maintaining physical hardware
    C. Securing application access and data
    D. Managing custom Amazon Machine Images (AMIs)

47. How would a system administrator add an additional layer of login security to a user's AWS Management Console?
    A. Use AWS Cloud Directory
    B. Audit AWS Identity and Access Management (IAM) roles
    C. Enable Multi-Factor Authentication
    D. Enable AWS CloudTrail

48. True or False: It is safer to use Access Keys than it is to use IAM roles.
    A. True
    B. False

49. True or False: Identity Access Management (IAM) is a Regional service.
    A. True
    B. False

50. True or False: Security in the cloud is the responsibility of AWS.
    A. True
    B. False

51. True or False: The Standard version of AWS Shield offers automated application (layer 7) traffic monitoring.
    A. True
    B. False

52. Which of the following AWS tools help your application scale up or down based on demand? (Choose 2)
    A. Agile Load Balancing
    B. Elastic Load Balancing
    C. Auto Availability Zones
    D. AWS CloudFormation
    E. Auto-Scaling

53. What is true about Regions? (Choose 2)
    A. Each region is located in a separate geographic area
    B. All regions are located in one specific geographic area
    C. They are the physical location of your customers
    D. They are the physical location with multiple availability zones
    E. Resources are replicated across all regions by default

54. Which of the following best describes Availability Zones?
    A. They are restricted areas designed specifically for the creation of Virtual Private Clouds
    B. They are distinct locations from within an AWS region that are engineered to be isolated from failures
    C. A Content Distribution Network used to deliver content to users
    D. Two zones containing compute resources that are designed to automatically maintain synchronized copies of each other's data

55. Which of the following is correct?
    A. # of Regions > # of Availability Zones > # of Edge Locations
    B. # of Edge Locations > # of Availability Zones > # of Regions
    C. # of Availability Zones > # of Edge Locations > # of Regions
    D. # of Availability Zones > # of Regions > # of Edge Locations

56. Which of the following data archival services is extremely inexpensive, but has a 3-5 hours data-retrieval window?
    A. S3-RRS
    B. S3
    C. Glacier
    D. S3-IA

57. Which of the following best describes EBS?
    A. A NoSQL database service
    B. A managed database service
    C. A virtual hard-disk in the cloud
    D. A bitcoin-mining service

58. Which of the following EC2 options is best for long-term workloads with predictable usage patterns?
    A. Reserved Instances
    B. Dedicated Host
    C. Spot Instances
    D. On-Demand Instances

59. In which of the following is CloudFront content cached?
    A. Data Center
    B. Edge Location
    C. Region
    D. Availability Zone

60. Which of the following best describes an AWS Region?
    A. It is collection of databases that can only be accessed from a specific geographic region
    B. It is a console that gives you a quick, global picture of your cloud computing environment
    C. It is a distinct location within a geographic area designed to provide high availability to a specific geography
    D. It is a collection of data centers that is spread evenly around a specific continent

61. There are at least _______ availability zones per AWS Region.

A. 2
B. 4
C. 1
D. 3

62. Which of the following best describes a resource group?
   A. A resource group is a collection of resources that share one or more tags (or portions of tags)
   B. A resource group is a collection of resources of the same type (EC2, S3, etc.) that are deployed in the same availability zone
   C. A resource group is a collection of resources of the same type (EC2, S3, etc.) that share one or more tags or portions of tags
   D. A resource group is a collection of resources that are deployed in the same AWS Region

63. Which of the following are valid EC2 pricing options? (Choose 2)
   A. On-Demand
   B. Stop
   C. Reserved
   D. Enterprise

64. Which AWS service is specifically designed to assist you in processing large data sets?
   A. EMR
   B. EC2
   C. AWS Big Data Processing
   D. ElastiCache

65. You have a mission-critical application that must be globally available at all times. Which deployment strategy should you follow?
   A. Multi-Availability Zone
   B. Multi-VPC in two AWS Regions
   C. Multi-Region
   D. Deploy to all availability zones in your home region
   E.

66. You need to host a file in a location that's publicly accessible from anywhere in the world. Which AWS service would best meet that need?
   A. S3
   B. EBS
   C. RDS
   D. EC2

67. Which of the following is an AWS managed database service that is up to 5X faster than a traditional MySQL database.
    A. MariaDB
    B. PostgreSQL
    C. DynamoDB
    D. Aurora

68. What is an AWS Region?
    A. A region is an independent data center, located in different countries around the globe
    B. A region is a subset of AWS technologies. For example, the Compute region consists of EC2, ECS, Lambda, etc.
    C. A region is a collection of edge locations available in specific countries
    D. A region is a geographical area divided into availability zones. Each region contains at least two availability zones

69. Which of the following is an AWS Data Warehousing service?
    A. Snowball
    B. Elastic Map Reduce
    C. S3 Big Data
    D. Redshift

70. Which of the following are AWS compute services? (Choose 2)
    A. EC2
    B. Lambda
    C. EBS
    D. SNS

71. Which of the following AWS services should you use to migrate an existing database to AWS?
    A. Route 53
    B. Storage Gateway
    C. DMS
    D. SNS

72. Which of the following is NOT an AWS Region?
    A. Frankfurt
    B. Ireland
    C. Oregon
    D. Virginia
    E. Moscow

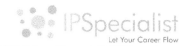

73. Which of the following statements are true about availability zones? (Choose 2)
    A. Multiple zones will fail if one zone fails
    B. Multiple zones are connected by low latency network links
    C. A single zone equals a single data center
    D. Multiple zones are physically connected on the same grid
    E. A single zone can span multiple data centers

74. What AWS tool utilizes edge locations to cache content and reduce latency?
    A. RDS
    B. EBS Storage
    C. EC2 Instances
    D. AWS CloudFront
    E. VPCs

75. How does an edge location help end users?
    A. Increases Latency
    B. Reduces Scaling
    C. Increases Storage
    D. Reduces Latency
    E. Reduces Power Consumption

76. Which of the following describes Elastic Load Balancers (ELB)?
    A. Translates domain names into IP addresses
    B. Creates new resources on-demand
    C. Launches or terminates instances based on specific conditions
    D. Distributes incoming traffic amongst your instances

77. Which of the following are high availability characteristics of Amazon Route 53? (Choose 2)
    A. Latency-based routing
    B. Geolocation routing
    C. Terminates instances based on specified conditions
    D. Masks failure of an instance/software
    E. Collects and tracks high latency metrics

78. What type of applications are recommended for Amazon EC2 reserved instances?
    A. Applications being developed or tested for the first time
    B. Applications that are only feasible at lower compute prices
    C. Applications that have flexible start and end times
    D. Applications with steady state or predictable usage

79. Which AWS service would simplify migration of a database to AWS?

A. AWS Storage Gateway
B. AWS Database Migration Service (AWS DMS)
C. Amazon Elastic Compute Cloud (Amazon EC2)
D. Amazon AppStream 2.0

80. Which AWS offering enables customers to find, buy, and immediately start using software solutions in their AWS environment?
A. AWS Config
B. AWS OpsWorks
C. AWS SDK
D. AWS Marketplace

81. Which AWS networking service enables a company to create a virtual network within AWS?
A. AWS Config
B. Amazon Route 53
C. AWS Direct Connect
D. Amazon Virtual Private Cloud (Amazon VPC)

82. Which component of AWS global infrastructure does Amazon CloudFront use to ensure low-latency delivery?
A. AWS Regions
B. AWS Edge Locations
C. AWS Availability Zones
D. Amazon Virtual Private Cloud (Amazon VPC)

83. Which service can identify the user that made the API call when an Amazon Elastic Compute Cloud (Amazon EC2) instance is terminated?
A. Amazon CloudWatch
B. AWS CloudTrail
C. AWS X-Ray
D. AWS Identity and Access Management (AWS IAM)

84. Which service would you use to send alerts based on Amazon CloudWatch alarms?
A. Amazon Simple Notification Service (Amazon SNS)
B. AWS CloudTrail
C. AWS Trusted Advisor
D. Amazon Route 53

85. Where can a customer find information about prohibited actions on AWS infrastructure?
A. AWS Trusted Advisor

B. AWS Identity and Access Management (IAM)
C. AWS Billing Console
D. AWS Acceptable Use Policy

86. True or False: S3 is object storage suitable for the storage of 'flat' files like Word documents, photos, etc.
    A. True
    B. False

87. True or False: To restrict access to an entire bucket, you use bucket control lists; and to restrict access to an individual object, you use object policies.
    A. True
    B. False

88. True or False: S3 can be used to host a dynamic website, like one that runs on a LAMP stack.
    A. True
    B. False

89. True or False: A Distribution is what we call a series of edge locations that make up CDN.
    A. True
    B. False

90. True or False: There are more regions than there are availability zones.
    A. True
    B. False

91. True or False: Objects stored in S3 are stored in a single, central location within AWS.
    A. True
    B. False

92. True or False: Both you and a friend can have an S3 bucket called 'mytestbucket'.
    A. True
    B. False

93. True or False: A CloudFront Origin can be an S3 bucket, an EC2 instance, an Elastic Load Balancer, or Route 53.
    A. True
    B. False

94. True or False: S3 Transfer Acceleration uses AWS network of availability zones to get your data into AWS more quickly.
    A. True
    B. False

95. True or False: Access Control Lists are used to make entire buckets (like one hosting an S3 website) public.
    A. True
    B. False

96. Which of the following AWS Support Levels offers 24x7 support via phone or chat?
    A. Developer
    B. Business
    C. Basic
    D. Individual

97. Which of the following are Support Levels offered by AWS? (Choose 3)
    A. Start-up
    B. Individual
    C. Basic
    D. Developer
    E. Business

98. Which of the following AWS Support Levels offers the assistance of a Technical Account Manager?
    A. Business
    B. Developer
    C. Elite
    D. Enterprise

99. By default, what is the maximum number of Linked Accounts per Paying Account under Consolidated Billing?
    A. 10
    B. 20
    C. 50
    D. 100

100. Which of the following support plans features access to AWS support during business hours via email?
    A. Basic
    B. Developer
    C. Business

D. Enterprise

101. Which of the following EC2 instance types will realize a savings over time in exchange for a contracted term-of-service?

A. Spot Instances
B. On-Demand Instances
C. Discount Instances
D. Reserved Instances

102. Which of the following AWS services are free to use? (Choose 5)

A. VPC
B. S3
C. Route 53
D. RDS
E. Auto-Scaling
F. Elastic Beanstalk
G. CloudFormation
H. EBS
I. EC2
J. IAM

103. Which of the following Support Plans features a < 4-hour response time in the event of an impaired production system?

A. Individual
B. Basic
C. Developer
D. Business

104. Which of the following are criteria affecting your billing for RDS? (Choose 3)

A. Additional storage
B. Data transfer in
C. Standby time
D. Clock hours of server time
E. Number of requests

105. Which of the following is not a fundamental AWS charge?

A. Data-in
B. Compute
C. Data-out
D. Storage

106. Which of the following AWS services should you use if you would like to be

notified when you have crossed a billing threshold?

A. CloudWatch
B. AWS Bugdet
C. AWS Cost Allocation
D. Trusted Advisor

107. Which of the following Support Services do all accounts receive as standard?

A. Technical support
B. Billing support
C. 24/7 support via phone and chat
D. Technical Account Manager

108. Your Development team uses four on-demand EC2 instances and your QA team has 5 reserved instances, only three of which are being used. Assuming all AWS accounts are under a single AWS Organization, how will the Development Team's instances be billed?

A. All the Dev instances will be billed at the reserved instance rate
B. The pricing for the reserved instances will shift from QA to Dev
C. All the Dev team's instances will be billed at the on-demand rate
D. The Dev team will be billed for two instances at on-demand prices and two instances at the reserved instance price

109. Which of the following support plans features unlimited (customer-side) contacts and unlimited support cases? (Choose 2)

A. Developer
B. Business
C. Enterprise
D. Basic

110. You have a project that will require 90 hours of computing time. There is no deadline, and the work can be stopped and restarted without adverse effect. Which of the following computing options offers the most cost-effective solution?

A. Spot Instances
B. ECS Instances
C. On-Demand Instances
D. Reserved Instances

111. When calculating the cost of Amazon EC2, what factors affect pricing? (Choose 2)

A. Number and size of objects stored in your Amazon S3 buckets
B. Number of hours Elastic Load Balancer runs
C. Number of items in your inbound data transfer
D. Number of instances

112. Which of the following is NOT included in the AWS Free Tier?
    A. AWS CloudFormation
    B. AWS Identity and Access Management (IAM)
    C. AWS Web Application Firewall (WAF)
    D. Amazon Virtual Private Cloud (VPC)
    E. Amazon Simple Storage Service (S3)

113. What AWS tool compares the cost of running your application in an on-premises data center to AWS?
    A. Total Cost of Operation (TCO) calculator
    B. Total Cost of Products (TCP) calculator
    C. Total Cost of Services (TCS) calculator
    D. Total Cost of Application (TCA) calculator
    E. Total Cost of Ownership (TCO) calculator

114. What is NOT a consideration when estimating the cost of Amazon S3?
    A. Number and size of objects
    B. Input Output Operations per Seconds (IOPS)
    C. Storage class
    D. Data transfer
    E. Requests

115. Which of the following is NOT available in the Business Support Plan?
    A. Access to Infrastructure Event Management
    B. Access to third-party software support
    C. Access to Cloud Support Engineers for technical issues
    D. Access to Well-Architected Review delivered by AWS Solution Architects
    E. Access to Personal Health Dashboard and Health API

116. What are the characteristics of the Developer Support Plan? (Choose 2)
    A. Assigned to a Technical Account Manager
    B. Unlimited contacts may open a case
    C. 24/7 access to Cloud Support Engineers via email, chat, and phone
    D. One primary contact may open a case
    E. Business hours access to Cloud Support Associates via email

117. As AWS grows, the general cost of running a business is reduced and savings are passed back to the customer in the form of lower pricing. What is this cost optimization called?
    A. Economies of Scale
    B. Economies of Optimization

C. Economies of Scope
D. Economies of Cost
E. Economies of Labor

118. What type of AWS data transfers are free? (Choose 2)
A. Inbound data transfer across all Amazon Web Services in all regions
B. Inbound data transfer between Amazon Web Services within the same region
C. Outbound data transfer across all Amazon Web Services in all regions
D. Outbound data transfer from S3 only
E. Outbound data transfer between Amazon Web Services within the same region

119. True or False: With Consolidated Billing, the Paying Account can make changes to any of the resources owned by a Linked Account.
A. True
B. False

120. True or False: With AWS Organizations, you can use either just the Consolidated Billing feature, or all the offered features.
A. True
B. False

Answers

1. **A** (Pay as you go)

Explanation:

AWS offers you a pay-as-you-go approach for pricing for over 70 cloud services.

2. **B** (High latency)
   C (Multiple procurement cycles)

Explanation:

AWS network offers performance (high bandwidth, low latency) and scalability. AWS provides an efficient cloud-centric procurement process.

3. **C** (Pay for racking, stacking, and powering servers)

Explanation:

The six advantages are:

1. Trade capital expense for variable expense
2. Benefit from economies of scale
3. Stop guessing capacity
4. Increase speed and agility
5. Stop spending money on running and maintaining data centers
6. Go global in minutes

4. **E** (Agility)

Explanation:

Increased agility, elasticity, focus on core business, optimized costs, and better security are all good outcomes when it comes to working with AWS.

5. **A** (The ability to 'go global' in minutes)
   B (Increased speed and agility)
   C (Variable expense)
   E (Elasticity)

Explanation:

The 'pay-as-you-go' nature of cloud computing ensures that a large up-front capital expense is not required.

6. **B** (Pay-as-you-go pricing)
   C (On-demand delivery)
   D (Services are delivered via the Internet)

Explanation:

Services incurred from a cloud services provider are operating expenses, not capital expenses. The other answers are correct.

7. **A** (Public Cloud)
   B (Hybrid Cloud)
   D (Private Cloud)

Explanation:
The three types of cloud deployments are Public, Hybrid, and Private (On-premises).

8. **B** (Platform-as-a-Service)

Explanation:
Lightsail is AWS' Platform-as-a-Service offering.

9. **A** (Disposable resources)
   B (Infrastructure as code)
   C (Assume *everything* will fail)
   E (Scalability)

Explanation:
Build your systems to be scalable, use disposable resources, reduce infrastructure to code, and, assume EVERYTHING will fail sooner or later.

10. **D** (Lambda)

Explanation:
Lambda is the AWS Function-as-a-Service (FaaS) offering that lets you run code without provisioning or managing servers.

11. **D** (Consumption model)

Explanation:
With AWS, you only pay for the services you consume.

12. **D** (Fault Tolerance)

Explanation:
Fault tolerance is the ability of a system to remain operational even if some of the components of the system fail.

13. **C** (Auto-Scaling)

Explanation:
AWS Auto Scaling monitors your application and automatically adds or removes capacity from your resource groups in real-time as demands change.

14. **C** (Traceability)

Explanation:
Performance efficiency in the cloud is composed of four areas:

1. Selection
2. Review
3. Monitoring
4. Trade-offs

15. **A** (Serverless architecture)
    E (Democratize advanced technologies)

Explanation:

Performance Efficiency principles are:

1. Democratize advanced technologies
2. Go global in minutes
3. Use serverless architectures
4. Experiment more often
5. Mechanical sympathy

16. **C** (Amazon EC2 instances can be launched on-demand when needed)

Explanation:

The ability to launch instances on-demand when needed allows customers launch and terminate instances in response to a varying workload. This is a more economical practice than purchasing many on-premises servers to handle the peak load.

17. **D** (AWS uses multi-factor access control systems)
    E (You retain complete control and ownership of your data region)

Explanation:

AWS uses Multi-Factor Authentication that adds an extra layer of protection on top of your user name and password. AWS manages security of the cloud, while security in the cloud is the responsibility of the customer.

18. **B** (Create individual IAM users)
    C (Activate Multifactor Authentication (MFA) on your root account)
    D (Use roles to assign permissions to IAM users)

Explanation:

The Root account should have MFA enabled; you should always create individual users (the root account should never be used for actual work); and roles should be used to grant permissions to the users you create.

19. **A** (Policy)

Explanation:

A Policy is the document used to grant permissions to users, groups, and roles.

20. **C** (JSON)

Explanation:

IAM policies are written using the JSON format.

21. **A** (Using the AWS Software Developers Kit)
    C (AWS Management Console access)
    D (Programmatic access via the command line)

Explanation:
The two types of access are AWS Management Console access and Programmatic Access via the AWS API, the CLI, and the SDKs.

22. **D** (PCI DSS Level 1)

Explanation:
A PCI DSS Level 1 certification attests to the security of the AWS platform regarding credit card transactions.

23. **A** (AWS Shield)

Explanation:
AWS Shield is AWS' managed DDoS protection service.

24. **B** (AWS Trusted Advisor)

Explanation:
AWS Trusted Advisor can help you assess the fault-tolerance of your AWS environment.

25. **D** (7)

Explanation:
WAF operates down to Layer 7.

26. **B** (AWS Inspector)

Explanation:
AWS Inspector assesses the security and compliance of your EC2 instances.

27. **A** (HIPPA)

Explanation:
A HIPPA certification attests to the fact that the AWS Platform has met the standard required for the secure storage of medical records in the US.

28. **B** (AWS Trusted Advisor)

Explanation:
Trusted Advisor helps you optimize your entire AWS environment in real time following AWS best practices. It helps you optimize cost, fault-tolerance, and more.

29. **C** (Trusted Advisor)
Explanation:
An online resource to help you reduce cost, increase performance, and improve security by optimizing your AWS environment, Trusted Advisor provides real time guidance to help you provision your resources following AWS best practices.

30. **B** (AWS Trusted Advisor)
Explanation:
The Trusted Advisor can assist you with the cost optimization of your AWS environment.

31. **C** (Customer data)
Explanation:
The customers are responsible for their own customer data.

32. **B** (All inbound traffic is denied and outbound traffic is allowed by default)
 C (Acts as a virtual firewall to control inbound and outbound traffic)
Explanation:
Security Groups acts as a virtual firewall to control both inbound and outbound traffic. It allows outbound traffic by default and denies all inbound traffic.

33. **D** (Manage services and their capacities)
Explanation:
Feature of AWS Identity and Access Management are:
1. Manage roles and their permissions
2. Manage users and their access
3. Manage federated users and their permissions

34. **B** (Online tool that helps you configure resources to follow best practices)
Explanation:
AWS Trusted Advisor is an online resource for optimizing your AWS environment by following AWS best practices.

35. **B** (AWS Management Console Access)
 D (Programmatic Access)
Explanation:
The two types of access that can be granted to a user when creating an IAM policy are:
1. The AWS Management Console
2. Programmatic Access (Command Line Interface and Software Development Kits)

36. **A** (Secure Global Infrastructure)

B (Meet Compliance Requirements)

Explanation:

Benefits of AWS Security are:

1. Secure Global Infrastructure
2. Meet Compliance Requirements
3. Save Money
4. Scale Quickly

37. **B** (Risk Management)
C (Control Environment)
D (Information Security)

Explanation:

AWS Risk and Compliance Program components are:

1. Risk Management
2. Control Environment
3. Information Security

38. **B** (Delete root user access keys)

Explanation:

This is recommended because anyone who has the access key for your AWS account will have unrestricted access to all the resources in your account, including billing information.

39. **C** (Which AWS services are used with the content)
E (In which country the content is stored)

Explanation:

AWS customer maintains ownership and control of their content, including control over:

1. What content they choose to store or process using AWS services
2. Which AWS services they use with their content
3. The AWS Region(s) where their content is stored
4. The format, structure and security of their content, including whether it is masked, anonymized or encrypted
5. Who has access to their AWS accounts and content and how those access rights are granted, managed and revoked

40. **A** (Laws, Regulations, and Privacy)
E (Certification/Attestations)

Explanation:

AWS Compliance and Assurance Programs include:

1. Certifications / Attestations
2. Laws / Regulations / Privacy

3. Alignments / Frameworks

41. **A** (Security of the cloud)
Explanation:
'Security of the cloud' is the responsibility of AWS, whereas 'Security in the cloud' is customer's responsibility.

42. **C** (AWS Enterprise Support)
D (AWS Trusted Advisor)
Explanation:
AWS provides customers with guidance and expertise through:
1. AWS Trusted Advisor
2. AWS Account Teams
3. AWS Enterprise Support
4. AWS Professional Services and AWS Partner Network
5. AWS Advisories and Bulletins

43. **A** (Only in the perimeter)
Explanation:
Regions, Availability Zones and Edge Locations are a part of the AWS cloud infrastructure.

44. **C** (WAF)
Explanation:
AWS WAF is a web application firewall that helps protect your web applications from common web exploits. All the rest of the services mentioned provides fault tolerance.

45. **B** (Identity and Access Management)
Explanation:
IAM controls who is authenticated (signed in) and authorized (has permissions) to use resources.

46. **B** (Maintaining physical hardware)
Explanation:
AWS is responsible for protecting the infrastructure that runs all of the services offered in the AWS Cloud. This infrastructure is composed of the hardware, software, networking, and facilities that run AWS Cloud services.

47. **C** (Enable Multi-Factor Authentication)
Explanation:
AWS Multi-Factor Authentication (MFA) is a simple best practice that adds an extra layer of protection on top of your user name and password

48. **B** (False)
Explanation:
It is safer to use IAM roles than it is to use Access Keys.

49. **B** (False)
Explanation:
Identity Access Management is a global service.

50. **B** (False)
Explanation:
AWS is responsible for the security of the cloud. The customer is responsible for security IN the cloud -- that is, the security of her AWS resources.

51. **B** (False)
Explanation:
Only AWS Shield Advanced offers automated application layer monitoring.

52. **B** (Elastic Load Balancing)
    E (Auto-Scaling)
Explanation:
Elastic Load Balancing handles varying loads of traffic by automatically distributing incoming application traffic across multiple targets. Auto-Scaling monitors applications and automatically adjusts capacity to maintain steady, predictable performance

53. **A** (Each region is located in a separate geographic area)
    D (Physical location with multiple Availability Zones)
Explanation:
Each region is a separate geographic area and has multiple, isolated locations known as availability zones

54. **B** (Distinct locations from within an AWS region that are engineered to be isolated from failures)
Explanation:
Availability Zones are distinct locations from within an AWS region that are engineered to be isolated from failures.

55. **B** (# of Edge Locations > # of Availability Zones > # of Regions)
Explanation:
There are more availability zones than regions and more edge locations than availability zones.

56. **C** (Glacier)
Explanation:
Glacier offers extremely inexpensive data archival, but requires a 3-5 hours data-retrieval window.

57. **C** (A virtual hard-disk in the cloud)
Explanation:
An EBS volume is best described as a virtual hard-disk in the cloud.

58. **A** (Reserved Instances)
Explanation:
Reserved Instances are the most economical option for long-term workloads with predictable usage patterns.

59. **B** (Edge Location)
Explanation:
CloudFront content is cached in edge locations.

60. **C** (It is a distinct location within a geographic area designed to provide high availability to a specific geography)
Explanation:
A region is a distinct location within a geographic area designed to provide high availability to a specific geography.

61. **A** (2)
Explanation:
There are at least 2 availability zones per AWS Region.

62. **A** (A resource group is a collection of resources that share one or more tags (or portions of tags)
Explanation:
A resource group is a collection of resources that share one or more tags (or portions of tags)

63. **A** (On-Demand)
C (Reserved)
Explanation:
On-Demand and Reserved are the valid EC2 pricing options.

64. **A** (EMR)
Explanation:
Amazon EMR is a web service that makes it easy to process large amounts of data

efficiently.

65. **C** (Multi-Region)
Explanation:
A Multi-Region deployment will best ensure global availability.

66. **A** (S3)
Explanation:
With S3, objects can be accessed from anywhere in the world via a dedicated URL.

67. **D** (Aurora)
Explanation:
Aurora is AWS managed database service that is up to 5X faster than a traditional MySQL database.

68. **D** (A region is a geographical area divided into availability zones. Each region contains at least two availability zones)
Explanation:
A region is a geographical area divided into availability zones. Each region contains at least two availability zones.

69. **D** (Redshift)
Explanation:
Redshift is AWS Data Warehousing service.

70. **A** (EC2)
B (Lambda)
Explanation:
EC2 and Lambda are AWS Compute Services.

71. **C** (DMS)
Explanation:
The AWS Database Migrations Service should be used for the migration.

72. **E** (Moscow)
Explanation:
Moscow is not an AWS Region, while the rest are.

73. **B** (Multiple zones are connected by low latency network links)
E (A single zone can span multiple data centers)
Explanation:
Multiple, physically separated and isolated availability zones are connected with low

latency network links that automatically fail-over between one another without interruption. Also, a single availability zone can span multiple data centers.

74. **D** (AWS CloudFront)
Explanation:
AWS CloudFront utilizes edge locations to cache content and reduce latency.

75. **D** (Reduces Latency)
Explanation:
User requests are served by the closest edge location resulting in reduced latency.

76. **D** (Distributes incoming traffic amongst your instances)
Explanation:
Elastic Load Balancing automatically distributes incoming application traffic across multiple targets, such as Amazon EC2 instances, containers, and IP addresses.

77. **A** (Latency-based routing)
B (Geolocation routing)
Explanation:
Amazon Route 53 uses a variety of routing types, including Latency Based Routing, Geo DNS, Geoproximity, and Weighted Round Robin, all of which can be combined with DNS Failover in order to enable a variety of low-latency, fault-tolerant architectures.

78. **D** (Applications with steady state or predictable usage)
Explanation:
Reserved Instances are recommended for applications with steady state or predictable usage as users can commit to a 1 year or 3-years term contract to reduce their total computing costs

79. **B** (AWS Database Migration Service (AWS DMS))
Explanation:
AWS Database Migration Service helps you migrate databases to AWS quickly and securely.

80. **D** (AWS Marketplace)
Explanation:
AWS Marketplace is an online store that helps customers find, buy, and immediately start using the software and services they need to build products and run their businesses.

81. **D** (Amazon Virtual Private Cloud (Amazon VPC))
Explanation:

Amazon VPC lets you provision a logically isolated section of the AWS cloud where you can launch AWS resources in a virtual network that you define.

82. **B** (AWS Edge Locations)
Explanation:
Amazon CloudFront delivers through a worldwide network of data centers called edge locations.

83. **B** (AWS CloudTrail)
Explanation:
CloudTrail logs, continuously monitors, and retains account activity related to actions across your AWS infrastructure.

84. **A** (Amazon Simple Notification Service (Amazon SNS))
Explanation:
Amazon Simple Notification Service is a notification service provided as part of Amazon Web Services. It provides a low-cost infrastructure for the mass delivery of messages, predominantly to mobile users.

85. **D** (AWS Acceptable Use Policy)
Explanation:
AWS Acceptable Use Policy contains information about prohibited actions on AWS infrastructure.

86. **A** (True)
Explanation:
S3 is object storage suitable for the storage of 'flat' files like Word documents, photos, etc.

87. **B** (False)
Explanation:
To restrict access to an entire bucket, you use bucket policies; and to restrict access to an individual object, you use access control lists.

88. **B** (False)
Explanation:
S3 can be used to host *static* websites.

89. **A** (True)
Explanation:
The collection of a CDN's Edge Locations is called a Distribution.

90. **B** (False)
Explanation:
As there are at least two Availability Zones (AZ) per AWS Region, there will always be more AZs than Regions.

91. **B** (False)
Explanation:
Objects stored in S3 are stored in multiple servers in multiple facilities across AWS.

92. **B** (False)
Explanation:
S3 bucket names are global, and must be unique.

93. **A** (True)
Explanation:
A CloudFront Origin can be an S3 bucket, an EC2 instance, an Elastic Load Balancer, or Route 53.

94. **B** (False)
Explanation:
S3 Transfer Acceleration uses AWS network of edge locations to get your data into AWS more quickly.

95. **B** (False)
Explanation:
Bucket Policies are used to make entire buckets (like one hosting an S3 website) public.

96. **B** (Business)
Explanation:
The Business and Enterprise Support Plans offer 24 X 7 support via phone or chat.

97. **C** (Basic)
D (Developer)
E (Business)
Explanation:
The AWS Support levels are Basic, Developer, Business, and Enterprise.

98. **D** (Enterprise)
Explanation:
Only Enterprise support offers the services of a Technical Account Manager.

99. **B** (20)

Explanation:
The default maximum is 20 linked accounts. This soft limit can be increased by contacting AWS.

100. **B** (Developer)
Explanation:
The Developer Support Plan features access to AWS support during business hours via email.

101. **D** (Reserved Instances)
Explanation:
EC2 Reserved Instances offer significant discounts for a contracted term-of-service.

102. **A** (VPC)
E (Auto-Scaling)
F (Elastic Beanstalk)
G (CloudFormation)
J (IAM)
Explanation:
The correct answers are VPC, Elastic Beanstalk, CloudFormation, IAM, and Auto-Scaling. Keep in mind that with VPC, Elastic Beanstalk, CloudFormation, and Auto-Scaling, the underlying provisioned resources will incur charges.

103. **D** (Business)
Explanation:
Both the Business and Enterprise support levels offer a < 4-hour response time in the event of an impaired production system.

104. **A** (Additional storage)
D (Clock hours of server time)
E (Number of requests)
Explanation:
Clock hours of server time, additional storage, and number of requests are among the criteria defining charges for RDS.

105. **A** (Data-in)
Explanation:
In AWS, data-in is always free-of-charge.

106. **A** (CloudWatch)
Explanation:
A CloudWatch alarm can be set to monitor spending on your AWS Account.

107. **B** (Billing support)
Explanation:
All accounts receive billing support.

108. **D** (The Dev team will be billed for two instances at on-demand prices and two instances at the reserved instance price)
Explanation:
Assuming all instances are in the same AWS Organization, the reserved instance pricing for the unused QA instances will be applied to two of the four Dev instances.

109. **B** (Business)
C (Enterprise)
Explanation:
Both Enterprise and Business Support Plans feature unlimited (customer-side) contacts and unlimited support cases.

110. **A** (Spot Instances)
Explanation:
Spot Instances would be the most cost-effective solution.

111. **B** (Number of hours Elastic Load Balancer runs)
D (Number of instances)
Explanation:
Factors that need to be considered for Amazon EC2 pricing are:
1. Clock Hours of Server Time
2. Machine Configuration
3. Machine Purchase Type
4. Number of Instances
5. Load Balancing
6. Detailed Monitoring
7. Auto-Scaling
8. Elastic IP Addresses
9. Operating Systems and Software Packages

112. **C** (AWS Web Application Firewall (WAF))
Explanation:
AWS WAF also follows the 'pay only for what you use' model and is not free.

113. **E** (Total Cost of Ownership (TCO) calculator)
Explanation:
AWS Total Cost of Ownership (TCO) calculator provides a comparative analysis of the

cost estimation by comparing on premises and co-location environments to the AWS.

114. **B** (Input Output Operations per Seconds (IOPS))
Explanation:
When estimating the cost of Amazon S3, the following are considered:

1. Storage Class
2. Storage (Number and size of objects)
3. Requests
4. Data Transfer

115. **D** (Access to Well-Architected Review delivered by AWS Solution Architects)
Explanation:
Access to Well-Architected Review delivered by AWS Solution Architects is available only for Enterprise customers.

116. **D** (One primary contact may open a case)
E (Business hours access to Cloud Support Associates via email)
Explanation:
24/7 access to Cloud Support Engineers via email, chat, and phone and unlimited contacts opening a case are available to Business and Enterprise customers, whereas Technical Account Manager is only available with Enterprise support plan.

117. **A** (Economies of Scale)
Explanation:
Economies of scale results in the transfer of savings back to the customer in the form of lower pricing.

118. **A** (Inbound data transfer across all Amazon Web Services in all regions)
E (Outbound data transfer between Amazon Web Services within the same region)
Explanation:
While Data Transfer Out comes with a price, there is no charge for inbound data transfer across all Amazon Web Services in all regions. In addition, there are no outbound data transfer charges between Amazon Web Services within the same region.

119. **B** (False)
Explanation:
The Paying Account cannot make changes to any of the resources owned by a Linked Account.

120. **A** (True)
Explanation:
With AWS Organizations, you can use either just the Consolidated Billing feature, or

all the offered features.

References

AWS Cloud Certifications

- https://aws.amazon.com/certification/
- https://cloudacademy.com/blog/choosing-the-right-aws-certification/

AWS Certified Cloud Practitioner

- https://aws.amazon.com/certification/certified-cloud-practitioner/

Cloud Concepts

- https://aws.amazon.com/what-is-cloud-computing/
- https://aws.amazon.com/types-of-cloud-computing/

Cloud Compliance

- https://aws.amazon.com/compliance/

Identity and Access Management

- https://aws.amazon.com/iam/

Security Support

- https://aws.amazon.com/products/security/

Cloud Deployment and Management

- https://do.awsstatic.com/whitepapers/overview-of-deployment-options-on-aws.pdf

AWS Global Infrastructure

- https://cloudacademy.com/blog/aws-global-infrastructure/

AWS Compute

- https://aws.amazon.com/products/compute/

AWS Storage

- https://aws.amazon.com/products/storage/

AWS Database

- https://aws.amazon.com/products/databases/

Amazon Virtual Private Cloud

- https://en.wikipedia.org/wiki/Virtual_private_cloud
- https://aws.amazon.com/vpc/

Network & Content Delivery

- https://aws.amazon.com/cloudfront/details/
- https://aws.amazon.com/elasticloadbalancing/
- https://aws.amazon.com/route53/

AWS Free Tier

- https://aws.amazon.com/free/

AWS Support Plans

- https://aws.amazon.com/premiumsupport/compare-plans/

AWS Organizations

- https://aws.amazon.com/organizations/

AWS Cost Calculators

- https://calculator.s3.amazonaws.com/index.html
- https://awstcocalculator.com/

Acronyms

- AAD Additional Authenticated Data
- ACL Access Control List
- ACM PCA AWS Certificate Manager Private Certificate Authority
- ACM Private CA AWS Certificate Manager Private Certificate Authority
- ACM AWS Certificate Manager
- AMI Amazon Machine Image
- ARN Amazon Resource Name
- ASN Autonomous System Number
- AUC Area Under a Curve
- AWS Amazon Web Services
- BGP Border Gateway Protocol
- CDN Content Delivery Network
- CIDR Classless Inter-Domain Routing
- CLI Command Line Interface
- CMK Customer Master Key
- DB Database
- DKIM DomainKeys Identified Mail
- DNS Domain Name System
- EBS Elastic Block Store
- EC2 Elastic Cloud Compute
- ECR Elastic Container Registry
- ECS Elastic Container Service
- EFS Elastic File System
- EMR Elastic Map Reduce
- ES Elasticsearch Service
- ETL Extract, Transform, and Load
- FBL Feedback Loop
- FIM Federated Identity Management
- HMAC Hash-based Message Authentication Code
- HPC High Performance Compute
- HSM Hardware Security Module
- IAM Identity and Access Management
- IdP Identity Provider

- ISP Internet Service Provider
- JSON JavaScript Object Notation
- KMS Key Management Service
- MFA Multi-factor Authentication
- MIME Multipurpose Internet Mail Extensions
- MTA Mail Transfer Agent
- OU Organizational Unit
- RDS Relational Database Service
- S3 Simple Storage Service
- SCP Service Control Policy
- SDK Software Development Kit
- SES Simple Email Service
- SMTP Simple Mail Transfer Protocol
- SNS Simple Notification Service
- SOAP Simple Object Access Protocol
- SQS Simple Queue Service
- SSE Server-Side Encryption
- SSL Secure Sockets Layer
- SSO Single Sign-On
- STS Security Token Service
- SWF Simple Workflow Service
- TLS Transport Layer Security
- VERP Variable Envelope Return Path
- VPC Virtual Private Cloud
- VPG Virtual Private Gateway
- WAF Web Application Firewall
- WAM WorkSpaces Application Manager
- WSDL Web Services Description Language

About Our Products

Other products from IPSpecialist LTD regarding Cloud technology are:

 AWS Certified Cloud Practitioner Technology Workbook

 AWS Certified Solutions Architect - Associate Workbook

 AWS Certified SysOps Administrator - Associate Technology Workbook

 AWS Certified Developer Associate Technology Workbook

 AWS Certified Solution Architect - Professional Technology Workbook

 AWS Certified DevOps Engineer - Professional Technology Workbook

 AWS Certified Advanced Networking – Specialty Technology Workbook

 AWS Certified Big Data – Specialty Technology Workbook

 AWS Certified Security – Specialty Technology Workbook

 Google Cloud Certified Associate Cloud Engineer Technology Workbook

Upcoming products from IPSpecialist LTD regarding Cloud technology are:

 Google Cloud Certified Professional Cloud Architect Technology Workbook

 Google Cloud Certified Professional Data Engineer Technology Workbook

Note from the Author:

Reviews are gold for authors! If you have enjoyed this book and it has helped you along your certification, would you consider rating and reviewing i

www.ingramcontent.com/pod-product-compliance
Lightning Source LLC
LaVergne TN
LVHW081656050326
832903LV00026B/1784

* 9 7 8 1 6 9 0 7 2 9 7 0 9 *